Praise for C

New York Times Editors Choice

Pacific Northwest Booksellers Association Award Winner

"A Harvard professor goes wide in this study of the humanities and human creativity, looking at standout moments and what they can tell us about our past and future. As [Martin Puchner] guides readers along a Nefertiti to TikTok continuum, he shows how cultural exchange and innovation help societies address some of life's most existential questions."
—Joumana Khatib, *New York Times*

"*Culture* is a breakneck, utterly captivating survey of the cultural transmission of ideas, stories, and songs—how they survive, change, vanish, and are borrowed, refined, coopted, and grafted through time. Reading this book was like taking a course in the history of humanities from a world-class professor with a rapacious, global, up-to-the-minute curiosity. I underlined sentences on every page."
—Anthony Doerr, author of *Cloud Cuckoo Land*

"Puchner is an adept storyteller who uses narrative to show that the common trait among all human cultures is skillful stealing in service of explanation." —Ismail Muhammad, *New York Times Book Review*

"This is a mighty, polymathic work, equally at home in all four corners of the globe. . . . Puchner has provided us a cultural map that traverses centuries and intercontinental byways and detours, always returning to what makes us human. It is a gift to be savored."
—Chris Vognar, *Boston Globe*

"Fearless and exhilaratingly erudite, Martin Puchner's panoramic tour of human culture across the millennia is a riveting page-turner. Revealing the beauty and necessity of cultural cross-pollination and borrowing, Puchner's tour de force is the perfect antidote to our increasingly dreary and close-minded times."

—Amy Chua, Yale Law School professor and author of *Battle Hymn of the Tiger Mother* and *Political Tribes: Group Instinct and the Fate of Nations*

"As much a book of philosophy as a sweeping history, Martin Puchner's *Culture* is calculated but bold in its approach to traversing and analyzing centuries of art, entertainment, and knowledge. *Culture* hops through countries and eras to deliver a resonant argument for the necessity of our common creativity."

—Lauren Puckett-Pope, *Elle*

"Why do we make art? Why do we tell stories? What is it about humanity that just has to build a pyramid or write a concerto or spray paint the side of a subway car? With *Culture*, professor and public intellectual Martin Puchner attempts to answer these questions—along with a seemingly infinite array of others—as he takes the reader through millennia of human creation, always wondering what's at the heart of our need to achieve."

—Jonny Diamond, *Literary Hub*, "Lit Hub's Most Anticipated Books of 2023"

"Cultures develop by sharing, borrowing, and collaborating—but also by conquest, appropriation, and theft. Martin Puchner's timely book takes us on a breathtaking tour of world history, reminding us that as we judge the past, one day we, too, will be judged, and that when we ignore or try to erase our cultural heritage, we are only impoverishing ourselves."

—Louis Menand, Pulitzer Prize–winning author of *The Metaphysical Club*

"If anyone wants to know what it is for comparative literature to encompass the globe, they need only read this remarkable book."

—Kwame Anthony Appiah, author of
The Lies that Bind: Rethinking Identity

"So many books these days are described as being 'sweeping histories'; *Culture*, which promises in its subtitle to take us from our most primitive artistic impulses all the way to the machinery of modern-day fandom. But what intrigues me most about Puchner's latest isn't its scope—it's its driving question: 'What good are the arts?' In my more hopeless moments, this question bubbles up inside me, and I'm chomping at the bit to hear Puchner's answer, grounded in history and informed by cultures around the world." —Sophia Stewart, *Millions*

"Martin Puchner has exceptional and invaluable gifts: intellectual fearlessness, dazzling erudition, trenchancy tempered by breadth of mind, and a humanist's eye for minute evidence that illumines huge problems. He leaps daringly among well-chosen vignettes to show us what cultural change is like: contingent, fragile, unpredictable, and always dependent on our willingness to exchange objects, people, and ideas." —Felipe Fernández-Armesto, author of
The Oxford Illustrated History of the World

"A thoughtful, generous vision of human creativity across centuries of culture." —*Kirkus Reviews*

"Puchner creates a perfectly balanced and incisively abridged version of the story of human culture. Ultimately, this is an examination of the making and transport of ideas, which is always an interaction between old and new. Each chapter builds a new layer, adding to the depth and complexity, while Puchner also provides a global who's who of cultural diffusion." —*Booklist*

CULTURE

ALSO BY MARTIN PUCHNER

Literature for a Changing Planet

The Language of Thieves

The Written World

The Drama of Ideas

Poetry of the Revolution

Stage Fright

AS EDITOR

Norton Anthology of World Literature

Norton Anthology of Drama

CULTURE

THE STORY OF US, FROM CAVE ART TO K-POP

Martin Puchner

W. W. NORTON & COMPANY
Independent Publishers Since 1923

For information about permission to reproduce selections from this book, write to
Permissions, W. W. Norton & Company, Inc., 500 Fifth Avenue,
New York, NY 10110

For information about special discounts for bulk purchases, please contact
W. W. Norton Special Sales at specialsales@wwnorton.com or 800-233-4830

Manufacturing by Lakeside Book Company
Book design by Daniel Lagin
Production manager: Julia Druskin

Library of Congress Control Number: 2023947080

ISBN 978-1-324-07450-2 pbk.

W. W. Norton & Company, Inc., 500 Fifth Avenue, New York, N.Y. 10110
www.wwnorton.com

W. W. Norton & Company Ltd., 15 Carlisle Street, London W1D 3BS

1 2 3 4 5 6 7 8 9 0

For the one to be loved

CONTENTS

===

Preface: How Culture Works   xi

Introduction: Inside the Chauvet Cave, 35,000 BCE   xiii

1. Queen Nefertiti and Her Faceless God   1

2. Plato Burns His Tragedy and Invents a History   23

3. King Ashoka Sends a Message to the Future   36

4. A South Asian Goddess in Pompeii   53

5. A Buddhist Pilgrim in Search of Ancient Traces   70

6. *The Pillow Book* and Some Perils
   of Cultural Diplomacy   87

7. When Baghdad Became a Storehouse of Wisdom   105

8. The Queen of Ethiopia Welcomes the
   Raiders of the Ark   123

9. One Christian Mystic and the Three
   Revivals of Europe   140

10. The Aztec Capital Faces Its European
    Enemies and Admirers   164

11. A Portuguese Sailor Writes a Global Epic   185

12. Enlightenment in Saint-Domingue and
    in a Parisian Salon   206

13. George Eliot Promotes the Science of the Past   227

14. A Japanese Wave Takes the World by Storm   246

15. The Drama of Nigerian Independence   266

Epilogue: Will There Be a Library in 2114 CE?   287

Acknowledgments   305

Notes   309

Index   337

HOW CULTURE WORKS

Here's one view of culture: the earth is populated by groups of humans, and these groups are held together by shared practices. Each of these cultures, with their distinct customs and arts, belongs to the people born into it, and each must be defended against outside interference. This view assumes that culture is a form of property, that culture belongs to the people who live it. One advantage of this view is that it encourages people to cherish their own heritage; it also gives them resources for defending it, as when museums are pressured to return objects acquired under dubious circumstances to their rightful owners. The assumption that culture can be owned has a surprisingly broad coalition of advocates, including nativists invested in their national traditions and those hoping to stop cultural appropriation by declaring one group's cultural property off-limits to outsiders.

There is a second view of culture that rejects the idea that culture can be owned. This view is exemplified by Xuanzang, the Chinese traveler who went to India and brought back Buddhist manuscripts. It was embraced by Arab and Persian scholars who translated Greek philosophy. It was practiced by countless scribes, teachers, and artists who found inspiration far outside their local culture. In our own time, it has been endorsed by Wole Soyinka and many other artists working in the aftermath of European colonialism.

Culture, for these figures, is made not only from the resources of one community but also from encounters with other cultures. It is forged not only from the lived experience of individuals but also from borrowed forms and ideas that help individuals understand and articulate their experience in new ways. When seen through the lens of culture as property, these figures might appear to be intruders, appropriators, even thieves. But they pursued their work with humility and dedication because they intuited that culture evolves through circulation; they knew that false ideas of property and ownership impose limits and constraints, leading to impoverished forms of expression.

This book is not a celebration of the great books, nor a defense of the Western canon. The view of culture that emerges here is messier, and I think more interesting: one of far-flung influences, brought together through contact; of innovation driven by broken traditions patched together from recovered shards. The figures who promoted this view were often unrecognized, and some remain unknown beyond a handful of specialists even today. Many were unfamiliar to me before I began to look beyond established canons and let the protagonists of this book lead me down less trodden paths and hidden byways. What I learned from them is that if we want to restrict exploitative tourism, avoid disrespectful uses of other cultures, and protect embattled traditions, we need to find a different language than that of property and ownership, one more in keeping with how culture actually works.

From the handiwork of these creators a new story of culture emerges, one of engagement across barriers of time and place, of surprising connections and subterranean influences. It's not always a pretty story, and shouldn't be presented as such, but it's the only one we've got: the history of humans as a culture-producing species. It's the story of us.

=

INSIDE THE CHAUVET CAVE,
35,000 BCE

Long before humans appeared on earth, the Chauvet cave, in the south of France, was filled with water. Over time, the water cut deep gorges into the brittle limestone and then drained away, leaving a system of hollows perched high above the Ardèche River that began to attract visitors. For thousands of years, families of bears retreated into its deep chambers to hibernate. When the bears were gone, a wolf came and left; once, an ibex walked deep into the dark interior, jumped, and landed hard, sliding into a narrow grotto.[1] Finding itself at a dead end, it panicked, quickly retraced its steps until it had freed itself again, turned around, and finally came to a complete stop.

When the bears, the wolf, and the ibex had abandoned the cave for good, humans dared to enter it for the first time.[2] They brought torches that illuminated the network of chambers with their surprisingly even floors and their bizarre columns growing from the ceiling and the ground, formed by millennia of dripping water.[3] The flickering light of the torches also revealed marks left by the cave's previous inhabitants. As hunters and gatherers, the torchbearers were expert readers of tracks. The eight-hundred-pound bodies of grown bears had made hollows where they slept, and their sharp claws had scratched the walls. The wolf had also left tracks, and the misadventures of the ibex were recorded step by startled step on the soft clay floor.

The humans didn't just read the animal markings; they added to them, beginning a long process of turning the cave into a new environment.[4] In some cases, they did as the bears had done and scratched the surface of the cave, its weathered limestone coated with a film of clay, engraving individual figures and scenes with fingers or simple tools.[5] They drew the outlines of bears, wolves, and ibexes as if to honor the previous inhabitants of the cave, but they also conjured up other animals—panthers and lions, mammoths and aurochs, reindeer and rhinoceroses—either alone or gathered in herds fleeing from hungry predators at their heels.

In addition to the engravings, humans used the coal from their spent fires to draw more elaborate figures and scenes, sometimes filling in the outlines with mixtures of clay and ash. The walls of the caves were not flat, and the artists incorporated their unevenness, surprising viewers with a herd of horses that suddenly appeared galloping around a corner. Some artists became better in the course of a single composition, capturing the muzzle of a lion or the mane of a horse with increasing precision. They placed these drawings at strategic locations around the cave, often high up on the walls, for maximum effect on torch-bearing humans, to whom the paintings would be disclosed one by one as they moved through these dimly lit spaces.[6]

Unlike the bears, humans never lived in the caves (none of the fire pits have animal bones or other signs of cooking); their fires were used only to illuminate these spaces and to produce the charcoal with which they were decorated. They began this work over 37,000 years ago and continued it for thousands of years, guided by a shared sense of how a particular animal—a rhinoceros, an ibex, a mammoth—should be drawn.

Then, 34,000 years ago, part of the mountainside came crashing down and sealed the entrance.[7] For the artists, none of whom were in the cave at the time, it was a catastrophe that shut them off from their multigenerational work. For us, it is a piece of luck because it preserved the cave from future generations of animals and humans who would have altered or destroyed it through continual use.

The Chauvet cave shows the central dynamic of culture at work. Originally, humans may have been inspired by random bear marks to undertake their work on the cave, but over time they turned these markings into deliberate artistry that was passed down through the generations with remarkable continuity. This is the fundamental difference between bears and humans: bears (and the other animals in the cave) developed through the process of natural evolution first outlined by Charles Darwin, a process so slow that it is measured in hundreds of thousands, even millions of years.

Humans, of course, are subject to the same slow process, but unlike other animals, we have developed a second process of evolution, one based on language and other cultural techniques. This second process depends on the ability to pass down information and skills from one generation to the next without having to wait for gene mutations to occur. It is a process of transmission that doesn't change the biological makeup of humans, or does so only minimally, but it enables them to accumulate knowledge, store it, and share it with others. This second process is infinitely faster than biology and allowed humans to become one of our planet's most widespread species (alongside microbes and earthworms, whose biomass exceeds that of humans).

Cultural storage and transmission require humans to accomplish the work of storing knowledge and passing it on to the next generation by means other than DNA. To that end, humans developed techniques of memorization, of transmitting knowledge through education and by using external memory devices. The Chauvet cave was such a device, a place that humans returned to generation after generation, cooperating on a project that none of them could have accomplished alone. Each generation of artists learned techniques and continued the work of previous ones, preserving and improving what their predecessors had wrought. For us, the idea that humans might work on a single system of caves for thousands of years in the same style is almost unimaginable. But these early humans were highly conscious of the importance of storing and preserving knowledge and of passing down ideas.

What was transmitted through intergenerational collaboration in places such as the Chauvet cave? From the first, humans transmitted know-how, knowledge of the natural world and how to manipulate it, including the art of making tools and of making fire. Over time, this know-how grew to include the cultivation of crops and finally science-based technology. This increase in know-how required more sophisticated institutions, such as temples, libraries, monasteries, and universities dedicated to preserving this knowledge and teaching it to others.

But know-how is not what was recorded on the walls of the Chauvet cave: it was something closer to what we today would describe as a combination of art and religion. In one of the chambers, the cave artists placed the skull of a bear on an exposed piece of rock as if on an altarpiece, remnant of a ritual enacted here. One drawing depicts the lower part of a woman's body entangled with a human-looking shape bearing a bull's head. This pair, clearly connected to fertility, doesn't represent the world of its creators the way other cave paintings of herds fleeing from predators do; it represents a myth, an image to which was connected a story of particular significance. A final group of marks consists of abstract symbols. Perhaps these symbols, too, acquired their meaning through ritual or stories that made them part of a symbolic order very different from the everyday life outside the cave.

The skull, the mythical figures, and the abstract symbols all suggest that this cave was part of a special experience involving ritual, light effects, and stories, as well as music.[8] Flutes and percussion instruments have been found in prehistoric caves, and some of the markings on the walls may have indicated places with particular acoustic effects, instructions for where singers and musicians should be positioned.[9]

Humans went to caves such as Chauvet to create their own version of reality and to make sense of life in the outside world, with its constant struggle against the predators also depicted on the walls. What drew these humans to the cave was not the hope of improving their know-how. It was something that answered fundamental questions of their existence: why they were on this earth; why they found themselves in a special relation to other animals; questions of birth and death, origins and endings; and why they had the capacity and need to understand their relation to the cosmos. The cave was a place for humans to make meaning. It was not know-*how* but what might be called know-*why*.

Over time, what began in caves with drawings, symbols, and rituals evolved into other practices. Increasing know-how allowed humans to build artificial dwellings, some of which were used for shelter, while others became places humans would visit only on special occasions for the enactment of rituals (temples and churches), performances (theaters, concert halls), and storytelling. As we developed more know-how, we also developed new ways of understanding our place in the universe, of making our existence meaningful.

From our perspective today, the story of know-how concerns tools, science and technology, the ability to understand and manipulate the natural world. The story of know-why concerns the history of culture as a meaning-making activity. It is the domain of the humanities.

Thousands of years after the landslide at Chauvet, a second group of humans temporarily found entrance to the cave, perhaps through another mud slide. This second group of humans was very different from the cave's original artists, separated from them by thousands of years. Coming from a different culture, with different myths, stories, rituals, symbols, and ways of understanding the world, these latecomers were probably as mystified by the elaborate paintings made by their distant predecessors as we are. But something drew them to the cave; they must have tried to interpret what they saw, bringing their own cultural understanding to these incomprehensible remnants from the distant past. It is likely that they even continued the work on the cave, adding their own decorations to the existing ones.

Then, a second landslide sealed the cave for the next 28,000 years, hiding its riches but also preserving them, until they were discovered in 1994 by a team of amateur explorers led by Jean-Marie Chauvet, after whom the cave is now named.

The landslide is a reminder of the fragility of cultural transmission, which usually depends on a continuous line of communication from one generation to the next. Unlike biological evolution, which moves slowly but preserves adaptive changes more permanently in DNA, cultural transmission depends on human-made memory and teaching techniques. These techniques, and the institutions within which they are practiced, can degenerate all too easily when people lose interest in them, or they can be destroyed by external force. If the line of transmission is broken, whether because of a landslide, changing climate, or war, knowledge is lost. It disappears unless there *is* a trace, such as the cave paintings, some material remnant that gives latecomers an inkling as to what it was that was once intended for transmission to later generations. The decorations of the cave are only fragments of a larger culture, fragments without explanation. What is missing is the person-to-person transmission of stories, performances, rituals, and myths that would give these traces their full significance. But the traces are better than nothing. They allowed the second group of humans—and a third group, us—to glimpse something of an earlier time.

In some cases, the cave artists sank their hands in clay or dye and made their marks on the walls—perhaps in memory of the bear marks of old. In other cases, they "spray-painted" around a hand placed on the rock, leaving its outline clearly set off from the rest. Some of these handprints are distinct enough that they can be attributed to a single person. They express something individual: *I was here. I contributed to making this symbolic world. I am leaving this trace for the future.*

A negative imprint of a hand "spray painted" inside the Chauvet cave. It bears the signature of a distinct individual. (PHOTO CREDIT: CLAUDE VALETTE)

The experience of the second group of humans of finding entry into the Chauvet cave speaks to another important aspect of cultural transmission: recovery. Since Chauvet, countless caves, temples, and libraries have been destroyed, whether by natural disasters or human-made ones. With each act of destruction, a line of cultural transmission was cut, sometimes to be resumed only after a long interruption, if at all, which means that time and again humans went through an experience similar to that of the second group of cave visitors, that of being confronted with the remnants of a forgotten culture. This experience has turned out to be widespread and surprisingly generative. Much of ancient Egypt took place in the shadow of the great pyramids erected in the distant past. Chinese literati revered the golden age of the Zhou dynasty. Aztecs honored the ruins of temples they encountered in the Mexico basin. Italians of the modern age have been fascinated by Pompeii, destroyed by a volcano that also preserved the city under its ashes. Looking into the past, trying to understand and even to revive it, has often led to astonishing innovations and revolutions—even the word "revolution" originally meant "return."

It so happens that the humanities as a discipline emerged through a desire to revive a newly recovered past—more than once. In China, the scholar Han Yu (768–824) rejected Buddhism and advocated a return to Confucian classics, whose fine example, he thought, had been lost.[10] For him and others, the task of reviving these old texts meant that an entire new discipline of commentary, interpretation, and teaching needed to be instituted. In the Near East, the philosopher Ibn Sina (980–1037) was part of a movement to translate and interpret texts from pre-Islamic times, including Greek philosophy, creating a new synthesis of different forms of knowledge in the context of Islam.[11]

Something similar happened in Europe, when a small group of Italian poets and scholars began looking for classical manuscripts, some of which had found their way to Italy through Arabic commentators. Slowly these curious Italians discovered a lost world (lost to them, that is), searching out and editing old manuscripts and using what they learned to transform their own culture. Later scholars marked the interruption by naming the period in between, calling it the Middle Ages, the age when classical knowledge was lost, followed by its rebirth, or Renaissance. What these terms obscure is that the Italian Renaissance was not an exceptional time of rebirth but simply one more encounter with dimly understood fragments of the past, and that recoveries had been taking place even during the so-called Middle or Dark Ages. Cultural history consists of interruptions and recoveries all the way back.

=

THIS BOOK TELLS THE STORY OF CULTURE BY FOCUSING ON THE interplay of storage, loss, and recovery, which in turn means focusing on special places and institutions of meaning-making, from the earliest marks left by humans in places like the Chauvet cave to human-made cultural spaces such as Egyptian pyramids and Greek theaters, Buddhist and Christian monasteries, the island city of Tenochtitlan (Mexico), Italian *studioli* and Parisian salons, as well as the collections, cabinets of curiosities, and museums that we can visit today if we crave the past. All served as institutions where art and humanist knowledge were produced, preserved, changed, and transmitted to the next generation.

These institutions were built on different storage techniques, from sculpture and painting to storytelling, music, and ritual, as well as what has arguably been the most powerful of them all: writing. The development of different writing technologies led to the creation of Mesopotamian and Egyptian scribal schools, Arabic libraries, medieval scriptoria ("places of writing"), Renaissance collections, Enlightenment encyclopedias, and the Internet. Print, first developed in China and then reinvented in northern Europe, became a prominent vehicle for increasing the availability of written stories, and enabled broad dissemination of images as well. But alongside writing and print, oral traditions and informal knowledge networks continued to exist into our own era, providing a second and significant method of passing knowledge down to the next generation.

No matter how good these memory and storage techniques were, cultural objects and practices continued to be lost, destroyed, or abandoned, forcing subsequent generations to make sense of cultural expressions they no longer understood or that had been preserved only partially and inadequately. The inevitable result of such degradation and loss was widespread misunderstanding, with each new generation developing mistaken beliefs about the past.

But interruptions and errors in transmission, though certainly deplorable, did not stop culture from evolving. In fact, they could be quite productive, leading to new and original creations. Just as biological adaptation proceeds by (random) errors in genetic sequences, so cultural adaptation proceeds through errors of transmission. These errors are the way in which culture experiments, allowing new generations to project their own concerns onto the past and to inject urgency into its continuation.

If one drama of cultural transmission has been preservation, loss, and (often error-prone) recovery, another drama has been the interaction among cultures. Such interactions were brought about by war and invasion, but also through commerce and travel, leading to new forms of culture. Some of the greatest civilizations developed by borrowing from others, as when an Indian king imported the art of erecting pillars from Persia, when the Romans imported literature, theater, and gods from Greece, when the Chinese went searching for Buddhist scripture in India, when Japanese diplomats crossed over to China to learn about texts, architectural styles, and new forms of worship, when Ethiopians invented a foundational story connected to the Hebrew and Christian Bible, and when the Aztecs borrowed from the preceding cultures they encountered in the Mexico basin.

As the advantages of cross-cultural interaction became evident, some forward-looking rulers deliberately encouraged it, among them the Japanese emperors who sent diplomatic missions to China and Haroun al-Rashid of Baghdad, who assimilated knowledge from across the Mediterranean and the Near East into what he called his Storehouse of Wisdom. All of these examples of cultural borrowing were accompanied by misunderstandings and errors, but these were often productive misunderstandings, leading to new forms of knowledge and meaning-making.

More troubling, cultural encounters also led to destruction, theft, and violence. This was especially the case with the rise of European colonial empires, which forced different parts of the world into contact with strangers who aimed to extract their labor and resources, including cultural ones. But despite the widespread violence that routinely accompanied cultural contact, cultures under assault developed astonishing strategies of resistance and resilience, demonstrating the rapid pace of cultural adaptation as opposed to the painfully slow course of biological evolution.

The history of culture sketched in these pages has plenty of lessons for us today. In some ways, we are more eager to track down and recover knowledge from the distant past than ever, even as important monuments are being lost with accelerating frequency through environmental forces, neglect, or deliberate destruction. New storage technologies make it possible to preserve texts, images, and music at minimal cost, and social media such as Facebook, Twitter, and You-Tube have made it simpler to share this stored content more widely than ever before. Never have previously produced cultural artifacts and practices been as readily available to as many people as they are now.

Yet, amid this digital abundance of cultural content, older file formats, websites, and entire databases are becoming unreadable at a frightening speed, raising the question of whether we're really so much better at preserving the past than our ancestors were. And while the technologies of cultural storage and distribution have changed, the laws governing how culture works—how it is preserved, transmitted, exchanged, and recovered—haven't. The interplay of preservation and destruction, of loss and recovery, of error and adaptation continues unabated in a world that has put almost all human cultures in constant contact. We fight over the past and what it means, over who owns culture and who has access to it, more than ever.

In our debates over originality and integrity, appropriation and mixture, we sometimes forget that culture is not a possession, but something we hand down so that others may use it in their own way; culture is a vast recycling project in which small fragments from the past are retrieved to generate new and surprising ways of meaning-making. This book tells of a sultan who stole an ancient pillar that was meant to be found; of an Arab archeologist who dug up an Egyptian queen who was meant to be erased from history; of a caliph who collected knowledge no matter who had produced it; of a Greek who invented a false story of Greece, and a Roman who invented a false story of Rome; of an Ethiopian queen who used the Ten Commandments to tell a new story of origin. These exemplary episodes in cultural history all feature humans who got their hands dirty with culture in the difficult work of meaning-making. How should we remember and judge them?

Above all with humility. Since the Chauvet cave, so much has been created and so little has survived, often because of the arrogance of later generations who neglected precious cultural artifacts and practices because they didn't conform to the religious, social, political, or ethical ideals of the moment. Will we do better? Will we let a greater range of cultural expressions thrive than they did?

The main lesson from cultural history is that we need engagement with the past, and with one another, for cultures to reach their full potential, despite the errors, incomprehension, and destruction that often accompany such engagement. If we were to divorce cultures from the past or from one another, we would deprive them of the oxygen that keeps them alive.

All creators put their trust in the future by trusting that the future will not destroy their works despite the differences in value they know will inevitably arise. *Culture: The Story of Us* aims to offer its readers the breathtaking variety of cultural works that we as a species have wrought, in the hope that we will carry our shared human inheritance into the next generation, and beyond.

CULTURE

CHAPTER 1

—

QUEEN NEFERTITI AND HER
FACELESS GOD

Mohammed es-Senussi was the first to lay eyes on her. Just after lunch break, he and his workers had dug up a bust of a king, badly damaged, and found evidence of other fragile pieces nearby. Clearly, they had hit on an unusual site. As the most careful and skilled of the excavators, es-Senussi sent everyone else away, afraid they might do damage to the delicate sculptures buried here, and continued on his own. The room was filled with three and a half feet of debris, which es-Senussi now cleared away carefully, as he had done so many times before, gingerly manipulating a hoe. Wearing his usual wide tunic, which had once been white but now showed signs of heavy use, and a cap that covered his large head and closely cropped black hair, he was slowly making his way towards the eastern wall of the room, finding several fragments of sculpture along the way.[1]

Es-Senussi and the workers entrusted to his care had been excavating in the area for over a year when they came across the remnants of a large complex that proved to be a treasure trove of sculptures, figurines, and reliefs. The small room in which es-Senussi was now working seemed to house an unusual number of them, packed closely together. After encountering some smaller fragments buried in the dry mud and sand, he came upon the neck of a life-size sculpture with astonishingly vibrant colors.

Es-Senussi put aside his hoe and continued with his hands. They weren't especially delicate hands and belonged to an imposingly tall and corpulent man, but es-Senussi could show exquisite finesse in handling fragile shards. He kneeled in the dirt and let his fingers feel their way around this sculpture. Slowly, a cone-shaped crown emerged.

Excavating the sculpture was difficult because other pieces were buried close by and had to be removed first, but finally es-Senussi was able to perceive the bust of a woman lying face down. When he lifted the sculpture from the ground and turned it over, he was able to look at her face: the first person to do so in some 3,244 years. A journal entry from December 6, 1912, notes: "the colors look as if they had just been applied. Exquisite workmanship. No use trying to describe it: you must see it."[2]

What es-Senussi saw was a face of astonishing symmetry, painted with a bronze skin tone, prominent cheekbones, oval eyes, and full but sharply drawn lips. There were slight creases around the sides of the mouth, not quite enough for a smile. The bust was almost miraculously preserved, with minor damage to the ears, and one of the eyes was missing. There was no name attached to the bust, but the regal crown made it clear that es-Senussi was holding a queen. A photo taken after es-Senussi had called others to inspect his find shows him cradling the queen in his arms, one hand supporting her weight, the other carefully balancing her large head, looking down on his treasure with an expression of intense pride and care. The queen does not return his gaze but looks serenely into the far distance, seemingly undisturbed by the excitement she is causing and unaware of the fact that she is, or will soon become, the most famous face of antiquity.

The sculpture was part of an ongoing puzzle. It was found in al-Amarna, equidistant from the two great cities of ancient Egypt, Memphis to the north and Thebes to the south. The ruins had long

Es-Senussi cradling the bust of Nefertiti, which he had just unearthed in the compound of the sculptor Thutmose. (UNIVERSITÄTSARCHIV, UNIVERSITÄT FREIBURG)

been neglected because they were insignificant compared to the great pyramids of Giza, near Memphis, or the palaces and temples of Thebes. But gradually, over the past century, the foundations of buildings and graves had been discovered, and archeologists suggested that there had once been a great city here, though no one knew its name.[3] Tombs and sculptures such as the one excavated by es-Senussi indicated that the city had been inhabited by a king and a queen. Finally, after years of searching, inscriptions were found that revealed a name. The bust depicted Queen Nefertiti, Lady of Grace, Great of Praises, Mistress of Upper and Lower Egypt, and wife of King Amenhotep IV. Who was this mysterious queen?

Egyptians had kept records of their kings and queens, but neither Nefertiti nor Amenhotep IV could be properly identified in them. As the excavations continued, more puzzles emerged. The city must have been built quickly, using mud bricks, which was why so little had remained. Apparently, it had been abandoned by the very people who had built it. Equally mysterious was the fact that their sculptures, such as the bust of Nefertiti, were unlike anything found in ancient Egypt. And why was one eye missing from her otherwise perfect face? A price was put on its recovery, but neither es-Senussi nor anyone else ever found it.

One thing became clear fairly quickly: Es-Senussi had dug his way into the storage room of a sculptor. Sculptors in ancient Egypt didn't sign their work, but the name tag on a harness found in this compound identified the owner as one Thutmose, making him a rarity, an artist from antiquity known to us by name. Judging by the size of his compound, Thutmose was well established. A wall surrounded the entire compound, which could be accessed only through a single gate, probably guarded. The complex contained a generous courtyard that provided access to several buildings, including workshops and narrow living quarters for apprentices. Most impressive were the living quarters of Thutmose and his family, which gave out onto a garden with a large well, crucial in this arid land. Right next to the living quarters was the granary, with four containers for holding barley and wheat. These grains did more than feed the members of the family and the workshop throughout the year. In an economy without money, grain could serve as a store of wealth, like gold, to be bartered for almost anything.[4]

Another sign of Thutmose's prominence was the location of his compound, far removed from the river Nile with its busy quays. Behind the quays were storage areas for different goods that arrived by boat, such as wheat, barley, beer, and cattle. Then came the part of the city mostly populated by workshops, though Thutmose's compound was

not among them. His was located in the quieter, residential area farther back, almost at the edge of town. Beyond his workshop, off at a
distance, were the workers' villages, nestled close to the quarries where
the heavy work of cutting stone was done. Given that other sculptures
of Nefertiti were found in Thutmose's workshop, it was clear that he
enjoyed the queen's particular patronage. Through the patient work
of excavators such as es-Senussi, one of the most unusual episodes in
Egyptian history was slowly coming to light.

Nefertiti and Amenhotep had grown up two hundred miles to the
south, in Thebes (today's Luxor), which at the time was one of the largest cities in the world, numbering some 80,000 inhabitants. It marked
the southern center of the Egyptian heartland, which stretched from
the mouth of the Nile in the north some eight hundred miles upriver
to Thebes in the south. Once a mere trading post with Sudan, Thebes
had become the capital many generations before Nefertiti, boasting
large temples with gigantic pillars and a processional avenue lined by
sphinxes. Across the river from the city was the Valley of Kings, where
pharaohs and nobles had been entombed for hundreds of years. For
Nefertiti and Amenhotep, growing up in Thebes meant growing up
amid the monuments of the past, latecomers to history.

If ancient history was present everywhere in Thebes, this was
nothing compared to the northern end of Egypt, in Giza, where the
kings of the Old Kingdom had built their three giant pyramids, one of
them guarded by a huge sphinx, over a thousand years earlier. In fact,
pretty much everything about Egypt was designed to make one feel the
weight of the past. More so than any other culture, Egypt had invested
its enormous resources into defying time. Not only pharaohs but also
nobles, and anyone, really, who could afford it, had their eyes set on
eternity (about the aspirations of the common people, those who built
the temples and burial chambers, little is known). Burial chambers
hidden deep inside pyramids and tombs carved into mountains were
outfitted with everything that might be useful in the future, from food

to naked female companions.[5] To be sure, burying and remembering the dead is something all human societies have done, but in Egypt, the dead were not only buried and remembered, but also preserved.

Amenhotep's father, Amenhotep III, was a typical representative of this worship of the past. He had inherited a unified Egypt with a host of vassal states reaching all the way to Mesopotamia. With enormous resources at his command, Amenhotep III had unleashed an ambitious building project, centered on the large, ancient temple complex of Karnak.[6] He restored some parts of it—restoration was one of the demands the monuments of the past placed on the present.[7] Not content with simple restoration, Amenhotep III rebuilt other temples, and in much grander style, including the ancient Luxor temple with its enormous colonnade.

When Amenhotep III died, in 1351 BCE, his son, Amenhotep IV, presided over his father's mummification and burial rituals, as was required, before ascending the throne. Then he married Nefertiti and designated her as his principal wife. For pharaohs, marriage was politics, and in the past many pharaohs had married their sisters or other relatives as their principal wives, in addition to secondary marriages to foreign princesses to forge advantageous alliances. Nefertiti was not of royal parentage, but perhaps grew up as ward, or even as daughter, of the influential scribe and administrator Ay.[8] The court was used to strong women—Amenhotep III's mother had been a power broker and continued to wield influence at court even after her husband's death. With the ascension of Amenhotep IV and his marriage to Nefertiti, the continuity of the line was assured.

But Nefertiti and Amenhotep were not interested in continuity. Instead, they wanted to break with tradition, at least when it came to buildings and institutions. They began by strategically neglecting one of the most visible monuments: the restored Karnak temple complex, which was dedicated to the important god Amun.[9] The priests in charge of maintaining his temple were correspondingly influential.

Neglecting the dwelling place of this god meant targeting a center of power. Adding insult to injury, Nefertiti and Amenhotep IV elevated a relatively minor god, called Aten. Within a few years, the old order of Thebes, with the god Amun and its gigantic temple complex at the center, had been upended, and worship of the new god took center stage.

In the polytheistic world of ancient Egypt, it was not unusual for gods to change. (Amun himself had been created by the fusion of two earlier gods.) But such changes had to be introduced gradually and carefully, not with the kind of violence that brought Amun down and elevated Aten to a supreme position. Yet Nefertiti and Amenhotep were not content even with this abrupt reversal. They neglected all other gods and increasingly came to view their Aten as the only important one. Unsurprisingly, everyone invested in the old order—not only the great number of Amun priests but also the larger part of the governing elite—was unhappy and fought back.

It was in the midst of this power struggle that Nefertiti and Amenhotep made the radical decision to leave everything behind: the temples; the burial tombs of their ancestors; the entire city littered with the monuments of the past, including many dedicated to Amun. They packed the entire court, including the sculptor Thutmose, onto barges and sailed two hundred miles downstream to make a fresh start.[10]

When Nefertiti and Amenhotep IV first arrived there, no habitation existed at all, only a stretch of desert bordered on one side by the Nile and on the other three by imposing cliffs.[11] The new city was going to be something unusual: a planned city built from scratch.

The new city would be free from the burdens of the past, uniquely focused on the new god after whom it was named: Akhetaten, Horizon of the Sun (Aten). (Today's name, Amarna, is derived from a tribe that subsequently settled there.) The city was constructed around a Great and a Small Aten Temple, between which was located the Great Palace. Everything else was oriented around this symbolic line. Akhetaten, the Horizon of the Sun, was a novelty, a city with precise geometrical axes, temples and government buildings arranged at right angles, and clearly delineated and planned workshops and workers' villages. Clearly, by leaving behind the old capital, Nefertiti and her husband had not left behind the passion for enormous building projects: their own plan to build an entire city was every bit as gigantic an undertaking as the great pyramids of Giza.

There was one significant difference: everything needed to happen quickly and was built in a rush, cheaply, for immediate use.[12] The result was that almost everything was constructed with mud bricks, stone being reserved only for pillars and large temples. This didn't mean that the palaces were not elegant. The walls of the palace were elaborately decorated, including the royal bedroom. Nefertiti was an unusual queen not only because she was not of royal blood but also because she and her husband apparently shared a bedroom; perhaps this was part of the revolution they had undertaken and that shook the country.[13] Their palace was situated right on the water, so that Nefertiti and her husband would have enjoyed whatever breeze this arid part of Egypt could summon up. (Nefertiti, like many Egyptian queens, had shaved her head, which was cooler in the desert heat and allowed her to wear different wigs for different occasions.[14]) To complete the revolution, Amenhotep IV shed the name of his ancestors and called himself Akhenaten. Nefertiti held onto her name but added the word for sun or disk (*aten*) as part of a second name, Neferneferuaten, or Fair is the Beauty of the Aten.[15] The two royals vowed never to leave the new city, with its new temples dedicated to their new god, ever again.

As part of their break with the past, Nefertiti and Akhenaten demanded that they be represented in a new style, which is why the new city was attractive to sculptors such as Thutmose who were eager to take on new commissions. While visual representation, in ancient Egypt, was by no means unchanging, there had been a remarkable degree of continuity over hundreds of years. Pyramids, sphinxes, obelisks, the decoration of burial caskets and chambers were part of an inherited repertoire. Pharaohs would take one step forward in three-dimensional sculpture or be turned sideways in two-dimensional reliefs so that they could be shown in their characteristic profile. Sculptors and painters weren't encouraged to innovate; originality was not a value, but a failing.

All this changed in the new city, where Thutmose and his colleagues were breaking with tradition and finding ways to signal to viewers that Nefertiti and Akhenaten were a different kind of ruler from their ancestors and therefore required a different kind of art. The new style sometimes strikes today's observers as exaggerated and strange.

When seen in profile, Nefertiti and her husband were depicted with elongated jaws and mouths, so that their faces almost resembled the snout of a dog; their heads were angled forward on unnatu-

Trial piece of Akhenaten, limestone, suggesting the elongated heads and snout-like faces typical of the Akhetaten period.   (METROPOLITAN MUSEUM OF ART, NEW YORK)

rally long necks. Strangest of all were the backs of their heads, which looked unnaturally long. Even Thutmose's painted bust of Nefertiti unearthed by es-Senussi bore traces of these features, including the elongated crown—who knew what kind of head was hiding underneath it—and the long neck, angled forward. Another innovation was the androgynous depiction of Akhenaten, who is often shown with breasts and wide hips; nineteenth-century archeologists sometimes mistook him for a woman.[16]

Egyptian painting and sculpture were not naturalistic and there is no reason to believe that Nefertiti and Akhenaten actually looked like that, just as there is no reason to believe that Egyptians walked sideways.[17] In ancient Egypt, painting and sculpture was closer to writing, a highly abstract system of visual communication. Hieroglyphics, after all, were standardized images that stood for ideas and combinations of sounds, so Egyptians were used to reading paintings, reliefs, and statues symbolically. Nefertiti's and Akhenaten's extended heads and elongated faces, for example, could be seen as fitting the shape of the crowns, as if these humans were predestined to wear them. Or they were depicted as having acquired their crown-like shapes because royalty had become second nature, making them look different from others. (Equally non-naturalistic was skin color. Egyptian artists used various shades, from light brown to almost black, but those tones said little about the race of the person depicted, in part because ancient Egyptians did not tie nationhood to a notion of biological race. People were Egyptian if they spoke Egyptian and lived like Egyptians.[18])

The new images were significant, also, because they were bound up with the new god Aten. Usually, other gods would be seen as intermediaries, but Nefertiti and Akhenaten, now firmly established in their new city, broke with this system and presented themselves as sole intermediaries between their god and everyone else.[19] In many images, they can be seen basking in Aten's rays, the only direct recipients of the god's life-giving power. Many of those images also include their children, something that was also quite unusual, making for intriguing family scenes. It is likely that many of these images, found in the houses of nobles, were used as devotional objects to which prayers and rituals would be directed.[20]

Thutmose's head of Nefertiti might have served a similar purpose, but more likely, this bust was used as a model with which he could show his assistants and apprentices how the queen should be molded—which would explain the missing eye, as an opportunity for Thutmose to demonstrate his craft. Es-Senussi found many other examples of models and works-in-progress in Thutmose's compound, which show us how stone sculptures were made. First, Thutmose would mold a face using wax or clay; then a gypsum cast was made, perhaps to be shown to Nefertiti herself; and only then would the sculpture be carved in stone.[21]

The use of the Nefertiti bust as model also explains the statue's

Carved limestone relief of Akhenaten, Nefertiti, and their three daughters basking in the rays of the sun god Aten.

(EGYPTIAN GALLERY, NEUES MUSEUM, BERLIN. PHOTO: GARY TODD, WORLDHISTORYPICS.COM)

extreme symmetry, which has struck so many observers as a sign of supreme beauty, but which is very different from the completed depictions of Nefertiti that Thutmose and other sculptors made. Sculptors used a system of measuring proportions with the width of a finger, and the Nefertiti statue fits that measuring system perfectly.[22] This suggests that the bust is a kind of abstraction, a demonstration model from which all idiosyncrasies and symbolic meanings, which make other depictions of the queen more difficult to understand, have been removed. Be this as it may, the new images of Nefertiti and Akhenaten helped establish Aten as a new god, but also as a new kind of god, which meant that Aten, too, required a new form of visual depiction. Aten had begun as a deity with a falcon head but had gradually assumed the shape of a disk, as in the disk of the sun. Then artists pushed this idea further by making him stand for light itself.

This process of abstraction could no longer be represented visually, which is why the supreme depiction of the new god was not in sculpture but in writing: "The Great Hymn to the Aten." This hymn was found inscribed in a burial chamber in Akhetaten, where otherwise passages from the *Book of the Dead* might be placed, to assure the dead person's passage to the underworld. (Some private tombs in Akhetaten do contain spells from chapter 151 of the *Book of the Dead*.[23]) It begins by praising Aten as other hymns might have praised an earlier sun god, namely by describing the defeat of darkness, the spectacle of sunrise, and the melancholy of sunset. But soon, the "Hymn" goes much further, elevating this god Aten as the sustenance of all life on earth, from plants and animals to humans. Aten is a god,

> *Who makes seed grow in women,*
> *Who creates people from sperm;*
> *Who feeds the son in his mother's womb*
> *Who soothes him to still his tears.*
> *Nurse in the womb,*

Giver of breath,
To nourish all that he made.[24]

This is a god who sustains all growth and, as the principle that makes possible every single breath, life itself.

The hymn is not done with its work of abstraction and concentration. Not only does this god sustain all life; he is responsible for having created the entire earth. "You made the earth as you wished, you alone / All peoples, herds, and flock." Aten is a creator god, who made everything, all by himself alone, without the help of any other god. It is difficult for us, who are so used to monotheism, to appreciate the radical nature of this thought. For a society used to multiple gods existing side by side and in complex relation with one another, it must have been a shock, almost incomprehensible.

The "Great Hymn" is sometimes attributed to Akhenaten, which makes sense given his close identification with this god, but it might also have been written by Nefertiti, who was associated with Egypt's most important scribe. In the past, royal wives usually played a minor or at least subordinate role in worship, but Nefertiti's function in the Aten cult was equal to that of her husband.[25] Intriguingly, the "Great Hymn" initially focuses on women's bodies, on what nourishes and sustains unborn life within them. It even describes the process of giving birth: "When he comes from the womb to breathe, / on the day of his birth, / You open wide his mouth, / You supply his need." While Aten is an increasingly transcendent god, here he is shown as giving birth in details that register experience. And the "Great Hymn" ends with an invocation of Nefertiti, "the great queen," "The lady of the Two Lands, / Nefernefru-Aten Nefertiti, living forever."

The revolution in art that took place in Akhetaten is a reminder of the close relation between art and religion as allied forms of meaning-making. In engaging the past, we tend to project our current ideas and categories onto societies that almost certainly would not have recognized them. The distinction between art and religion—implying that art can be disconnected from religion, and religion from art—is one of these projections. The Akhetaten revolution shows that in the distant past, and indeed in many of today's societies, making meaning is an exercise in orientation that involves fundamental questions that cut across neatly distinguished areas of art and belief.

The Akhetaten revolution ended almost as suddenly as it had begun. Nefertiti and Akhenaten were more interested in building their new city, worshipping their new god, and commissioning new sculptures than in maintaining their empire. Increasingly desperate for military aid, their vassals wrote to them from across the region, often in Akkadian, the lingua franca of the Middle East at the time, and on clay tablets using the cuneiform script. Old enemies, in Thebes, must have used the neglect of the empire to their advantage.[26]

On top of these pressures came disease. Tuberculosis, malaria, and other unnamed plagues were endemic in Egypt, the result of concentrated urban living. There is even speculation that Nefertiti's and Akhenaten's decision to start a new city was an attempt to escape from these diseases. But the diseases followed, and soon their city, too, was subject to them.[27] Nefertiti and Akhenaten still stayed true to their vow never to leave their new city, despite these scourges. When Akhenaten died, he was ceremonially buried, and his body preserved in the royal tomb that had been built for the purpose. His break with the past had not been absolute, and he thought about eternity in the traditional way. Perhaps he had even imagined that his city, once established, would be rebuilt on a more permanent basis.

As always with the death of a pharaoh, succession was of crucial importance. Akhenaten was succeeded by two very short-lived pharaohs, each ruling less than a year, and there is some speculation that Nefertiti may have been one of them. Greater stability was ensured only when Akhenaten's son Tutankhaten, who was still a child, took the throne, under the guidance of the high-ranking scribe and administrator Ay (who would himself accede to the throne at a later point).

But stability required the undoing of everything Nefertiti and Akhenaten had created. Tutankhaten changed his name to Tutankhamun, to signal that he was abandoning the new faith of his father and returning to the god Amun. More significantly, he moved the court and everything belonging to it back to Thebes. He didn't go so far as to outlaw the Aten cult entirely, and his own tomb, spectacularly discovered in the early twentieth century, even contained a depiction of Aten, as if in memory of his father's extraordinary experiment. But for all intents and purposes, the Aten era had come to an end.

With the court gone, there was less and less reason for anyone to live on this harsh desert plateau, and so the city of Akhetaten was gradually abandoned. This was certainly the case for Thutmose, who depended on royal patronage. He didn't leave in a hurry, but carefully selected what he would take and what he would leave behind.[28] The gypsum casts of his works-in-progress were useless and didn't need to be transported, at great cost, to Thebes or Memphis. All unfinished or finished sculptures and reliefs of Akhenaten and his god were now obsolete; they, too, would be left behind.

The same was true of the beautiful model bust of Nefertiti. No longer would Thutmose show his apprentices how to use the precise finger-method of measuring proportions using this bust, nor would he demonstrate how to add an eye to its face. To honor his years of service to the two revolutionary royals, he carefully placed all these statues in a storeroom and sealed it with a wall. The court might be abandoning the city and everything it stood for, but Thutmose did not want looters to defile the remnants of his handiwork. And there, in the sealed-off storeroom, the bust remained, safe from interference. At some point, the wooden shelf which held the Nefertiti bust crumbled and the bust fell to the ground, where it was gradually covered by mud brought by the Nile. Fortunately, the mud also preserved it for the next three thousand years, until es-Senussi, with his large but careful hands, cleared the mud away, turned the bust over, and gazed at it in astonishment.

It's not so easy to get rid of the past, even though we keep trying. The past lies buried underground, sometimes for thousands of years, waiting to be dug up again.

THOU SHALT NOT HAVE OTHER GODS BEFORE ME

Egyptian rulers and scribes didn't pay much attention to the people living in the periphery of their empire. The same was not true the other way around: different groups of semi-settled shepherds knew that their fate was closely bound up with that of their Egyptian overlords. One such group in particular told a story of their people in which Egypt played an outsized role. The story features a shepherd by the name of Joseph, son of Jacob, who is sold into Egypt as an enslaved laborer. A willing and industrious worker, he manages to rise in the administrative apparatus of the empire and ends up occupying one of the highest positions in the land. He attracts the attention of the (unnamed) pharaoh thanks to his careful management of resources.

Joseph's use of storage is striking because it is historically true that Egypt had profited from a storage revolution. At the base of this revolution was agriculture, which had allowed humans to settle down and crowd together in urban spaces. The Nile, which supplied Egypt not only with water but also with nutrient-rich floodplains, was perfect for this new mode of living.

The storage of grain and other foods made possible a different kind of storage, namely of wealth. Nomadic peoples had been comparatively egalitarian. While they had their leaders, differences in wealth were restricted to what people could carry on their backs or their horses (they could, of course, own several horses). But now, with the storage revolution, discrepancies in wealth could, in principle, be infinite.[29]

Those with control over land and labor could extract enormous riches that could be stored in granaries.

Joseph, according to these stories, understood the power of storage and induced the pharaoh to store grain during good years as a hedge against calamity. When a drought hit the region, he was able to feed Egypt and extend its power. During this time of hardship, Joseph brought his tribe of shepherds from Canaan to the Egyptian heartland, where they were allowed to settle. When he died, Joseph was embalmed and buried in the Egyptian fashion, as befitted his station.

After Joseph's death, and the death of the friendly pharaoh, Egypt turned against the foreigners. Fortunately, one of them, by the name of Moses, had been adopted by a new pharaoh, and enjoyed the privileges and education of a member of the royal household. After much back and forth, he finally managed to convince the pharaoh to let the shepherds return to their ancestral homeland in Canaan, whither he led them and their religion based on a single god.

There is no mention of these Canaanite shepherds anywhere in the ample records kept by Egyptian scribes, nor would one expect there to be. Semi-pastoralists from the periphery of this far-flung empire came and went without leaving a trace in the minds of pharaohs and the annals of their affairs of state. Without an ethnic conception of nationhood, Egyptians married foreign women and bought foreign enslaved people depending on their needs. (There is some speculation that Nefertiti may have been from Mesopotamia because her name means "The Beautiful One Has Come," suggesting her arrival from abroad.) The only record of these complicated relations between the shepherds and their Egyptian lords is to be found in the later writings of the shepherds, which would come to be known as the Hebrew Bible, once they had settled in Canaan and founded a small kingdom centered on the city of Jerusalem.[30]

Two important figures of this group—Moses and Joseph—are described, according to their own scriptures, as Egyptian administrators and scribes. Moses, whose name means in Egyptian "child," as in "child of," is the one who, according to tradition, wrote down the story of these people, thereby bringing the scribal culture of Egypt to a group whose lifestyle did not depend on writing.

The religion defined in the Hebrew Bible, based on a single god, was radically different from anything else at the time—with one exception: Nefertiti's short-lived god Aten.[31] Could it be a coincidence that these two cultures, so closely interlinked, came up with the radically novel experiment in a form of monotheism? Egyptian records, of course, erased the Aten experiment. The Hebrew Bible, in turn, might have wanted to emphasize its people's independence from Egypt (even though it admitted to the outsized role of Egypt in the lives of Moses and Joseph), and might have wanted to avoid references to Egyptian models. If borrowing occurred, all traces of it have disappeared.

Ever since the Aten experiment was uncovered in the late nineteenth century, different cultural figures have been intrigued by a possible connection between the Aten cult and Judaism. The Nobel Prize-winning novelist Thomas Mann spent over a decade turning the story of Joseph and his brothers into a four-volume novel, in which he places Joseph at the court of Akhenaten.[32] His contemporary Sigmund Freud went further and suggested that Moses was quite simply an Egyptian, a staunch supporter of the Aten experiment who went into exile after the death of Akhenaten and proselytized the new monotheistic faith to a group of Canaanites, where it slowly became what we know as Judaism.[33]

I don't think it is necessary to go quite so far. Despite the radical nature of the Aten cult as established by Nefertiti and Akhenaten—and sculptors such as Thutmose—this cult wasn't anything like the monotheism we associate with Judaism and its successor monotheisms, Christianity and Islam. While Nefertiti and Akhenaten neglected other gods, they did not outlaw their worship, as the Hebrew Bible does in its first commandment—"Thou shalt have no other gods before me."[34] In contrast to Judaism, the Aten cult was not mandatory for the common people, only for courtiers and the elite (no statues either of Nefertiti and Akhenaten, or of Aten, were found in the houses of workers). Worshippers of other Egyptian gods continued to play a role outside the newly-built capital city.

The Aten experiment also did not include anything like the radical law against any depiction of divinity we know from Judaism and Islam (otherwise sculptors could not have depicted Nefertiti and Akhenaten basking in the rays of their god). Finally, Judaism, Christianity, and Islam developed into religions based on a text: sacred scripture. Egypt did associate some texts with the sacred, but the *Book of the Dead* and the "Great Hymn" were nothing like the Hebrew Bible or the Qur'an—namely, the sole source and intermediary between a god and its people.[35]

Yet the intriguing fact remains that two intensely intertwined cultures developed versions of what we call monotheism, though probably at different times. Perhaps the question of influence, of direct borrowing, is not the most important one. Everyone is influenced by someone; every instance of originality can be traced to things borrowed from others. We're all latecomers, ever since we evolved techniques of cultural storage that put the past at our disposal. What is important is not *what* we borrow but *how* we borrow, what we make of what we find. What the group of Jewish exiles made of the Aten experiment, if they encountered it at all, is utterly distinct from it and deserves to be remembered as a great achievement regardless.

The importance of how we borrow from others is related to how we borrow from the past, that is, how we remember. In the case of Nefertiti and Akhenaten, they were almost forgotten because their names were deleted from the king lists, from statues, and from other records. If there was mention of these two radicals at all, it was to denounce them. For the next several thousand years, Akhenaten was known only as "the criminal of Amarna."[36] This erasure was surprisingly effective and managed to remove Nefertiti, Akhenaten, and their experiment from history, creating a puzzle that was gradually solved only in the nineteenth and twentieth centuries. It was a bitter irony: the two royals who had done everything to break with the past were themselves erased from it.

If Nefertiti's and Akhenaten's experiment in monotheism was the reason why they were almost forgotten, it's now the reason why we remember them. We care so much about this brief episode in Egyptian history because we now live in a world shaped by monotheism. If the world had continued to live in a polytheistic manner, the Aten experiment would be little more than a curiosity, a footnote in history. We bring our own values and experiences to the past. It was the future, our future, that made Akhetaten not only a great rebellion against the past, but also the first glimpse of something new.

The Akhetaten episode reminds us that the past is never just there, to be discovered or ignored. We constantly fight over it. Just as Nefertiti and Akhenaten abandoned the Amun temples and let them crumble, so their successors let the new city decay. One person's criminal is another person's hero of innovation. In using the past, we constantly make and unmake it according to our needs and prejudices.

The willful erasure of Nefertiti, Akhenaten, and their god, and the abandonment of their city, paradoxically also helped preserve it. To be sure, graverobbers devastated many graves, which is why Tutankhamun transferred his father's mummy to Thebes.[37] He knew that the abandoned city would be undefended and open to looting.

But an abandoned city, even one that is looted, reveals to later archeologists much more than a city continually in use. Continual use tends to be surprisingly destructive, as artistic models get recycled and new buildings are constructed from the materials of the old. Even though not much remains of Akhetaten, due to its cheap and temporary building materials, the city, untouched, frozen in time, has given us unprecedented insight into the lives of royals and commoners alike, including into the working techniques of sculptors such as Thutmose.

Today, the Nefertiti bust resides in the Neues Museum in Berlin, where she has a small room to herself. The room is darkened, with careful indirect lighting that brings out her radiant colors. The story of how she ended up there also speaks to a dynamic of preservation and destruction. The work of es-Senussi's hands was financed and overseen by Prussian archeologists—the latest of a series of Europeans fascinated with ancient Egypt and eager to excavate its monuments.

A first wave of Europeans had come in the wake of Napoleon's invasion of Egypt, when Jean-François Champollion managed to decipher hieroglyphics, which had passed from human knowledge for thousands of years. Many European Egyptologists, however, also acted, in the way of colonial powers, like graverobbers, transporting their findings to European museums with impunity while justifying themselves as preservers. Only gradually did Egypt—and other countries visited by these rapacious scientists—institute laws that prevented the theft of cultural objects. By the time es-Senussi unearthed Nefertiti in 1912, arrangements had been made to divide whatever treasures might be found in this Prussian-financed excavation, with some going to Egypt and others to Germany. Nefertiti ended up in the German pile.

Nefertiti's century in Germany has been a tumultuous and dangerous one. Archeologists are by necessity destructive: once they remove the layers of dirt that preserve a site, the site is forever disturbed and exposed. Only the most meticulous documentation and the most careful procedures can possibly justify this intrusive search for the past. Meanwhile, fragile objects such as Nefertiti's bust, once they are unearthed, are exposed to all the dangers of life on the surface of the earth, from harsh weather to human destruction. In Berlin, Nefertiti faced two world wars. The Neues Museum was bombed in the near-total destruction of Berlin at the end of World War II. Fortunately, most of the objects, Nefertiti among them, had been removed and placed in safe locations.

The Neues Museum was left as a ruin in East Berlin throughout the existence of the Communist state and carefully restored only in 2008, in a way that treated it exactly as we now treat ancient statues, by making visible what is old and what is new. When one visits Nefertiti today, therefore, one has to pass through the ruin of a museum, walk up the stairs through a courtyard that was until recently open to the elements, to arrive at the darkened chamber where this serene bust now resides, seemingly undisturbed by the tumult of the ages. But then again, Nefertiti was used to upheaval and revolution. She had been a central player in the construction of a new city, as well as of a new god and new art, created from almost nothing within a few years in one of the most extraordinary experiments undertaken by humans, whose true significance would only be appreciated in the distant future.

CHAPTER 2

PLATO BURNS HIS TRAGEDY
AND INVENTS A HISTORY

"O Solon, Solon," the priests of the Egyptian goddess Isis laughed at their Athenian visitor, "you Greeks are always like children. There is no such thing as an old Greek." Solon asked for an explanation. The priests replied: "You are young in soul, every one of you. For therein you possess not a single belief that is ancient and derived from old tradition."[1]

According to this story, Solon, one of the founding figures of Athenian democracy, had traveled to Sais, an imposing city located in the Nile delta, expecting to receive some ancient, gnomic wisdom. Over the past centuries, Greek city-states had established trading posts and settlements throughout the eastern Mediterranean, outposts of a rising Greek culture. The Greeks generally looked down on other cultures, calling them "barbarians"—a term which, although it originally meant simply non-Greek-speaking, had taken on negative associations of inferiority.

But Egypt was sometimes excepted from Greek arrogance perhaps because it was seen, even by Greeks, as singularly ancient, mysterious, and possessed of a sacred writing system guarded by priests, which was why Solon had traveled there. He got what he asked for when

the priests of Isis went on to school him: Egypt enjoyed a continuous
cultural tradition of great antiquity. Egyptian records dated the origin
of Egyptian culture eight thousand years back, and since then, Egypt
had created institutions assuring cultural continuity from generation
to generation, above all great temples that housed its scrolls, such as
the one in which they were speaking (the priests didn't mention that
sometimes they would erase a name from king lists, as had been the
case with Nefertiti). Where less fortunate cultures, including Greece,
were visited by fires and floods, Egypt was safe from both, the periodic
flooding of the Nile being well under control and in fact beneficial for
agriculture. Blessed with a stable environment, Egypt had created a
culture of great longevity. Compared with Egypt, Greece was a latecomer, a mere child.

The Egyptian priests had a point. Solon's Greece had come into
possession of a widespread writing system only recently (two earlier
systems, now called Linear A and B, had been of limited use). For the
longest time, Greece had relied on charismatic singers, who recited
mythological stories and accompanied them with music, sometimes
becoming as famous as rock stars are today. These trained singers
remembered long tales by splitting up stories into self-contained episodes and associated important characters with phrases that could be
repeated throughout a recitation. Oral tradition was one of the key
storage techniques used by humans ever since they had evolved language to tell stories, and it had proved to be remarkably effective. This
was how stories of the Trojan War had been transmitted for generations. But, at least according to this account, Egyptian priests, like
most representatives of cultures based on writing, looked down on oral
transmission as fleeting and unreliable.

Traders from Phoenicia (today's Lebanon) had brought a new writing system to Greece: one based on sounds. Over the next few hundred years, this alphabet, so much easier to use than other writing
systems, proved revolutionary. While earlier writing systems had been

the domain of specialized scribes, the new alphabet made reading and writing much faster to learn, ushering in an age of widespread literacy.

So, in a sense, the Egyptian priests were right: Greece did not have a continual tradition of literacy and seemed to have forgotten or abandoned its previous writing systems only to adopt a new, imported one. Perhaps the priests also looked down on the simplicity of the new alphabetic writing, so different from their own difficult and ancient script.

The person who reported—or, rather, invented—the conversation between Solon and the Egyptian priests was the philosopher Plato. In recounting the story in his dialogue *Timaeus*, Plato clearly identified with the Egyptian priests and their laughter at Greece's youthful forgetting. But Plato didn't leave it at that. He had his Egyptian priest reveal to the startled Solon that Greece was actually as old as Egypt. Greece, too, had a deep history—but it had been forgotten. Greece was caught in a state of perpetual youth, unaware of its great past, because Greece lacked the institutions and cultural techniques capable of storing and transmitting its past into the present. Fortunately, Egypt had recorded Athens's ancient history, and the priests of Isis were now ready to disclose it to Solon. Plato had done something audacious: he had invented a glorious history for Greece and put it in the mouth of Egyptian priests.

Athens, according to this story, had once been a powerful and well-organized state. Its most heroic moment had come when it took a leading part, along with Egypt and other countries, in the war against the military aggressions of Atlantis, a now-lost island off the coast of Africa. Athens had fought valiantly against Atlantis and, at great cost, defeated this common foe. Earthquakes and a flood had since sunk Atlantis, just as they had destroyed all Athenian records of these great deeds. It was only thanks to Egypt's unbroken memory, its ancient writing, and its priests that knowledge of Atlantis had survived and could now be communicated to Solon. Plato faced a dilemma that was the opposite of Nefertiti's. While Nefertiti felt the burden of Egypt's ancient past, Plato craved just such a past. Since no such past was available, he simply made one up, claiming its records could be found in the archives of Sais.

But what was wrong with a culture that enjoyed perpetual youth? It could be seen as a great asset, allowing a culture to invent new arts and new expressions, free from the burden of the past. In a way, this was exactly what had happened in the two hundred years between Solon and Plato, when Greece had gone through a breathtaking burst of creativity, giving birth to a new form of theater, among other innovations.[2] But Plato was having none of it. He revered antiquity and invented the story of Athen's war against Atlantis specifically to belittle his own contemporaries, including many of the things we now celebrate as Greek achievements, such as the Homeric epics, Greek tragedy, and democracy. Plato is often seen as a representative of classical Greece. In truth, Plato was an anomaly, an admirer of Egypt, craving its ancient writing system, temples, and priests. He used his admiration for Egypt to attack his own culture.

≡

PLATO HADN'T ALWAYS BEEN AT ODDS WITH GREECE AND ITS ARTS. AS a young man, he was fully immersed in the cultural activities he would later scorn, above all Athenian theater. According to his biographer, he became the leader of the chorus, which consisted of roughly two dozen citizens who acted and danced together as a group and represented the larger community. Being leader of the chorus meant that he was responsible for providing costumes, masks, and lodging, with the backing of a wealthy patron who could afford these extravagant expenditures. Because theater was a highly public art, performed live in front of large audiences, the leader of the chorus enjoyed public admiration. At a young age, Plato had managed to establish himself at the center of an art form that prized immediacy, the ultimate art of the present.[3]

Greek theater was performed as part of the city's most spectacular festival. Held in the spring when the seas became navigable again after the winter season of storms, the Dionysia festival was dedicated to the god Dionysus, patron of revelry and theater. The festival attracted throngs of visitors, some walking in from surrounding villages, others riding in on donkeys or mules, and still others coming by boat from nearby islands or from farther-flung settlements and trading posts. No matter where they came from, visitors would be wearing their best clothes, sometimes even theatrical masks, while those who could afford it would be riding in chariots.

The festival encouraged widespread participation from across Athenian society, including not only citizens (exclusively male) but most likely also women, *metikoi* (foreigners who did much of the manual as well as skilled labor), and *douloi* (enslaved people who mostly worked in agriculture).[4]

As a leader of the chorus, Plato occupied an important role in organizing the festival, which would open with a statue of Dionysus being paraded through the streets. Crowds would stand on either side to witness the sacrifice of goats and sheep, and then follow the statue up the hill to the great Dionysus Theater, an open-air arena carved into the mountainside surrounded by fragrant cypress and olive trees. From there the audience could see as far as the harbor, the source of power for this seafaring empire. Above them was the ancient citadel, or Acropolis.

But Plato was not content to serve as leader of the chorus; he had also written a tragedy and hoped that it would be performed as part of the festival.[5] Plato lived toward the end of the golden age of Greek playwriting. In previous generations, the three great tragedians, Aeschylus, Sophocles, and Euripides, had created a new powerful formula for tragedy. The protagonists, often kings or other personages of high standing, were played by male actors wearing masks that exaggerated their facial expressions and amplified their voices. The stage had almost no scenery or props, but a shed toward the back had been gradually repurposed to serve as backdrop.[6] Since only two or three actors were allowed to participate, the shed (called *skene*, the origin of our word "scene") enabled them to change character. Violent scenes were never enacted on stage, but took place off-stage, for example in the *skene*, from which a dead body could then be wheeled out and displayed to the audience. A dancing and speaking chorus of about fifteen male citizens, such as the one led by Plato, would represent the citizenry and comment on the action.

Athenians could watch Agamemnon, who had led the Greeks against Troy, return home after a bitter ten-year war. In another play, audiences could watch the struggle between Creon, who had become the ruler of Thebes after a bloody civil war, and Antigone, who insisted that her brother be given a proper burial even though he had betrayed the city. Or audiences could witness in horror how Medea, the wronged wife of Theseus, punished her husband by murdering their children.[7]

The combination of dance and speech, chorus and actors, masks and music, proved to be deeply engrossing. The crowd assembled in this special location was watching their fellow citizens perform in the chorus, but it was also watching itself, conscious of its own significance. The plays were sometimes so effective that they riled up the crowd and caused public unrest. Assembling some 17,000 Athenians from different classes in a single space made for a combustible situation that could be set off by a single stirring performance. In response, authorities outlawed contemporary topics, which were more likely to cause trouble. Only a single tragedy survives that is set in the recent past: Aeschylus's *Persians* (very few Greek tragedies survive as complete texts; those that survive were collected in libraries and recopied). *The Persians*, too, may have led to scenes of disorder. Even though the play depicts a victory of the Greeks over the Persians, it is set in Persia and tells the story from the perspective of the losers. All later tragedies that survive are set in the mythological past, presumably to avoid riling up the Athenian audience. But other types of plays, including comedies, continued to take place in present-day Athens, and all plays, no matter when they were set, were performed as if the actions were happening in the here and now.

Greeks were easily moved by theater because they lived in a culture based on performance. On a regular basis, they would participate in processions, rituals, or the recitation of hymns such as the ones associated with the Dionysia festival. But even though Greek theater continued to be performed in the context of religious festivals, playwrights began to address topics that had little to do with a particular god or a particular ritual. This meant that the close connection between theater and religion was becoming looser, though it was never completely severed. The looser connection meant that Greek plays could be understood and appreciated outside the context of the Dionysia, which in turn meant that they became a highly portable, adaptable art form, one that would subsequently find followers who knew little about the original Dionysus cult from which Greek theater had emerged.

The impact of Greek tragedy beyond Greek culture is in many ways surprising since the art form was highly local, designed for a specific theater and audience, and regulated, with rules dictating precisely how many actors could be used (two or three), how large the chorus should be (twelve to fifteen), what kind of theater the performance should take place in (the stage empty but for the scene shed), where violence should occur (off-stage), and what shape the story should take (based on a high-ranking individual who falls). But somehow, this specific formula traveled beyond its origin. Writing helped, because it allowed plays to be read as well as performed. As Greek writing spread thanks to the alphabet and also to trade and conquest, written plays spread along with it and were stored in faraway libraries.

Other traditions would go through similar stages. Egypt, so revered by Plato, also had a form of performance that combined dance, song, and storytelling in the context of religious festivals, and some of those performances had been written down. In South Asia, plays written in Sanskrit, such as *Shakuntala* by Kalidasa, were based on epic stories, while Japanese Noh theater, equally circumscribed by rules and conventions, evolved a type of play that could be compared to Greek tragedy. Ultimately, all of these plays left their original contexts, traveled farther and farther afield, and mingled, especially in the twentieth century, when directors created fusions between Greek tragedy and Noh, and the Nigerian playwright Wole Soyinka connected Greek tragedy to Yoruba performance traditions.

These developments were in the future. If Plato's Egyptian priests had heard about Greek theater and its tendency to move beyond its ritualistic context, they might have been confirmed in their suspicion that the Greeks had no sense of deep history, felt unburdened by it, and blithely chose to adapt their own stories for new purposes.

=

PLATO'S DEEP INVOLVEMENT IN THEATER WAS SHAKEN BY AN encounter that changed his life. It occurred just as he was about to submit a tragedy he had written, when he chanced upon a group of people engaged in a heated debate with the notorious troublemaker Socrates. Socrates didn't come from the higher echelons of society. He was the son of a sculptor and a midwife, wore eccentric clothes, and sometimes walked around without sandals. But despite these peculiarities—or because of them—he had become a fixture in the marketplace and in front of the gymnasium, where male citizens exercised naked (the Greek verb *gymnazein*, the origin of our word *gymnasium*, means "exercising naked").[8] There, he managed to draw people into conversation by asking simple questions. Often, those questions revealed that people were contradicting themselves or didn't realize that their most cherished beliefs made no sense.

Socrates challenged not only the opinions of ordinary people, but also those of the most important cultural authorities, above all Homer.

The stories of the Trojan War and the difficult return home had been told for generations by singers but had been written down, and shaped into coherent works, shortly after phonetic writing was introduced to Greece. The name to which those written versions were attributed was Homer, even though little external evidence exists that such a person ever lived. But no matter who the author or authors of the written versions of those stories really were, the two epics, the *Iliad* and the *Odyssey*, had become foundational texts of Greek culture: anyone who learned to read and write did so by studying those texts; playwrights were heavily influenced by Homer; and sculptors and painters frequently used scenes from Homer to decorate temples as well as everyday objects such as storage jars, mixing bowls, and drinking cups. Over time, Homer had become the most important cultural authority. Many Greek tragedies were set in the Homeric world.

But just because Homer (or his scribe) had written something down, Socrates proclaimed, didn't necessarily make it right. Everyone should have the right to ask questions, to probe assumptions, to tease out consequences. People didn't always thank Socrates for his services; some were annoyed and stopped talking to him. But Socrates always found new interlocutors and even acquired a following among the privileged youths of Athens. Perhaps this was why Plato was drawing nearer, curious to hear what Socrates had to say.

Of all the cultural institutions attacked by Socrates, theater fared the worst. Socrates was concerned by its power, especially over impressionable youths like Plato. He feared that large audiences could easily be incited to violence (much like the earlier authorities who had declared contemporary topics off-limits for tragedy). He distrusted actors who skillfully slipped into different roles, merely feigning their emotions. More fundamentally, he regarded theater as a space of mere illusion that gave audiences the impression that they were witnessing real events taking place live, in the present, when in fact everything was made up by ambitious playwrights whose only interest was to win first prize.

The longer Plato listened, the more he was mesmerized by this uncouth teacher, and by the time the conversation was over, he decided to become Socrates's student. There was only one problem: with his involvement in the chorus and his recently completed tragedy, Plato had been caught red-handed as an enthusiast of theater. He now had a choice: theater or philosophy. Abruptly, he took his tragedy, over which he had labored so much, and set it on fire. While his play went up in flames, he shouted, as if conducting an important ritual: "Come hither, god of fire, Plato is in need of thee."[9] He had chosen philosophy.[10] From the fire was born Plato's second career, the one that would make him famous: the career of a critic, of a contrarian, of someone who openly admired Egypt and who would invent an alternative history of Greece. It was Socrates who turned Plato against the most important cultural institutions of Athens.

In his new role as a follower of Socrates, Plato attacked theater as well as another Greek institution that can be seen as related to it: democracy. Because theater enjoyed such broad participation, and because the chorus consisted of citizens, theater could appear to be an art form particularly suited to democracy. (The connection also worked the other way around: just as only privileged male inhabitants of Athens could act in the chorus, so only they were allowed to vote.)[11] No matter how tight the connection between theater and democracy really was, one thing was certain: after becoming a student of Socrates, Plato turned against both. Later in life, he would try to work as an advisor to Dionysus I, the tyrant of Syracuse, a Greek colony in Sicily. The effort didn't go well and Plato, according to some sources, was sold into slavery as a result (a friend later bought his freedom).

Plato had an additional reason to oppose democracy when the democratically elected leadership of Athens condemned Socrates to death on trumped-up charges of introducing new gods and misleading the youth. Socrates's students and followers, in their desperation, hatched a plot to bribe the prison guards and help him escape, but

Socrates refused to go along with it. Instead, he spent his last hours in the company of his students, some of whom had started to cry. Socrates was doing what he had always done: abstract from a particular situation—one person's death—and examine the principles at stake.

Plato, who had given up his career as a playwright to follow Socrates, was not with him that day. Perhaps he couldn't bear to watch his teacher die. Or perhaps he had already started to mourn Socrates in another way: by writing about him. First, he wrote about the trial and about Socrates's refusal to play along with the judges. Later, he wrote about the escape plot and Socrates's heartbreaking final hours. Over time, Plato would turn Socrates into the personification of philosophy, especially through the events surrounding his death. As a former tragedian, he realized that Socrates's death would make Socrates into the tragic hero of philosophy.[12]

Plato carefully set these dialogues in the places Socrates had frequented, such as walks outside the city or the busy harbor and the marketplace, making his teacher come to life in the imagination of his readers. He was moving from writing tragedies to codifying something more disruptive: the philosophical dialogue.[13] Over time, Plato used his philosophical plays to belittle the cultural achievements of classical Greece. He attacked actors; he attacked singers who recited Homeric songs; he attacked teachers, whom he called sophists.[14] This, for him, was the true meaning of philosophy: a critique of everything.

This critique even included writing. Plato questioned whether writing was an unmitigated good, claiming that the more we trust to written words, the more our memories will atrophy. In making this argument in writing, Plato knew that he was not heeding his own advice. As in the case of his alternative history of Greece, he put this argument in the mouth of an Egyptian priest; since Egypt had much longer experience with writing, it would also have a much better sense of its drawbacks.

Plato's philosophical critique of everything ultimately extended to all of reality and led him to envision a world of pure forms of which our world is but a shadow. Platonism, as this view came to be called, was the grandest of his alternative visions. Just as Atlantis was his alternative to the actual history of Greece, so his world of pure forms was an alternative to reality. Plato didn't just tear down; he built up an entire philosophical edifice that has shaped philosophy ever since.

≡

DESPITE PLATO'S OBJECTION TO THEATER—IN HIS DAY, THE MOST potent medium for creating simulated reality—and worries about the widespread use of writing, his philosophical dialogues survived alongside Greek tragedies in libraries and private collections, above all in the Library of Alexandria, near Sais, where the discussion between Solon and the Egyptian priest was said to have taken place.[15] The survival of Greek plays and of Plato's dialogues was greatly aided by the fact that the Greek alphabet, much easier to use than Egyptian hieroglyphics, had led to much higher literacy rates, which meant that plays and philosophical dialogues circulated widely. (For the same reason, Egypt developed the much easier demotic script). Broad distribution was as effective a survival mechanism as a well-guarded bastion of learning such as an Egyptian temple.

But there was yet another—and perhaps even more effective—way for culture to survive, namely through imitation, by inspiring new generations to keep cultural practices alive. This person-to-person process—call it education—was much less reliant on stone or the alphabet and instead bet on large numbers of people. To this end, Plato founded a philosophical school right outside Athens, in an olive grove that came to be known as the Academy, which is why that word has been used to describe philosophical schools of all kinds. One of his students was Aristotle, who significantly revised his teacher's philosophy. (He also was more positive about theater, giving us the most detailed account of tragedy; adaptations of this work, the *Poetics*, are still used by Hollywood screenwriters today.)

Much of what survives of Plato and Aristotle was due to their commitment to education, their ability to appeal to new generations of students. This legacy taught an important lesson to Egyptian priests and all others who put their trust in writing and temples: don't rely solely on cultural storage, because temples and libraries can be destroyed and writing systems can be forgotten, as happened with Egyptian hieroglyphics. Even the Library of Alexandria burned down, destroying many Greek texts, while countless others perished when Christian monks refused to copy material from the pre-Christian era. Plato survived in part because he had been able to inspire a generation of students who in turn had inspired others, making his philosophy to be widely known and shared.

Thanks to these modes of transmission, Plato has exerted a varied and sometimes unexpected influence on subsequent thinkers and writers, both inside and outside philosophy. Visionaries intent on constructing utopian societies have been inspired by his myth of Atlantis, while science fiction writers have been drawn to him for alternative visions of the future. Meanwhile, Plato's critique of simulated reality, originally born from his own experience with theater, has been updated to suit new media. In 1998, the film *The Truman Show* imagined a character growing up in a typically American suburb only to discover that what he took for reality was nothing but an elaborate reality TV show. One year later, *The Matrix* took on computer simulation, offering the red pill to those willing to recognize computer-simulated reality for what it really was. Should the metaverse, recently announced by Facebook, come into being, we can be sure that Plato, playwright and philosopher, inventor of false histories and of alternative futures, would have much to say about it.

CHAPTER 3

===

KING ASHOKA SENDS A
MESSAGE TO THE FUTURE

DELHI, 1356 CE

For Sultan Firoz Shah Tughlaq, hunting was a festive undertaking, both a pastime and an affair of state, allowing him to display his skill, courage, and power. He would set up a large base camp somewhere outside the city, with a whole army of attendants catering to his every need, before sending scouts to look for prey. If they located one of the more impressive predators, such as a wolf, a lion, or a tiger, the sultan would insist on encircling the animal, carefully arranging the members of the hunting party, before killing it, and then moving on to stalk lesser animals such as deer or wild asses.[1] The most formidable animal to hunt was the elephant. Once, the sultan had killed seventy-three elephants, almost too many to bring back across a challenging mountain range to Delhi, where he proudly displayed them.[2] Hunting put him in a good mood and his subjects knew it. If you wanted to beg the sultan for forgiveness, it was best to seek him out during a hunt. If you were in luck, he might not only forgive you but also give you one of his stunning Arab horses as a gift.[3] Perhaps the reason for his magnanimity on such occasions was the knowledge that hunting connected him to his predecessors, who had come from Central Asia on swift horses to conquer much of the Indian subcontinent.

Today's hunt had taken him far from Delhi, a hundred miles north into the foothills of the Himalayas. It was in the middle of this hunt that the sultan came across an unexpected specimen near the village of Topra: not a tiger or an elephant but an enormous pillar. It seemed to rise almost miraculously from the ground and shoot up straight up into the sky. It was massive, over forty feet high, and made from sandstone, the exterior skillfully finished, surprisingly smooth to the touch. Who had made it? And how had it stayed up?

Even after the sultan returned to Delhi, he couldn't get this mysterious pillar out of his mind. There were other manifestations from the distant past in his realm, ruins of forts and remnants of settlements that testified to a civilization from the time before India had been conquered by his Muslim ancestors. But this pillar seemed different from these other remnants of the past, so tall and self-contained, seemingly untouched by time. What should he do with it? Pillars were not part of Islamic architecture.[4] Should he knock it down to show who was the ruler of these lands now?

Such an act of vandalism was against his nature. Some parts of his empire had recently rebelled, but Sultan Firoz had decided to let those portions of his domain break away without a fight. Instead of war, he had staked his reign on building and infrastructure projects, digging canals and wells, establishing rest houses and gardens, even founding entire cities. After contemplating what to do with the pillar, he came up with a plan much more in line with these activities: he decided to bring it to Delhi and incorporate it into his own palace, placing it near a mosque. The transport would be an almost impossible challenge and demonstrate his prowess much more effectively than toppling the pillar.[5]

A builder at heart, Sultan Firoz planned the operation in detail, mobilizing hundreds of workers. First, he had the pillar secured with silk ropes to keep it from collapsing. Then his workers started to dig. Soon they discovered why the pillar had stood upright for so long:

buried in the earth was a stone base that consisted of a single massive slab. Once they had dug out this base, they slowly lowered the pillar to the ground until it rested on cotton supports constructed especially for the purpose. Then they carefully encased the pillar in reed and bark and hoisted it onto a custom-built carriage. The pillar was ready to go.

The carriage itself was a marvel, so long that it required forty-two wheels, with each wheel attached to a massive rope pulled by two hundred men, at least as reported in an eyewitness account. Moved step by step by the muscle power of thousands of workers, the pillar edged its way toward the river Yamuna. The whole time, Sultan Firoz did not let it out of his sight. A flotilla of boats and barges took the massive load to the new capital, Firozabad (today's Delhi), where the pillar was hauled inside the palace gates and finally came to rest near the Jama Mosque.

Pillar erected and inscribed by Ashoka in Topra and transported to its current location in the Kotla (citadel) of Firozabad, in today's Delhi, by Firoz Shah Tughlaq. (PHOTO: VARUN SHIV KAPUR)

The final task was to set it upright again. To this end, a supporting structure was built out of stone, and another army of men pulled up the pillar inch by inch with thick ropes and wooden pulleys until it finally stood erect again, rising above all other buildings. Sultan Firoz added a golden cupola to top off his latest acquisition. The pillar now reflected the sun, a reminder of the glories of the sultan's benevolent rule.

The sultan imagined that the feat of transporting and erecting this pillar would ensure his fame for all eternity, and the pillar still stands today, eight hundred years later. There is a lesson for all who want to commune with the future: use the most durable material and make sure it calls attention to itself, attracting future rulers to preserve it and to adopt it, making posterity curious as to its provenance and history.

While contemplating the future, Sultan Firoz was also curious about the past. The pillar bore regular inscriptions that seemed to be writing but in a system unknown to him. Curious as to the meaning of this ancient message, he invited scholars versed in different pre-Islamic traditions, those who knew Sanskrit and other languages of the subcontinent, to decipher it. But none could read this script. Flummoxed by the writing, the sages instead relayed stories about how the pillar had been used by a giant figure (the character Bhima in the *Mahabharata*) as a walking stick—this, at least, was all they would divulge.[6] There were other pillars such as this one, and in one case the sultan even had it inscribed himself, as if wanting to add words to his architectural message.

The Sultan wasn't the first to be struck by these ancient pillars and their mysterious messages. Centuries earlier, another man had found such a pillar: Xuanzang, a visitor from China who had traveled to India to find the origins of Buddhism. He encountered several pillars around the middle of the seventh century and asked the same question the sultan would ask seven hundred years later: what did their inscriptions say? Xuanzang claimed to be able to read them, or had them translated, but these translations seem to have been highly inaccurate.[7] Like the sultan, Xuanzang probably relied on local lore for information, and here Xuanzang was at an advantage, being closer in time to the pillars' origins. In the year 640, orally transmitted knowledge had a different explanation for who had left behind these pillars: not a giant from an ancient epic, but the great Mauryan king Ashoka.[8]

If the sultan had been in a position to know about the ancient provenance of his pillar, he would have been impressed that by his time, in 1356, it was already some sixteen hundred years old. The pillar had survived thanks to its heft, its impressive size, and its solid stone base, but its writing had been forgotten.

=

THE ORIGINAL CREATOR OF THE PILLAR, KING ASHOKA, WHOSE reign lasted from around 268 BCE to 232 BCE, had inherited a large kingdom from his father and grandfather, the founders of the Mauryan dynasty.[9] His deeds were celebrated by Buddhist monks in a text called *Legend of Ashoka* (which was how Xuanzang had heard of this king).[10] The *Legend* told a story of a sudden turn in the king's life. Originally, Ashoka had defended and extended the boundaries of his realm through violence, making a name for himself as an ugly and cruel king known as Ashoka the Fierce.[11] His cruelty was directed not only at external enemies but also at his subjects; at one point, he was reported to have killed five hundred ministers suspected of disloyalty, and at another, an equal number of women after he felt disrespected by one of them.

But one day, Ashoka chanced upon a Buddhist monk and became a follower of the Buddha. After convincing those close to him to do likewise, he went on a pilgrimage to various sites associated with the Buddha, including his place of birth and the bodhi tree where the Buddha had experienced enlightenment. He also collected, according to the *Legend*, relics of the Buddha and built 84,000 stupas, dome-shaped temples, to house them. Shortly before his death, he gave most of the state's funds to Buddhist monasteries. True to the doctrine of Buddhism, the *Legend* also told readers about Ashoka's previous lives. In one of his earlier incarnations young Ashoka had met the historical Buddha. A dirt-poor boy at the time, he had wanted to give something to this radiant being, but the only thing he had to offer was a handful of dirt. An impure offering, the dirt explained why Ashoka was a mixture of good and bad, Ashoka the Fierce and Ashoka the Righteous.[12]

Even though the *Legend* cannot be taken as historically accurate and didn't mention the pillar specifically, it cast, for anyone who knew it, some light on the pillar's origins in that the pillar clearly fit Ashoka's building program, his dedication to marking and commemorating sites associated with the Buddha.[13] But when the pillar's original inscription was deciphered in the nineteenth century, it became clear that it reflected not only the piety of a Buddhist king but a most unusual and rare voice of ancient times, one proclaiming an entirely new idea of kingship and of being in the world.[14]

In his inscription, Ashoka begins by ruminating on matters of morality, invoking such ideas as happiness, good deeds, and truth. Again and again he mentions *dharma*, the term Brahmin priests had originally used to mean duties of a king but which to Buddhists meant the teachings of the Buddha.[15] Passions such as cruelty and anger, Ashoka declares, should be avoided, and suffering everywhere reduced. The king's language is reflective, philosophical, religious—quite different from other public declarations in the ancient world.

As a king speaking to his subjects, Ashoka outlined a program of welfare that extended from humans of all classes to animals and even plants, based on the respect that was due to all living things. This was an extraordinary and radical idea, one that had been powerfully formulated by the Buddha hundreds of years before Ashoka. This idea went against everything human society was built upon.[16] Humans were not treated equally, and Ashoka himself, at least according to the later *Legend*, had killed enemies, disloyal servants, and disobedient consorts with impunity.[17] Animals were treated worse, slaughtered for food or sacrificed in rituals, and forests were routinely cut down for lumber.

It was one thing for otherworldly Buddhist monks to rail against this order of things and quite another for a king to do the same. Realizing the extraordinarily radical nature of his new belief, Ashoka signaled a willingness to compromise. He specified on his pillar that it was *needless* suffering, not all suffering, that should be avoided, and only *certain* animals should be exempted from slaughter. He used the precious space on the pillar to list seemingly random groups of animals that should be spared, including parrots, bats, queen ants, and skate fish, adding "all quadrupeds that are neither useful nor edible."[18] One can feel his underlings breathing a sigh of relief. Brahmin priests derived their income from the fees they collected for performing the ritual sacrifice of animals; local economies depended on the use of forests and domesticated animals for sustenance; an entire culture and way of life had been built on these resources.[19] With this new compromise version, there was enough wiggle room to muddle through. But if his subjects believed that this more lenient tone meant that Ashoka had given up on radically transforming their lives, they were wrong. His pillar left no doubt that he was putting the power of the entire state behind his new conception of dharma.[20]

Ashoka was lucky in that he had inherited from his grandfather and father the first centralized and unified kingdom of the subcontinent; it even extended into Afghanistan. Eager to implement his vision of universal welfare, Ashoka decided to create a new structure: an imperial bureaucracy with different types of emissaries, who were empowered to bring wayward local rulers to heel. These inspectors reported only to himself, giving him an unprecedented level of central command. The pillar later found by Sultan Firoz reminded everyone of the long reach of Ashoka's state.[21]

Ashoka's new vision of a welfare state didn't rest on just this one pillar. He wrote proclamations on rocks located alongside well-traveled roads. Even for the majority of the people who couldn't read them, these markers signaled that a central ruler had taken control over a territory. But it was his pillars that attracted the most attention. He placed them at strategic locations, marking the territory where the new dharma would prevail (Sultan Firoz would eventually find another pillar, somewhat smaller than the first, and transport it to Delhi as well).

Stone pillars must have been particularly striking to Ashoka's subjects, because hitherto most building in India had been done with mud bricks and wood. These materials could be used to build elaborate, multistory houses and palaces, but they were not made to last. This is the reason why we have comparatively little knowledge of India's early civilizations and their building styles, only hints of settled cities along the Indus Valley as well as across Rajasthan, Gujarat and as far as Haryana. Ashoka's decision to use stone opened up new possibilities of endurance over time, the ability to contemplate how future generations might see these pillars and admire them as the product of his building prowess.

Most likely, Ashoka got the idea of erecting stone pillars from Persian travelers and craftsmen.[22] Persia's capital, Persepolis, had been founded as a grand, ceremonial city and was studded with pillars and columns, some as much as sixty-five feet tall. Typically, they were topped by carved animal heads, and they sometimes carried inscriptions. Even though most of Ashoka's pillars have tumbled or been broken, we know that they originally featured carved animals reminiscent of Persian models. Without a tradition of building in stone, let alone building and erecting pillars, Ashoka likely relied on Persian workers to manufacture his pillars and carve the lions sitting on top. The pillars came late in his reign, after he had been proclaiming dharma on rocks. Perhaps he felt that these earlier rock edicts had not been heeded sufficiently and that a new, more spectacular form of display was needed, something that had never been seen before in these lands.[23] (It is possible that Ashoka also knew about Greek columns and Egyptian obelisks.)

Some of the edicts carved into rocks and pillars elaborated on the administrative structure Ashoka had created to govern his empire more tightly. Others specified the institutions he had created for the welfare of humans and animals, putting the resources of the state behind his lofty ideals. A third group urged tolerance among the subcontinent's divergent belief systems, including Jainism, Buddhism, and Hinduism, along with other faiths like that of the Ajivikas, suggesting that Ashoka didn't seek to create division with his radical ideas. While the *Legend* portrays him as a pious follower of the Buddha, the pillars show an independent mind and vision, one informed by Buddhism but by no means limited to it.

Most surprising, perhaps, is the intensely personal tone Ashoka struck in some inscriptions, chastising himself for the cruelty he had shown during the conquests of his early kingship—perhaps in this instance anticipating the story later told in his *Legend*.

The Kalinga country was conquered by King Priyadarsi [Ashoka], Beloved of the Gods, in the eighth year of his reign. One hundred and fifty thousand persons were carried away captive, one hundred thousand were slain, and many times that number died. Immediately after the Kalingas had been conquered, King Priyadarsi became intensely devoted to the study of Dharma, to the love of Dharma, and to the inculcation of Dharma. The Beloved of the Gods, conqueror of the Kalingas, is moved to remorse now. For he has felt profound sorrow and regret because the conquest of a people previously unconquered involves slaughter, death, and deportation.[24]

A king proclaiming his deep remorse for having caused suffering during a successful military campaign—this was an entirely new way for a ruler to speak to his subjects.

This personal tone was part of the change Ashoka wanted to bring to the idea of kingship. In conquering the Kalingas, Ashoka had acted like a typical king, the kind of king his father and grandfather had been, embodying ideals of kingship outlined in a treatise called *Asthasastra*.[25] War and conquest were considered legitimate means of ruling and of extending an empire. Even though Ashoka regretted the violence associated with this conquest, he didn't release the Kalingas from his empire; he merely injected a new moral dimension into the calculation of war.

Ashoka used Buddhism to create a new cohesion among his subjects, bringing his vast and extremely diverse empire under a unifying vision. Dharma didn't mean, simply, what Brahmin priests or Buddhist monks thought it meant.[26] The inscriptions show a new style of rule, allowing Ashoka to assert a change in the understanding of kingship.

Unlike Nefertiti, who only changed the belief system of the ruling class, Ashoka wanted to change the hearts and minds of all his subjects. He was trying, desperately, to institute new ways of thinking, which was hard enough, but also new ways of living, which was infinitely harder. For this, he needed to speak to his people directly. This use of public writing was very different from that practiced by Egyptian priests or the storage techniques of great libraries. In the past, rulers had erected monuments inscribed with laws, a history beginning with Hammurabi's Code in Mesopotamia (in 1754 BCE). But Ashoka was using the idea of dharma and of writing in a new way: to mark territory; to make the land speak his words, narrating his change of heart. With pillars and stones, stories could be inscribed directly into the landscape.

Ashoka's public inscriptions were particularly daring given that writing had hitherto been far from widespread. The earliest writing on the subcontinent is shrouded in mystery because most writing was done on palm leaves—the paper of the ancient world—a highly perishable material.[27] Some fragments of clay bearing abstract signs have survived, but whether those signs were part of a full writing system, and if so, what they said, remains unknown to this day.[28]

In the absence of widely used writing, India produced a civilization based on sophisticated methods of memorization (as Greece had done before the arrival of writing). The oldest stories of the creation of the world, the Vedas, were carefully preserved generation after generation through oral transmission. Initiates had to learn to recite them verbatim, even backward. These stories were preserved with astonishing accuracy, along with commentaries. One of the first treatises in linguistics, explaining the structure of sounds and meaning, was composed by the great scholar Panini and transmitted orally for generations.[29]

The teachings of the Buddha were memorized by generations of students who had systematically organized themselves not to lose a single word the Buddha had spoken during his life. Periodically they came together in a Great Council to compare what they remembered and preserve the store of conversations of their dead leader. But ultimately, writing systems emerged and were adopted more widely for recording everything from Buddhist sutras to royal proclamations. One alphabet, Kharosthi, was based on Aramaic models, and Ashoka used it for two of his stone edicts.[30]

≡

EIGHTY YEARS BEFORE ASHOKA'S REIGN, THE POLITICAL AND CULtural worlds of Persia and India were interrupted by Alexander the Great and his relentless drive eastward to Persepolis, then to what is today Afghanistan, and all the way to northwestern India. Having created a short-lived empire that stretched from Greece to India,

Alexander increased contact between these disparate cultures.[31] The most enduring effect was on writing, facilitated through the spread of the Greek alphabet. (Alexander had studied with Aristotle and carried a copy of Homer, annotated by his teacher, on his conquest, and slept next to it every night.[32]) This alphabet likely influenced Brahmi, the writing system used by Ashoka for most of his edicts, including the large stone pillar later found by Sultan Firoz.[33]

Instead of promoting the Brahmi script exclusively, Ashoka was pragmatic about which writing system to use. Near Taxila, a cosmopolitan town that included many Greeks who had come in the wake of Alexander's conquest, he had a stone edict written in Greek using the Greek alphabet.[34] Ashoka was, after all, an inheritor of the dynasty Alexander had left behind and therefore felt no compunction about using a Greek writing technology when it suited his purposes. But even with Ashoka's canny and flexible use of different writing systems, one problem remained. Ashoka knew that literacy, no matter in what script, was confined to relatively small groups of people. How to reach the illiterate masses? He solved this problem by proclaiming—in writing—that his edicts should be read aloud by his emissaries on regular occasions. In fact, many of the edicts were placed so that there would be room for a large crowd to gather.[35] With this new communication technology, Ashoka was able to engage with his subjects, hoping to influence their behavior and thought. Using the accelerating network of cultural exchange begun by Alexander the Great, Ashoka combined India's past with select Persian and Greek imports to create something new, a targeted, highly specific use of cultural techniques adapted to new purposes.

Cultures often develop by confronting their own distant past: rejecting it as Nefertiti and Akhenaten did; inventing it, as Plato did in the case of Greece; or recovering it, understanding it anew, adapting it to new circumstances. Ashoka's pillar exemplifies a different, but related drama: encountering fragments of an earlier period, only dimly understood, and using them for new purposes, as Sultan Firoz would do. As cultural contact across large geographic areas spread, more and more people encountered relics of cultures they did not understand. Sometimes, they would simply reject those fragments and remain happy with what they knew (and didn't know). But more often, they encountered these objects with curiosity, trying to make sense of them as best they could. Sometimes, they even decided to adapt them to their own purposes.

The Eurasian exchange network, which intensified in the wake of Alexander and which soon extended well beyond the boundaries of his realm, became the largest and most closely knit network in the ancient world.[36] It enabled trade in everything from agricultural crops and domesticated animals to technologies and cultural forms of expression, as well as exchange of diseases.[37] Northern India, Persia, Mesopotamia, and the Near East were all roughly in the same climate zone, which meant that crops and domesticated animals could be easily adapted across these regions (though not all: while Greek travelers didn't say much about Buddhism, they admired Indian kings because of their elephants).[38] This put some of the earliest civilizations, from the Indus Valley to the so-called Fertile Crescent, into contact—often violent, as recorded in the history of conquest and occupation, from Alexander the Great to Sultan Firoz. Yet it also facilitated exchange and advances in technology and culture, from stone pillars and writing to new ideas of kingship and religion.

In some ways, the Eurasian exchange network put those cultures participating in it at an advantage over those living on other continents such as the Americas and Africa, which stretched not from east to west but from north to south, traversing different climate zones.[39] Africa and the Americas were also, for the most part, much more difficult to cross and navigate. To be sure, humans living in relative isolation also cultivated crops, domesticated animals, and developed new technologies and cultural practices. And cross-cultural contact across large distances often came with significant drawbacks, including not only violence but the spread of disease, which could make isolation seem a blessing.[40] But over the long term, cultural contact unleashed a dynamic process that increased the ways in which humans could interact and profit from one another.

Ashoka's role in this new exchange network was not only that of an importer. Once he had adapted the art of making stone pillars and of using different writing systems to his own purposes, and combined them with the oral traditions of Buddhism, he proceeded to send this new cultural package abroad.[41] Buddhist ideas about overcoming suffering and achieving enlightenment were well suited to export because they were not directed at a specific group or class. Ashoka became their most important early advocate, putting the power of a king behind this missionary movement with universal appeal.[42] In one stone edict, he is proud of the common appeal of his philosophy:

> everywhere people are following Beloved-of-the-Gods' [Ashoka's] instructions in Dharma. Even where Beloved-of-the-Gods' envoys have not been, these people too, having heard of the practice of Dharma and the ordinances and instructions in Dharma given by Beloved-of-the-Gods, are following it and will continue to do so. This conquest has been won everywhere, and it gives great joy—the joy which only conquest by Dharma can give.[43]

In another edict, Ashoka declares that he has brought the new idea of kingship, the dharma, to Persia and Greece, precisely the cultures from which he borrowed certain cultural techniques. Even though Ashoka correctly identified Buddhism as a potentially successful export product, he was wrong about the direction in which it would move. Only few sources in the West mention Buddhism, and there are few indications that Ashoka's dharma had lasting impact on Mesopotamia, Greece, or Egypt, though there are Buddhist traditions in Persia.

While Ashoka was looking west, the greatest success for Buddhism waited in the east. Buddhist monks traveled to China, and later to Korea and Japan as well as to Southeast Asia, spreading the word of the Buddha (and ultimately drawing the pilgrim Xuanzang to India). This export created a second, updated exchange network, the Silk Road, which accelerated the integration of the Eurasian continent.[44]

Ashoka was thinking of exerting his influence not only across space, but also across time. The ability to project his thought into the future, after all, was a major appeal of writing on stone pillars. On his magnificent pillar, the one later transported to Delhi by Sultan Firoz, Ashoka proclaimed: "I have ordered this edict on Dharma inscribed in order that it may endure forever," echoing, almost verbatim, Sultan Firoz's desire, fifteen hundred years later, that the pillar be a monument to himself until Judgment Day.[45] In another edict, Ashoka elaborated on the same idea: "Wherever there are stone pillars or stone slabs, there this Dharma edict is to be engraved so that it may long endure."[46] Writing on stone created a new sense of permanence. Ashoka's writings are the earliest written records in the Brahmi script and the earliest surviving use of writing by an Indian king.

And yet, Ashoka overestimated the longevity of writing over oral transmission—as is not atypical of cultures shaped by writing. (Plato overestimated writing, even though he was also critical of it.) What Ashoka didn't quite appreciate was that writing had to withstand not only the corrosion of time—a problem that could be solved by writing on stone—but that there had to be people capable of deciphering it. If you wanted to talk to the future, you needed to put your trust in the existence of an entire writing infrastructure, with schools and other functioning lines of transmission from one generation to the next. Ashoka's edicts, even though they endured physically, became illegible. It was oral tradition that had preserved the connection between

Ashoka and the pillars, while the writing on the pillars had become impossible to read.

Finally vindicating Ashoka's belief in the endurance of writing, his script was decoded in the 1830s, as part of another violent cross-cultural encounter. By the nineteenth century, Muslim rule over Ashoka's realm had ended and India was controlled by a vast British company, the East India Company, which used the subcontinent to enrich its shareholders in a new, rapacious form of colonialism.[47] Control of territory and people also requires cultural knowledge, which is why the East India Company began studying India's distant past, collecting manuscripts and cultural artifacts and transporting many of them to London (just as the bust of Nefertiti was later transported to Berlin). This act of cultural requisition was accompanied by efforts to decipher the Brahmi script. James Prinsep, an archeologist, philologist, and official of the East India Company, contributed significantly to decoding this writing system,[48] using statistical methods as well as drawing on the work of a Norwegian scholar, Christian Lassen, who used a bilingual Greek–Brahmi coin from the reign of the Indo-Greek king Agathocles (190–180 BCE), much as Jean-François Champollion used the Rosetta Stone to decipher Egyptian hieroglyphics. And so it was that over two thousand years after Ashoka's death, his voice, his idea of kingship, and his efforts on behalf of Buddhism became legible again.

Ashoka raises many intriguing questions about the past and cross-cultural contact. What happens when one culture sends missionaries to another? Should cultural objects such as Ashoka's pillar be left where they were originally put, or removed to new locations? To be sure, Sultan Firoz simply seized the pillar and used it for his own purposes; but then again, one might argue that the pillar was meant to be found and used in the future, that Ashoka had put it there for precisely this purpose. Each generation must work through the uneasy entanglement of destruction and creation that cultural contact produces. When seen in hindsight, much of culture involves interruption, misunderstanding, and misreading, borrowing and theft, as the past is dug up, taken, and used for new purposes. Awareness of these entanglements is the true lesson to be learned from this extraordinary king and his pillar, which was erected, abandoned, misunderstood, forgotten, rediscovered, moved, and finally deciphered again. May its message endure forever.

CHAPTER 4

=

A SOUTH ASIAN
GODDESS IN POMPEII

The statue is small, nine and a half inches tall, and intricately worked, a female figure facing forward in a complicated pose. Her left foot has stepped across her right one and her right arm reaches down her back while her left hand is reaching up. The head is slightly turned towards the left. She is flanked by two small attendants, reaching only up to her waist, one holding a cosmetics box. The woman has long hair, which she wears in braids, and is elaborately bejeweled, with rings on both lower legs and arms, pearls around her neck, and a belt around her waist. Made from the ivory of the Asiatic elephant, which is now on the list of endangered species, the statue bears the single letter *sri* in the Kharosthi script, used in the northwest of India (including by Ashoka for two of his northern rock edicts), indicating the statue's origin. This suggests that the figure may represent the goddess Lakshmi or another figure associated with fertility from the pantheon of South Asian goddesses and spirits.[1]

From the northwest of South Asia, the statue began its voyage westward. She probably traveled by land via Bactria to Persia and from there to Mesopotamia, traversing high mountain ranges and deserts before arriving in today's Turkey. Alternatively, she might have chosen

the sea route, which would have involved traveling by land southward
to the Indian Ocean and taking a boat to the Persian Gulf or around
the Arabian peninsula into the Red Sea, braving the seasonal monsoon
winds as well as pirates.[2] There, she would have been picked up by
merchants and brought across the eastern desert to the Nile, where she
would have been transported on a flat barge to Alexandria, the great
port city founded by Alexander the Great. From Alexandria, she would
have been loaded onto a boat to be rowed and sailed across the Mediterranean Sea into the heart of the Roman Empire.[3]

By the first century CE, the Roman Empire had expanded into
Egypt and Palestine in the south, Greece, Asia Minor, and Mesopotamia in the east, Gaul in the north and the Iberian peninsula in the
west. It was an irresistible-looking rise that would soon reach its point
of greatest territorial expansion. Exchange of people and goods in the
empire was brisk, drawing people living thousands of miles apart into
a single network.

But even this extended network wasn't enough to satisfy the
Romans' demand for luxury goods, which was why traders had established relations with places far beyond the empire, including India.
Imports from India included raw cotton, precious stones, raw silk,
and silk garments (perhaps originally brought from China), as well
as spices such as pepper, ginger, turmeric, and cardamom, some used
for cooking and others for medical purposes.[4] Roman coins have been
found in India, an indication that Rome had few goods to trade to
India in return and needed to spend hard currency.[5] Pompeii's villas,
with their Greek mosaics and Eastern luxury goods, were a perfect
example of this trade imbalance. While Romans paid for these commodities in hard currency, they also exoticized India as the land of
spices, medicines, and magic.[6]

Located 150 miles south of Rome, Pompeii had a complicated
relationship to the capital. Thanks to the nearby volcano Vesuvius,
it enjoyed an especially rich soil, which lured settlers to these foot-

hills around 800 BCE, while the nearby gulf of Salerno provided easy access to the Mediterranean. By 523 BCE Pompeii had become Etruscan, as the dominant civilization of northern Italy spread southward. But as the reach of Rome expanded, Pompeii was slowly incorporated into the Roman Empire, which meant that Pompeiians began to adopt Roman ways. After a civil war in which Pompeii found itself on the losing side, Pompeii was forced to give up its independent status and was formally annexed as a colony.

Pompeii, then, was a lively, Romanized town when the Indian statue arrived. Many houses boasted an atrium-style covered central court with a roof, and the busiest part of town contained bars and restaurants, one of which was equipped with an elegant marble bar (in 2020, new evidence of a "snack bar" was discovered).[7] We don't know exactly when the Indian statue completed its long journey to Pompeii, but we know that it must have arrived before the autumn of 79 CE, because that's when the volcano erupted.

It started with small tremors. They should have been a familiar warning, since a major earthquake causing widespread destruction in Pompeii had occurred just seventeen years earlier. But perhaps the tremors were too small, or they were not recognized as harbingers of something worse. When the volcano finally erupted, it released dense clouds, sometimes light and sometimes dark, depending on the composition of the materials from which they were composed, which shot up into the air like the trunk of a pine tree. Once this ominous tree of clouds had reached the extraordinary height of twenty miles, the trunk grew branches that spread out in all directions, creating a broadening canopy that blocked out the sun. The wind blew from the northeast, driving the canopy in a southerly direction, along the coast. The direction of the wind proved fatal for Pompeii, which began to receive a rain of ash and light volcanic rocks, formed from the gas-rich froth of lava. Some inhabitants tried to hide from the infernal bombardment inside their homes. But as ash and rock started to accumulate, many fled the city, trying to take their most precious possessions with them, protecting themselves by covering their heads with pillows and by breathing through moistened cloth.

Amidst the general panic, no one paid attention to the Indian statue, which was probably part of a small piece of furniture—there is a hole in the back that suggests that it was part of a larger object—making transportation impractical. Or its owner had immediately—and wisely—fled, leaving everything of value behind.

The rain of rock and ash continued hour after hour, the debris accumulating foot by foot, but no hot stream of lava emerged from the mouth of the volcano that would have engulfed the city in a river of fire. Perhaps this emboldened some residents, who had run to the shore to flee by boat, to return to the burning city to rescue more possessions. This proved fatal, because some eighteen hours after the original eruption, a second and even more lethal phase began, as one side of the volcano ejected a surge of hot gas and lava fragments that raced down the mountainside, burning everything in its track with temperatures of up to 500 degrees Fahrenheit. The gas first hit the town of Herculaneum, which had been spared most of the ash and rock due to favorable winds, incinerating everything in its path. The cloud of gas moved so fast that those inhabitants who had remained in town or returned had no time to seek shelter and were burned wherever they were caught. Their clothes, skin, and flesh were incinerated at once in the extreme temperatures. Their corpses came to rest in grotesque postures because their muscles contracted in the heat before being burned off their bones; their brains exploded, leaving their skulls looking like cracked eggs.

Once the gas cloud was done with Herculaneum, it came for Pompeii. Because the city was several miles farther from the volcano, temperatures were somewhat lower by the time the cloud reached the city, which spelled a different kind of death for its inhabitants. They suffocated from the hot gases and fell to the ground dead, but their clothes didn't burn off their bodies, the muscles didn't contract wildly, and their brains didn't explode. The volcano kept emitting ash that accumulated on top of the corpses and eventually buried them under nine feet of debris. Pompeii and Herculaneum had to be abandoned, never to be inhabited again.

There was one piece of luck involved in the destruction of Pompeii, an unusual eyewitness, only seventeen at the time, who would become one of the great writers of his generation: Pliny the Younger. He watched the eruption from just far enough away to survive. At the behest of a historian, he wrote about it afterward, combining precise description with evocative images. It is thanks to his observations that we can reconstruct the two phases of the eruption that brought life in Pompeii to an abrupt halt.[8]

If Pliny's quill was one way in which the destruction of Pompeii was preserved, the other was the eruption itself, which sealed off the city, all that remained of it, under a protective layer of ash, giving us a rare snapshot of life in the Roman Empire. From the point of view of historical preservation, earthquakes, floods, and erupting volcanoes are bad because they destroy, but the one thing that will destroy more thoroughly is continual use by humans. If Pompeii had not been buried under ash, life there would have gone on, which would have meant that existing houses would have been torn down and replaced by new ones, and sooner or later almost all traces of art and culture would have disappeared.

Over time, the ash served like a seal that protected the statue, along with the rest of Pompeii, from the elements—and from humans. Whatever piece of furniture she may have been part of was burnt, but the ivory goddess herself survived, miraculously unscathed under a bed of ash. And there she lay hidden for the next eighteen hundred years. Without the volcano, how long would she have survived? It is difficult to say. Most likely, the statue would have been broken or discarded in favor of a new fashion in luxury goods.

The snapshot provided by Pompeii—like a time capsule—is so unusual that historians speak of a "Pompeii bias": what we know about everyday life in 79 CE is mostly based on this one provincial town, and extrapolating from it to the entire Roman Empire may be misleading. But Pompeii is simply too good a time capsule not to be used.

The town reveals an empire that drew its arts and goods from around the world, even from its rivals. The Indian statue was not the only foreign art object in the city. One of the first temples to be excavated was dedicated to an Egyptian god, Isis; its walls were inscribed and painted with Egyptian hieroglyphics, which probably no one could read.[9] In the polytheistic world of Rome, it was not unusual to incorporate foreign gods. Often gods would acquire new names and attributes suited to their new worshippers. Here, Isis and Osiris were fused with their son Horus, the Egyptian god of the sky as well as of kingship typically depicted with a falcon head, creating a kind of trinity. Their temple is a reminder of how open to foreign influence Rome was, even from its long-time enemy, Carthage. Perhaps the inclusion of foreign gods into the Roman pantheon was even a sign of military triumph, though it was also sometimes fraught, as when the highly popular cult of Dionysus was banned.

The Egyptian influence paled in comparison to that of Greece. Rome had defeated Greece a little over two centuries before the volcano erupted, in the same year (146 BCE) that it had finally managed to destroy Carthage.[10] Emboldened by its final victory over Carthage, Rome had turned its eyes on a smaller but nonetheless recalcitrant enemy, the Achaean League, an alliance of all major Greek city-states, led by Corinth. Roman legions, some 3,500 cavalry and 23,000 infantry soldiers, attacked from Macedonia in the north, defeated the League, then marched on Corinth, located on the Peloponnesian peninsula, and took the city. The defeat and destruction of Corinth had lasting consequences. It cemented Roman control over the Eastern Mediterranean and led to the long-term eclipse of Greece as a military and political force. To make the humiliation complete, most Corinthian men were killed, the women enslaved, and the city razed to the ground.

But apparently, this defeat did not lead Romans to treat Greek culture with contempt. On the contrary, a walk around Pompeii would give any citizen a crash course in Greek culture, just by looking at the paintings alone. In one house, they could have enjoyed scenes from a play by Euripides, one of the playwrights who had excited Athenian audiences to the dismay of Socrates and his student Plato.[11] The scenes were painted in the typical fresco style, where paint is applied to moist plaster and hardens with it. Thanks to this style of painting, and the protective layers of ash, the mosaics and fresco paintings from Pompeii are still remarkably vivid in color and expression after almost two thousand years.

One house would have provided a particularly good introduction to one of the most significant Greek imports: theater. The house, now called the House of Menander because it contains an incredibly well-preserved portrait of the Greek writer of comedies, boasted a grand interior courtyard, columns at the entrance, and a generous atrium, much larger than that enjoyed by the owner of the Indian statue. Menander is painted in the ochre hues often found in Pompeii, sitting on a chair with one elbow, which rests on the back of the chair, lightly supporting his head, and the other hand holding a text, presumably a play, a toga casually thrown over one shoulder. Besides the portrait, this house has trompe l'oeil columns, arches, niches, and windows opening onto imaginary vistas.

Menander wasn't the only element of Greek drama of interest to Pompeiians. Along with Romans living elsewhere, they copied Greek theaters, with their semicircular stalls, side entrances, a semicircular playing area, and a building at the back of the stage, though they decided to close off the stage entirely so that the audience was no longer looking out past the action into the distant landscape. For centuries, Roman theaters were made of wood, temporary structures that could

Fresco painting of the Greek comedic writer Menander found in a private villa in Pompeii now called the House of Menander.   (PHOTO: WOLFGANG RIEGER)

be erected for festivals. Only later—though before the eruption of the volcano—were they built in stone, as Greek theaters had been. Even though Pompeii was just a provincial town of about 12,000 inhabitants, it boasted two theaters in addition to the larger amphitheater that was built to house gladiatorial combats, the latter a genuine Roman invention.[12]

The Greek influence on Rome extended to other areas as well, especially to education. After Rome's military victory, Greek educators came to Rome, often as enslaved teachers, while educated Pompeiians might complete their education in Greece, enabling them to switch to

Greek, and quote Greek writers in the original.[13] Many fresco paintings in Pompeii depict scenes from the two Homeric epics, especially the *Iliad*, and Homer was also a major source of knowledge about the Greek gods. A well-preserved fresco shows the earliest existing depiction of Alexander the Great, whom Romans admired. Many temples in Pompeii were dedicated to Greek gods, all of them now given Roman names and sometimes new functions. (It is likely that the owners of the Indian statue would have interpreted her as a version of Venus, the Roman adaptation of the Greek goddess Aphrodite.[14])

The Roman infatuation with all things Greek was surprising since the Greeks themselves, even at the height of their power, had shown relatively little interest in other cultures (except for Egypt, so admired by Plato), and rarely learned another language. Judging by the common trends of history, it might seem more natural for Rome to have turned to cultural resources native to the Italian peninsula, such as Etruscan culture, of which traces remained in Pompeii and many parts of Italy, including Rome, where Etruscan rulers had once held sway. But this didn't happen, and instead Romans chose to graft a culture produced

Mosaic found in Pompeii, in the House of the Faun, depicting the Battle of Issus between Alexander the Great and Darius of Persia. The painting was a copy of a Hellenistic original. (NAPLES NATIONAL ARCHEOLOGICAL MUSEUM. PHOTO: MARIE-LAN NGYUEN)

in a different language and based on a different history onto their own, homegrown traditions.

The choice of Greece over the local past is surprising, also, because it seems to fly in the face of geography. To be sure, there existed various Greek settlements on the Italian peninsula, above all in Sicily, dating back to archaic times, with Syracuse founded in 734 BCE, creating channels by which Greek culture reached early Rome. (Even today, some of the best-preserved Greek temples are in Sicily.) Syracuse finally fell to Rome after the defeat of Carthage, but maintained its Greek character. But Syracuse, along with other Greek settlements, was too small to explain the outsized influence of Greece on Rome.

Above all, the Roman use of Greek culture seems to upend our intuition about military power and its relation to cultural imports. Often one culture encroaches on another when an empire extends its reach by conquest and thereby brings its own culture to a foreign land as, for example, Alexander did with his Greek settlements across Asia. Pompeii itself was on the receiving end of such an imposition centuries before, when it was still an Etruscan town, making Etruscan art, and praying to Etruscan gods before being Romanized by the rising Roman city-state. But with Rome and Greece, the opposite happened: the Greek alliance in Corinth was defeated and yet Greece managed to sustain and even extend its cultural influence. Having achieved a stunning and lasting military victory, Romans decided to defer to their former enemy in almost all cultural matters, from religion and art to literature.[15] (Etruscans had been responsible for some early Greek imports, including the twelve Olympian deities.) The Roman poet Horace, in a letter to Augustus, wittily expressed the surprising Greek presence in Rome: "captive Greece captured the savage conqueror and brought the arts to rustic Latium."[16] The common story of Greece influencing Rome hides something much more unusual in human history: a country actively and deliberately grafting the culture of a defeated foe onto its own institutions and practices.

The grafting included theater, which began when a writer and actor by the name of Livius Andronicus started to write and perform plays in the Greek style and based on Greek topics, plays with titles such as *Achilles*, *Aegisthus*, *Andromeda*, and *Troianus*.[17] He also wrote comedies, drawing on Greek models. Livius Andronicus was likely an enslaved Greek who had taken the Roman name of his owner, Livius, when he became a freedman; his biography bears witness to the entanglement of political power and cultural influence.[18]

The performances of Livius Andronicus's plays attracted attention, and other writers followed suit, above all Terence and Plautus, neither of whom was Greek. Terence (Publius Terentius Afer) was born in North Africa, in Carthage, while Plautus was born in what is now northern Italy. But they both made sure that Roman drama drew on Greek models, flooding the market with plays that sometimes were adaptations of comedies by Menander but more often were new plays loosely inspired by Greek models (some fifty-three play titles attributed to Plautus have come down to us, though only twenty actual plays survive. One early source claims Plautus wrote 130 plays.)[19] Terence and Plautus made Menander so well known that the owner of the House of Menander in Pompeii decided to give the playwright pride of place in his home.[20] It is unlikely that Menander's plays themselves were performed in the theaters of Pompeii; Menander was known primarily through his devoted followers Livius Andronicus, Plautus, and Terence. The same is true of the other scenes from Greek theater that can be found in Pompeii: these scenes and plays were recognizable reference points for the cultural elite. If you wanted to be an educated Roman, you needed to know these names, even if you didn't go to watch the plays being performed. (Roman theater also drew on Etruscan dance and performance traditions.[21])

The grafting of Greece onto Rome also extended to Homer. Again, it was Livius Andronicus who obliged his target audience by translating the *Odyssey*. By our standards, it was a free translation, which Romanized everything from the names of gods and humans to the meter: rejecting the Greek hexameter, Livius opted for a Roman meter, thus easing the work's passage to Rome.

Translating texts from another language and culture seems to us the most natural thing in the world. After all, this is how most of us read both Greek and Roman literature now. Translation is how literature circulates outside its sphere of origin, becoming what we now call world literature.[22] But translating the literature of another culture was rare in the ancient world.[23] The most common exceptions were translations of manuals of practical knowledge, such as agriculture and medicine, and religious texts. Buddhist texts were translated from Indian languages into Chinese, and Greek-speaking Jews living in Alexandria translated the Hebrew Bible into Greek. But translating the entire canon of another culture had never happened before; at least, there is no record of such an undertaking. If we now routinely enjoy the literature of another culture in translation, we are doing as the Romans did for the first time in human history.[24] It was part of their extraordinary experiment in cultural grafting. The mistaken idea of a natural cultural progression from Greece to Rome is due to the success of this experiment: the cultural graft worked.[25]

The graft had unexpected consequences. Usually, cultural objects such as plays, epics, sculptures, and paintings evolve along with the culture that produces them, adapting to changing circumstances in their home audience. Collections of oral stories emerge when literacy spreads, while oral epics are transformed into written texts, allowing later literatures to refer back to these early texts but also to regard them as passé, the product of an earlier time.

When one culture adopts the entire spectrum of art from somewhere else, those artworks, which in their original context evolved gradually over time, now arrive all at once, confronting the grafting culture with a dazzling and confusing array of options. These options may seem like a wonderful boon, but they can also feel overwhelming.

Both reactions can be observed in Rome. While many Romans clearly welcomed Greek-inspired plays and literature, others experienced this influx as a loss of innocence, as if Rome hadn't been allowed to develop a literature on its own.[26] Some, like Cato the Elder (234–149 BCE), rejected the influx of Greek culture entirely. Others responded by returning to the earliest stories of the founding of Rome, the myth of the twins Romulus and Remus suckled by a female wolf, and erected, in the middle of bustling Rome, the simple hut that had allegedly served Romulus as his dwelling place long ago, before the rise of Rome and its adoption of Greek culture.[27] Many Romans did both, feeling nostalgic about the lost origins of their city while at the same time enjoying a dizzying array of literature imported and translated, or newly produced based on foreign models.

The grafting of Greek culture onto Rome raised a crucial question: how should Romans think of their own history in relation to the culture they had adopted with such enthusiasm? The person who provided an answer to this question was Virgil. He realized that Rome needed a fuller story of its own origins—one that explained its strange relation to Greece. The myth of Romulus and Remus suckled by a wolf was not enough. Virgil decided to write this story as an epic poem in the manner of the *Iliad* and the *Odyssey*.

The fact that Virgil was able to make this choice was itself an effect of the experiment in cultural grafting, facilitated by Livius Andronicus's translations. Normally, epic stories of origin emerged from oral stories that were gradually turned into longer written accounts. This is how the Homeric epics emerged centuries ago, and how other epic stories, from the Mesopotamian *Epic of Gilgamesh* to the Indian *Mahabharata* and *Ramayana*, came into being as well. Epics weren't planned and written by an author using other epics as a model.

But this was precisely what Virgil decided to do: to write an epic in the Homeric style, using an assortment of local legends.[28] This was a radically new type of epic: the epic of a latecomer. Doubly strange, Virgil was a latecomer not with respect to his own past, but with respect to the past of another culture, perhaps a bit like Plato felt in relation to Egypt.

There are immense advantages to being a latecomer. You have all kinds of models and options at your disposal. Virgil had the two Homeric epics before him, which put him in the unique position of being able to pick and choose from both. In the *Iliad*, Homer described an episode near the end of the Trojan War when Achilles withdraws from battle because he feels slighted in the distribution of loot. His refusal to participate places the Trojans at an advantage, and it isn't until Achilles relents that the Greeks have the upper hand again, leading to their ultimate victory. In the *Odyssey*, Homer described the long, difficult wanderings of his hero as he slowly makes his way home, overcoming all kinds of impediments along the way.

Drawing on both models, Virgil has his hero, the future founder of Rome, undergo a period of wandering across the Mediterranean Sea, tossed about by storms and adverse gods, as in the *Odyssey*. Along the way, he is nearly sidetracked from his purpose, above all by Dido, queen of Carthage, just as Odysseus almost forgets about home when on the island of the nymph Calypso. But once Virgil's hero arrives in Italy, he must fight its inhabitants in a series of battles reminiscent of the *Iliad* and the siege of Troy depicted there. In addition to picking plots and scenes, Virgil also borrowed the invocation of the muses, the frequent interventions of the gods, and Homer's famous similes, extended metaphors in which a poet could take flights of fancy.

In order to explain and justify—after the fact—Rome's cultural graft, Virgil did more than simply combine the two Homeric epics into a new Roman one. He directly connected the plot of his epic to Homer's world. His epic starts, in Homeric fashion, "in the middle of things," when Aeneas is within sight of Sicily, but then moves back to the chronological beginning of the story, in the burning city of Troy. It was the perfect setting—the ruins of the city described by Homer—

enabling Virgil to create an arc that stretches from the Homeric world to Italy, where Aeneas's descendants will found Rome. Like Plato, Virgil created a false backstory for his own culture.

In implementing this cunning plot device, Virgil made a surprising decision: he did not choose as his protagonist one of the Greek heroes, which might seem the obvious thing to do given the importance of Greek culture. In doing so, Virgil would have signaled to his readers: see, our origins actually lie not in the Etruscan past, or the local prehistory of the city of Rome, but rather in these ancient Greeks, one of whom subsequently sailed to Rome and founded our lineage and empire. But Virgil did not choose this path. Instead, he selected one of the losers: the Trojan Aeneas. To be fair, Homer did not vilify the Trojans. Even though he wrote as a Greek and for a Greek audience about a great and costly war which the Greeks finally won, there was never a sense that Trojans were fundamentally different. The Trojan War was not a culture war or a religious war, nor was it a war between different political systems or different ethnic groups. As represented by Homer, Trojans and Greeks spoke the same language, prayed to the same gods, had the same values, and recognized each other as groups of equal worth. All of this is quite different from much of the subsequent literature of war, certainly in modern times.

Still, it may seem surprising that Virgil would choose Aeneas, whom we last glimpse, in the *Iliad*, giving up the fight and fleeing the burning city of Troy. This hardly seems to recommend him as the founder of a rising empire. Why not, say, have Odysseus set out from Ithaca, restless at home after twenty years of adventure, and found Rome?

Virgil was not the first to establish a relation between Rome and Aeneas. There were legends of Rome's Trojan origins, and the emperor Augustus, along with the other Caesars, liked to trace his origins to Aeneas, based on a questionable etymology of his name. Virgil took these legends and genealogies and wove them into a full storyline, one that quickly became canonical.

The choice of Aeneas also allowed Virgil to gain something valuable: distance from Greece. While suturing Rome's prehistory to that of Greece, he also wove into the fabric of the story a new thread, a non-Greek thread connecting Troy to Rome, leaving the Greeks as victors but also as bystanders in the drama of Rome's founding. In Homer, the Greeks are drunk with victory and let Aeneas slip away; his role in their story is over. But not for Virgil, not for Rome. For Rome, the story is just beginning, and despite the overwhelming importance of Greece, despite the fact that Virgil tells this story in an epic closely inspired by the two foundational stories of Greece, showing that Rome is different from Greece after all. Choosing one of the losers of the Trojan War was a sign not of weakness but of confidence. We, Romans, aren't just imitating Greece; we're using it actively, deliberately, to tell our own story. They did the same with respect to their supposed Trojan ancestry. By the end of the *Aeneid*, Trojans must give up their language and culture and become assimilated to Italy.

Virgil's *Aeneid*, which became the foundational story of Rome, illustrates the glories of a cultural graft, its possibilities and subtle maneuvers, the fact that it doesn't have to be an act of defeat or inferiority. The same is true of Roman culture in other domains. Terence and Plautus wrote plays that outstripped in influence anything written by Greek dramatists for hundreds, even thousands of years (until Greek tragedy was revived and performed again beginning in the nineteenth century).[29] Roman architects created new types of buildings and temples by drawing on Greek models, and the same is true of Roman sculptors and painters. Plutarch tied the two cultures together by writing a book of biographies in which he paired a Greek and a Roman figure, showing how similar they were.

Pompeii, with its intricate fresco paintings, atrium buildings, and theaters, remains the best place to admire the result of Rome's cultural graft. A large building next to the Forum of Pompeii has inscriptions that borrow from Virgil, describing the mythological origins of Rome in the Trojan Aeneas, just as the entire town, from its frescoes to its theaters, is a testament to this cultural experiment.

Today, we admire Rome for its advances in statecraft, in infrastructure (from roads to baths), in military organization, in political acumen. But Rome's most remarkable legacy is the art of the graft. In fact, when historically and geographically distant cultures such as that of the United States returned to Rome for inspiration, they indirectly paid homage to this legacy, grafting Rome's culture, across vast distances, onto their own, just as Rome had once done with Greece.

The South Asian statue, meanwhile, has taken up residence in the archeological museum of Naples, the large city that has sprung up not far from Pompeii, within sight of the volcano, which sooner or later will erupt again. If it does, we must hope that the statue will not be looted or otherwise taken away, because that would increase the likelihood of her getting lost. Ideally, in such a future eruption, she would remain exactly where she is, ready to be excavated by archeologists yet again.

CHAPTER 5

===

A BUDDHIST PILGRIM IN
SEARCH OF ANCIENT TRACES

When Xuanzang (602–64) arrived on the shores of the Indus River, he was eager to get home.[1] The Indus was wild, fed by glaciers from the highest mountain range in the world, and hundreds of yards wide. Xuanzang knew that the crossing would not be easy. But there was no other way. If he ever wanted to make it back to China, he would have to ford the river in order to reach the Khyber Pass, which would take him to the Hindu Kush, one of the great barriers of the world. From there he would be able to turn east and, after traveling thousands of miles across mountains and deserts, hopefully arrive in Xi'an, the capital of China.

Xuanzang was unsure what would await him at home. The emperor might have him arrested because he had left China in secret, violating an explicit decree against foreign travel, the result of continuing wars between China and Turkic nomads and kingdoms in the west.[2] Xuanzang had almost been caught as he snuck out of the Jade Gate and entered the wild lands beyond the empire, but a foreigner had come to his aid, helping him to begin his travels to India.[3]

His escape through the Jade Gate had taken place sixteen years before. Sixteen years of travel, mostly on horseback and on foot; sixteen years, and thousands of miles, that took him across the Indian subcontinent from Nashik in the west, to Kanchipuram (in today's Tamil Nadu) in the southeast, and up the eastern coast to Tamralipta in Bengal before he turned northwest to cross the Indus again and head home. Perhaps his unusual experience, the information about foreign lands he could provide, and his heavy burden of foreign treasures would convince the emperor to overlook his unauthorized departure. This meant that the seeds, manuscripts, and statues he had patiently collected were his best hope of survival.

Xuanzang loaded his precious goods onto a boat, which he left in charge of a trusted overseer. He himself would cross the river using a more dignified method: astride an elephant. Even though the river was wild, a fully grown elephant could usually cross it without being swept away. The plan worked. Xuanzang made his way across the expanse of gushing waters and reached the other side safely. It was a dramatic way to reach "his" side of the Indus, the side pointing homeward.

When Xuanzang looked back to make sure his goods were making their way across as well, he saw that suddenly intersecting currents had created a wave that tossed the boat violently about. His possessions were coming loose, and some started to fall overboard. The overseer, who tried to secure the cargo, was himself swept into the water. For a moment, it looked as though everything would perish. But then the moment of greatest danger passed, fellow passengers managed to rescue the overseer, and the boat finally reached the other side. The damage was considerable. A significant number of scrolls, which Xuanzang had collected and copied with great effort, were lost to the river. Among all the things he had accumulated, they were the most important, and he knew that he could not face the emperor without them. Should he turn back and never see his homeland again? Was he wondering why on earth had he chosen, all those years back, to violate the imperial decree and undertake his long journey to India?

Much later, after he had finally returned home, Xuanzang would record this disastrous river crossing, along with many other observations, reflections, and descriptions, in *Record of the Western Regions*. In this work, Xuanzang took pains to describe each region, providing geographic information and commenting on the inhabitants and their culture, their language, and writing systems. *Record of the Western Regions* became a classic, exemplifying an important genre of world literature: the travelogue. Travel writing of the kind produced by Xuanzang played an outsized role in the mobility of culture.

Why did Xuanzang embark on his travels?

Xuanzang had grown up in a culture based on the study of texts. His family belonged to the so-called literati (*wenren*), a class unique to China (in a different form it also existed in Korea and Vietnam). Entry to government service and advancement depended on having mastered a group of ancient texts. An extensive examination system had been set up to select those who excelled at these literate arts, taking young men—women were excluded—through grueling multiday ordeals. If they passed, they would be allowed to sit for the next set of exams, which advanced them from the local to the provincial level and finally to the highest, imperial one. The system had been created to take power away from the military class and from local strongmen by ensuring that only educational sophistication, not brute military power, paved the way to lucrative government posts. The result was the first government system based on educational meritocracy—a meritocracy grounded in literature.

The texts at the heart of the exam, the so-called Confucian classics, hailed from the distant past and celebrated that past as an ideal: a book of poems set in the time of the early Zhou dynasty, a thousand years before the Common Era; a book of speeches and documents attributed to the early Zhou rulers; books of rites, detailing court ceremonies and protocols, as well as forms of social behavior; the so-called *Book of Changes*, or *I Ching*, containing a divination system; and a historical record of the state of Lu.[4]

The Confucian classics created a culture based on worship of the past. They were called Confucian classics because Confucius, a sage who lived in the fifth century BCE, had admired them and was subsequently seen as their editor (his home state was Lu, which strengthened his association with the historical records of that state). Technically, this was not quite true, since Confucius did not write anything but instead imparted his teachings orally to his students (much like the Buddha, Jesus, and Socrates).[5] But he had instilled in his followers a deep reverence for the past, especially the early Zhou dynasty so vividly evoked in these texts. The early Zhou, according to Confucius, was a period of order and harmony, a prime example of a well-governed state, very much in contrast to Confucius's own time, in which rival states were locked in a protracted phase of fighting. For Confucius, the past was an ideal born from disgust with the present.

It is difficult to appreciate just how revolutionary was this attitude toward the past. We're very used to the idea that things were better in the past, that some sort of golden age of yore has given way to our own fallen age, such as Eden in the Hebrew Bible. Confucius did something different: he singled out a distinct historical period, from which some alleged records and other remnants had survived, as an ideal. This was radical. Confucius was one of those, like Plato a continent away and over a hundred years later, who looked backward in order to find fault with the present.

The idea was astonishingly powerful. The teachings of Confucius spread and were written down after his death; and they were combined with books of ancient texts. The canon that resulted from this process was then placed at the center of an examination system, which oriented an entire culture toward the past, instilling in it a sense of tradition and continuity.

For Xuanzang, drilled in the Confucian classics from an early age, the worship of this ancient canon of texts was connected to an extraordinary flourishing of culture in the present.[6] A new dynasty of emperors had recently been established, the Tang dynasty (618–907), which had reunited the country. Their capital, Xi'an, became one of the largest, most developed cities in the world. A new type of poetry had emerged that would be recognized by subsequent generations as a high point of Chinese literature. While Rome fell, China was reunified and experienced a golden age, one that far exceeded the Zhou dynasty so admired in the Confucian classics in wealth and cultural production.

But Xuanzang was content neither with the Confucian classics nor with the new age of letters taking form in the capital, where he had moved. Through his brother, he was introduced to another strain of thought, one that would ultimately bring him to India: Buddhism.[7]

Buddhism had been brought to China haphazardly along the same route that Xuanzang would later retrace, via the Hindu Kush and Afghanistan.[8] At the time, this type of cultural import was unusual. Soon, it would happen with increased frequency, as Christianity was accepted by the Roman Empire, and Islam by much of the Middle East and North Africa. But in the centuries before the Common Era, the mobility of religious belief was rare. Few religions aspired to win converts from other cultures. Buddhism was one of the first of these new proselytizing religions, something King Ashoka had recognized early on when he tried to export Buddhism to distant lands.

The most important innovation Buddhism had brought to China in the second century CE was probably not its doctrine of dharma, rebirth, and nirvana, but the institution in which this doctrine was practiced: the monastic community. Shedding all possessions, taking a vow of poverty and celibacy, shaving the head, and living on the charity of others: such modes of living had been unknown in China (just as they were new to India, where there had existed individual ascetics living in poverty, but no monastic community of worshippers until communities of Buddhists emerged in the centuries after the Buddha's death). Initially there was strong opposition to this new way of life, which went against the most important Confucian precepts. While Confucianism was geared toward government service, Buddhism advocated withdrawal from the world. While Confucianism preached political stability, Buddhism saw worldly arrangements as necessarily fleeting and unstable. While Confucianism demanded reverence for parents, Buddhism asked converts to leave their families behind and become celibate. Despite the discrepancy between Buddhism and Confucianism, Buddhist communities of seekers had formed across China and become part of Chinese culture, even drawing adepts from the established literati class, the one most entrenched in Confucian training. Perhaps it was the radical difference between Buddhism and Confucianism that had led literati such as Xuanzang's brother to embrace this new way of life.

Buddhists eagerly spread their doctrine and way of life, which was why Xuanzang's brother introduced Xuanzang to Buddhism. Xuanzang was ordained at the age of twenty, shaved his head, took a vow of celibacy, and began to devote significant time to the study of Buddhist texts.[9] He also learned Sanskrit, one of the languages in which some of the Buddha's conversations had been written down after generations of oral transmission.[10] Having mastered the Confucian classics, Xuanzang was now mastering the classics of Buddhism. He spent seven years as a Buddhist monk, devoting his life to the practice of meditation, renunciation, and recitation that defined what it meant to be a member of this devotional community.

Then he became restless. Devoting his time to following the precepts of the Buddha had oriented his mind to the west, the homeland of this man who had achieved enlightenment. The Buddhist texts Xuanzang studied revolved around the places associated with the Buddha: where he had been born; where he had achieved enlightenment, sitting under a bodhi tree; where he had preached particular sutras. True, Buddhism was a portable system of thought that could be practiced anywhere, especially in places where communities of Buddhists had formed. But there was a particular mystique associated with the original sites of the religion, the landscape that was commemorated in its scriptures. Xuanzang began to feel the urge to go to these places himself. At this point, his plan was not necessarily to bring back an elephant-load worth of treasures or even to return home at all. What he wanted, by his own account, was to seek "sacred traces."[11] With the life of the Buddha, an extraordinary event had taken place in India. Xuanzang wanted to witness whatever remained of that event hundreds of years later.

Xuanzang was drawn to India by a power that is an inevitable result of cultural mobility: the lure of the distant origins of an import. Those in the thrall of a foreign import often worry that what they know is only a shadow of the real thing, something partial, filtered, and fundamentally changed by its passage across time and space. Hence the yearning for the source, the place where the cultural innovation, whatever it is, can be enjoyed in its original state, or at least through whatever traces remain of it. Xuanzang simply had to adore what was left of the Buddha, becoming a figure that is familiar to us today: a pilgrim.

Xuanzang chose to walk a portion of the Silk Route that rounded the Taklamakan Desert in the north and continued to the Jade Gate, so called because caravans bearing jade would pass through this outpost of Tang-era China, of which ruins are still visible today. This was the border he was not supposed to cross. Beyond it was the Tarim Basin, an area that had seen many recent battles as it was fought over by different Turkic tribes. China was encroaching upon the territory of these groups, leading to constant conflict. By the time Xuanzang returned from his travels sixteen years later, the area had been annexed by China. (Today it is known as the Xinjiang region in China's northwest. Tarim Basin is also known as Altishahr, which means "six cities" in Uyghur.)

Once Xuanzang was beyond the Jade Gate, he was in constant danger of being drawn into skirmishes or otherwise attacked. And

Xuanzang knew how vulnerable he was: alone, a fugitive, and a devoted Buddhist. Xuanzang knew that Buddhists could be the victims of persecution. By keeping his head down, he made his way through this war-torn territory relatively unscathed. Often, he was aided by Buddhist communities that had sprung up in oases and towns, and local kings and rulers provided him with provisions and letters to other rulers, some of whom maintained friendly relations with the Tang emperors.

For Xuanzang, the main risk came from common highway robbers, who accosted him not as a potentially hostile Chinese intruder but simply as an easy mark. The other peril came from the difficult terrain. He almost died in the desert, and was rescued only at the last minute by other travelers. He described the events after his return thus: "we enter on a great sandy desert, where there is neither water nor grass. The road is lost in the waste, which appears boundless, and only by looking in the direction of some great mountain and following the guidance of the bones which lie scattered about, can we know the way in which we ought to go."[12]

As Xuanzang got closer to India, he sought to gauge the level of support for his cause, the existence of Buddhist communities, and the attitudes of rulers toward the religion. Among the most striking signs of Buddhism were statues. In the Bamiyan Valley (in today's Afghanistan), Xuanzang was astonished by a gigantic stone figure of the Buddha which had been carved directly into the mountainside. Framed by the Snowy Mountains, "its golden hues sparkle on every side, and its precious ornaments dazzle the eyes by their brightness."[13] The statue was cut from the sandstone mountain and refined with mud and stucco, with parts of it, including an outstretched hand, painted gold, and other parts decorated with gemstones sparkling in different colors. It was part of a group of such statues, one of them 140 feet high, majestic and powerful, a testament to the long-standing importance of Buddhism in this region.

The "western" Buddha, one of the two large statues of the Buddha carved into a sandstone cliff in the Bamiyan Valley in today's Afghanistan, as it looked in 1940 before its destruction in March 2001 by the Taliban.

(ANNEMARIE SCHWARZENBACH, SWISS NATIONAL LIBRARY)

The "western" statue of the Buddha in the Bamiyan Valley after its destruction in March 2001 by the Taliban.

(PHOTO: SQUAMARABBAS)

These statues were so large and solid that they remained part of the cultural landscape even when the people of the region converted to Islam, centuries after Xuanzang's visit. Some used them as refuge and even lived permanently in the large niches that had been carved into the mountainside. In 2001, Taliban forces used anti-aircraft guns and heavy artillery to demolish them, but even these modern weapons did not manage to destroy them entirely; the statues, still visible in outline, haunt these sites to this day and there has been talk of rebuilding them.

Xuanzang was fascinated by these statues not only because they were extraordinarily large but also because they were as close as he could ever hope to seeing the Buddha, to beholding his radiant face. Buddhists had created different styles of visual representation, of depicting the Buddha as a person, evolving particular gestures and poses deemed fitting to his teachings, another example of the close connection between religion and art. Xuanzang absorbed these developments with the eagerness of a pilgrim in an early phase of his journey.

But Xuanzang knew that he was still not in India proper and pressed on. After crossing the Shibar Pass and reaching the area of today's Kabul, he felt that he was getting closer to the heartland of the Buddha. Finally, he crossed into Gandhara (in today's Pakistan), which had been part of Ashoka's realm eight hundred years earlier. Xuanzang knew about this legendary king from the *Ashokavadana*, the *Legend of Ashoka*, one of the Buddhist texts that had been translated into Chinese. The *Legend* had praised Ashoka for having erected 84,000 stupas, the round temples housing alleged relics of the Buddha. As an attentive reader of this text, Xuanzang now attributed many of the stupas and gigantic stone pillars he encountered to Ashoka.[14] Thanks to these pillars, as well as statues, temples, and monasteries, Xuanzang had the feeling of traveling through a sacred landscape. He had finally arrived at his destination: the place where Buddhism had reigned the longest, the land of the Buddha.

Yet Xuanzang reported with great chagrin on the countless structures that had fallen into disrepair, ruins of their former splendor. (He also noted how a king deliberately sought to erase Buddhist inscriptions made by Ashoka.)[15] The sense of disappointment and disapproval helped Xuanzang remember part of his original plan, which did not depend on the survival of statues, pillars, or stupas. Given his upbringing in two text-based traditions, Confucianism and Buddhism, he had meant to recover Buddhist texts. Once he was in India, the search for manuscripts became paramount.

Different traditions and schools of Buddhism had grown up in different regions of India over time, and the teachings that had reached China depended on which monks brought back which scrolls and how they were translated into Chinese. When compared to the long-established canon of Confucian classics, which had remained surprisingly stable over time, the new and emerging body of Buddhist texts seemed unreliable, eclectic, prone to error and misunderstanding, unmoored from its original context. The earliest Buddhist text to be translated into Chinese, for example, was one that did not exist in India at all, but was a "best-of" anthology, a compilation of famous passages from across the Buddhist canon called the *Mahayana*, or "Great Vehicle." As in the case of Rome, where Livius Andronicus translated Homer into Latin, a famous translator was associated with this original transfer of texts: Kumarajiva. Kumarajiva himself grew up in Kucha, in the Tarim Basin (traversed by Xuanzang), but was captured, imprisoned, and finally transported to the Chinese capital, where he was honored by the emperor for his translation of Buddhist texts into Chinese (which he had learned in prison).[16]

Since the time of Kumarajiva, cultural exchange between China and India had intensified. Several hundred years before Xuanzang, a traveler by the name of Faxian had set out with the same purpose: locating sacred Buddhist texts.[17] By the time of Xuanzang, China could boast a tradition of translating Buddhist texts going back hundreds of years. It wasn't just Chinese Buddhists who were drawn to the heartland of the Buddha. Xuanzang learned that pilgrims had come from Ceylon in the south, and since those pilgrims encountered hostility, their king had accommodation built for them.[18]

Xuanzang's own induction into Buddhism had occurred mostly through this same canon of Mahayana texts, and it was through the lens of these excerpts that he now observed the Buddhist practices he encountered in India. While generally curious about all forms and manifestations of Buddhism, he was surprised by the number of different schools, each with its own set of sacred writings. Favoring the Mahayana, he was dismissive of other schools, including the so-called "Small Vehicle," or Hinayana. He was even more dismissive of other religious practices he encountered, above all those of Hindu Brahmins, whom he regarded as the enemies of Buddhism. Despite all this, Xuanzang was kindly received wherever he went. A traveler from China in search of Buddhist manuscripts was unusual and accordingly treated mostly with respect.

After Xuanzang had visited most of the places associated with Buddhism, studied with famous Buddhist scholars, and collected precious manuscripts, statues, and other goods such as seeds, he started to wonder what he should do. Should he stay in India or return home? His Indian hosts couldn't understand why he would want to return to China. Hadn't Xuanzang come all this way to live in the heartland of Buddhism? What was there for him in China, so far from the sacred landscape he cherished?[19]

Xuanzang's response to these well-meaning entreaties is one of the most dramatic moments in his travelogue, because it shows him to be a Confucian still. China, he explained to his baffled hosts, was an extremely well-ordered country, ruled by virtuous emperors, with children venerating their parents. Chinese astronomers had devised a sophisticated calendar, musicians played delicate music, and everywhere people were trying to balance the yin and the yang. His Indian hosts must have had trouble understanding this speech, based as it was on values and terms alien to them, though they might have thought that they, too, had delicate music and obedient children.[20]

As a cultural go-between, Xuanzang couldn't just praise a foreign culture; he also had to praise the culture of his intended audience, back in China. But there was something else behind this turn: after having absorbed as much of the foreign culture as he could, he was now turning inward, reflecting on his experience, and realizing that for all his dedication to Indian Buddhism, his own formation had fundamentally shaped his travel experience and the account he would give once he had returned home. When, in his travel records, he explains his desire to offer more accurate versions of the Buddhist scriptures, he quotes Confucius on the importance of getting names right.[21] The search for better, more authentic versions of foundational texts and more accurate translations of these texts have remained central concerns for the humanities ever since, making Xuanzang a central figure in the formation of the Chinese tradition of humanities knowledge.

Xuanzang's reflection on his own Confucian formation also made him view his travels in a new light. He agreed with his hosts that India was blessed by being the birthplace of the Buddha. This, after all, was why he had gone to so much trouble to travel there. But this didn't mean that Buddhism should be permanently tied to India. Even though Xuanzang had devoted the better part of his life to searching for origins, he came away with the conviction that origins, in the form of Buddhist texts and small, portable statues, could be transplanted.

Thus Xuanzang undertook his journey home, across the Indus River astride his elephant while he watched his precious cargo, the fruit of sixteen years of travel, fall overboard. Since his new understanding of Buddhism was premised on his ability to bring back manuscripts and devotional objects, the loss of his cargo was doubly painful. His load was important to placate the emperor, but also to ground his new understanding of Buddhism, replacing the adoration of sacred locations with the adoration of portable objects and translatable texts, and, ultimately, with his own travelogue.

With part of his cargo irretrievable, Xuanzang stopped his journey and sent messengers to some of the monasteries that had supplied him with manuscripts before, begging them to send new ones. Over the next several months he managed to assemble a sizable trove of scrolls and small statues. Even though he was not able to replace everything he had lost, it was enough.[22]

With his new, smaller collection of texts and statues, Xuanzang could finally undertake the crossing of the Hindu Kush. In preparation for this journey, he had written for help and received horses and camels to transport his remaining possessions.[23] On the far side of the Khyber Pass, he diverged from his previous path and rounded the Taklamakan Desert via a southerly route, which brought him to Khotan, a largely Buddhist kingdom built around an oasis lush with mulberry groves, a center of silk production (conveniently located on the Silk Road), and the Dunhuang Caves, a crucial location for Buddhism marked with an imposing stupa.[24] Dunhuang was also near the Great Wall and the Jade Gate, through which Xuanzang had passed sixteen years earlier. After slipping through this border gate again, he found himself in China once more.

He still had to make his way to the capital and face the emperor. Fortunately, a new emperor had taken the throne during Xuanzang's absence and was willing not only to overlook Xuanzang's violation of the travel restrictions sixteen years ago but also to appoint Xuanzang to a government post. Xuanzang's early Confucian training had prepared him for that job, but his immersion in Buddhism and his years in India had given him a more powerful sense of mission. He refused the appointment and instead asked permission to join a Buddhist monastery with the hope of spending the rest of his life translating the texts that he had collected abroad.[25]

For Chinese Buddhists, Xuanzang became an almost mythical figure, a traveler and pilgrim who had managed to correct, improve, and expand the Buddhist canon available in Chinese. Because translators tend to be seen with misgivings—in Italian, there is a joke premised on the similarity in sound between translator and traitor, *traduttore, traditore*—people tend to forget the pioneering work of translators. (Few remember Livius Andronicus but everyone knows Homer and Virgil.) Even today, the names of translators are often omitted from book covers, almost as if we want to believe that we always have access to the original, that books are created by individual geniuses without the help of cultural go-betweens. This attitude is all the more surprising since we live in a world in which translators have multiplied and all cultures rely on their often unappreciated labors. In the ancient world, wholesale translation was nearly nonexistent. Along with Latin translations of Greek literature, the importation of Buddhist texts into China was one of the major exceptions.[26] It is a tribute to Tang-era China that it not only relied on translators and travelers such as Xuanzang but turned them into cultural heroes.

Even more important than Xuanzang's work as a translator was what he represented: someone who had followed a cultural import back to its source (just as Christians would later undertake travels to the Holy Land). Cultural imports create complicated force fields in which a distant origin promises access to the source of a movement or faith even when the cultural import has long been assimilated by a new host culture. Chinese Buddhists felt the pull of India, but few dared undertake the perilous and forbidden journey westward. Xuanzang went on behalf of all of them. More important, he returned with the news that visits to the sacred landscape were overvalued. Thanks to the texts and objects, observations and experiences he brought back, Chinese Buddhism could flourish without having to feel inferior to that of Buddha's original homeland. Xuanzang was a pilgrim who assured Chinese Buddhists that it was fine to stay home.

=

BECAUSE XUANZANG'S TRAVELS WERE SO LOADED WITH SIGNIFI-cance, it became crucial for him to record everything he had experienced, resulting in *Record of the Western Regions*. That work would shape China's view of India and become a classic in cultural mobility. It is also a good example of the fraught nature of cultural encounters. Like translators, travelers are figures who cross cultural boundaries and are often accused of harboring divided loyalties. In wartime, both translators and travelers are particularly scrutinized and often seen as spies (Xuanzang was suspected of this as well). More recently, travelers tend to be accused of projecting their home culture onto foreign lands. And it is true: formed by their own upbringing, travelers and travel writers get a lot of things wrong. Xuanzang was no exception. He approached India through his Confucian training as well as through the lens of the distinct form of Buddhism that had emerged in China. He also falsely attributed many monuments to Ashoka.

But while travelers get things wrong, they also notice things that locals don't pay attention to, often out of sheer familiarity. As a traveler, Xuanzang bothered to describe in his travelogue many things that Indian writers didn't record because they were taken for granted, including stupas, monasteries, and Buddhist statues. For people who lived among these monuments, it would have been pointless to detail them in writing. For a traveler such as Xuanzang, they were fascinating and therefore at the center of his account.

Unwittingly, Xuanzang produced an account of India that became important not only for his contemporaries in China but also for all posterity. Many of the buildings and statues Xuanzang described have since perished without a trace—we wouldn't know that they had ever existed if not for his account. Thanks to Xuanzang, we have a much better idea of architecture and sculpture in India than in many other places at the time. His descriptions of Buddhist statues became even more precious than the actual statues he managed to rescue from the boat on the Indus River and haul across mountains and desert to the Chinese capital. His descriptions survived. The statues themselves did not.

The transfer of Buddhism from one culture to another, as facilitated by translators and travelers, turned out to be crucial for the preservation of Buddhist thought, which declined in India in the centuries after Xuanzang. Traditional Brahmins managed to reform their Hindu faith and win new converts, draining support from Buddhism. Then much of India was invaded and ruled by successions of Muslim rulers, including the ancestors of Sultan Firoz. They didn't outlaw Buddhism or other local faiths and practices, but they didn't support them, either. Xuanzang had complained about the many ruins of temples and monasteries across India; in the centuries following his visit, many more Buddhist monasteries and communities disappeared.

While Buddhism diminished in India, it flourished in the East, not only in western China but throughout the Chinese Empire, all the way to the Korean peninsula and Japan, far from the sacred traces the Buddha had left. This long-distance impact was Xuanzang's most important legacy.

Xuanzang's status grew in the centuries following his death, based on his travel writing and the massive translation work he accomplished upon his return. His fame received a further boost in the sixteenth century, when another genre of literature burst onto the scene: the prose novel. *Journey to the West*, attributed to the author Wu Cheng'en, enlivens Xuanzang's journey with fantastical encounters and a group of amusing companions, including a monkey; it became an early success in the history of the novel and has remained the most popular classical novel in China, with countless adaptations ranging from theater to animation and film.

As a traveler who became a mythic figure, Xuanzang is a reminder that the culture of China, whose Great Wall is sometimes taken as a sign that it tends to close itself off from the world, is in fact a major example of cultural importation. In honoring Xuanzang, China took a translator and traveler who went on a secret journey and turned him into a hero of cultural mobility.

CHAPTER 6

THE PILLOW BOOK AND SOME PERILS OF CULTURAL DIPLOMACY

Once upon a time, the emperor of China challenged the ruler of Japan to a duel of wits. First, he sent a wooden log that looked entirely symmetrical and demanded to know, "Which is the top and which the bottom?" A young Japanese captain, after consulting with his clever father, suggested that they throw the log into a river and observe which end turned downstream. The experiment completed, they sent the log, properly marked, back to China. Next, the emperor sent two identical snakes and asked which was male and which was female. Again, the young captain, with the help of his father, came up with a solution: if they held a twig near their tails, the female would react and the male wouldn't. Pleased with the success of the experiment, the Japanese sent the snakes back.

Finally, the emperor of China sent an intricate jewel with seven curves and a tiny passage running through them, demanding that the Japanese pass a thread through this labyrinthine path and adding that everyone in China would be able to do so easily. This time it seemed that the Japanese would be unable to rise to the challenge, but the father of the captain once more came to the rescue by recommending that they tie a thread to two large ants and send them crawling through the winding passage. When the emperor of China was confronted with their success, he decided that the Japanese were smarter than he had thought and stopped threatening them.[1]

This story is included in Sei Shōnagon's *Pillow Book* and speaks to the complicated relations between Japan and China. *The Pillow Book* is a unique record of life at the Heian court in the tenth century, and Sei Shōnagon was in a perfect position to write it. As a lady-in-waiting at the court of Japan, including to an empress, she spent most of her time in the exclusive world of the capital, today's Kyoto. Sei Shōnagon would leave this enclave only for brief visits to outlying temples and shrines. (The story about the Chinese emperor is occasioned by a visit to a shrine called Two Ants, dedicated to the Japanese victory over the Chinese emperor.)

In addition to collecting stories such as the one about the arrogant Chinese emperor, Sei Shōnagon recorded the minutiae of court life, noting which of her fellow ladies-in-waiting had found favor with an empress, the comings and goings of high government officials, and the jockeying for position. But court gossip was only a small part of the diary. Sei Shōnagon created lists of things she admired, from fireflies dancing in the dark to particular clothes, such as "a girl's over-robe of white on white over pale violet-grey."[2] As Sei Shōnagon captures moments of exquisite natural and human-made beauty, she also comments on the social graces and pleasing moments of court life: how a lover is supposed to leave in the morning (reluctantly); how a young girl is supposed to dress (somewhat casually, without the stiff formal skirted trousers);[3] and how an expedition to a shrine is supposed to unfold (according to strict protocol). While other women in her position turned inward, keeping diaries about their internal struggles and feelings, Sei Shōnagon turned her gaze outward, describing the world around her, though never as a neutral observer. Quick to pass judgment, she offers us the world as seen through her own discriminating mind.

China is everywhere at the Heian court as represented in *The Pillow Book*. Many types of clothes and screens were inspired by Chinese models—Sei Shōnagon particularly admires exquisite Chinese-style paper and fans—but the influence of China is strongest when it comes to poetry. At court, poems are written and recited many times a day, to mark the first snow or the first day of spring as well as other minor and major occasions.[4] Sometimes, an empress asks several of her attendants to compose short poems on the fly and judges which one is the best, dress rehearsals for more formal poetry competitions.[5] Poems are used in other situations as well, for example, to solve a tricky situation. Sei Shōnagon describes how one night, the emperor was rudely awakened by a rooster that was being chased by a dog, making a racket. A member of the court intervened "by loudly declaiming the words from the Chinese poem, 'The prudent monarch rises from his sleep.'" "My own eyes were heavy with sleep," Sei Shōnagon continues, "but the magnificent way in which he recited the line made me open them wide. Their Majesties were both delighted and complimented the Counsellor on his apt quotation."[6]

Above all, poems were social. They were often addressed and sent via messenger to particular people, who were then expected to respond in kind. The skill was in communicating indirectly, by subtly alluding to or quoting from classical Chinese poems and then adding a short line of commentary to give the quoted poem a new twist. Such exchanges, not unlike text messages today, took place between friends, between court ladies and their superiors, and between lovers. Sei Shōnagon reports being won over by a beautiful poem and agreeing to spend the night with the man, who was then expected to compose a "morning after" poem, hopefully equally apt.[7] Many pages of *The Pillow Book* are devoted to such exchanges and trysts, which were common in the permissive if highly regulated world of the court, a deeply patriarchal society in which proximity to the emperor was everything.

Chinese poetry was important for this practice of communicating via short poems because Japan had adapted the Chinese canon of poetry, as well as of ritual and historical records, as a basis for its own writing culture. At the Heian court, official documents were written in characters derived from China and organized along Chinese formats, which meant that all members of the court were expected to know China's writing system and literary traditions. Sei Shōnagon's story of the Chinese emperor challenging Japan to a battle of wits was a response to the omnipresence of Chinese culture, expressed in the Chinese emperor's arrogance as well as in the Japanese desire to demonstrate their superiority.

=

THE PREVALENCE OF CHINESE CULTURE IN JAPAN WAS THE RESULT of centuries of deliberate cultural diplomacy between the two countries. Exchange between them had started in the first century CE and had accelerated during the Sui and Tang dynasties, when diplomatic talks became an institution. These cultural missions represent an unusual strategy of cultural transfer. Along with Rome's relation to Greece, Japan's relation to China is the other great example of a wholesale cultural import not driven by conquest of the importing culture. Even though, in Sei Shōnagon's story, China is seen as overbearing and potentially threatening, in truth it never attempted to invade Japan. Rather, Japan willingly undertook diplomatic missions charged with bringing back cultural objects and new knowledge.

Unlike Rome with respect to Greece, Japan as the importing culture didn't dominate China militarily. And while, in Rome, the import of Greek culture was the work of individuals, albeit influential ones, in Japan it was the state itself, as represented by the emperor, that organized the transfer of culture. In Japan, cultural import was government policy.

There is one figure who captured how Japan executed its policy of cultural diplomacy, because, like Sei Shōnagon, he kept a diary of his experiences: a monk named Ennin. Ennin's travels (838–47) offer a glimpse of the hazards involved in the cross-cultural missions that would shape Japan for centuries, all the way to the time of Sei Shōnagon and beyond.

Ennin's mission was typical in that it was planned years in advance, involving complicated selection mechanisms as to who would be allowed to go and the work of over a hundred people, including sailors, soldiers, manual laborers, artisans, scholars, and monks.[8] Preparations began with the building of unusually large boats and extended to a careful selection of presents, such as ornamental knives, rock crystals, brushes, and conch shells.[9]

Then came the hazardous crossing of the Yellow Sea. Even though the compass was not yet known in Japan, Japanese sailors gradually acquired enough experience to risk travel via the Japanese Okinawa islands and then across 450 miles of open ocean, a route that got them to Suzhou, the southern center of power (near today's Shanghai).[10] In Ennin's mission, two early attempts at the crossing saw the ships stranded and forced to return. Only the third attempt finally reached its goal, barely. Ennin's ship was tossed about by a storm, then ran aground. The mast and anchor had to be capped, which meant that the boat could no longer be steered, leaving it at the mercy of waves and wind. Fortunately, another boat from the same party came to the rescue, allowing the crew and cargo to arrive safely on the eastern shore of China.

The next difficulty was communication. None of the Japanese spoke Chinese, and vice versa. On occasion, Koreans, who had more contact with both cultures, were able to act as intermediaries, but for the most part, Ennin and his fellow travelers depended on a particular form of communication. Even though the language spoken in Japan was unrelated to Chinese, Chinese characters were the basis for Japan's own writing system, which meant that Chinese was a lingua franca and the Chinese classics a common reference point.[11] The shared writing system allowed Japanese diplomats to communicate with their Chinese hosts by writing the Chinese signs on paper, even though they pronounced them in a mutually incomprehensible manner, much as speakers of two different languages can negotiate over price by writing numbers on a piece of paper. Because writing was done with brushes, this form of communication, which is impossible in writing systems based on phonetic alphabets, was called "brush talk."[12]

Ennin recorded one of his first exchanges of brush talk, which took place upon their arrival in China: "We Japanese monks now meet with you monks because in the past we had important affinities with you. We know for certain that one must dwell in the emptiness which is the nature of the Law. Our meeting is most fortunate."[13] This exchange, something of a mission statement, reveals that while the imperial missions to China were interested in all kinds of cultural developments, Ennin's particular interest was Buddhism, here referred to simply as "the Law."

Buddhism was another import from China. As a Buddhist monk, Ennin hoped to bring back the latest forms of worship and devotional art. For Ennin, Buddhism was more than a religious doctrine. It was a way of life and a source of innumerable artworks, since the cultural development of both China and Japan was inextricably linked to this faith. (Buddhism, especially the recitation of the Lotus Sutra, was omnipresent in Sei Shōnagon's *Pillow Book*, which also mentions many Buddhist paintings, statues, and festivals.)

In order to learn the latest developments in Chinese Buddhism, Ennin hoped to travel to monasteries on Mount Tiantai, which he believed to be the center of Buddhist learning. Quickly it became clear that he needed to obtain permission from several functionaries. Thus began Ennin's great paper war with the Chinese bureaucratic machine, a by-product of its exam system and writing culture. He pursued his goal doggedly, slowly making his way up the hierarchy by sending innumerable letters requesting permission. After many months, the reply finally came back: permission denied.[14] Disappointed, Ennin spent the remainder of the mission collecting manuscripts, devotional objects, and paintings while the rest of the delegation undertook its diplomatic work.

When it came time to return home, Ennin busied himself with packing, along with his companions. He brought on board the ship a bamboo box full of scrolls as well as two mandalas, geometric charts used in Buddhist meditation that represent the cosmos. In order to provide extra security, he put these treasures in a Chinese leather box which he had acquired for the purpose.[15]

When the boats, with their heavy baggage, left, three Japanese visitors secretly remained on shore: Ennin and two of his students. After waging and losing a paper war against the imperial administrative system, Ennin had decided to go rogue.

Until this point, Ennin's experience in China was typical of the cultural missions sent by Japan, though Ennin cared more exclusively about Buddhism than about other aspects of Chinese culture. But when Ennin decided to stay behind, he was on the wrong side of the law; he and his students were on their own. After a while, a boat approached and inquired what they were doing. Were they lost? Had they been shipwrecked? Unprepared, Ennin muttered that they were Koreans. As a friendly gesture, they were marched to the next village, an arduous hike across mountains. There, they were presented to the locals, including a government official. The official quickly ascertained that the three monks were not Korean. Embarrassed, Ennin changed his story, now admitting that he had been part of a Japanese mission but claiming that he had been left behind due to illness. Finally, he mumbled that he was simply a Japanese monk seeking wisdom from Chinese Buddhism.

What should be done with these suspicious foreigners? After spending a winter at a local monastery, Ennin was allowed to travel to a center of Buddhist learning on Mount Wutai, in northern China.

Studded with pagodas, temples, halls, and monasteries, Mount Wutai was named after its five terraces, one for each direction, and a central terrace, which were reached via steep mountain trails. Its flat peaks were covered with snow most of the year and rose majestically from thick green forests of pines, firs, poplars, and willow trees.

Ennin and his two students would stay in a monastery to receive instruction, study scrolls, and learn new ritual practices before moving on to the next. In one of the temples he visited, Ennin was particularly impressed by a sixteen-foot figure of the historical Buddha in the process of dying and attaining the state of nirvana. Usually, a figure of the Buddha attaining nirvana was in a supine position. But in this case, the Buddha was lying on his side, "his right side beneath a pair of trees." The sculpture also included his mother, who is "swooning to the ground in anguish" as well as a large number of demigods and lesser saints, "some holding up their hands and weeping bitterly, some with their eyes closed in an attitude of contemplation."[16] It was all startlingly novel, precisely the kind of innovation Ennin had come to observe.

The question of how the Buddha and famous bodhisattvas—those on the path to achieving enlightenment—should be represented had been debated for centuries and turned out to be central for the development of the arts across Asia. As in so many cultures, especially in the ancient world, questions of religion and of art were closely intertwined. Originally, Buddhist artists had not wanted to represent the Buddha at all and restricted themselves to depicting the bodhi tree under which the Buddha had received enlightenment, the wheel of dharma, and the round stupas symbolizing entry into nirvana.[17] But soon, an elaborate system of portraying the Buddha evolved, with significant local variations. Painters and sculptors simply could not resist creating images of the Buddha at various stages of his life, as described in scripture. Because achieving nirvana was associated with meditation, with the desire to dissolve the ego and its attachments to the world, images and sculptures of the Buddha emphasized stillness, depicting him in postures of remote quietude. Often, he is sitting in the lotus position, but even when he is standing, he is engaged in minimal activity. Motion, or any form of drama and agitation, is reserved, if at all, for the lower beings and students who are often seen crowding around the Buddha or bodhisattva, as in the sculpture admired by Ennin.[18]

While seeking to achieve complete composure, Buddhist artists evolved an elaborate system of rendering the Buddha's face, poses, and other characteristics. The goal was not to capture details of anatomy, but to express visually the detachment so central to this doctrine. To express stillness, the Buddha was almost always represented frontally, with complete symmetry, and his limbs and body shaped with a soft roundness that indicates rest, without any suggestion of muscles or sinews used in exertion or motion. There was no reason for artists to worry about human anatomy, much less dissect corpses, as some European painters would begin to do a few hundred years in the future. Any attempt at realism would go against everything Buddhists believed in: it would focus the viewer on the particular, the striking, the unusual; it would emphasize individuality and bodily quirks. Buddhist sculpture tried instead to capture what the Buddha signified: a philosophy of emptiness.[19]

The same was true of his face. The Buddha's dark blue eyes looked straight out at the viewer below a wide forehead, with a white lock of hair between the eyebrows symbolizing the third "wisdom eye." The Buddha wore a modest monk's robe, without ornaments. Only his hands assumed striking poses, codified by mudras, the hand gestures or "hand yoga" that allow the artist to signal a particular inner attitude.[20] Everything signified an aspect of Buddhist philosophy.

While Ennin was absorbed by his studies of Buddhism, the mood in China turned. In 840, a new emperor, Wuzong of Tang, took the throne. Unlike his predecessor, Wuzong was partial to Taoism, the Chinese philosophy based on the book *Daodejing* (or *Tao Te Ching*) by the sage Laozi that had taken root centuries earlier. Over time, followers of the Tao (or the Way) had absorbed folk rituals, astrology, and medicine, as well as elements from Buddhism, combining philosophy and religion. Less numerous and less well-endowed than Buddhists, Taoists tended to view Buddhists as rivals and resented their access to power and privilege, above all in the capital. The ascension of Wuzong provided an occasion to settle old scores and resentments and to extract more resources.

Besides the newly emboldened Taoists, Confucians remained hostile to Buddhism. Their belief system, based on government service and filial piety, tended to view Buddhism, with its emphasis on individual enlightenment, with suspicion. In addition, Buddhist monasteries such as the ones in the capital and on Mount Wutai had acquired significant wealth. Confucian administrators now hoped to confiscate and redirect some of this wealth with the support of the new emperor.

Buddhists, of course, had their own advocates, including eunuchs, who held significant positions at court, but increasingly it became clear that Buddhism was on the defensive. Even though it had existed in China for hundreds of years, both Confucians and Taoists branded it as a foreign import.

In 842 the first anti-Buddhist edicts were passed, forcing the closure of monasteries, the confiscation of assets, and the burning of scriptures. Ennin recorded the persecution of his fellow monks in his journal without betraying much emotion. Sometimes, he even blamed the victims, as when he frowned on some Buddhist scribes who were foolish enough to present the emperor with Buddhist scriptures knowing full well how hostile the emperor was to their faith.[21] His own strategy was to keep his head down, throw himself into his studies, and hope that the anti-Buddhist wave would finally ebb away.

The opposite happened. In 844 the persecutions entered a more extreme phase, with the wholesale destruction of smaller temples, the confiscation of all wealth held by monasteries, the mass defrocking of monks, and the destruction of Buddhist sculptures and images. The precious bells of Buddhist monasteries were removed and given to Taoist temples. Only gradually did Ennin wake up to this new reality, admitting to himself that clearly the new emperor loved Taoism and hated Buddhism.[22] The destruction of Buddhist art was particularly hard on him: "Moreover they have peeled off the gold from the Buddhas and smashed the bronze and iron Buddhas and measured their weight. What a pity! What limit was there to the bronze, iron, and gold Buddhas of the land? And yet, in accordance with the Imperial edict, all have been destroyed and have been turned into trash."[23] The world of Buddhist art that Ennin had come to observe was crumbling before his eyes. (Christians were also persecuted, to devastating effect.)

It was only a matter of time before the anti-Buddhist campaign came across this Japanese monk hiding out in the capital. Ennin was defrocked and sent home. He left the capital empty-handed. In the eight years since his arrival, he had amassed scriptures and art objects to take back to Japan, but he realized that he had to leave them all behind. Buddhism had been officially abolished and he couldn't be found on the road laden with images and scrolls. All that he would be able to bring back with him was what he had stored in his own mind. In parting, a sympathetic Chinese citizen, a chief administrator, left him with a rueful thought: "Buddhism no longer exists in this land. But Buddhism flows toward the east. So has it been said since ancient times."[24]

Ennin was still in China when, in 846, Emperor Wuzong passed away, bringing the most severe phase of persecution to an end. Contrary to the dire assessment of the Chief Administrator, Buddhism in China survived the great persecution of 845, though it never again regained the power and significance it had enjoyed under the previous Tang emperors. Mount Wutai was largely destroyed. Ennin's diary became the most detailed record of this extraordinary assemblage of mountains and monasteries, of nature and art. (Over the ensuing centuries, some monasteries were rebuilt, drawing on his diary, and the area is now a UNESCO World Heritage Site.) As in the case of Xuanzang, a foreign visitor had recorded an art and culture more thoroughly, in more detail, than a native would have had reason to do, leaving not only his Japanese readers but all of posterity with a unique record of this magical place.

As the Chief Administrator had predicted, Buddhism continued to flow to the east. Having emerged in India, it gradually lost ground there, only to be taken up in the mountain regions of today's Afghanistan, in Tibet, and then in China, before moving on to Korea and Japan and from there to the rest of the world. What the Chief Administrator didn't say, but implied, was that the enablers of this eastward flow were travelers such as Xuanzang and Ennin, people who had gone west in order to bring Buddhism east.

≡

ENNIN'S WAS THE LAST JAPANESE IMPERIAL MISSION TO TANG-ERA China. Another mission was planned a few years later but it was abandoned, in part because of the danger of the sea voyage, but also because of the uncertain situation in China. By the time Sei Shōnagon wrote her diary, the period of cultural diplomacy and the import of Chinese culture to Japan, from poetry to Buddhism, had drifted into the past.

In the intervening centuries, Japan took increasing pride in cultural independence. To this end, it developed a new script, the kana script, a phonetic syllabary that doesn't rely on Chinese characters and is keyed to the Japanese language. (The script was said to have been developed by a Buddhist priest who brought the idea back from India, inspired by its phonetic alphabets.) The kana script broadened literacy in Japan. While in China literacy was predominantly restricted to men, the new script allowed women to enter the literary world in greater numbers. Among them were court women such as Sei Shōnagon who wrote diaries, while Sei Shōnagon's younger contemporary, Murasaki Shikibu, wrote the first great novel in world history, *The Tale of Genji*.[25] Even though the new script was initially seen as less sophisticated, it ended up giving rise to works of the greatest originality and significance, in part because it created a space for women writers to innovate outside the strictures of male, Chinese-oriented literature, with its set canon and literary conventions. (It also gave rise to the first court-sanctioned Japanese poetry anthology, the *Kokinshū*.) The mostly female diaries written in the kana script were so fresh and successful that male writers started to imitate them.

Despite this newfound independence, Chinese culture continued to be a hugely important reference point in Japan. Murasaki's *Tale of Genji*, for example, includes almost eight hundred Chinese-style poems and makes frequent reference to Chinese literature.[26] Murasaki is also one of the few contemporaries to have written about Sei Shōnagon, whom she regarded as a rival: "Sei Shonagon has the most extraordinary air of self-satisfaction. Yet, if we stop to examine those Chinese characters of hers that she so presumptuously scatters about the place, we find that they are full of imperfections." Even centuries after the end of imperial missions to China and the flowering of the kana script, the best way to put down a rival was to criticize her faulty Chinese writing.

=

THE CLEAREST EXPRESSION OF THE NEW SPIRIT OF INDEPENDENCE is another account of an imperial mission, one produced with considerable hindsight around the same time as *The Pillow Book* and comparable to its story of the Chinese emperor's testing of the Japanese. It is a scroll combining text and image to recount the travels of one Kibi no Makibi, a legendary minister who went on an imperial mission to China.

According to other sources, the historical Kibi had mastered thirteen areas of Chinese learning, which included the five Confucian classics, history, yin–yang, calendars, astronomy, and divination, as well as the game of Go.[27] This impressive knowledge of Chinese culture served

him extremely well because the scroll describes his mission to China
as going terribly wrong. Initially, all seems well: the crossing of the sea
between Japan and China goes smoothly, the boat bearing the Japanese
visitors arrives on the shore and is met by a smaller boat that takes them
to land, where they are cordially received. But then, trouble begins. Kibi
is taken to a tower and effectively imprisoned. Warned by a ghost of his
own impending death, Kibi knows that to survive he must impress his
murderous hosts, who subject him to various tests and ordeals.

First, he will be tested on his knowledge of an anthology of Chinese literature. Fortunately, he knows how to fly, so he and the helpful ghost get airborne to spy on their Chinese captors as they prepare
the literary test. After passing the test, Kibi must show his mettle in
a game of Go, which he does by swallowing a crucial piece. His hosts
suspect what has happened and intend to prove it by inspecting, after
an appropriate interval, his excrement. The artist shows us a group of
inspectors gazing intently at the ground but is discreet enough not to
render the object of their scrutiny. In the event, the Chinese don't know
that among Kibi's many admirable talents is complete control over his
bowel movements, which has allowed him to hold back the Go piece.
Through these and similar tricks, Kibi impresses the Chinese so much
that they become truly afraid of him, and when he threatens to destroy
the sun and the moon, they let him go.[28]

The scroll, despite its humor, paints a relentlessly negative picture
of China and warns of the dangers Japanese visitors might encounter
there, including a deadly battle of wits much like the one Sei Shōnagon
recorded in her diary. This negative picture of China is remarkable
because there is no indication that the historical Kibi was imprisoned
in a tower or almost starved to death.

Rather than depicting historical events, the scroll, with its suspicion of the Chinese, expresses how fraught cultural import can be.
Cultural imports tend to entangle two cultures in a complicated operation of borrowing and influence, often eliciting anxieties over superior-

ity and dependency. What does it mean to borrow technology, culture, and art from another country? What happens if you borrow someone else's literary canon?

The case of Japan—like that of Rome—shows that borrowing can be a great asset, enriching a culture that choses to borrow from another voluntarily. At the same time, such borrowing, almost inevitably, creates a sense of rivalry, of being latecomers, of having to prove one's worth. Perhaps this sense of rivalry is especially strong if the imported culture does not come from a defeated military foe, as was the case with Greece for Rome, creating a backlash against fears of being dominated by another. Ennin's diary records the backlash, in China, against the import of Buddhism, while his own diary became, indirectly, subject to a backlash against Chinese imports to Japan.

The anxiety of cultural imposition was pervasive, but also misplaced. True, Ennin's diary changed the face of Buddhism in Japan in part by strengthening the Tendai school of Buddhism, but this influence, based on his original writings and the scrolls he shipped back, evolved into new forms in Japan. Over time, Japanese Buddhism would give rise to other, distinct types of Buddhism, above all Zen Buddhism—the name derived from the Chinese *chan*, for meditation—which developed its own forms of worship and art.

The Kibi scroll itself is a work of great originality. Even though the practice of creating narrative picture scrolls, combining calligraphy and ink drawing, originated in China, nothing quite like this scroll exists there and picture scrolls became a distinctive Japanese art form. Skillfully alternating text and images, it evokes movement everywhere: boats arriving and being met by a crowd of people; the guests being transported by a cart, accompanied by horses; the traveler and the ghost flying through the air, their hair blown back by the wind. In the crowd scenes, everyone is busy doing something, whether it's holding an umbrella, bending down, leading a water buffalo by the reins, galloping toward a palace, climbing the steep steps of a tower, or reading

Portions of the scroll depicting Minister Kibi's Adventures in China (Kibi daijin nittō emaki), from the twelfth century.

(MUSEUM OF FINE ARTS, BOSTON. PHOTO: MUSEUM OF FINE ARTS, BOSTON)

a scroll. Even the people who seem to be waiting or sleeping are doing so in dramatic poses, draped over stairs or leaning on lances, ready to spring into action at any moment.

The scroll was produced in the workshop of Tokiwa Mitsunaga, who had perfected the art of kinetic flow by giving the format of the scroll a forward drive, a sense of motion that anticipates manga, the graphic novels created in Japan that took the world by storm in the twentieth century.

Ennin's diary and the Kibi scroll, though they express anxiety over cultural imports, demonstrate that there was nothing derivative about Japan, neither in its literature, painting, sculpture, and architecture, nor in its forms of Buddhism and Buddhist art. As in the case of Rome, a voluntary import helped create a new and original culture of lasting significance.

Of these original creations, Sei Shōnagon's *Pillow Book* has remained one of the most significant, securing her a firm place in world literature. Toward the end of the diary, Sei Shōnagon tells her readers the story of how the diary began.

Palace Minister Korechika one day presented to the Empress a bundle of paper.

"What do you think we could write on this?" Her Majesty inquired. "They are copying *Records of the Historian* over at His Majesty's court."

"This should be a 'pillow' then," I suggested.

"Very well, it's yours," declared Her Majesty, and she handed it over to me.

I set to work with this boundless pile of paper to fill it to the last sheet with all manner of odd things, so no doubt there's much in these pages that makes no sense.

Overall I have chosen to write about the things that delight, or that people find impressive.[29]

The anecdote registers the importance of paper (a Chinese invention). It lets us know that the paper is available because the emperor no longer needs it for copying *The Records of the Historian*, one of the core documents of the Chinese canon, which clearly remains important even though imperial missions have long ceased. Originally intended for a Chinese classic, the paper has, by chance, ended up in Sei Shōnagon's hands, where it will be used to produce an entirely different type of historical record, one not of arms and battles but of culture and art, of poems exchanged, of aesthetic ideals and social decorum, of scents and sounds and sights, of everyday observations and lists of charming (and un-charming) events. It is a record written not by a Chinese man but by a Japanese woman, and written not in Chinese characters but in a Japanese syllabary, affording us a rare glimpse into a hidden world that was closed to all but very few contemporaries and that would have vanished from history if not for the bravery and ingenuity of this acute observer and extraordinary writer.

In evaluating culture, we tend to overemphasize originality: when and where something was first invented. Claims of origin are often used to prop up dubious claims of superiority and ownership. Such claims conveniently forget that everything comes from somewhere, is dug up, borrowed, moved, purchased, stolen, recorded, copied, and often misunderstood. What matters much more than where something originally comes from is what we do with it. Culture is a huge recycling project, and we are simply the intermediaries that preserve its vestiges for yet another use. Nobody owns culture; we merely pass it down to the next generation.

CHAPTER 7

=

WHEN BAGHDAD BECAME A
STOREHOUSE OF WISDOM

One night, the caliph al-Ma'mun had a dream. He saw a man with a high forehead, bushy eyebrows, bald head, dark blue eyes, and handsome features. His skin tone was reddish white. The dreamer reported that he was filled with awe standing in front of the apparition, and asked: "Who are you?" The apparition replied: "I am Aristotle." The caliph further reported that he was delighted and proceeded to ask the philosopher all kinds of questions, before waking up.[1]

The caliph dreamt this dream during his twenty-year reign, from 813 to 833, in the city of Baghdad. He found the dream significant enough to report it to his attendants but seemed remarkably unfazed to have been visited by a Greek philosopher. On the contrary, he was, by his own account, pleased by the visitation. Al-Ma'mun was clearly conversant with Aristotle and knew exactly how to handle him, even in a dream.

Why would a caliph of Baghdad dream of a Greek philosopher who had been dead for twelve hundred years?

Al-Ma'mun's rise to power was swift and brutal. He had been named Abu al-Abbas Abdallah ibn Harun al-Rashid: the son, as the last part of his name indicated, of Harun al-Rashid, the fabled ruler who had consolidated the rapidly increasing Arab Empire. Harun al-Rashid bequeathed to his sons the Arabian peninsula as well as Egypt and northern Africa in the west and what is today Syria, Iraq, and Iran in the east. But even though al-Ma'mun was the firstborn son of Harun al-Rashid, his father decided to put his younger half-brother in charge of the realm, centered in Baghdad, leaving al-Ma'mun only with central Persia. The inevitable followed. Al-Ma'mun eventually invaded Baghdad, beheaded his brother, and took the title of caliph. To cap off the success of the campaign, he adopted his new, regal name, in 813.

Since the death of the Prophet Muhammad less than two hundred years earlier, Arab forces had conquered oasis after oasis, city after city, with breathtaking speed. Unusually mobile due to their semi-nomadic lifestyle and expertise in long-distance trade, they quickly took control of trade routes, which set off a cascade of victories, making it difficult for local rulers to resist. Many also recognized the advantages of becoming part of a single trade-based empire and willingly surrendered.

As the empire expanded westward, along the northern coast of Africa, and eastward toward Mesopotamia and Persia, it became increasingly clear that what had driven this stunning success—mobile forces on horseback organized along tribal or regional lines, without central command—was ill-suited as a system of rule for what was becoming a world empire. A new political organization was necessary to consolidate the changes that had taken place on the ground. The answer to this challenge, in the generations before al-Ma'mun, was Baghdad.

Founding a new city is an architect's (and a ruler's) dream. Rather than following the natural outline of the landscape, Baghdad was constructed by the second Abbasid caliph, al-Mansur, along a completely different principle: geometry. The city was built as a perfect circle, symbolizing the rising power of Arabia in a single center.[2] Building a new city signaled a new phase in the young history of the empire.

Starting from scratch had the advantage that the new city didn't have to contend with an old architectural layout or an existing ruling class. Its ruler could envision a new type of center, one specifically designed to control a new type of empire, concentrating political and material power in a single focal point.[3] (This was not dissimilar to what Nefertiti and Akhenaten had done by moving their court to the new city of Akhetaten, what Brazil would do in 1960 by founding Brasilia, and what Myanmar has been doing since 2002 when it established a new capital, Naypyidaw.)

The new, circular city represented a larger ambition: the concentration of knowledge. In Baghdad, rulers would preside over an ambitious undertaking of amassing information from across their rapidly growing realm and even beyond its boundaries. The unprecedented accumulation of texts from different cultures required new methods of categorizing discrete types of knowledge, leading to a new genre: the *summa*, or summation of all knowledge. Aristotle played a central role in this endeavor.

By founding a new city in which to consolidate an empire, al-Ma'mun's ancestors had chosen the right place. Baghdad was located on the river Tigris, in the fertile floodplains of Mesopotamia, near the ancient city of Babylon. It was here that the first cities had arisen some five thousand years earlier, nourished by plentiful water, with clay, a cheap building material (the same material used for building Akhetaten) readily available.[4] It was the beginning of a new phase in human history: the urban revolution.

The most important technique behind the urban revolution was intensive agriculture. In order to support a city, it was necessary to transport enough food from the surrounding area to feed a large population that was stuck in place, unable to follow a herd or move to new hunting grounds. Urbanism didn't rely on military conquest. It relied on the ability to grow food.

But growing food was not enough. Another technique was necessary: storage. The best storage could be achieved with grain (as Thutmose, the sculptor of the Nefertiti bust, knew—his compound included storage for grain). Once grain had been harvested, it could be preserved for long periods of time. Soon it became clear that storing grain did more than provide safety against droughts and pests. Those who controlled the storage of grain gained immense power, which created hierarchical social structures, making it possible for individuals or groups of people to own wealth that was limited only by the size of storage and the ability to control it by force.[5] The rise of a centralized state in Egypt was one early consequence of the storage revolution.

In founding Baghdad, al-Ma'mun's ancestors drew not only on the ancient storage revolution with respect to controlling grain, but also with respect to information. Mesopotamia had given rise to the first full writing system, a system of signs capable of capturing speech, allowing for the storage of stories and other forms of verbally transmitted knowledge. One of the first libraries in the world was created by the Assyrian king Ashurbanipal in the city of Nineveh (also built from scratch to facilitate his reign).[6] It is not surprising, therefore, that the new city of Baghdad included an ambitious palace library whose goal was to preserve the written record of the past: the Storehouse of Wisdom. It was the place where knowledge would be accumulated but also organized, with the help of a new system of categorizing different types of information.

What did the new rulers of Baghdad wish to store? Initially, records from the past, from a time before the birth of Muhammad and Islam. This meant mostly writings in Persian, since Mesopotamia had long been influenced by Persia, whose literature included the *Kalila wa-Dimna*, a story collection of entertaining and instructive animal fables. Once Arabs had taken Mesopotamia and Persia, this Persian past was translated into Arabic.[7] Translation was an act of homage on the part of the new Arab rulers, but it was also a canny move that allowed them to tap into the cultural resources of the conquered region. Soon, translations from Persian became the building blocks for a new Arabic literature, above all, *One Thousand and One Nights*, which would eclipse its much smaller Persian antecedent and become a classic of world literature. Along the way, it immortalized al-Ma'mun's father, Harun al-Rashid, who appears in many of the stories that are set in Baghdad.

Harun al-Rashid was crucial in facilitating another import from the east, this one from China: paper. Not just the Storehouse of Wisdom, but the entire expanding bureaucracy centered in Baghdad increased the demand for writing material. The most widespread writing material was made from papyrus, cross-cut leaves of the plant that grew best in swampy conditions such as those prevailing in the Nile delta—one reason why the Library of Alexandria was situated there— but was much less common in Mesopotamia and Persia.

Paper didn't rely on the papyrus plant, which was difficult to grow outside Egypt, but on a whole range of plant fibers which were pulped, combined with water, and pressed through a mesh to create a smooth yet flexible writing material. Harun al-Rashid quickly recognized the advantages of paper and turned Baghdad into a center of paper-making.[8]

The Storehouse of Wisdom was not devoted exclusively to the local (Persian and Arabic) past but to a much wider set of cultural influences. This wider intellectual horizon was aided by its location on the Silk Road, which had long connected Mesopotamia to Asia. Some of the stories included in the two Persian story collections, for example, came from India. The Storehouse also contained Indian tracts on astronomy, including the *Surya Siddhanta*, which described ways of calculating the orbits of various celestial objects, translated from Sanskrit into Arabic.[9] One of al-Ma'mun's predecessors created an institute of astronomy in Baghdad, demonstrating the extent to which this new city aimed to gather and store knowledge.

While many of the texts came to Baghdad from the east, some hailed from the opposite direction, including Euclid's *Elements*, with its famous definition of the circle as a collection of lines of the exact same length emanating from a single point. Inhabitants of Baghdad may well have appreciated Euclid's definition of the circle because the city, too, sought to be the central place from which all lines radiated equally, and not just architecturally.[10] The city's scholars wanted to assemble knowledge from everywhere and bring it to what Euclid would have called "the point," which he defined as "the center of the circle."

While initially Euclid was the only Greek author to be thus honored, soon translations from Greek into Arabic, sometimes via Persian, started to increase—above all, of the works of Aristotle. (Euclid had drawn on Aristotle as well.) Thanks in part to these translations, Aristotle became known, simply, as the Philosopher.[11] No one was more enthusiastic in promoting this increasingly expansive translation project than al-Ma'mun.

The kind of knowledge accumulated in Baghdad cut across what we today would call STEM (science, technology, engineering, and mathematics) and the humanities, a reminder that our current system is not the only way of organizing knowledge. In Baghdad, astronomy and mathematics, as well as treatises on medicine, were transmitted side by side with texts of literature and history. Scholars considered these areas of knowledge to be interrelated. One thing was clear: the rulers and scholars of Baghdad had decided that different areas of knowledge produced in the past could be useful in the present.

The increasing dominance, in this translation project, of Greek texts wasn't all that surprising given that the Arab conquest had quickly expanded eastward, incorporating Persia and Bactria (today's Afghanistan), and, finally, reaching India. In connecting India to the Middle East, this new Muslim Empire reconstituted the vast territory where Alexander the Great had scattered Greek settlements, the Greek language, and Greek learning.[12] After Alexander's death, his empire fractured into different parts, each headed by a different general, but it had the long-term effect of making the Greek language, and therefore Greek learning, a shared language across a wide region (inducing Ashoka to inscribe one of his pillars in Greek). The center of Alexander's Greek world was the Library of Alexandria, which was now incorporated into the Arabic world.[13] In drawing on Greek culture, Arab rulers didn't have to go beyond the boundaries of their own realm, but only into the past: their new empire was built on top of a number of previously existing ones. Rather than eradicating what went before, they preserved it, translated it, and incorporated it into their own view of the world.

The other empire on which the new Arabic world was stacked was the Roman Empire. The western part of the empire had been in decline, invaded by Goths from central Europe. Only the eastern part, centered on Byzantium, survived, though much of its territory fell to the Arabs.[14] In its diminished state, Byzantium closed in on itself and lost interest in preserving the full body of Greek thought. Part of the problem was that the city saw itself as the last defender of Christendom in the east, which meant that it became increasingly suspicious of its own pre-Christian past. In 529, Emperor Justinian forbade pagans from teaching, including scholars steeped in texts that had survived from the pagan past such as those of Euclid, Ptolemy, and Aristotle—precisely the thinkers who would soon be translated into Arabic.[15] This meant that pagan texts would have to be transcribed by Christian scholars, if at all. (It wasn't just knowledge of the pre-Christian canon that was lost; Byzantium also lost the art of erecting large stone columns, central to building Greek temples and marketplaces, and of casting in bronze, as the city's economic and artistic ambitions diminished.[16])

Fortunately, Baghdad's Storehouse of Wisdom took over the job of preserving the classical world at a time when the Eastern Roman Empire seemed to be abandoning it. The situation was not so different from the way Buddhism lost ground in India but flourished, in translation, in China and then, when Buddhism was persecuted in China, continued in Japan. In this way Baghdad grew in knowledge, translating and storing learning from different cultures in its center of power no matter where this knowledge came from. In pursuing knowledge from afar, scholars in Baghdad were following a famous statement attributed to the Prophet Muhammad: "Seek knowledge, even if it be [as far away as] China, for seeking knowledge is a religious duty for every Muslim."[17]

Despite the advantages of Baghdad's collection project, the influx of foreign texts eventually resulted in a backlash. Emperor Justinian, with his edicts against pagan teaching, wasn't the only one worried about the existence of pagan traditions; Islamic scholars were as well, and for similar reasons: the problem was how to reconcile monotheism with pagan knowledge. Islam was now dominant across a vast territory and eager to find converts. Its adherents found few difficulties with works such as Euclid's geometry or Indian methods of calculating the movements of celestial bodies. But Aristotle had created a system of thought that included fundamental views about the nature of the universe, an account of why things were the way they were, which could be seen as clashing with basic tenets of Islam (or perhaps this was just another version of how Socrates had clashed with his own city for having introduced new gods). It was at this juncture that the difference between more technical forms of knowledge and fundamental beliefs, between know-how and know-why, came to the fore.

The promoters of the Baghdad translation project were undeterred, in part because they realized that bringing Greek knowledge into the Arab Empire didn't weaken Islam. Harun al-Rashid and his son saw that in the competition between different religions and philosophies, Islam needed sharper tools, and they were willing to find them either in distant lands or in the intellectual remnants of the past. There was a competition between different traditions of know-why; learning what earlier cultures had produced would add to the sophistication and force of current ones. Also, there were a lot of technical aspects to know-why—forms of argument, logical consistency, techniques of writing and thinking—that could be transferred from one culture to another. The tools of thought made available through the translation project helped Islamic clerics and rulers to debate the representatives of other religions.

Byzantium was a cautionary example of how an inward turn and closing of intellectual possibilities accompanies and sometimes precipitates decline. Harun al-Rashid and al-Ma'mun realized that if they wanted to create a world empire, they couldn't shut themselves off from the world. (Byzantium experienced a revival of interest in texts from classical antiquity a few centuries after Justinian's edict, driven by Empress Irene, who took power in 780 and recalled exiled scholars. In addition, there was money to be made in selling copies of classical texts to collectors from Baghdad.[18])

The Baghdad translation project was a demonstration of an important principle in cultural history: borrowing cultural products can be an immense source of strength. Instead of weakening the borrowing culture, borrowing can bolster it, supplying it with cultural resources, insights, and skills that are lost to those who are worried about provenance, ownership, or ideological purity.[19]

It was this open-minded attitude that conspired to turn Aristotle into a figure who could haunt al-Ma'mun in a dream. In recounting this dream, actual or invented, the caliph signaled that Aristotle had been driven out of Byzantium and had found refuge in Baghdad, that the Arabs were the true heirs of ancient Greece.

=

IBN SINA (980–1037) NEVER REPORTED ANY OF HIS DREAMS, BUT he must have dreamt of Aristotle frequently because he devoted his entire life to the Philosopher. Better known in the West by the Latin version of his name, Avicenna, he grew up in the city of Bukhara in northeastern Persia (today's Uzbekistan), the region that had been given to al-Ma'mun by his father.[20] Like most inhabitants of that region, Ibn Sina spoke Persian, but he adapted to the new rulers by conducting most of his writing in Arabic. His education and his life's work exemplified the result of the Baghdad translation project and demonstrated what could be done with the knowledge accumulated through it. For it was not enough to preserve the wisdom of ancient Greece, India, and other traditions: this wisdom had to be processed and adapted to new circumstances. It had to be used.

Initially, Ibn Sina studied the Qur'an, which, according to the dominant method of instruction, meant learning portions of it by heart. By age ten, he was able to recite the entire text, which laid the foundation for his later writing in Arabic. The next step in his education he owed to a merchant, an Indian who taught him arithmetic. Then, he was lucky to have the privilege of a tutor who introduced him to other fruits of the Baghdad translation project, what was by then known in Arabic as *falsafa*, an adaptation of the Greek word *philosophia*.[21] Absorbing these extremely different traditions and modes of knowledge was exciting to the teenage Ibn Sina, but also confusing. In particular, he struggled with Aristotle's metaphysics, whose abstract arguments about cause and effect he found intriguing but difficult to follow. Fortunately, he encountered a bookseller hawking a treatise by al-Farabi, one of the first self-declared Islamic scholars of *falsafa*, who explained Aristotle to his Arabic-speaking audience.[22]

As a budding scholar, Ibn Sina got another lucky break when he was allowed access to the local sultan's library. Local authorities across the Arab world, including those of Bukhara, were imitating Baghdad, with its concentration of manuscripts and scholars. The translation project had radiated outward, reaching students in different parts of the empire.

The Baghdad translation project not only created the conditions for the education of someone such as Ibn Sina; it also created a market for explaining what all this new learning was about. A merchant of his acquaintance, who had always been curious about *falsafa*, commissioned Ibn Sina, still in his teenage years, to write a summary and explanation. This assignment spoke to Ibn Sina's particular talent: showing how different traditions and modes of knowledge could be made to fit together. Over the next several decades, he became a great synthesizer of knowledge. In the process, he developed a new form of thought.

Just when Ibn Sina delivered that first commission, the world around him—his access to the sultan's library, the network of his teachers in Bukhara—started to fall apart. Squabbles among local rulers meant that he had to flee. He would spend the rest of his life essentially stateless, looking for new patrons who could provide him with commissions and with access to books. There were periods of relative stability, as when he was able to live and work in Isfahan, but overall, his life was marked by flight and imprisonment, and by the desperate search for safety. Late in life, he suffered from debilitating illness that made it difficult for him to write by hand.[23] He recorded these experiences in a short autobiography, in which he also gave an account of his education, but he refused to dwell on his hardships. "Necessity led me," is all he would say about being chased from town to town, sometimes escaping unrest at the last moment.[24] These things could not be helped, but they were not worth dwelling on. The only thing that mattered was *falsafa*.

Throughout his volatile life, Ibn Sina never stopped reading, teaching, and writing. That early commission had set his mind on thinking about how different traditions and branches of knowledge could be combined. For this task, Aristotle was the perfect guide, because in a sense this was what Aristotle had done, the reason why he was simply called the Philosopher; he had created a system of thought—one that was elaborated by scholars in Alexandria before it reached Ibn Sina. Such a system was precisely what the concentration of knowledge in the Storehouse of Wisdom needed, a way of classifying and integrating what would otherwise be nothing but a grab bag of historical curiosities.

Ibn Sina understood knowledge as falling into the following categories, which had been created by Aristotle, but which were now used more systematically:[25]

1. **Logic.** This branch of knowledge is the backbone of the art of reasoning, first developed by Aristotle. It includes other forms of organizing thought through language, including Aristotle's books on rhetoric and poetics and his treatise on Greek tragedy. (Aristotle's *Poetics* was difficult for most Arabic commentators since there was no equivalent of Greek theater in the Arab world.)

2. **Mathematics.** Here, Ibn Sina didn't confine himself to Aristotle but also drew on astronomy, optics and the theory of music, understood as the relation between scales, often expressed as mathematical fractions. Soon, Arabic mathematicians would lead the world in their field, among other things by utilizing the value of zero—the reason why Arabic numerals are used in most parts of the world today.

3. **Physics.** Based on Aristotle and others, this branch concerned the observable part of the universe, what we might call nature, including the nature of bodies, both animate and inanimate, their motion and behavior, different types of causes, changes and continuities, but also the nature of the universe in general, the notion of time, and eternity.

4. **Metaphysics.** This branch of knowledge was initially called metaphysics because Aristotle's books on this matter were placed after (*meta*) those on physics. They included much of what has since come to be known as philosophy—or *falsafa* in Arabic—namely reflections (what we sometimes call meta-reflections) on existence, on knowledge, and on reason. This part of Aristotle's philosophy was also a response to his teacher Plato and his theory of eternal forms.

The division into four branches was only a simplified scheme. Ibn Sina also needed to accommodate more mundane forms of knowledge, such as medicine, which played an important part in his work, as it did for the Baghdad translation project more generally. Finally, Aristotle had written on ethics, the principles governing human behavior toward other humans, which also included politics, the science of government, and economics, the word derived from the Greek word *oikos*, for household.

While some aspects of this scheme may seem familiar, others, such as the inclusion of music as part of mathematics, are not. This is a reminder that philosophy, as conceived of by Aristotle and adapted by Ibn Sina, is another discipline that has undergone significant change before it ended up in the humanities in today's university system. For Aristotle and Ibn Sina, it encompassed many parts of what today we would call the natural and social sciences, which were spun off from philosophy over the course of the sixteenth and seventeenth centuries under the label of "natural philosophy." Meanwhile other parts, such as logic and mathematics, ended up among today's STEM subjects. And while the modern research university prides itself on interdisciplinary work, it does not encourage the creation of a unified system of knowledge, as Aristotle and Ibn Sina did.

Ibn Sina always acknowledged Aristotle as the creator of this system, but Ibn Sina wasn't, and didn't see himself as, simply repeating or popularizing Aristotle's system; instead, he elaborated it, expanded it, and incorporated into it other sources of knowledge.[26] More important, Ibn Sina reflected on different types of knowledge, and on the question of how we can know things in the first place. He concluded that all humans are uniquely endowed with the capacity for rational thought, which can be elaborated by the rules of logic, what Aristotle had called the rational soul.

Above all, Ibn Sina needed to address the question that haunted all who participated in the Baghdad translation project: how did this system relate to Islam and its conception of a creator God, as revealed to the Prophet Muhammad, transmitted to scribes, and written in the holy Qur'an? For one thing, Islam, as elaborated by scholars devoted to *kalam*, Islamic theology, had placed a premium on knowledge (*'ilm*), which made their thought compatible with what Ibn Sina was proposing (it's possible that the importance of knowledge for Islamic theology was itself an indirect result of the Baghdad translation project).[27] To further relate Aristotle to Islam, Ibn Sina seized Aristotle's emphasis on causes and proposed that God was the ultimate cause of them all. This was why the universe could be known rationally, for example through the rules of logic. But God, the ultimate cause, could not.[28]

For all his admiration for the Philosopher, Ibn Sina didn't follow Aristotle blindly. This was the point of being a rationalist: you examined an argument and adjusted it or changed it if necessary. Ultimately, Aristotle was important not because he was an authority but because he had come up with an incredibly useful method of reasoning, one that could—and needed—to be adapted to the here and now. Ibn Sina had a genius for placing each science in a larger scheme. His works became models for what the Latin Middle Ages would call *summa*, the sum of knowledge.

Writing a *summa* wasn't merely a matter of explaining someone else's thought. Even though Ibn Sina allowed himself increasing leeway to depart from Aristotle, he nevertheless felt that he had to justify these departures. Sometimes, he explained that Aristotle had left things deliberately unsaid, afraid that his work might fall into the wrong hands. Only now could commentators bring these hidden dimensions into the open. At other times, he complained that he didn't have the right books to consult—a plausible excuse given his chaotic life—and therefore might depart from the Philosopher more than he would want to.[29] But he never gave up on the goal of the *summa*, the most pressing intellectual challenge for someone who had grown up amid the compilation of knowledge brought about by the Baghdad Storehouse of Wisdom.[30]

Ibn Sina's work is a good example of the creative powers unleashed by commentary and interpretation. His use of Aristotle was more than simply paying homage to an ancient philosopher; it was an active process that involved much original work. In fact, it wasn't that Aristotle had hidden important parts of his work for later interpreters such as Ibn Sina to discover; Ibn Sina chose to disguise his original thought by pretending that all he was doing was teasing out points that had originally been made by Aristotle.

In creating an all-encompassing synthesis of available knowledge, Ibn Sina shaped how philosophy would be done for the next several hundred years. Even today, much work in the humanities proceeds by way of commenting on a canon (Ibn Sina imported the term into Arabic as *qanun*), albeit one that is always changing. It is a mode of doing philosophy that enacts the desire to preserve the past but also to use it actively for the present; it is born from our ability to store thoughts and arguments, and to translate them into the present and across cultures. It is a mode of conducting humanistic research that places a premium on collecting, preserving, combining, and concentrating intellectual resources from different places and different times as the most likely path to meeting the challenges of the present.

The *summa* was a mode of information management born from a sense that there existed important work that needed to be collected and preserved for later use. This sensibility is perhaps overly familiar to us, who appreciate the importance of storage but also of search, of collections and metadata, who know what it is to feel thrilled and overwhelmed by a surplus of information. We have access to so much, but we don't always know what to search for and what to do with it.

It makes sense that this sensibility would have been developed by someone who lived on the Silk Road, who lived in an empire that connected India to Greece, prized the storage of culture as an ideal, and saw the transfer and translation of ancient and foreign texts not as a threat but as an enrichment—albeit one that required new modes of information management.

As someone whose mode of doing philosophy depended on collecting texts that had been preserved from long ago, Ibn Sina was exceptionally bad at collecting and preserving his own work. Mostly, this wasn't his own fault. Keeping track of an entire career in the age before print wasn't easy in the best of circumstances. Some of Ibn Sina's early summaries, for example, were commissioned by specific patrons, who would pay once they received a single handwritten manuscript. If Ibn Sina wanted to keep a copy for himself, he would need to write one out, or hire someone to do it, which meant that there might exist only a couple of copies of any of his texts in the world. The additional copy could easily be lost in the many sudden departures and flights that Ibn Sina was forced into throughout his life. If Ibn Sina lost his only copy, he would have to track down his former patron, or the patron's descendants, which was often impossible given the political unrest. In such a situation, he might try to recreate the work from memory, but why would he do that? Wouldn't it be better to refashion everything in a different way, perhaps improving upon it, and essentially write a new work? Such rewriting characterized several of Ibn Sina's treatises.

The people who were supposed to sort through this mess, make copies of Ibn Sina's works, and hunt down lost works were his students.[31] In his autobiography, Ibn Sina recounts convivial evenings spent in discussion with a whole group of students, while drinking wine (apparently seen as compatible with Islam). But he mentions only one by name there, al-Juzjani, who bore the brunt of collecting and copying the master's work. As Ibn Sina's fame increased, a new problem emerged: some texts were falsely attributed to him. This meant that frequently al-Juzjani had to authenticate works as actually having been written, or rewritten, by Ibn Sina. Finally, al-Juzjani took it upon himself to encourage Ibn Sina to write new works or to recreate lost ones, often taking dictation himself.

Al-Juzjani's efforts are the reason why some works have survived, and others are known to us by name via later bibliographers. (The golden age of Arabic letters gave rise to extensive bibliographies, yet another attempt to collect and catalogue different forms of knowledge.) Other students worked mostly by writing their own commentaries and summaries of Ibn Sina's work, including Bahmanyar, possibly a Zoroastrian, Ibn Zayla, who commented on Aristotle's more elusive works, and al-Lawkari, whose own *summa* did much to spread the method at the heart of Ibn Sina's work, the method of rational argument.[32] In this way, Ibn Sina's thought survived in ways similar to the work that had been cultivated in the Baghdad translation project—through an effort of summarizing and synthesizing.

≡

MEDIEVAL BAGHDAD, THE CENTER OF THE GOLDEN AGE OF ARABIC letters, with its paper industry, its Storehouse of Wisdom, and its concentration of translators, commentators, and scholars, did not survive the ravages of time. The fault was, once again, with the building material, mud bricks, which were abundant and had given rise to the very first urban spaces, but which did not last more than a few generations. In contrast, say, to Nefertiti's Akhetaten which was abandoned, Baghdad had the misfortune—from the point of view of preservation—of being continually occupied ever since its foundation by al-Ma'mun's ancestors, which meant that the city was constantly being rebuilt. In the process, all traces of its original architecture were irrevocably destroyed, leaving us with no sense of what the Storehouse of Wisdom looked like, or whether it ever existed as a single distinct building.

Fortunately, we can see this storehouse through the imprint it left. That imprint was enormous, turning not only Baghdad but the entire Arab Empire into a center for learning, the place where new forms of knowledge preservation and production were developed. Perhaps it was never a single storehouse, anyway, but an idea of collecting, translating, and synthesizing knowledge, something that ultimately was not dependent on a single place but on an attitude toward the past and the products of other cultures. Ibn Sina did not have the luxury of working in a single place or of remaining in possession, even, of his own work, yet his work turned out to be crucial.

Thanks to the Arab Empire, the translation project begun in Baghdad and brought to fruition by Ibn Sina radiated outward, to the remote edges of an increasingly enormous area. In Delhi, where soon Islamic dynasties assumed control, a sultan heard about Ibn Sina's most influential *summa*, titled *The Healing*, and commissioned an elegant copy for himself.[33] The sultan was Muhammad ibn Tughlaq, whose son would take such an interest in Ashoka's pillar: perhaps his father's copy of Ibn Sina stirred Sultan Firoz's interest in the distant past.

At the same time, the Storehouse of Wisdom projected its influence westward, all the way to the Iberian peninsula, where Arab forces had established the largest Islamic province in Europe. This became the route through which Ibn Sina's work, and other results of Baghdad's translation project, reached western Europe. The result was an act of cultural borrowing that was called, falsely, a rebirth, or renaissance.

Bust of Queen Nefertiti (fourteenth century BCE), excavated by Mohammad es-Senussi in 1912 at Amarna, Egypt. The bust has since become the most famous face of antiquity.

Head of a princess from Akhetaten (fourteenth century BCE), with the prolonged head typical of the work done in the workshop of the sculptor Thutmose.

This mosaic (100 BCE–79 CE) found in Pompeii depicting Plato's Academy is an example of Romans adapting Greek culture as their own.

(NATIONAL ARCHAEOLOGICAL MUSEUM, NAPLES)

A 2017 concert in the ancient Roman theater of Taormina, Sicily (third century BCE), is just one example of the many ways contemporary Italians reuse Roman ruins.

(ITALIAN G7 PRESIDENCY 2017)

A multicolor print (1840) by Hokkei Totoya depicting Sei Shōnagon, author of *The Pillow Book*, which captured life at the Heian Court.

A multicolor print by printmaker Suzuki Harunobu (1725–1770) depicting Murasaki Shikibu, the author of the *Tale of Genji* (ca. 1000 AD), the first great novel in world literature.

A library with pupils depicted by illustrator Yahyá al-Wastiti in a 1237 work by Arabic poet al-Hariri of Basra. The depiction is reminiscent of the Storehouse of Wisdom in Baghdad.
(NATIONAL LIBRARY OF FRANCE)

Raban Maur (left) supported by Alcuin (middle) hands his work to the Archbishop Otgar of Mainz. Alcunin was one of the most prominent scholars whom Charlemagne attracted to his court as part of his program of cultural revival. The illustration is from Maur's ninth-century work *De laudibus Sanctae crucis* (In Praise of the Holy Cross). (NATIONAL LIBRARY OF AUSTRIA)

Illustration from the *Liber Divinorum Operum* (Book of Divine Works) by Hildegard of Bingen, composed between 1163–74, in which she described her visions. (LIBRARY OF CONGRESS)

A page from the Codex Borgia (thirteenth–fifteenth centuries) depicting the sun god Tonatiuh. The Codex Borgia is an example of Aztec picture-writing, a highly complex script that is still in the process of being deciphered and interpreted today. (VATICAN LIBRARY, ROME)

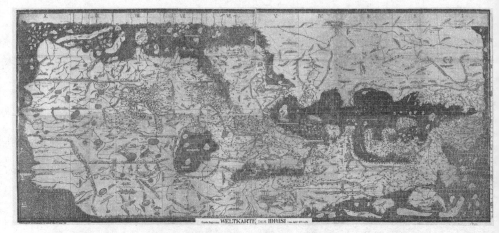

World map by the Arab geographer Muhammad al-Idrisi, from the year 1154, depicting Asia, North Africa, and Europe "upside down," with south at the top. The map shows the expanded Arab trading network before the Portuguese circumnavigation of Africa. (LIBRARY OF CONGRESS)

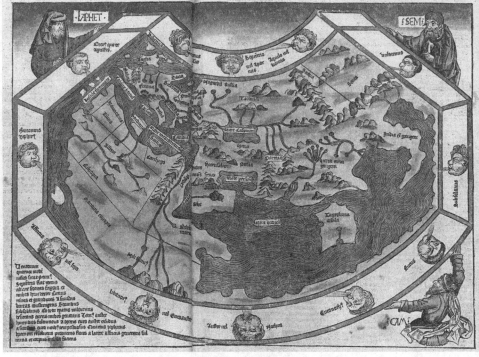

The Nuremberg Chronicle by Hartmann Schedel, printed in 1493. It depicts Asia, Europe, and Africa in a way that forecloses the possibility of circumnavigating Africa to enter the Arabian Sea by ship, as Vasco da Gama would do.

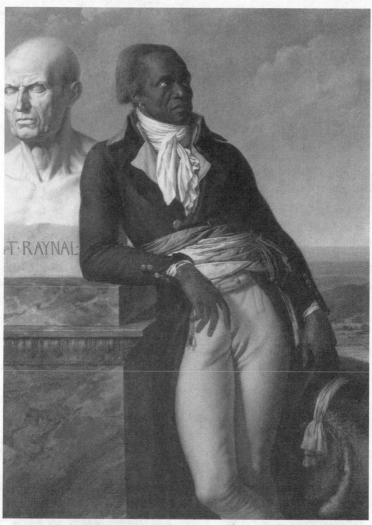

Anne-Louis Girodet de Roussy-Trioson, Portrait of J.B. Belley, Deputy for Saint-Domingue, 1797. The marble bust of Raynal pales in contrast to the vivid color palette of the painting. Belley is clothed in the garments typical of the French Revolution.

Noh mask of Oji, the old man, from the Edo period (1603–1868), made from wood and paint. Noh theater prized stylization, with highly codified gestures and movements supplementing the use of masks, which were painted in different colors.
(GUIMET MUSEUM. PHOTO CREDIT: MARIE-LAN NGYUEN)

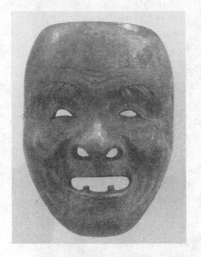

Edmund Dulac's frontispiece for the 1921 edition of William Butler Yeats's Noh-inspired play, *At the Hawk's Well*.
(EDMOND DULAC, MACMILLAN AND CO.)

Kim Tae-hyung (V) performing "Singularity," his 2018 solo track. V plays with masks to emphasize the public roles K-pop performers have to contend with. Noh theater used white masks for the role of young women or supernatural beings, conveying innocent beauty. In Korea, masks featured in regional dance dramas.
(STILL IMAGE FROM MUSIC VIDEO "SINGULARITY" (2018) BY V, A MEMBER OF BTS)

CHAPTER 8

＝

THE QUEEN OF ETHIOPIA
WELCOMES THE RAIDERS OF
THE ARK

The Old Church of Our Lady Mary of Zion, in Aksum, Ethiopia.   (PHOTO: SAILKO)

The city of Aksum, on the Tigray plateau of Ethiopia, houses the Church of Maryam Syon, or Our Lady Mary of Zion. The center of Ethiopian Christianity, the church has been rebuilt many times. Its most recent version dates from 1965, when Emperor Haile Selassie constructed an airy modern domed structure supported by large arches and windows.[1] This building is situated near an older one, which also features arched windows but in a darker, smaller, rectangular building that dates from the seventeenth century. But even that church took the place of several older ones, ultimately going back to the fourth century, when Christianity first arrived in Ethiopia.

Throughout the volatile history of razing and rebuilding this church in different styles and materials, one thing has remained the same: the church contains a *tabot*, which refers both to the stone tablets on which were written the Ten Commandments and to the Ark of the Covenant, that is, the box that houses them.[2] In fact, the church is named after this *tabot*, since Syon (or Zion) here means the Ark, not Mount Zion in Jerusalem.[3] Every Ethiopian church contains a symbolic *tabot*, but the one in the Church of Maryam Syon was allegedly the original Ark containing the original Ten Commandments.[4] How did this sacred object of the Jewish people end up in an Ethiopian church?

According to the Hebrew Bible, Moses constructed the Ark of the Covenant following the specifications given to him by God near Mount Sinai. The Ark was a gold-covered wooden chest meant to house the two stone tablets onto which Moses wrote the Ten Commandments, as dictated to him by God.[5] The Ark was carried on two long poles wherever the Israelites went, hidden from sight by thick veils made from animal skins and cloth forming a tent, or tabernacle. It was the closest thing the Israelites had to an idol and was guarded with vigilance. Once, the Ark was captured by the Philistines, but it brought such plagues upon them that they quickly returned it, glad to be rid of this mysterious object. King David took it to Jerusalem, where King Solomon constructed a temple to give it a permanent home.

The Ark remained securely in the temple until the city was destroyed by Nebuchadnezzar in 587 BCE, at which point the Hebrew Bible loses track of this precious box. It is not mentioned among the articles brought back when the Jewish people returned from Babylonian exile to rebuild their city and their temple.[6] Other sources are equally uncertain what happened to it. When Titus Vespasianus, the Roman general, sacked Jerusalem in 70 CE, he destroyed the temple and brought its most valuable objects, including a golden candelabrum, with him to Rome, but the Ark was not among his loot. Sometime between the first and the second destruction of the temple, the Ark of the Covenant between God the Jewish people, this holiest of holies, was lost. Who was responsible?

A solution to this puzzle is provided by an intriguing text written in Ge-ez, the ancient scribal language of Ethiopia. Called *Kebra Nagast*, it reveals that the Ark was stolen in the time of King Solomon. As for the culprit, the text proudly identifies Ethiopia, ruled by a legendary queen.

The Queen of Sheba is described in the Hebrew Bible when she paid a visit to King Solomon, arriving with many attendants and camels bearing spices, gold, and precious stones as diplomatic offerings. Before giving him these rich presents, she cross-examined him until she was convinced that King Solomon was really as wise as he was reported to be. The king, no doubt flattered by this judgment, responded to the queen's generosity by giving her many presents in return. He also showed her his palace and the temple, of which he was justly proud, before sending her back to her own country.[7]

The *Kebra Nagast* tells a different story. It says that the story refers to an Ethiopian queen who allowed herself to be embraced by King Solomon and was with child by him by the time she arrived home. Once their son, Menelik, came of age, the queen sent him to Jerusalem, along with a ring given to her by King Solomon, so that Menelik would be identified by his father. True to his much-praised wisdom, King Solomon recognized Menelik, welcomed him as his son and even declared him to be his official firstborn, which meant that Menelik would ultimately inherit the kingdom and rule over the Israelites.

But Menelik did not want to rule in Jerusalem; he wanted to return home to his mother. Reluctantly, Solomon let his son go and provided him with a group of young men to accompany him, a kind of honor guard composed of the sons of the most noble families of Jerusalem. The sons felt somewhat ambivalent about being sent away and, perhaps out of resentment or to carry with them something from home, hatched a plan to steal the Ark.

Days after Menelik and his entourage had left, Solomon noticed the theft and sent warriors after them. But they were too late. The Ark had given Menelik and his companions wings, allowing them to arrive safely in Ethiopia, where Menelik was crowned king. All this might well explain why the Ark wasn't actually in the temple when Jerusalem was destroyed first by Nebuchadnezzar and then again by Titus. It had been sitting quietly in Aksum, the capital of Ethiopia, for centuries.[8]

Who would have written such an unusual and ingenious text? The version of the text that survived was used and promoted under King Amda Seyon, or Pillar of Zion (1314–44), but most likely it drew on earlier versions and materials.[9] Unlike more distant predecessors, Amda Seyon claimed to be a descendant of King Solomon, and the *Kebra Nagast* was the means by which he reinforced this lineage. But this text did much more than simply confirm his royal pedigree. It provided the different language groups and tribes that made up the high plains of Ethiopia with a shared sense of the past; *kebra nagast* means "greatness of kings," but its purpose was to establish the greatness of Ethiopia. The success of the Solomonic dynasty of Ethiopia is a good example of the power of a shared foundational story, something the compilers of this text may have learned from their own source text, the Hebrew Bible.

In telling the story of the theft of the Ark, Ethiopia connected itself to a Jewish dynasty by declaring direct descent from it—supported by a story of dynastic succession, much more concrete than mere translations of texts or import of artifacts. The *Kebra Nagast* is not alone in pursuing this type of cultural graft or transfer: Virgil declared the founder of Rome to have been the Trojan Aeneas, while the Persian *Book of Kings* claims that Alexander the Great was secretly the child of a Persian princess and should therefore be celebrated as a Persian king named Iskandar. The *Kebra Nagast* merely goes one step further by combining dynastic descent with the theft of the Ark. In doing so, it allows Ethiopia both to claim biblical origins and to shift the religious center of gravity from Jerusalem to Aksum. The *Kebra Nagast* is a fascinating example of what one might call strategic borrowing, disguised as theft.

The other remarkable thing about this story is the fact that the *Kebra Nagast* was not used by Ethiopian Jews, who might have an understandable investment in claiming a close connection to Jerusalem. It was used by Ethiopian Christians. The stolen Ark is the foundation on which Ethiopian Christianity is built.

The *Kebra Nagast* is a good reminder that cultural borrowing occurs in all domains of meaning-making, from philosophy and wisdom literature to art and religion. This is nowhere as clear as in the case of Christianity itself. Originally, Christianity was an offshoot of Judaism, the product of a wave of messianic Judaism of which Jesus of Nazareth was one of several examples. Jesus had learned to read the Hebrew Bible and saw himself, in light of this ancient text, as the Messiah predicted by the prophets.[10] In the century after his death, Jesus's followers slowly drifted away from the mainstream of Judaism and finally broke with it under the guidance of Paul, giving birth to a new religion.[11] But the rupture was not absolute. Jesus, after all, had seen his own life as the fulfillment of the Hebrew Bible. Creating a new scripture that would serve as the foundational text of a new religion would never have occurred to him. In fact, he did not write a single word.[12] It was only after his death that his followers wrote down stories about his life, to which were added letters and other texts from people who had never known the historical Jesus in person. Eventually these texts became a new scripture.

While the Hebrew Bible was a patchwork of texts put together by scribes over a period of hundreds of years, and written in Hebrew, these new accounts of Jesus were composed over a much shorter period, and in Greek.[13] The difference in style wasn't the only problem. Among the new accounts of Jesus were many not written by eyewitnesses, and several disagreed on essential points. Christian scholars sorted out these problems in several gatherings, called Councils, which took place across the Middle East, where they decided which texts about Jesus should be deemed authentic and which were inauthentic, or apocryphal, how they should be arranged, and how they should be interpreted (similar to the councils held by the followers of the Buddha after his death). The scholars didn't always agree, leading to sharp divisions, even breakaway sects. Different Councils sought to adjudicate these disputes and patch over divisions, not always successfully.

Another problem was how this new canon of texts should relate to the old one. The solution was to rename the Hebrew Bible the Old Testament and the Christian canon the New Testament. Despite their differences in age and style, these two groups of texts had to be stitched together so that Christians could still feel themselves connected to the faith of the historical Jesus as well as his Hebrew Bible, and yet know that that Bible served only as a foundation on which they had built a different religion.

The work of stitching the two texts together was undertaken by commentators, who combed the Hebrew Bible for figures and images that could be seen as an anticipation of Christianity. The work succeeded to the satisfaction of Christians, thanks to the ingenuity of these interpreters who lived in places such as Alexandria, Jerusalem, and Antioch, as well as further east (including the Nestorian monastery south of Baghdad, where monks would later translate Greek texts into Arabic).

This was the context in which Christianity reached Ethiopia, sometime in the fourth century, probably through Syria. The particular branch of Christianity was called Miaphysite, whose adherents believed that in Christ the human and the divine formed a single nature, while orthodox Christians insisted on keeping the two natures distinct.[14] The *Kebra Nagast* is a Miaphysite text, but that's not the main reason why it is significant. Its ingenuity lies in the fact that it came up with a different, and in many ways superior, method of connecting the Old and the New Testaments.

The *Kebra Nagast* moves back and forth between stories from the Old Testament and the New Testament, weaving the two texts closer together by using some of the interpretations undertaken by commentators throughout the Near East. The *Kebra Nagast* makes these connections not through commentaries but through storytelling. Adam is described as a king, the original monarch from whom all future kings, including King Solomon, are descended. Solomon is seen as a Christlike figure, and many episodes from the Hebrew Bible are characterized in Christian terms, such as the delivery of Daniel from the lion's den as a kind of resurrection. Other figures from the Hebrew Bible seen in a distinctly Christian light are Noah, Samson, and Moses. In this way, the *Kebra Nagast* constantly moves between episodes based on the Old and the New Testaments, using the latter as a lens through which to view the former.[15]

This strategy undergirds the central story of the theft of the Ark, which became the most important link between the Old Testament and Ethiopian Christianity. Since the Ark and the Commandments were important for Judaism and Christianity, the authors of the *Kebra Nagast* were able to claim that their practice of Christianity, which was being dismissed as a strange sect, was actually a more ancient and authentic form of Christianity, making Ethiopia one of the earliest Christian nations.[16]

Yet, for all its desire to claim direct descent from King Solomon, the *Kebra Nagast* turns against the wise king by presenting him as a sinful person who tricks the Queen of Sheba into a sexual union. These fissures—deepened by the theft of the Ark—will ultimately turn into an actual war between Ethiopia and the Jewish people. In other words, the *Kebra Nagast* wants to claim a close connection to a Jewish dynasty and, at the same time, denounces Judaism as a misguided religion and Jews as a people against whom wars must be fought.[17] This is yet another consequence of strategic borrowing: often the borrowers will seek to prove their independence by turning against the culture from which they have borrowed.

Even though the *Kebra Nagast* is sometimes dismissed as an eccentric amalgamation, when it is read at all, it is a perfect example of the dynamics underlying religious and cultural borrowing. The *Kebra Nagast* can be explained as an act of borrowing that turns against the source (the Hebrew Bible) it sought out, creating both continuity and rupture, admitting to being derived from a culture (Judaism) to which it then declares itself superior—not unlike the Japanese Kibi scroll and its satire of a cultural mission to China. The *Kebra Nagast* is also a literal version of what Christianity did with Judaism: claim descent from it and at the same time compete with it over possession of its sacred past (and, repeatedly, the people who held onto the original tradition). Descent and theft: the *Kebra Nagast* turned these two operations of cultural borrowing into tangible form through its story of Solomon's Ethiopian son and the theft of the Ark. Far from being eccentric, this is how latecomers deal with the fear of being derivative—and ultimately we're all latecomers to the world of culture, always confronted with something that came before and to which we must now create a meaningful relation.

=

LIKE ALL FOUNDATIONAL STORIES, THE *Kebra Nagast* IS SELECTIVE and leaves out a lot of things, including Islam. This is all the more surprising since a note attached to the earliest existing manuscript states that even though it was originally written in Coptic, derived from ancient Egyptian, it was then translated into Arabic before being translated into Ethiopian Ge-ez in the thirteenth century. Amda Seyon, under whom the *Kebra Nagast* found its final form, had conquered Muslim territories, which makes the omission of Islam from this text all the more remarkable.

The absence of Islam from the *Kebra Nagast* can mean two things: the text, or at least the stories from which it was derived, might have been written much earlier after all, at a time when Ethiopia had recently been Christianized and was seeking to define its relation to other Christian centers such as Byzantium and Alexandria (where Coptic was a rather widespread language). In this scenario, the earliest parts of the *Kebra Nagast* would have been produced before the rise of Islam in the seventh century.[18] Alternatively, and more likely, a version of the text was composed in Arabic and then translated and adapted into Ge-ez at a moment when Ethiopia felt embattled by Islam and wanted to create for itself a history that had nothing to do with the new religion (many scholars now doubt that a Coptic version ever existed).[19] But in either case, the role of Arabic is central for the history of transmission because the Ge-ez version, the only one we have, contains a number of words and grammatical constructions that come from Arabic. The *Kebra Nagast* seems to be an unusual example of the Arabic translation project, even if its Christian editors sought to erase that legacy.[20]

Geographically, Ethiopia had always been closely connected to the Arabian peninsula, from which it is separated by the Red Sea, an easily navigable waterway whose narrowest point is barely sixteen miles across.[21] In fact, it is possible that early forms of Christianity might have reached Ethiopia via southern Arabia, where both Jewish and early Christian influences were strong.[22] The Ethiopian heartland was not located on the coast, however, but on a plateau that was more difficult to access, a geographic position that allowed the inhabitants to create and defend an independent empire connected both to Egypt via the Nile valley and to Arabia via the Red Sea. Geographic indepen-

The Stelae Park in Aksum, Ethiopia. Visible in the foreground are the remains of the Great Obelisk. (PHOTO: SAILKO)

dence also expressed itself in linguistic independence. Both the Old and the New Testaments were translated into Ge-ez, and the *Kebra Nagast* uses these translations as its source material.[23]

The position of the Ethiopian heartland became crucial during the period of Islamic expansion beginning in the seventh century. Muslim influence came from the east, across the Red Sea, via a network of Arab merchants and ports. Later Arab influence also came from the north, via Egypt, with which Ethiopia had always had economic and cultural ties (Aksum was a city of Egyptian-style obelisks, some of which have survived). One reason for the northern connection was the slave trade, since Egypt used enslaved Ethiopians to man its army.[24] Another longstanding influence on Ethiopian intellectuals were scholars working in Alexandria, with its significant scribal traditions reaching far back into antiquity.

The rise and expansion of Islam can be seen as a parallel experiment in religious transfer and selective fusion. Even though the Prophet Muhammad was never an adherent of the Hebrew Bible, his prophecy, dictated to scribes who turned it into the Qur'an, subtly drew on its material as a resource, borrowing several of its stories and figures. Though much more distant from the Hebrew Bible than Christianity is, Islam could still be regarded as a selective transfer project, a religion that regarded the older scripture as a narrative resource. This selective borrowing included the story of the Queen of Sheba and her visit to Solomon (though not their sexual union or the theft of the Ark, which are exclusive to the *Kebra Nagast*).[25]

Ethiopian Christians coexisted with Muslims even as Islam expanded westward across the northern coast of Africa and into Spain, and eastward toward Mesopotamia, Persia, and India. Ethiopians held onto Christianity by moving further inland, ceding control of the coast to Arab traders.[26] This retreat almost inevitably turned into a feeling of being embattled, whether real or imaginary, and the *Kebra Nagast* helped Ethiopians maintain a distinct cultural identity. The text borrows (allegedly steals) from one culture, Judaism, while maintaining its distance from another, Islam.

In 1450, an Ethiopian monarch articulated the sense of impending doom in no uncertain terms: "Our country Ethiopia [is surrounded by] pagans and Muslims."[27] Doom came in the person of Ahmad ibn Ibrahim al-Ghazi, a local ruler allied with the Arabs, who defeated the Ethiopian emperor Lebna Dengel with a force composed of Ottoman Turks, Arabs, and various African forces.[28] He conquered Aksum and destroyed its central church, Our Lady Mary of Zion, guardian of the Ark, in the 1530s. Dengel and the ruling class fled into the mountains, where he died in 1540. The unlikely story of Ethiopia seemed to have come to an end.

But there was another geopolitical development under way: the Portuguese sailor Vasco da Gama had managed to round Africa and make his way up the western coast of Africa. His goal was to cross the Indian Ocean and establish a sea route for the lucrative Indian spice trade, now that the rise of the Arab Empire had made the land

route difficult and costly. In addition to this mercantile motive, he
was driven by stories: tales of a fabled Christian kingdom in eastern
Africa. Soldiers returning from the Crusades in the twelfth century
had brought back reports of a Christian king called Preste Joao, or
Prester John (an overland expedition had made contact with Prester
John in 1490).[29] As Gama was making his way up the coast, he heard
confirmation from Muslim traders that there was indeed such a kingdom further north, inland from the Horn of Africa. Gama did not
stop to explore because he was eager to cross to India, but in the wake
of his voyage, more Portuguese ships came and established contacts
in eastern Africa.

It was a group of those Portuguese that the Ethiopian court called
on for help, which came in the form of Cristovao da Gama, Vasco da
Gama's son. Aided by four hundred muskets, he freed the court from
its mountain retreat, rescued Dengel's wife, and managed to defeat
Ahmad ibn Ibrahim al-Ghazi.[30] Cristovao gave his life to the cause: he
was captured and beheaded in 1542. But he had managed to establish
an Ethiopian–Portuguese alliance.

The defeat of Muslim forces helped Ethiopia maintain its Christian
orientation (though Portuguese Jesuits were taken aback by the specific
form of Ethiopian Christianity, so different from European Catholicism).[31] The Portuguese were the first to translate the story told in the
Kebra Nagast into a European language, in the seventeenth century. In
Europe, the story was taken as further proof that the legends of Prester
John, which had long fired the European imagination, were true.

Ethiopia encountered another adversary in the form of the British Empire. In 1868, British forces launched a "punitive" mission in
response to reports that Ethiopia had imprisoned several missionaries
in a mountain fortress. Queen Victoria sent General Robert Napier,
whose army managed to take the fortress; the defeat drove Emperor
Tewodros II to suicide.[32] Following their usual procedure, the British
combed the ancient city of Aksum for cultural treasures to ship home,

while installing another ruler, Emperor Yohannis. Among the stolen treasures were two copies of the *Kebra Nagast*. When Yohannis discovered the theft, he wrote to London:

> There is a book called "Kivera Negust" which contains the Law of the whole of Ethiopia, and the names of the Shums [Chiefs], and Churches, and Provinces are in this book. I pray you find out who has got this book, and send it to me, for in my country my people will not obey my orders without it.[33]

Without its foundational text, Ethiopia could not be governed. The British returned the two copies, a rare example of Europeans giving up their cultural loot.

The extraordinary story of the *Kebra Nagast* and how it shaped the fortunes of Ethiopia has largely been neglected. The Ethiopian form of Christianity became peripheral to both the Greek Orthodox faith and the Catholicism propagated by Rome. But the neglect of the *Kebra Nagast* was due also to a more general dismissal of African cultural history that began in antiquity and continues to this day. In Homer, the Ethiopians are described as the *eschatoi andron*, the most remote men.[34] Even the biblical story of the Queen of Sheba, and the rumors of Prester John and a Christian kingdom in Africa, did not dislodge the idea that Ethiopia was a remote, peripheral, and eccentric case, nor did it dislodge the European idea that Africa was a continent without history, or literature, or civilization, and somehow disconnected from the cultural exchange that was drawing different parts of the world into an ever thicker web of exchange. When the Renaissance painter Piero della Francesca, along with other European artists, depicted the encounter between Solomon and the Queen of Sheba, he painted her in light skin tones.

=

Piero della Francesca, *The Meeting between the Queen of Sheba and King Solomon* (c. 1452–66). The painting depicts the embassy by the Queen of Sheba to King Solomon described in the Latin Bible, I Kings 10.   (BASILICA OF SAN FRANCESCO, AREZZO)

THERE EXISTS ONE EXCEPTION TO THE GENERAL NEGLECT OF THE *Kebra Nagast*, halfway around the world from Ethiopia, in Jamaica. As was the case with other Caribbean islands, Jamaica's native population was decimated after the arrival of European settlers, due to their enslavement on sugar plantations and their lack of immunity to smallpox. To make up for the missing labor, Europeans brought enslaved people from the western coast of Africa, today's Ghana and Nigeria. Despite the brutal living conditions—worse, even, than those on the American mainland—these enslaved Africans preserved their cultural expressions and memories.

After the formal end of slavery in 1838, the quest for forging a new cultural identity continued. How should the descendants of enslaved Africans relate to the continent from which their ancestors had been taken? While the schooling set up by European colonists promoted the superiority of their European culture, some Jamaicans turned to Africa as a source of identity.

One of them was Marcus Garvey, a labor organizer, printer, editor, and orator who founded the Universal Negro Improvement Association; he also spent several years in the United States and set up a chapter of the UNIA in Harlem, New York. Over time, it became the most important pan-African movement of the early twentieth century.[35] Even though he had never set foot on the African continent, Garvey had heard intriguing accounts that contradicted the widespread dismissal of Africa propagated by most colonial educators. Ethiopia, with its ancient history and scribal tradition, became an important reference point for Garvey. To be sure, very few of Jamaica's inhabitants had ancestors from Ethiopia specifically, which was located far from where slave ships picked up captured Africans for the Atlantic slave trade, but Garvey found in Ethiopia's history a tradition that placed Africa at the center of some of the world's most important cultural and religious developments, and could serve as a historical model of Black Christianity.[36] (Garvey also started a shipping line to facilitate renewed contact between Africa and Jamaica.)

At the time, Ethiopia was governed by a king called Lij Tafari Makonnen, who legitimized his rule, as his many predecessors had done, with the *Kebra Nagast*, claiming descent from the Queen of Sheba. Upon ascending the throne, he adopted the title Ras Tafari, and when he was declared emperor, he used his Ge-ez name, Haile Selassie.[37] For Garvey and many others, Ras Tafari was a representative of an ancient African culture, an African emperor who could claim a cultural tradition going back to antiquity.[38] When Ethiopia was attacked by Italy in that country's brutal attempt to extend its African colonies in 1935, Garvey and others rallied to its cause (though Garvey was also critical of Haile Selassie): ancient history had become a matter of resistance to European colonialism that connected the Caribbean and East Africa.[39]

In Jamaica, the fascination with Ethiopia ultimately led to the creation of a movement, based on Ras Tafari's name, called Rastafari. In addition to their long-distance devotion to Ras Tafari, Rastafarians devote themselves to natural living, often growing vegetables and cannabis. (The international success of reggae musician Bob Marley firmly connected, in the minds of many, Rastafarianism and his music.) Dreadlocks, the distinct hairstyle of many Rastafarians, are sometimes seen as originating in Ethiopian Christianity, by way of the Bible's mention of the Nazarites, who equally abstain from wine and from cutting their hair.[40] Rastafarians also observe Ethiopian Christmas.[41] Thanks to this movement, the *Kebra Nagast* enjoyed a second life in Jamaica.[42]

As was the case with Ethiopian Christianity, Rastafarianism is sometimes seen as a hodgepodge, a grab bag of practices, but, like ancient Ethiopia, it should be regarded as a prime example of cultural transfer and fusion. The descendants of enslaved people from Africa needed to forge a past that promised them a different future than what European colonists had to offer. Even though Ethiopia was far away, it was a useful cultural resource for their needs, an example of strategic borrowing in many ways similar to what the *Kebra Nagast* itself had undertaken. Rastafarians recognized something unusual in this faraway country, an opportunity to rewrite their own cultural history across vast distances of time and space. The result was something very different from a simple return to Africa or African history; it was something highly original, combining an ancient Ethiopian text with the experience of Jamaica, including its distinct music and other traditions. It responded to the violence of the trans-Atlantic slave trade and colonial exploitation with a blend of ancient legends and early-twentieth-century ideas about the distinct identity of Black Jamaicans and their descendants. Since then, Rastafarians have inspired other cultural and political independence movements, including the Black Panthers. Through these and other readers and intermediaries, the *Kebra Nagast* has continued to do its work and draw new readers into its orbit. It is high time that it is recognized as a crucial text in the canon of world culture.

CHAPTER 9

═

ONE CHRISTIAN MYSTIC AND THE THREE REVIVALS OF EUROPE

The Coronation of Charlemagne, painted in the workshop of Raphael (Raffaello Sanzio da Urbino).   (RAPHAEL ROOMS, PONTIFICAL PALACE, VATICAN)

The Coronation of Charlemagne was painted by Raphael and members of his workshop to decorate several rooms of the Vatican at the height of the Italian Renaissance in the early sixteenth century. But the scene depicted in the fresco had taken place some seven hundred years earlier, in the year 800. That year, Charlemagne had traveled a thousand miles from Aix-la-Chapelle to Rome to provide military assistance to the pope, Leo III, who had been threatened by an internal revolt. In return, Charlemagne was being crowned Emperor of the Romans, the first ruler to receive that distinction since 476, placing him in the coveted line of Roman emperors.[1] The coronation signaled that the Roman Empire was rising again, after a period of decline.

Most people living through the decline and fall of Rome would have been puzzled by this description (just as they would have been puzzled by the terms Middle Ages or Dark Ages). Historical events tend to happen slowly, almost imperceptibly. An inhabitant of Rome living through the attacks by the Visigoths would know that a new ruling class had arrived in the capital, but for most inhabitants this meant just one more change in a world marked by constant ups and downs brought on by good and bad harvests, periodic flooding and famines, good and bad emperors. True, the population of the Eternal City would shrink from a height of one million (a number not achieved again until the eighteenth century) to 50,000 in the sixth century.[2] But Romans living in other parts of the empire would have been affected only indirectly by these so-called historic changes.

Perhaps the clearest, telltale sign that a decline is felt to have taken place in the past is an attempt at revival, at returning to former days of glory, whether real or imagined. This was the case with Charlemagne, who had consolidated his rule over most of what is today France, Italy, Germany, Austria, the Czech Republic, and Croatia, and liked to think of his realm very much as an inheritor of the Western Roman Empire. Even though Charlemagne held court far from Rome, in Aix-la-Chapelle, his imperial seal proclaimed the *Renovatio imperii Romanorum* (renewal of the Roman Empire).[3] Charlemagne's project of renewal didn't just include crowns and seals. He also wanted to "renew literary production, which through the neglect of our fore-fathers is now almost forgotten."[4]

Charlemagne was telling a story, a story of revival. But all stories are selective, cherry-picking events and placing them in a neat story-line. Stories of revival are no exception. Charlemagne didn't call the preceding period "dark" or "middle"—those terms were invented in the eighteenth century—but he laid the foundation for them by claiming that his forefathers had neglected literary production so that it now needed to be restored to its former splendor.

For Charlemagne, reviving literary production was not an easy task because he himself could not write, something that would have been unthinkable of the Roman emperors of old (as well as of Chinese emperors or Arab sultans ruling at the time).[5] Charlemagne knew that not knowing how to write cut him off from a significant cultural tech-nology and tradition, one that had once been much more widespread.

This meant that if Charlemagne wanted to revive literature, he needed to start with himself. Laboriously, he underwent the process of learning to write. Frustrated by his lack of progress, he kept writing tablets and leaves of parchment under his pillow so he could practice. Unfortunately, as his biographer Einhard observed, he never man-aged to master this skill because he had taken it up too late in life.[6] It is likely, however, that he did learn to read, which primarily meant reading Latin, and would therefore have had at least partial access to the world of learning he created. It was also common to have texts read aloud publicly, and we know that Charlemagne enjoyed such read-ings.[7] Charlemagne also made sure that his daughter, Rotrude, was instructed by the Italian scholar Paul the Deacon in reading and writ-ing as well as in the higher literary skills.[8]

The experience of failing to master writing taught Charlemagne how difficult it was to access literature, how much it depended on institutions of education and an entire infrastructure of literary pro-duction. To create such an infrastructure, he built up an impressive court library (just at the time when the Storehouse of Wisdom was created in Baghdad), which included not only Christian literature but also pre-Christian writing, including Aristotle and Roman literature.[9] From his own experience he knew that simply collecting books was not enough. Books needed to be studied, copied, illuminated with images, and freed from the accidental errors made by inattentive scribes. In response, Charlemagne turned his court into a center of literary activity, attracting scholars and writers from abroad, including the English scholar Alcuin, and providing them with whatever resources they needed to unlock the knowledge contained in the impressive volumes of his literary hoard. (Alcuin had previously benefited from an influx of texts from Spain, where Christians were fleeing from Arab invaders and bringing their texts with them.)

There was an additional difficulty, one that Charlemagne experienced at first hand as well: the books and manuscripts that were being brought to his court were often difficult to decipher. Scribes working in different parts of Europe used radically different hands, abbreviations, and scripts. In this situation, Charlemagne and his advisors decided that what they needed was an entirely new writing culture, and this meant a new script. The new script would increase legibility, it would ensure that scribes from across Charlemagne's realm would be able to decipher one another's writings, and it would enable students to improve more quickly.[10] The new script came to be known as Carolingian minuscule.[11] (I am typing these lines in a font called Times New Roman, which is the most recent version of Carolingian minuscule, an apt name for a script that was created by a new Roman emperor whose writing reform was intended to create a new Roman writing culture.)

This literary revival radiated outward to minor courts that sought to imitate what was happening in Aix-la-Chapelle. Charlemagne encouraged other courts to adopt his new script and to collaborate with his court in the cultivation of the literary arts. While writing culture stood at the center of this renaissance, Charlemagne also promoted the visual arts and architecture in what was considered the Roman style and is known today as Romanesque.

The program of cultural revival promoted by Charlemagne, which also included political and social reforms, was so significant that it is now often referred to as the Carolingian Renaissance. When examined more closely, it's not so much a rebirth as a strategic decision, made by Charlemagne, to connect his realm to the history of the Roman Empire. His revival was also based, in part, on borrowing knowledge from al-Andalus, Arab-occupied Spain, to which pre-Christian learning had been brought from places such as the Storehouse of Wisdom in Baghdad.[12]

=

AMONG THE INSTITUTIONS THAT CHARLEMAGNE PROMOTED WAS one that had not existed during the height of the Roman Empire: the monastery. The monastic movement emerged during the waning years of the Roman Empire, and became a central institution for storing and transmitting culture for more than a millennium. It was in monasteries that most works of literature were copied and thereby preserved for the next generation. Even Charlemagne's highly literary court did not possess its own scriptorium, or place of writing. For the actual work of copying, he relied on monasteries. Nuns working in convents played an important role as well, including Charlemagne's sister, who was abbess at the Convent of Notre-Dame in Chelles.[13]

The significant role of monasteries in the aftermath of Charlemagne's reforms is exemplified in one of their most striking leaders: Hildegard of Bingen (1098–1179). Born three hundred years after Charlemagne's coronation in Aix-la-Chapelle, she unleashed the power of the scriptorium by using it not only as an institution of copying old books, but also of producing new knowledge. To be sure, monasteries had always combined preservation with innovation, but what Hildegard would do with this institution was strikingly unusual.

The first eight years of Hildegard's life would have been enviable to most of her contemporaries. She was born into an aristocratic family with extensive holdings across southern Germany and a stately main residence. Her parents' privileged status meant that they were not subject to anyone except His Majesty the Holy Roman Emperor—the successor of Charlemagne.[14]

Hildegard's life changed radically at the age of eight, when her parents decided to offer their youngest daughter to God, as a kind of tithe.[15] This meant that the eight-year-old Hildegard was legally given to the Church and destined for a life in a monastery. This act of oblation was accompanied by a monetary gift, and any inheritance that might come to Hildegard in the future would be automatically directed to the monastery.[16] Hildegard had ceased to be the child of free aristocrats and become a possession of the Church.

Initially, the eight-year-old child was placed in the care of a novice, Jutta von Sponheim. Hildegard was formally inducted into a small female "enclosure" attached to a monastery, "confined" as the term had it, around the age of fourteen, which was considered adulthood in medieval law.[17] She was now a member of a new Benedictine community, Disibodenberg, which meant she was formally married to God. For the rest of her life, Hildegard would live within the confines of monastic life.

Hildegard's life in the monastery was highly regulated. Precisely formulated rules told her when to get up, when to eat, when to pray, what prayers to say, and what songs to sing. No moment of monastic life was free, since its regulations were designed to forestall idleness.[18] These rules had been set down toward the end of the Roman Empire by Benedict of Nursia (480–550) in the so-called *regula Sancti Benedicti*. They prescribed the rhythms of everyday life but also the organization of the monastery itself, which was controlled by an abbot. (Promoting the *regula Sancti Benedicti* had been part of Charlemagne's renewal of learning.)

At the time of Benedict, monastic life was relatively new to Christianity, though it was well established elsewhere. Buddhism, in particular, had grown out of a monastic movement that started in the last centuries BCE, with followers of the Buddha giving up their old lives and swearing an oath of poverty.[19] Strictly speaking, only monks living in such a community could really call themselves Buddhists; everyone else, including King Ashoka, was a mere layperson whose purpose was to support monastic Buddhists.[20] Neither Judaism nor early Christianity were built around monastic life or required its strictures for someone to be considered Jewish or Christian. If Christian monasticism was influenced by Buddhism, the influence would have been indirect, perhaps via hermits in Egypt and other parts of the Near East, whose ascetic practices found their way into Christian Europe as the western part of the Roman Empire crumbled. Be that as it may, it was Benedict, who lived near today's Perugia in Italy, who shaped those practices into a distinct institution.

For Benedict, the monastery combined several purposes in one. The most important one was to enable a life dedicated exclusively to God, in contrast to worldly purposes. But what would it mean to dedicate your life to God? One component was prayer (*orare*), which included performing the liturgy and praying for the wider community. Equally important was work (*laborare*), which would depend on the location and size of the monastery. Often monasteries provided secure accommodation to travelers at a time when roads were dangerous; they would offer food to the poor; and they would seek to educate members of the populace. Benedict realized that to bring together these different purposes, he needed to formulate rules that would create an entirely new type of cultural entity. He succeeded beyond his wildest dreams as more and more monasteries and convents adopted the *regula Benedicti*, creating an institution that would shape Christian Europe.

Benedictine monasteries and convents were much more than a way for devoted Christians to dedicate their lives to prayer and to engage in good works. They were also places in which knowledge was preserved, modified, and transmitted. The Benedictine fear of idleness could be channeled into a strict regime of physical labor, especially in monasteries with extensive agricultural operations, but labor could also mean reading and writing. While the old institutions of literacy in the Roman Empire, such as schools and private libraries, were in decline, monasteries emerged as a new alternative. Conscious of this role, the *regula Benedicti* took great care to specify how books should circulate, how they could be borrowed, and when they needed to be returned, making the library the beating heart of the Benedictine monastery, or at least one of its chambers.

Adjacent to the library was the scriptorium, the place where monks and nuns would do their mandated labor in the form of writing. Before the widespread use of print, the preservation of knowledge depended on long hours spent copying books by hand. There were too many books to preserve and never enough time to recopy them all, leading to a brutal process of selection. Not all monks and nuns working in a scriptorium were involved in copying books. Others supplied these books with commentaries. While ostensibly meant to elucidate an important text, commentaries were often used to articulate new ideas, thinly disguised as remarks on existing ones. A third group of monks would add illuminations, turning capital letters at the beginning of chapters into entire visual worlds while sprinkling other illustrations, often miniscule figures and scenes, around the edges of texts. The books produced in monasteries were multilayered, multimedia creations.

But what kind of books were selected for survival? Particularly difficult was the question of whether Benedictine monasteries should preserve Greek and Roman literature. From a Christian perspective, everything predating Jesus, except for Judaism, was pagan and therefore seen as deficient if not outright misguided and deplorable. (Dante would place pre-Christian writers, including

Homer and Virgil, in Limbo, the first circle of hell, not because they had committed specific sins but simply because they had lived before Christ and therefore did not have access to the privilege of being Christian.) At the same time, Greek and Roman thought had shaped early Christian writers, beginning with the Gospel according to John, as well as the writings of the so-called Fathers of the Church such as the North African bishop Saint Augustine, who particularly admired Plato. Through the classical influence on the work of these early Christian writers, substantial amounts of classical learning were preserved, copied, and commented on in the libraries and scriptoria of Benedictine monasteries—in addition, of course, to the Old and New Testaments, in Latin translation.

Many other authors from Greek and Roman antiquity survived only through quotation. Of Plato's extensive oeuvre only one dialogue, the *Timaeus* (in which Plato bemoaned Greece's youthfulness and created the alternative history of Atlantis), was available in Latin translation, though significantly more of Aristotle and other writers, often via Roman translators. The Benedictine monastery, after all, was primarily designed to promote Christianity, not to preserve the widest range of knowledge (in this respect, it was very different from the Storehouse of Wisdom in Baghdad). What survived of pre-Christian antiquity did so often accidentally or indirectly, sometimes when precious parchment bearing works from antiquity was written over with Christian texts. The reused material, called a palimpsest, often bore traces of the original script, which allowed later generations to rediscover and breathe new life into older works.

By the time Hildegard was inducted into monastic life, many centuries after the origin of the monastic movement and its expansion by Charlemagne, there existed a network of some thousand monasteries following Benedict's rule, all organized into the powerful Benedictine Order. Over time, Hildegard mastered those rules and the mode of life created by them, rising to become Magistra, the head of the group of nuns attached to the monastery of Disibodenberg, at the age of thirty-eight.[21]

Nuns were usually under the control of an abbess, but Disibodenberg was a dual monastery, with separate sections of nuns and monks, which meant that the nuns were beholden to an abbot. Hildegard was not content with this subservient position. Again and again, she clashed with the abbot of Disibodenberg on the interpretation of specific rules, and pleaded for the relaxation of the most draconian of them; she even wrote a commentary on the *regula Benedicti* to capture her own distinct take on how a monastery should be run, namely, more leniently.[22] After years of petitioning the authorities, she was finally allowed to found a cloister of her own in Rupertsberg, near Bingen, around 1150, when she was in her early fifties.[23] Having spent almost her entire life within an institution not of her own making, she was finally in a position to remake that institution in her own way.

While Hildegard cherished the monastery as an institution of cultural storage and transmission, she was particularly aware that cultural storage was not an end in itself but could be used for the production of new knowledge and insight. Even though much of what she was able to read was preselected by Christianity, as filtered through the Benedictine library system, there were other types of knowledge that had found a home in monasteries, including medicine. As centers of learning, monasteries attracted people with severe or unusual illnesses who hoped that the knowledge collected in these institutions might produce a cure. Monks and nuns had diligently recopied treatises on medicine, which were considered unlikely to interfere with Christian beliefs. Monasteries also collected information on successful cures and passed it down to the next generation, making their books of medicine highly prized possessions. Hildegard drew on this knowledge.

Medicine was unusual in that it was based not only on book-learning but also on practical expertise. Many monasteries maintained herb gardens and attracted monks and nuns versed in their application.

The practical knowledge would often be passed down orally, especially among populations that had difficulties accessing literacy, including women.[24] Part of Hildegard's written oeuvre, to which she owed her growing fame, was on medicine, combining practical experience acquired in the herb garden and in curing patients with knowledge acquired from books.

Hildegard's writings on medicine, despite their influence, were not why she would become one of the most widely known women of her time; that fame rested on her visions. From a relatively young age, Hildegard had had visions that suggested a distinct view of the world, of history, and of how to live. (Even her writings on medicine are embedded in a larger view of the cosmos.[25]) Later, toward the end of her life, she explained how these visions came to her:

> In the year 1141 of the incarnation of Jesus Christ the Son, of God, when I was forty two years and seven months of age, a fiery light, flashing intensely, came from the open vault of heaven and poured through my whole brain. Like a flame that is hot without burning it kindled all my heart and all my breast, just as the sun warms anything on which its rays fall. And suddenly I could understand what such books as the Psalter, the Gospel and the other catholic volumes both of the Old and the New Testament actually set forth; but I could not interpret the words of the text; nor could I divide up the syllables; nor did I have any notion of the cases or tenses.[26]

What were these visions? One could interpret them religiously, as visions bestowed upon Hildegard by God. One could interpret them psychologically, as the product of a life spent in the heightened religiosity of a cloistered community or, as some have suggested, as extreme migraines. But I would suggest that we approach them in a different manner: as a particular kind of cultural project (these approaches are not mutually exclusive). Even though the visions seem to have come to Hildegard directly, they were in fact deeply shaped by the library and the scriptorium, the core of the Benedictine monastery. The visions were the way in which Hildegard used the scriptorium for a completely new purpose.

Some of the images Hildegard reported were drawn from long-standing traditions of apocalyptic Christianity, including God as a shower of light or the Holy Spirit giving birth to the soul, but other images were of her own making, some elaborate and baroque, others strikingly simple: "the soul in the body is as the sap in the tree."[27] There were visions of cosmic creation and of the salvation of humankind through Christ, but also of the struggle between good and evil and of giving birth to monsters. Hildegard's visions culminated in scenarios of the end of times, inspired by the book of Revelation.

Presented as divine messages, Hildegard's visions came with huge risks: they had to be declared authentic by the Church, otherwise they would be denounced as false, even heretical. Through her administrative duties, Hildegard knew what she needed to do and began a careful campaign to get her visions authorized.[28] Her letters to authorities, including Bernard of Clairvaux, the most important Church intellectual at the time, were masterpieces of diplomacy, the same skill she would use when seeking authorization to found her own convent. She even managed to gain approval of her visions from Pope Eugene II during his visit to Trier.[29] In this way, she managed to get her visions recognized as authentic.

Gaining recognition outside the thick walls of the monastery was important for another reason: it allowed Hildegard to travel, to accept invitations to present her visions and ideas, to meet with learned Church scholars and to engage in an extensive correspondence. All of these were means by which Hildegard could add to what she had been able to learn within the confines of the library and the scriptorium, expanding her intellectual horizon as well as her sphere of influence.

Visions such as Hildegard's were a delicate matter, also, because they were so different from the kind of learning ordinarily produced by monasteries, focused as they were on the copying of scripture and the writing of commentaries. In contrast to commentaries, visions didn't use quotations from other texts, at least not overtly. For the same reason, they did not claim literary authority, which was mostly exercised by men. Even though Hildegard came from an aristocratic family and hence had access to educational resources, as did most members of her convent, she never felt fully immersed in the world of writing and scholarship more easily available to her male colleagues—at least, that's what she claimed. She tended to downplay her literary learning and her literary sources.

Her humility is to be taken with considerably more than a grain of salt. Perhaps she felt that this was what her male superiors wanted to hear; perhaps she really had difficulties with the finer points of Latin grammar. She summed up these shortcomings as her "ignorance," but what did this mean? It is not certain to what extent she was educated in the so-called seven liberal arts, the basic curriculum that was divided between the fundamental three arts (*trivium*)—rhetoric, grammar, and logic—of manipulating language and thought, and the four arts (*quatrivium*) of arithmetic, geometry, music, and astronomy. These seven were called *liberal* arts because they were meant to educate free people, as opposed to servants, serfs, enslaved people, and others who were considered dependents (including most women). They were called *arts* in the sense of "areas of knowledge," without any relation to what we consider works of creative art. Even music, as it was taught in the *quatrivium*, was seen as an offshoot of mathematics, concerned with proportions and harmonies that could be expressed in numbers, not with the composition or performance of musical artworks. Even though Hildegard was the daughter of aristocrats, almost her entire life had been lived in the monastery, where emphasis was placed more on the *trivium* part of the liberal arts—rhetoric, grammar and logic.

No matter what her formal education included or neglected, Hildegard read and knew much more than she herself admitted, including, of course, the Latin Bible and the works of Benedict, but also the writings of other Christian commentators, such as Saint Augustine.[30] If Hildegard was conscious of the fact that she did not have the same education as the most learned men of her age, there was nevertheless more than mere submissiveness at work in her professed ignorance. While evading the question of how much she had studied, or should have read, she developed a different source of authority through her visions, which were not dependent on the ability to rattle off strings of quotations and other techniques of argumentation.

The visions, at least in their written form, were nevertheless produced in the scriptorium. Hildegard could have written them down herself but she probably dictated them to scribes, including Volmar, her assistant, who carefully oversaw the production process of the visions, an oeuvre of enormous size and complexity. While most of her visions were evoked through verbal description, some were also captured visually through illuminations, which include cosmic symbols and religious figures, using the techniques developed by scribal monks and nuns for capital letters and marginalia.[31] Writing down extensive visions of this scope and novelty wasn't what the Benedictine scriptorium had been designed to do, but Hildegard was using that institution for her own ends.

Finally, in addition to the intensely visual nature of Hildegard's experiences, there was also an auditory component that needed to be captured. As an ephemeral art form, music disappears, often without a trace. Of the music produced by humans, only the tiniest fraction has survived, and only from the last two thousand years, since humans evolved forms of musical notation that at least give us an inkling of what the music of the past may have sounded like. This doesn't mean that we don't know anything about music before musical notation. Sometimes, fragments of instruments survive, or images of instruments, such as flutes used by cave-dwelling humans and images of Egyptian lute players, giving us small hints of the musical culture of a given society. Where speech was written down, especially in ceremonial contexts, it sometimes included clues about performance. Later, a burgeoning culture of writing would include descriptions of musical events.

Fortunately, Hildegard lived at a time when a musical notation had been developed, allowing her to record the songs that accompanied her visions. Many of her songs are in so-called plainchant, featuring a single voice. Her musical work includes seventy-seven such liturgical chants, to be performed on specific feast days, and a liturgical drama to be performed by an assembly of nuns written on the occasion of the founding of the new community at Rupertsberg. (Only the devil does not get to sing and must content himself with ordinary speech.)[32] Her plainchant is distinctive because of its variety, including its extraordinary melodic range.

After Hildegard, musical notation would lead to a flourishing of complex compositions and ever more refined forms of harmony and polyphony, the simultaneous expression of different voices. While Hildegard's compositions might look simple in comparison, they were unusual, deviating from the standard repertoire. But what is most unusual about them is that we have them at all, that they were written down, and connected to a particular person. Hildegard is one of the earliest composers we know by name.[33]

Hildegard's dedication to writing took one more unusual form: she created a secret language, including an entire alphabet. Begun perhaps on a whim, she developed it seriously over her entire life. In keeping with her recurring claims of ignorance, she called it *lingua ignota*. The phrase is usually translated as "unknown language," but it can also mean a language of unknowing.[34] This language reminds us that Hildegard attached positive value to unknowing and how much she thought about different writing techniques, from the regular Latin alphabet and musical notation all the way to her secret language.

The comprehensive nature of Hildegard's work can be compared to another genre of the age: the *summa*, or summary of all knowledge, developed by Ibn Sina as he was integrating different forms of knowledge from across the vast Arab Empire and beyond. Neither the Carolingian revival nor Benedictine monasteries had been particularly focused on recovering Greek philosophy. While Aristotle was read, interpreted, and used by Arab and Persian scholars such as Ibn Sina, he remained less known in Christian Europe, except for very few texts, mostly on language and logic.

All this changed over the course of Hildegard's life due to increasing contact between Christian Europe and the Arab Empire. To be sure, the two realms had never been completely isolated from each other. Part of the Iberian peninsula, after all, was under Arab rule—an ideal breeding ground for cultural production, spurred by frequent contact between Islamic, Jewish, and Christian scholarship, writing, and art. Scholars from across Europe would go to Spain and bring back information and even manuscripts from this extraordinary combination of traditions.

In the century preceding Hildegard's life, another form of contact had arisen: the Crusades. These military missions aimed to free Jerusalem from the Muslims, but never achieved their goal permanently. While Christian soldiers managed to establish temporary strongholds, most of those had fallen by the end of the twelfth century. Along the way, the Crusades caused widespread suffering and destruction; despite their professed Christian mission, they did not spare Constantinople, still Christian at the time, which was badly ransacked by the Fourth Crusade in 1204, shortly after Hildegard's death.

As so often in the history of culture, forces of destruction can have unintended consequences. The Crusades brought back reports of the new science that had been developed in the Arab world, the summaries of knowledge written by scholars, and the existence of Greek philosophy in Arabic translation. The result was an increasing influx of texts from Byzantium, Baghdad, Cairo, and al-Andalus, above all Aristotle. Christian writers discovered the Philosopher's lost works (lost to them, not to Arab scholars), and started to write *summas* in the style of Ibn Sina. This influx transformed knowledge production in Europe and can be regarded as a second revival—not a rebirth, exactly, but a dual act of revival and borrowing brought about by a renewed interest in classical writing, such as Cicero, as well as cultural contact between rival empires.[35]

The impact of this revival—if that term still makes sense given that it was both a revival and an import—made itself felt in convents and monasteries and at courts, but above all, it made itself felt in universities, institutions that were emerging in Italy (Bologna), Spain (Salamanca), France (Paris), and England (Oxford). These new centers of learning, which have shaped knowledge production ever since, were crucially influenced by the Arab Storehouses of Wisdom in ways that are not sufficiently recognized by a wider public even today. Some forms of public debate and of writing (the *summa*), and even some titles and rituals associated with universities, such as special robes or the dissertation defense, were borrowed from Arab models.[36] (Another strain of thought impacting universities was Jewish theology, with its distinctive reading practices and commentaries, developed on the Iberian Peninsula and in other centers of learning throughout Europe.)

The influence of Arab thought and institutions on twelfth-century Europe is especially important in light of the continuing debate, in Europe, of whether that continent should consider itself exclusively Christian, or, in any case, not Islamic. Put either way, the distinction doesn't make sense. The twelfth-century revival crucially shaped Christian Europe; because of that revival, Europe inherited philosophical writing composed by Muslim thinkers, who combined influences from Greece and Rome with others from Persia and as far away as South Asia and North Africa. European and Islamic history and thought are inextricably intertwined. They cannot, and should not, be disentangled now.

=

RENAISSANCE: WE ORDINARILY RESERVE THE TERM FOR AN EVENT that, at the time of Charlemagne's literacy program or Hildegard's use of the monastery, was still in the future: the Italian Renaissance of the fifteenth and sixteenth centuries. As with the earlier revivals, the Italian Renaissance was not so much a rebirth as a reuse of knowledge that was only half remembered and needed to be reimported from elsewhere. It was, if anything, a borrowed renaissance that took place among a number of Italy's independent city-states, where ambitious rulers practiced a form of politics that would soon be defined, and made notorious, by Niccolò Machiavelli. This ruthless form of politics included culture.

Federico da Montefeltro (1422–82) is a perfect representative of this era. He didn't have to look far to be reminded of the hazards of living in Italy, with its warring city-states, conspiracies, assassinations, and duels. In fact, he didn't have to look farther than his own nose, whose bridge he had lost in a duel, along with an eye. Far from hiding this injury, his portraitists did their best to foreground it, above all his friend Piero della Francesca, who featured the extreme hook of Federico's reconstructed nose in profile maximally visible against a light sky. Federico was not a major player in the game of power, but was important enough to become, through intrigue and violence, ruler of the city of Urbino.[37] His control over Urbino, where Raphael would soon be born, allowed him to amass enough resources to shape his life and work according to his ideals.

To conduct his complicated affairs of state, Federico had two palaces at his disposal, one in Urbino and one in the smaller town of Gubbio, with large, impressive rooms in which he could receive visitors to plan his next move. Off to one side, and not intended for the public, was a small room, one in each palace. He called each a *studiolo*, or study, and they were carefully decorated to capture the understanding of culture that would be known as the Renaissance.[38] The word is a

Piero della Francesca, portrait of
Duke Federico da Montefeltro, whose
nose and one eye were damaged in a
duel. (UFFIZZI GALLERY, FLORENCE)

misnomer in that it describes a new concentration of knowledge and
art, but in fact only some of it was revived from the past, while other
parts were borrowed from elsewhere, and a third group startlingly new.

The *studiolo* in the Gubbio palace included an ensemble repre-
senting the seven liberal arts, on which the medieval curriculum had
been based (and which Hildegard probably only enjoyed in parts),
showing that Federico did not intend a rupture with the learning of
the previous centuries. If there was anything new, it was the compre-
hensiveness of knowledge assembled here. Both *studioli* contained a
number of well-chosen books, including Virgil's *Aeneid* (effectively
rescued from Limbo, to which Dante had confined it). Federico had
assembled, through book hunters, one of the most impressive libraries
of the time outside the Vatican, with a total of 900 volumes, of which
600 were in Latin, 168 in Greek, 82 in Hebrew, and two in Arabic.[39]

This was very different from what a Benedictine library, let alone the books assembled by Charlemagne, would have looked like, especially the large number of texts in Greek and Hebrew and the existence of original works in Arabic. Federico had many of those books copied on especially high-quality vellum, the durable and expensive writing material made of carefully prepared animal skins, as opposed to cheap and less durable paper.[40]

For all his love of books, Federico rejected a new technology that was revolutionizing the production of books: the printing press. Originally invented in China hundreds of years earlier, it had recently been adopted by Johannes Gutenberg, who had turned this old technique into an industrial production process that could churn out cheap copies of astonishing quality. Gutenberg's success was due, additionally, to another imported technology, namely paper, which had also originated in China and had then reached Europe via the Arab world. Federico looked down upon such manufactured books, but he purchased several printed books nevertheless—only to have them recopied by hand.

While rejecting print, Federico embraced another innovation in the realm of writing: the new science of words. This science was crucial for a group of scholars who had developed sophisticated techniques for studying old manuscripts, including the ability to date manuscripts based on a detailed understanding of how language had developed over time. By comparing phrases, idioms, and other often minor details of a written document, they were able to deduce where and when it had been composed. They applied the same technique to comparing different versions of the same text, ferreting out later additions and mistakes made in the process of copying. (They also rediscovered Carolingian minuscule, and it was thanks to their efforts that that script became dominant.)

The new science, known by the Greek word for "love of words," or philology, had already led to a spectacular triumph.[41] The power of the pope, and of the Church, had been based on a document known as the Donation of Constantine, according to which Constantine, the Roman

emperor who converted to Christianity, had given authority over Rome
to the Church. This document had been used by generations of popes
to claim dominion over Christendom, but it looked suspicious to those
versed in the new science of philology, including the priest Lorenzo
Valla. He subjected the text to a rigorous analysis and was able to prove,
to those who could follow his reasoning, that the document must have
been produced hundreds of years later. Valla's proof was spectacular
because it undermined the authority of the pope.[42] For this reason, Valla
was later seen as a predecessor of Martin Luther, whose attacks on the
papacy were fought not with philology but with the printing press.

Even though humanists such as Valla could be seen, in retrospect,
as critics of the Church, that wasn't how most of them thought of
themselves. They weren't looking to redefine Christian theology, but
to develop a new approach to thinking and writing, an alternative to
what Christian universities were teaching. These writers and scholars
were hoping to found new centers of learning. In Florence, there was
an attempt to revive Plato's Academy, and Federico was doing something similar in Urbino.

The term most often used to describe these scholars and writers
intent on reviving antiquity is humanist. Why? Above all, classical
learning was seen as enhancing the humane qualities of humans. But
there was another aspect to the term: the new classical learning would
not directly interfere with theological matters.[43] For Petrarch (1304–
74), what mattered above all was the elegance of classical Latin, as
represented in its original sources; he did not try to reinstitute Greek
or Roman gods. Humanists such as Valla might challenge a worldly
document like the Donation of Constantine, but they would not present themselves as priests or compete with the Church.

While Federico underestimated the new science of texts and the
power of the printing press, he knew that a new age was dawning. His
studiolo in Urbino was fitted with two walls of portraits that included
Greek sages such as Plato and Aristotle, Romans such as Cicero, and

Christian writers such as Saint Augustine, but also, and prominently, Petrarch. While Petrarch is now primarily admired for his own poetry, particularly his love sonnets, Federico and others admired him for his revival of the past. Over a century earlier, Petrarch had begun the search for old manuscripts, especially those of Roman times. (Petrarch was also interested in Greek authors, including Homer, but never learned Greek himself.) A particular find of his were hitherto unknown letters by Cicero, and, inspired by them, Petrarch sought to emulate the Roman writer's language and style. He used that style to write letters to long-dead authors, including many who would grace the portrait gallery of Federico's *studiolo* at Urbino. (The *studiolo* at Gubbio features allegorical paintings of the liberal arts.)

The most astonishing thing about the books in Federico's *studioli*—as opposed to those in his library—was that they weren't real. They, like almost everything else, were worked in wood, in the form of intricate intarsia, by which differently colored pieces of wood depict objects—paintings in wood. The *studiolo*, a place to withdraw and contemplate the different forms of art that a Renaissance ruler could enjoy, was itself a triumph of artisanship.[44] Not only books, but all kinds of objects and instruments were depicted in intarsia, even a mirror. Among them were musical instruments; the *studiolo* also served as a place for chamber performances. Prominently depicted was the lute, an instrument adapted from, and named after, the Arabic oud.

These intarsia were striking, also, because they used the relatively new technique of central perspective. Italian painters were now able to capture depth with unheard-of precision, constructing their paintings—with the help of an apparatus—for the eye of the beholder. It was one thing to use central perspective in paintings (including Piero della Francesca's portrait of Federico); it was another to attempt it in intarsia.

But that was not all. While the technique of central perspective usually assumed that the viewer would be standing directly in front of the painting, some painters had begun to employ the technique in more intricate ways, such that an image became legible only when the beholder assumed an extreme position; anyone standing in front of the painting would see only distortions. This extreme use of perspective, called anamorphosis, also found its way into the woodwork of Federico's *studiolo*, where it was used to depict a lute.

The *studiolo* assembled these various arts to inspire Federico when he withdrew there after affairs of state had been completed. In addition, this ingeniously constructed space also served as a gigantic memory device, calling to the owner's mind different arts and artistic figures as well as memorable sayings, which were displayed, again in intarsia, in prominent places. Theorists of memory had long conceived of so-called memory theaters, spaces that would help orators remember long

Studiolo in the ducal palace in Gubbio. The original now resides in the Metropolitan Museum of Art, New York. (METROPOLITAN MUSEUM OF ART, NEW YORK)

speeches by breaking them into small units and associating those units with memorable features of an interior space such as columns or corners. Over time, these memory theaters became more elaborate devices for arranging, storing, and accessing all kinds of information, distant predecessors of computer storage.[45] Federico's *studiolo* served him as such an external memory device, a storage and retrieval mechanism for a new range of knowledge.

=

THE COURT LIBRARY OF CHARLEMAGNE, THE BENEDICTINE SCRIPtorium, twelfth-century universities, and finally the Italian *studiolo*: each of these institutions embodied different ways of preserving, reproducing, and expanding knowledge, but each also had a different purpose and therefore a different strategy for reviving the past. They complemented one another, each prioritizing different texts and modes of knowing within the framework of Christianity. That framework meant different things to each of them, allowing them to understand the pre-Christian past in different ways. The three waves of borrowed revival—three renaissances—managed to preserve, and import, a growing number of texts from antiquity. That these revivals were undertaken at all shows that Europeans as different as Charlemagne, Hildegard, and Federico felt that something of the past had been lost and needed to be recovered from elsewhere. They all thought of themselves as latecomers, looking back at what had been lost and seeking to restore it.

Federico's studio included not only books, painting, and musical instruments, a chess set (a game imported from Arabia) and a spherical model of the sky, but also a representation of an astrolabe, an instrument used for navigation. Little did he know that this inconspicuous device, captured, like everything else in the *studiolo*, in wood, would soon be taking explorers around the southern tip of Africa and across the Atlantic, thereby transforming the world yet again.

=

CHAPTER 10

THE AZTEC CAPITAL FACES ITS EUROPEAN ENEMIES AND ADMIRERS

TENOCHTITLAN, 1519

When Emperor Moctezuma took stock of his expanding empire, he could be proud of what the Aztecs had accomplished. More than two hundred years before, they had left their homeland in the north and slowly made their way southward until, several generations later, they had arrived in the Mexican basin with its intricate ecological system of lakes surrounded by mountains and two snow-capped volcanos. At first, the Aztecs had made arrangements with local rulers, paying tribute and offering themselves as mercenaries.[1] But then, about a hundred years later, they had rebelled against their overlords and become independent. Initially, their new power barely reached beyond the basin, but over the subsequent decades, these trained mercenaries managed to raid and threaten neighboring towns and extend their realm to the Gulf coast in the east, the Pacific in the west, and to the Maya-speaking peoples in the south. This was the realm over which Moctezuma now presided.

The greatest achievement of the Aztecs was not control over territory but Tenochtitlan, the floating city. The city was built in the middle of two connected lakes that were fed by streams rushing down from the mountains. Without an outlet, the water collected in the lakes and slowly evaporated. The larger lake was therefore saltwater, and only the smaller lake to the south, the first to receive the meltwater from the volcanoes, contained freshwater. Engineers had created three causeways connecting the city with the mainland; the causeways also slowed the flow from the freshwater lake, which was slightly higher, to the saltwater lake. As the city grew, a large dike, some twelve miles long, had been constructed to create marsh-fields in which food could be grown.

The city, surrounded by marsh-fields traversed by the causeways, was a miracle of geometry, engineering, and imagination. Sustaining life for some 50,000 inhabitants in the island city, plus another 50,000 in nearby towns and settlements, required impressive logistics.[2] Everything had to be brought in from outside. Because there existed no beasts of burden in the Americas beyond the llama, in the Andean region, food and water had to be carried by some 5,000 human porters, who either walked across the causeways or paddled canoes to the city each day.[3] At the center of the city stood a large temple complex built around the Great Pyramid, which was topped by a large platform holding two large shrines. Approaching the city either by causeway or by canoe, this was the first thing one would see: the dual shrines, about two hundred feet high, rising from the lake.

The city existed in a carefully balanced ecosystem that could be easily overturned. A generation before, one of Moctezuma's predecessors, Ahuitzotl, had undertaken the construction of an enormous stone aqueduct to bring fresh water from the springs of nearby Coyoacán directly into the city. The inauguration of this new engineering miracle was a festive affair, and artists commemorated the occasion by creating a stone relief depicting the aqueduct.[4] Initially the aqueduct worked as intended, but as soon as heavy rains started to fall, the lifesaving fresh water it brought to the city turned into a devastating flood, disturbing the city's carefully managed system of lakes, dikes, and causeways. Some said that Ahuitzotl himself died in the flood caused by his own hubris.[5]

For Moctezuma, the disaster of the aqueduct served as a reminder that Tenochtitlan relied on a precarious balance of water and stone, vulnerable to nature but also to human mistakes. He would be the emperor who rebuilt the city and saved it from disaster. This meant further expanding the empire, so that new resources, including food, would stream into the city, and it meant being careful with future engineering projects. The aqueduct incident showed how quickly the city could turn into a trap.

Controlling the flow of water was not only a matter of concern for engineers and emperors, but also for gods. There was, for example, Chalchiuhtlicue, the water goddess, who represented fertility but also freshwater, the management of which was so important to Tenochtitlan. But the main pyramid-temple of the city was dedicated to two other gods: Huitzilopochtli, the god of war, and Tlaloc, the god of rain and agriculture. It was the god Huitzilopochtli who had directed the Aztecs to found the city in this spot and who demanded the greatest sacrifices, mostly captured soldiers from the outer reaches of the empire.[6] The sacrificial victims would be drugged and taken up the steps of the pyramid to the large platform, where priests would wait to cut out their beating hearts with knives made from sharp flint or obsidian. Blood was known as "precious water," so offering pulsing hearts, sometimes dozens at a time, was a way of ensuring that the balance of the empire would be sustained, that wars would be won and yield prisoners and tribute, and, above all, that the waters of the lake would remain quiescent.[7]

Water, food, and captives were not the only things brought into the lake city. As latecomers to this region, the Aztecs were everywhere confronted with remnants of past civilizations. Not far from the Aztec capital, near the northern shore of the lake, was Teotihuacan, a site with ruins of enormous pyramids and temples lined up along a wide ceremonial avenue.[8] Impressed with the antiquity of this site, Aztecs incorporated it into their own mythology, declaring it the origin of the world.[9] (It was here, amid the ruins of this earlier civilization, that Moctezuma had been inaugurated.) Aztecs also undertook excavations and placed relics inside their own massive temple as an offering to their gods. They did the same with other cultural remains, including the mysterious carved stone heads of the Olmec civilization, some of them over two thousand years old at the time.[10] Aztecs also copied from the Olmecs architectural forms and sculptural techniques, including serpent heads.

Some of the most intriguing cultural objects of the region were its books, in which painter-scribes told stories of their gods, of their people, and the calendars by which they lived. These books were written in a combination of images and pictorial signs that functioned as a form of writing. The picture-symbols didn't capture individual words or syllables the way alphabetic writing or Egyptian hieroglyphics did. (In Mesoamerica, only the Maya to the south had developed such a system of written language.) But the painted symbols recorded ideas, events, and dates, functioning as precise memory-aids for priests and painter-scribes. When the Aztecs overthrew their former rulers, they decided to burn their books as well.[11] Here, as elsewhere, history was often written—or painted—by the winners.

This fight over stories meant that the Aztecs didn't just want to erase the past, but also to rewrite it. For the Aztecs not only burned the books of their former overlords but also created new ones in their stead, books that set down their calendars (the word for reading also meant counting), their gods, their myths, and their history.[12] Because Aztec painter-scribes used red and black ink, written stories were called "stories in red and black." Moctezuma's priests, living in the large temple complex surrounding the main pyramid-shaped temple, were trained to paint and draw these books and to interpret them, and also to use them for purposes of ritual and divination.

It was from this miraculous city with its temples and books that Moctezuma expanded his empire. His soldiers sent back tribute extracted from the surrounding region, concentrating more and more resources, and thus power, in this one place. Within Moctezuma's lifetime, Tenochtitlan grew to become the largest city in the Americas, and larger than many cities in Europe. Wealth brought with it new specializations, division of labor, and cultural achievements. While canoes and porters brought in food and raw materials, artisans manufactured ever more sophisticated commodities, from elaborate pieces of clothing to weapons and art objects. These were sold in a large central market that could accommodate thousands of people. Moctezuma also prided himself on his impressive personal zoo, which contained all kinds of wildlife, including deer, fowl, little dogs, and many species of birds, whose feathers were highly prized.[13]

Even as Moctezuma's realm grew, sometimes by force but also through the advantages of being a powerful trading empire, this expanded realm was far from unified. Some of the more remote, tribute-paying groups such as the Maya in the south or the Totonac on the Gulf coast never felt that they were part of a unified whole. There was no sense of shared citizenship (as ultimately evolved, for example, in the Roman Empire) or of language. Despite the sophistication and size of Tenochtitlan, Moctezuma did not have at his disposal a state bureaucracy that might have created a sense of unity or even of sustained control. Moctezuma's empire was held together by a fragile combination of force and self-interest, along with the radiance of his greatest creation, the water city itself, which was the beating heart of the empire.

This was the situation of the Aztec world when Moctezuma first heard reports that floating castles had been sighted again on the coast. Two years earlier, inhabitants of the coastal regions had seen enormous ships for the first time. Ever since, Moctezuma's scouts had been on the lookout, and now they heard rumors that accompanied the ship-sightings of pale-skinned people astride large deer and aggressive dogs trained for battle.

Moctezuma decided to do two things. He sent one of his painter-scribes to document the unbelievable reports of the scouts. Images would enable him to understand it all better: the people, their animals, their clothes, their ships, their weapons.[14]

The other thing Moctezuma did was to send elaborate presents, hoping to impress these strangers and demonstrate to them the cultural resources at his command. He included samples of his most talented artisans, including an enormous disc-shaped representation of the sun, in gold, and one of the moon, in silver; gold figurines of ducks, lions, panthers, dogs, and apes; finely worked jewelry; weapons, especially arrows with ornamental feathers; a staff, also in gold, and a collection of his best feathers, which had been turned into artworks with gold additions. Moctezuma also included samples of the elaborate clothes, finely worked, that only nobles were allowed to wear.

Would the foreigners put on these ceremonial clothes? Would the presents be enough to convince them of Moctezuma's power and make them turn back?

NUREMBERG—BRUSSELS, 1520

Less than a year after Moctezuma sent his presents to the foreign visitors, Albrecht Dürer found himself in financial difficulties. Despite his position as one of Europe's most famous painters, he relied on a stipend from the Holy Roman Emperor for financial support, and for several years now the Nuremberg magistrates had refused to pay. Nuremberg was a "free city," essentially an independent city-state, and was reluctant to make payments on behalf of the emperor.[15]

Nuremberg was not only independent but also well connected, a center of trade in constant exchange with eastern and western Europe and even the Arab world. Following Middle Eastern models, Nuremberg had established the first paper mill in Europe north of the Alps.[16] More recently, enterprising residents of the city had seized on Gutenberg's use of movable type only a few hundred miles away and developed one of the earliest centers of print publishing.[17] With 40,000 inhabitants, Nuremberg had become one of the largest and most significant cities in Europe. Some considered it the secret capital of northern Europe.[18]

In the middle of Dürer's standoff over his stipend, the emperor had died. The artist would have to make his case directly to a new emperor, Charles V, who was holding court in the Netherlands.

There was another reason to leave Nuremberg temporarily: plague had struck again. The Black Death had first arrived in Europe in 1347 and had never gone away entirely, sweeping through regions and cities with almost predictable frequency. It was currently spiking in Nuremberg; everyone who could afford it was fleeing into the countryside or to some faraway place.[19]

Seventeen years earlier, Dürer had fled another wave of plague by traveling to Venice, a city even richer than Nuremberg and more international, located right on the contested but also lucrative border between Europe and the Middle East. For a painter, Italy was especially important since it had been part of a revolution in art, the place that had developed a new, geometrically precise form of perspective in which all lines converged onto a single vanishing point, which allowed painters to turn canvases into windows looking out onto endlessly receding vistas. At the same time, some Italian painters, above all Leonardo da Vinci, had gone into the body-snatching business to learn about bone structure, muscles, and sinews through dissection, which put them in a position to capture the human body with unheard-of precision. On his travels, Dürer had managed to meet the city's great painters, Mantegna and Bellini.[20] Mantegna used vivid colors to create paintings with unusual constellations, while Bellini focused on the kind of receding, atmospheric landscapes that used the new perspective to maximal effect. (The two were connected by marriage—Bellini's sister had married Mantegna.[21])

From this center of world trade and art, Dürer had returned to a Nuremberg decimated by plague. Inspired by what he had learned, he had worked hard to become the chief representative of the new painting north of the Alps. His portraits showed the anatomical knowledge acquired by Italian painters and his landscapes used the depth made possible by central perspective. The revolution in painting also brought with it a new self-awareness, which Dürer expressed in his lifelong predilection for self-portraits, which chronicled his rise as a painter and the development of his technique.[22]

Italy was not the only source of inspiration. As Dürer was now preparing to escape from plague once more, he wanted to use his travels to Brussels to learn about the latest developments in Dutch art. Two generations earlier, Jan van Eyck and his students had stunned the world with their sympathetic portraits of commoners, lively town scenes, and depictions of nature. The Dutch were his only true rivals in northern Europe; it would be good to see what they were up to.

In order to facilitate artistic exchange, but also to demonstrate his superior skill, Dürer would bring an unusual asset: a trunk full of prints. The Italian painters he admired, Mantegna, Bellini, and Raphael, with their emphasis on composition and color, were also interested in the new technology of print, as were some of his Dutch rivals. But Dürer felt he was at an advantage. He had recognized early on the potential of print and learned how to turn wood, copper, and stone to his will, mastering the technique of carving that would look good in print. With astonishing precision, he captured the organic forms of plants, the ears of hares, and the poses of humans, bringing the dead materials to life. Best of all: these images could be reproduced at will, allowing for an entirely new source of income and distribution. Dürer also produced images for printed books, profiting from Nuremberg's position at the center of the print revolution. In turning print into high art, Dürer recognized that print was changing not only writing and literature, but also visual representation.

During his trip, Dürer's prints served another purpose as well: he treated them almost like cash, doling them out to landlords and patrons as compensation for services rendered. He recorded these transactions in a diary, a reminder that the primary purpose of his trip was money. His diary was a kind of account book, in which he gave a precise reckoning of his expenses, down to every meal and overnight stay.

On his way north, Dürer heard shocking news: Luther had been arrested. It had been only a few years since the friar Martin Luther wrote to his bishop to protest the sale of indulgences (mass-produced, thanks to print) and other abuses of the Church. Since then, things had happened very quickly. A lack of response from the bishop had prompted Luther to write more and more letters of protest, and some of his associates had taken those letters to the newly established printing presses, turning Luther into the first populist of the print era.[23]

In Nuremberg, where many of Luther's letters and tracts were printed and where Luther had gained early followers, Dürer had observed this process with interest and sympathy. Along with some of his friends, he had supported Luther's call for a renewal of Christianity. Word of the arrest prompted Dürer to pen a long screed in favor of Church reform, supporting Luther's cause. Little did he know that in this particular instance, he was worrying too much.[24] Luther had been arrested by a sympathizer, who had taken Luther into "protective custody" at Wartburg Castle. There, Luther would translate the New Testament from Greek into the German vernacular with astonishing speed. Once completed, he would give it to printers, above all those located in Nuremberg, who demonstrated what mass production could do. Luther's Bible would become the first bestseller of the age—the vanguard of a revolution that would reshape Europe.

On his journey north, Dürer was thinking not only of Luther, his stipend, and the work of Dutch painters. He also took pains to record in his diary an unexpected encounter in Brussels, where Holy Roman Emperor-elect Charles V was holding court. Charles's rule extended from Burgundy to Austria (he allegedly bragged: "I speak Spanish to God, Italian to women, French to men, and German to my horse"), and four years earlier, in 1516, he had also become King of Spain, thereby acquiring Spain's growing possessions in the New World. Dürer wrote:

> I have also seen the things which have been brought to the King from the new land of gold, a sun entirely in gold, almost six feet wide, and a silver moon of similar size, two closets full of armor and various kinds of arms, shields, bows and arrows, astonishing and strange clothing, blankets, and other astonishing tools, much more worth seeing than miracles. These objects are so valuable that they are estimated to be worth one hundred thousand guilders. In my entire life, I haven't seen anything that so delighted me as these things. What I saw among them were astonishing objects of artisanal craft, and I was astonished by the subtle genius of the people in this foreign land. I don't even know how to express in words what I saw.[25]

What Dürer saw were the gifts Moctezuma gave to the strangers who had arrived on his coast less than a year earlier. The gifts had been eagerly received by Hernán Cortés, the Spanish soldier in charge of the expedition, who had set out from Cuba to explore the coast and trade with the inhabitants. Cortés had no intention of sticking to this official charge. He had already made an agreement with his crew to create an illegal colony and to extract as much from this land as possible. As was usual, the emperor would get one-fifth of the proceeds. Of the remaining four-fifths, Cortés would try to claim a generous portion for himself. In establishing a permanent settlement and getting ready to move inland, Cortés had exceeded his charge and become a fugitive from the law.

There was only one way in which this daring endeavor would not end badly: he would appeal directly to Charles V, present himself as a brave conqueror and send the king samples of the riches to come. To achieve his goal, Cortés composed a long account of the expedition so far, how he had arrived at the coast, his various encounters with native inhabitants, and what had prompted him to exceed the official brief. As a further enticement, he sent an itemized list of presents he had received.[26]

Cortés entrusted the letter and the presents to two loyal followers. They were instructed to sail directly to Spain, without going via Cuba where they might attract unwanted attention from Cortés's superiors. For some reason, they landed in Cuba anyway, perhaps to acquire provisions, and were almost intercepted. Somehow, they managed to get away and sail to Seville, the city in southwestern Spain that dominated the new trans-Atlantic exploration, where they learned they would now have to travel half-way across Europe to deliver the gifts personally to Charles. Charles was soon to be crowned emperor in Aix-la-Chapelle, just like Charlemagne before him. (Like Charlemagne, Charles V would be crowned again, by the pope in 1530, the last Holy Roman Emperor to receive that additional distinction.[27]) In order to commemorate that occasion, Charles decided to exhibit the presents sent to him by Cortés as a way of boasting about his newest possessions, which was how Dürer came to see them.

But what was it that Dürer thought he saw? In his diary, he used words such as *wunderlich* (wonderful) and *seltsam* (strange). Dürer was aware that he knew nothing about the people who had wrought these objects—no one in Europe did. This didn't mean that Dürer had no conception of the New World. As a citizen of Nuremberg, Dürer was in a good place to have received some news from Spanish and Portuguese sailors. (Fellow citizen of Nuremberg Martin Behaim had created one of the first globes, in 1492.)

Dürer might also have read the accounts of the New World that had been written and printed by Christopher Columbus, who depicted

the inhabitants he encountered as noble savages, and by Amerigo Ves-
pucci, who described them as dangerous cannibals.[28] Two years after
Dürer's encounter with Moctezuma's gifts, he would have occasion to
look at a woodcut printed in Nuremberg that depicted children being
sacrificed, and two years after that, a first map of Tenochtitlan was
printed in Nuremberg, allowing Europeans to imagine this miraculous
city in the water, probably at least as large as Nuremberg. And even
though Venice was likely larger, Tenochtitlan was sometimes called
"the Great Venice," turning the Italian original into the lesser one.[29]

But if Dürer had come across the depiction of Native Americans
as either noble savages or ignoble cannibals, neither characterization
seems to have informed how he perceived their artworks. While freely
admitting to total ignorance, he looked at them, simply, as objects
made by skilled artists and artisans such as himself. As someone who
was always thinking about money, especially on this trip, he assessed
the value of what he saw as extremely high (about 10 million dollars

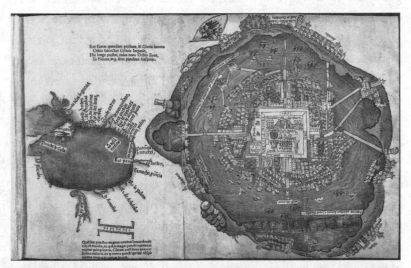

Map of Tenochtitlan included with a Latin translation of Hernán Cortés's "Second
Letter to Emperor Charles V," printed in Nuremberg in 1524. (LIBRARY OF CONGRESS)

today), but above all he admired the workmanship, the "subtle genius" of those who had made the objects. It is clear, from these gushing lines—and Dürer was not someone prone to gushing—how much he admired the craft of these artists. He especially appreciated the works in gold. Although he himself was a painter and engraver, he had grown up in a goldsmith's household and married the daughter of a goldsmith.[30] He knew how to evaluate work in gold.

What Dürer brought to these objects, which were entirely detached from all cultural context, was a highly developed sense of artisanal skill and artistic imagination, but also a sense of humility about his own ignorance. This allowed him to avoid some of the clichés about the Americas circulating around him—noble savages, bloodthirsty cannibals—and to come to this extraordinary encounter, the first time that a first-rate European artist interacted with the highly developed arts of Mesoamerica, with unusual openness and appreciation.

Dürer's sight of Moctezuma's gifts in Brussels was not his only encounter with strange objects brought back by Spanish and Portuguese sailors. A few years earlier, he had received a breathless account of a new species of animal from the far east. It was called a rhinoceros and was a colossal giant with a threatening horn and a skin as thick as armor. A German merchant saw this creature disembark in Lisbon and described it to Dürer in great detail. Dürer decided to make an engraving based on this description—an unusual decision for an artist who wanted to create lifelike images such as his depiction of a hare, so precise that today it almost looks like a photograph.

In the case of the rhinoceros, too, the result was striking. Dürer started with a sketch and then reworked it as a woodcut. Clearly, this was a perfect opportunity for mass reproduction, for who wouldn't want to see this monster of a beast? The woodcut captures the incredible heft of the animal, its bulk supported by four legs that look like towers, its large head equipped with the threatening horn. Only the ears, sticking up like those of a donkey (or hare?), give the animal a slightly friendlier, perhaps even ridiculous demeanor. But all this is dwarfed by the heavy armor that makes it impervious to attack, armor that looks like the plates of a tortoise and that covers the bulk of the creature.

In creating this woodcut without seeing the animal, Dürer took a calculated risk. It reflected his interest in foreign forms, but also his commitment to making things visible: to demonstrate that everything could be shown given the right technique and vision, even something that he had not seen with his own eyes. The risk paid off. Dürer's rhinoceros became a big success, an emblem of the wonders of the East.[31] It was only in the eighteenth century, when more Europeans saw rhinoceroses in the flesh, that people noted that the actual animals didn't

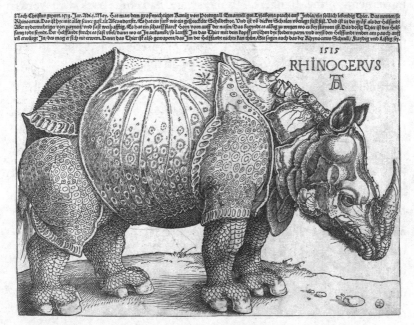

A woodcut by Albrecht Dürer of a rhinoceros. Dürer never set eyes on a rhinoceros and instead based this rendering on a written account. He captures many details correctly, but mistakenly thinks the animal has plates similar to those of a tortoise instead of thick skin. (ROSENWALD COLLECTION, NATIONAL GALLERY OF ART, WASHINGTON DC)

have armor plates, just thick skin (Dürer captured many other features of the animal quite accurately, a feat given that he had to rely on a verbal description). Through the power of reproduction, Dürer had created a misleading image of this animal in Europe for several centuries.

Dürer's rhinoceros print was among those he brought along to the Netherlands, where he gave them to Margaret of Austria, Charles V's aunt, who successfully interceded on his behalf. Dürer was able to return to the parsimonious Nuremberg magistrates with an imperial writ instructing them to pay out the required sum.

TENOCHTITLAN, 1519

Meanwhile, back in Tenochtitlan, Moctezuma was watching the movements of the strangers. His messenger had come back with words and paintings of what he saw, but the rendering didn't tell Moctezuma how to deal with these people. Clearly, his presents had not had the intended effect of displaying his might, satisfying their desire for gold, and making them turn back. On the contrary, the newcomers had demonstrated their might in battle, attacking some of Moctezuma's tributaries with their armored deer, their shooting balls, their bloodthirsty dogs, and their powerful crossbows. It was now their declared purpose to come to Tenochtitlan to meet him in person.

Moctezuma sent more messengers, with more gifts, hoping that the strangers would turn around and go home, but they continued making their way inland. Clearly, they had learned something about the lay of the land, and before long they had made allies, especially the Tlaxcalans, whom Moctezuma had tried, unsuccessfully, to turn into tributaries. Moctezuma had been harsh with the Tlaxcalans, and had repeatedly made incursions on their territory in search of people to sacrifice on special occasions.[32] Even though the strangers initially attacked the Tlaxcalans, they quickly recruited them as allies against Moctezuma, and so they crossed into Aztec home territory.

The strangers seemed intent on entering Tenochtitlan. Moctezuma decided that perhaps it would be better to have them where he could examine them and more easily handle them, at the center of his power.

The first meeting, outside Tenochtitlan, was awkward. The leader of the pale-faced strangers sought to embrace him, an enormous breach of protocol. Fortunately, at the last moment, Moctezuma's underlings prevented this from happening.[33] Then Moctezuma took them into the city, which clearly impressed them. Nothing they knew came close to what he showed them, from the dikes and causeways to the central temple and palace. (Spanish accounts describe this encounter, falsely, as a surrender.)

Once the foreigners were inside the city, things started getting out of control quickly. First, they confined Moctezuma to his palace, essentially making a prisoner of him. Moctezuma still had access to his staff, but he did not have freedom of movement, which was beginning to undermine his authority. At least his network of messengers was still in place, and he received regular updates on what was happening across his realm. For example, he knew that a flotilla of ships much larger than the previous one had arrived on the shore. The news seemed to make the foreigners uneasy, and before long, their leader, Cortés, left the city in the company of a substantial force of both foreigners and their new allies.[34]

Meanwhile, the situation in the city was deteriorating. With Cortés gone, the Spaniards became riotous, interfered with a religious festival, and massacred many Aztecs. Moctezuma knew that his position was becoming increasingly untenable, given the open hostilities. There was talk that a new emperor would have to be found since he was a captive and incapable of acting as sovereign.

Then Cortés reappeared. Apparently, he had won a battle against the new arrivals and his ranks had swelled. But conditions in the city had gone from bad to worse. The previous stalemate had given way to new hostilities and before long there was open war, as the city was rising up against the murderous foreigners. Street by street, canal by canal, causeway by causeway, the foreigners were being driven out of the city. There were heavy casualties, but the Aztecs had won.

Moctezuma was not among those to witness this final triumph: he was killed, either by the foreigners or by his own people. He, Moctezuma II, who had rebuilt the city after the disaster with the aqueduct, who expanded the Aztec realm, and who had fought foreign intruders, had died defending the city that many regarded as the highest achievement of Aztec civilization.[35]

Driven out of the city, the foreigners regrouped. They continued their policy of terrorizing different groups, coercing them into new alliances, turning former tributaries of the Aztecs into rebels by promising them revenge for past humiliations. Then a plague arrived.[36] This was a different plague from the Black Death that had been stalking Europe. It was smallpox, to which the Spaniards, unlike the inhabitants of the Americas, had higher levels of immunity. Perhaps it was best that Moctezuma did not live to see the population of Mesoamerica decimated by this pestilence. His successor probably succumbed to the illness. The old system of alliances that had created the Aztec Empire frayed badly, and the plague put additional pressure on a civilization under threat.[37]

It was in this situation that the foreigners launched their final assault on the city, using specially built boats to give their cannons and other firearms maximum effect. Weakened by the plague, the city could not withstand the assault. The Spaniards and their allies didn't just take the city; they burned it to the ground, including Moctezuma's palace, his collection of books, and his zoo. When the battle was over, the foreigners had destroyed the miracle they had admiringly called "the Great Venice."

What remained? After the destruction, a new battle began, one over history. Hernán Cortés continued writing letters to Charles V justifying his actions, boasting of his exploits, ingratiating himself, and creating facts on the ground that no one would dare to change.[38]

Some of his companions would pen their own histories, including the soldier Bernal Díaz, who had less to prove than Cortés and who wrote his account of the conquest toward the end of his life, with the benefit of hindsight that made the historical outcome seem inevitable.[39]

These accounts are a far cry from the books Aztecs had created before the downfall, with their intricate picture-signs that recorded calendars, histories, and myths. Knowledge of this complicated system of writing and reading was gradually lost, and most of the books were burned or disappeared. Only very few Aztec books survived the destruction of Tenochtitlan.

In an extraordinary effort to preserve the Aztec experiences of the destruction of Tenochtitlan, a Spanish friar, Bernardino de Sahagun, conducted an oral history project, interviewing aging eyewitnesses, assembling voices and images. The result was an immensely valuable book, documenting not only the battles against the Spanish and the disease they brought to the Americas, in Nahuatl and Spanish, with over two thousand images, but also the life of the Aztecs before the destruction of the empire, including everyday activities, agricultural and fishing practices as well as musical instruments such as drums and rattles.[40] (My account relies on all the sources mentioned above, but especially on this one.)

This book project, too, was blinded by its own skewed vision of events, and was undertaken decades after the fall of Tenochtitlan; it relied on translation and was, of course, assembled by a Spaniard, and one who reported on pre-conquest cultural practices so that Christian priests could better convert the Aztecs and, if necessary, stamp out their culture.[41] His Aztec sources had their own investments in depicting recent history, trying to blame the downfall of their civilization on Moctezuma alone, as if only a bad emperor could explain so extraordinary an occurrence.[42] But all histories have their own purposes, leading to distortions, skewing perspectives as they attempt to explain things in hindsight.

Bernardino's work of oral history is called the Florentine Codex, after the Italian city in which it now resides. Both Spanish and Nahuatl are written in the phonetic alphabet the Spanish brought with them, and the images, painted by Aztec painters, are illustrations of the text. Because these Aztecs were encouraged to record and explain their culture to outsiders—a culture they knew was disappearing— they depicted and described it in a way they would never have done if the Spanish had not arrived on their shores, recording many things that might otherwise have gone without saying. Once again, destruction and preservation, disappearance and recording, were strangely entangled.

Of the few surviving Aztec books, many were later destroyed by Spanish priests and friars, who wanted to eradicate the worship of Aztec gods and rightly recognized Aztec books to be intimately connected with the old religion. Those that remained were taken to Europe and dispersed among various libraries, including the well-guarded vaults of the Vatican. There the books lay more or less forgotten until they caught the interest of a Mexican monk, José Lino Fábrega, in the eighteenth century.[43] This is the thing about libraries and archives: they can be used to steal and bury cultural objects, but libraries cannot control how future generations will use their treasures, at least not entirely so.

Since Fábrega's pioneering work, scholars have tried to reconstruct the lost art of Aztec picture-writing, painstakingly wresting meaning from carefully arranged symbols that are striking in their symmetry and intricate design, complementing the account given in the Florentine Codex. The process is still going on.[44] We know that the few, precious Aztec books that have escaped destruction harbor much of the way in which Aztecs made sense of the world, their assumptions about their place in the universe, the stories of creation and destruction, the meaning of their rituals and art. The process of reading and reconstruction is not simply a matter of deciphering a script; it is a matter of deciphering an entire world.

=

DÜRER NEVER HAD A CHANCE TO SEE ANY OF THESE BOOKS, EVEN though Cortés had included two in his shipment to Charles V. Apparently, they were seen as less valuable than weapons, clothes, and objects made from gold. Some of Dürer's greatest engravings were allegories, images that use symbols that must be read like signs, so it is intriguing to speculate what he would have made of the image-symbols in these books. When he returned to Nuremberg after receiving his stipend, he had only eight more years to live. While he had escaped the plague ravaging Nuremberg, it is likely that he contracted, on his travels to the Netherlands, the illness that would eventually kill him. If that is the case, he paid a heavy price for securing Charles V's favors, and for seeing Moctezuma's golden art.

The clash between Cortés and Moctezuma, the Spanish Empire and the Aztec Empire, was also a clash between the new European mass production of books and the handmade books of the Aztecs. Mass production became a way of assuring the survival of books and images, an alternative to institutions such as museum or library vaults designed to preserve unique artifacts. (The Nuremberg map of Tenochtitlan likely survived because it was mass-produced.) Mass production soon swept the world, generating an unprecedented flood of books and images, a process that has accelerated again recently with our current storage and media revolution.

At the same time, mass reproduction has not eliminated but, on the contrary, raised the value of the original, the unique, the irreplaceable object (including, perhaps paradoxically, mass-produced books in the form of first editions and editions signed by the author or by famous previous owners). For the same reason, we continue to spend considerable resources on preserving originals in manuscript libraries and museums, and not just those from the distant past. It's almost as if the greater the ease and prevalence of mass production, the more precious originals have become.

The fragile, irreplaceable nature of artistic originals is nowhere as clear as in the case of the Aztecs' greatest creation: their floating city. And yet, the city is also an example of how hard it is to destroy something completely, even through continual use. Tenochtitlan was rendered uninhabitable by the Spanish and their allies, but it was rebuilt. If destruction sometimes preserves, continual use often destroys, which is why it's been so difficult to excavate the burnt city in the middle of a heavily populated area.

But some of the urban structures of Tenochtitlan still exist in the bustling megalopolis of Mexico City. In the 1970s, excavations began in the temple complex not far from the city's central square. Just as we are still learning to read Aztec codices, we're still discovering lost traces of the past. Even when it looks as if the past is gone, there is often something that remains, and from those remains, a lost world can be glimpsed and reconstructed.[45]

There is a square in Mexico City called Plaza de las Tres Culturas, on the site of a battle between Spanish and Aztec soldiers. The three cultures referred to are the Aztecs, the Spaniards, and the mixed Mexican population of the present. An inscription reads: "This [battle] was neither victory nor defeat. It was the painful birth of the mestizo people that is Mexico today."

CHAPTER 11

A PORTUGUESE SAILOR
WRITES A GLOBAL EPIC

When Luís de Camões (c. 1524–80) set out from Macao for India, he was facing an uncertain voyage across the South China Sea. Having been born into the intoxicating boom of Portuguese exploration, Camões had spent the better part of his life harnessing the power of the winds. He had braved the mistral of the Mediterranean, which could carry sand from the Sahara Desert all the way to southern Europe; the trade winds of the Atlantic, which had taken him close to the coast of Brazil; the treacherous cross-currents of the Cape of Good Hope; and the seasonal monsoon of the Indian Ocean. In due course, he would turn this experience into the most important piece of Portuguese literature, *The Lusiads* (which means *The Portuguese*), becoming the country's national poet. Today he is being rediscovered as a witness to the first age of globalization, as someone who shaped how we view the world empires of the past and also our own contemporary forays into the expanses of space.

Camões was traveling across the South China Sea during the season of what the Chinese called *ta feng*, the great wind, a word Portuguese sailors had translated as *tufão* (typhoon).[1] Typhoons announced themselves with stronger winds, storm surges, and a front of dark clouds. When those signs appeared, the only hope was to strike sail immediately. If the wind caught a ship under sail, it could break the mast and leave the ship unnavigable, at the mercy of giant waves that would crush wooden decks and hulls as if they were made of paper.

On this particular voyage, Camões didn't have to worry about keeping watch because he was traveling as a prisoner. A superior had accused him of embezzling money in Macao, and since there was no Portuguese court in this remote trading post, he would have to return to Goa, on the western coast of India, in order to be brought to justice. Camões hated Goa, where he had seen what the Portuguese, with their cannons, armor, and battle tactics, had done to the local population.[2] His accuser was well-connected, so there was little hope of getting off easy. Camões had spent some time in prison back in Portugal, which was why he had embarked on a life at sea two decades earlier. But prison in Goa was certain to be much worse.

Camões's one consolation was that he had been allowed to bring his Chinese wife, Dinamene, with him.[3] For most of his life, he had been unlucky in love. As a young man, after leaving university and joining court society as tutor to a high aristocrat, he had fallen in love with a woman out of his reach. It was only decades later and halfway around the world that he had found a true companion. If the trial in Goa ended well after all, perhaps he could return with Dinamene to Macao, the one place where he had found something close to happiness.

Despite the uncertain season, Camões's ship made its way across the South China Sea without major incident and now, over a thousand miles later, found itself close to the southern tip of Indochina, today's Vietnam. They still had another thousand miles to Malacca, in today's Malaysia, where they would take on provisions and make repairs, before they could risk the long voyage around the southern tip of India and up the coast to Goa. But for the time being, Camões could enjoy being close to land, taking in the enormous delta where the Mekong

River empties into the sea. Having spent half his life at sea, Camões had experienced many times the thrill of seeing land after weeks of staring at the endless expanse of ocean, the joy of being greeted by birds and fish that only live close to shore.

Perhaps their tantalizing proximity to land was why the watchman relaxed his attention. Suddenly, the strong winds and threatening clouds turned into a full-blown typhoon. The bosun was shouting. Sailors tried to climb up the masts to take in the sails, but it was too late. As the great wind seized their vessel, men were swept overboard into the gushing waves, and the ship would soon be crushed beyond hope. Amidst the chaos, Camões somehow managed to escape and get himself ashore. Local fishermen found him half dead and nursed him back to life over the course of many weeks. He was one of the few to survive. Dinamene was nowhere to be found.

It wasn't just wind power that had brought Camões to Asia; it was also the will of kings. The Portuguese kings presided over a small strip of land at the westernmost periphery of Europe, far removed from the centers of trade. Portugal didn't even border the Mediterranean Sea—"our sea," as the Romans had called it. The Mediterranean was not without its dangers, but it was ringed by ports, carefully recorded in so-called portolan charts, which a ship in need could reach with relative ease. Those port towns, above all the republic of Venice, were lucky to be part of a lucrative trade network that reached, indirectly, all the way to India, bringing spices and gems via Arab traders to Europe.[4] Portugal, by contrast, faced only the endless and unprofitable expanse of the Atlantic Ocean.

Out of frustration over this unfortunate position, Portuguese kings had sent ships into the Atlantic, not straight out west—nothing was to be found there, they believed—but on a southerly route, along the coast of Africa. Arab travelers had talked about a land of gold south of the Sahara Desert; perhaps something profitable could be found there.

Step by step, the Portuguese had managed to capture forts and establish a presence along the coast, beginning with Ceuta, in Morocco, in 1415. (Camões would serve in Ceuta over a century later, in 1547, losing one eye in battle.[5]) The assault on Ceuta was a mere dress

Fourteenth-century Catalan atlas attributed to Abraham Cresques.

(NATIONAL LIBRARY OF FRANCE)

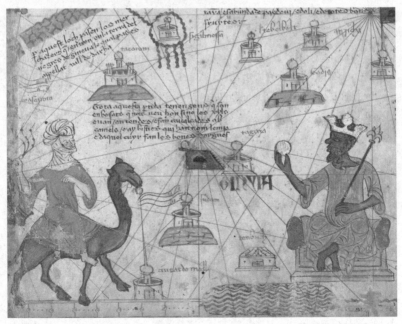

Detail from the fourteenth-century Catalan atlas depicting western Africa and its king. (NATIONAL LIBRARY OF FRANCE)

rehearsal for more ambitious plans. The Portuguese kings sent their captains further and further down the coast, into the unknown. It was clear that the African landmass was large, but how large exactly? And where would it end? Contrary to later belief, people at the time didn't think that they would simply fall off the earth if they ventured past the limits of the known world. There existed circular maps and spherical models of the world, but at some point the landmasses gave way to undefined space, and the sailors had no idea what they would find there. Continuing beyond this point meant literally going off the charts.

Increasingly, the Portuguese kings were ready to run this risk—or have their ships run it for them—hoping to find a sea passage into the Indian Ocean. If they did, Portugal could trade with India directly, without having to go through Venetian and Arab intermediaries. If such a route could be found, Portugal's unpromising geographic position on the left-hand side of the Ptolemaic map would suddenly put them at an advantage.

It was Vasco da Gama who found a way in the last years of the fifteenth century. Equipped with four state-of-the-art ships, he sailed down the African coast, then turned westward into the open Atlantic. This route was counter-intuitive, given that he was ultimately hoping to travel east, but Gama had realized that it was useless to fight against the Atlantic wind system that was driving them southwest. Against the opposition of his sailors, he let himself be carried to within a few hundred miles of the coast of Brazil before finally turning east. The maneuver eventually landed him on the southern tip of Africa and allowed him to round the Cape of Good Hope—all unknown territory to the Portuguese at the time. From there, he crept up the coast cautiously, taking in fresh provisions in Mozambique, Tanzania, Kenya, and Somalia before crossing the Indian Ocean to India.[6]

After Gama's triumphant return two years later, more and more Portuguese ships followed the same route around Africa, establishing trading posts along the way, often against local opposition. A settlement in Goa, on the western coast of India, became the first territorial possession and therefore the center of an expanding trading empire, which soon stretched southeast to Indonesia, with an outpost in Malacca, and even to faraway Macao. This was the Far Eastern world where Camões, who had been born and raised in Portugal, would spend much of his adult life, before being transported as prisoner and shipwrecked in the Mekong delta, uncertain what to do next. Should he remain with the fishermen who had saved him, or continue to Goa and face trial?

Portugal was able to project its power across vast distances because its kings understood the importance of information. Every voyage they sent into the unknown was painstakingly documented, every part of the African coast transposed into new charts, every new anchorage recorded, and every new insight into the wind systems of these distant oceans noted with care. Scribes also recorded the price of commodities, what the Portuguese could trade, and what they could buy. And when the voyagers returned home two years later (if at all—of Gama's fleet of four, only two vessels returned, with a third of the original crew), all this precious knowledge was collected and classified in one building located right at the center of Lisbon: India House.[7] In order to speed up the exchange of information, India House devised a relay system by which ships left messages at improvised ports of call along the coast of Africa. At one point, a Portuguese captain put a written note in an old shoe suspended from a tree.[8]

Thanks to the information collected at India House, Lisbon prospered greatly in the half-century between Gama's first voyage and Camões's own travels. Fortune hunters and traders, along with scholars and geographers, came to Lisbon from across Europe to learn of the latest developments. The world was changing, requiring new maps to be drawn, with far-reaching geopolitical consequences. It was here, in Lisbon, where the Nuremberg-born mapmaker Martin Behaim went to gather the information needed to make a new model of the world.[9]

Because information was so crucial to an expedition's success, it became important to control it and keep it from the eyes of rivals. King Manuel, who had sent Gama around the Cape of Good Hope, was the first to realize just how valuable information was and to forbid new maps and globes such as Behaim's "earth apple" from circulating.[10] He also tried to swear returning sailors to silence. But silence was hard to enforce.

Writers were the biggest problem. Many explorers brought along scribes to document their discoveries, and accounts of these early voyages had made some of these scribes well known. King Manuel sought to suppress their accounts before other empire-builders took advantage of the new knowledge first. But the world-altering information collected at India House couldn't be kept from the public forever. (Of the few actual documents about Camões's life that survived, for example, most are from the archives of India House.)[11] Many sailors and soldiers were former convicts (including Camões himself), which perhaps made them more likely to scoff at the law and sell valuable intelligence to rival powers, such as Venice, who were ready to pay a high price for it. When the ship of Portuguese explorer Ferdinand Magellan, the first to circumnavigate the globe on a westward course by going around South America and then across the vast Pacific Ocean, returned from its epic voyage, a Venetian scribe managed to get some of the (few) sailors who had made it back to talk, and published an account.

From then on, India House was guarded more and more jealously even as it became clear that maintaining secrecy was impossible. Meanwhile, new sets of maps and globes were being made.

≡

IN THE SHIPWRECK, CAMÕES HAD LOST EVERYTHING: HIS WIFE, and all of the worldly possessions he had accumulated during his three years of service in Macao. But there was one thing he managed to salvage from the sinking ship: a wooden box containing a manuscript.[12]

After reading the accounts of earlier explorers such as Gama, and having become a foot-soldier in the Portuguese trading empire, he had decided to see if he could make money by describing Portuguese exploration. And the writing would not be mere reportage. He did not, for instance, want to write a travelogue. Those reports tended to be factual, prosaic affairs, which was not what Camões had in mind. He wanted to ask what it all meant, to make sense of his experience. He wanted to turn the new map of the world into literature.

Camões had been drawn to literature throughout his life. His preferred form was poetry, especially love poetry written to women who were out of his reach. (After the loss of Dinamene, he wrote several poems about his dead wife.) In his heyday at court, he had also written a play, making indirect stabs at his social superiors which led to his exile from Lisbon, his army service in Ceuta, and the loss of his eye.[13] Drama held no appeal after this experience, and in any case, neither poetry nor drama was the right form for capturing an experience of global proportions.

At this crucial moment, to make sense of the extraordinary discoveries of his time, Camões turned to the distant past—not even the past of his own people, but of people living thousands of miles away. Why?

Camões lived at a time when the art and literature of Greece and Rome had suddenly become vitally interesting again. The rediscovery of the ancient world had begun in Italy, when scholars and poets went searching for lost manuscripts and other artifacts of Roman and Greek culture, some of which they imported from Constantinople and Baghdad. Letters of Ovid, dialogues of Plato, and of course the *Odyssey* and the *Aeneid*, were held up as models. The turn to the past was called a renaissance because those at the forefront of this rediscovery thought of it as a rebirth, conveniently ignoring earlier revivals and the fact that this rebirth included a lot of borrowing from intermediaries.

Portugal was a latecomer to this renaissance, but as soon as riches from the Far East began pouring in, it caught up quickly. Just as merchants and geographers were attracted to Lisbon to learn of the newest discoveries in the East, so scholars and teachers from across Europe came to Portugal to practice what we now call the humanities, a form of knowledge mostly based on the recovery of old manuscripts and other forms of editing, commenting on, and thinking alongside material from the past. The University of Coimbra, which had been founded hundreds of years earlier, became the center of this form of knowledge, one based on thought and argument, on debating the answers past generations had given to fundamental questions regarding the place of humans in the cosmos—their know-why. Two colleges were set up inside a grand monastery, one for the higher nobility and one for the lower nobility and the bourgeoisie, but the center of the university was an extraordinary collection of over 100,000 books and manuscripts. Like India House, the University of Coimbra stored knowledge with the purpose of using it and passing it down to the next generation.[14]

Sometimes the two institutions even worked hand in hand. The maps created by Ptolemy in the second century CE had been brought to Italy in 1397 as part of the rediscovery of ancient texts.[15] Even though the shapes of the continents known to Ptolemy were soon revised, and a sea route was added to the white spaces on the map, Ptolemy's system of longitudes and latitudes remained a valuable invention and could now be used to create more accurate maps that would equip modern merchants and voyagers to reach their destinations and navigate challenges along the way.

It was here, at the University of Coimbra, where Camões had learned to revere the classics. His uncle was the rector of the university, which meant that young Camões had access to the immense concentration of knowledge accumulated in the library. Classical learning left such an impression on him that decades later and halfway around the world, he decided to use Homer and Virgil as models for how to tell the story of Portuguese exploration. He chose as his subject Gama's first voyage to India—a stand-in for a hundred years of exploration done by an entire people, which is why he called his work *The Lusiads*, which is to say, "The Portuguese." To make sure that his readers knew how much he was drawing on Coimbra, he included a description of the city's natural setting and celebrated it as a new Athens.[16]

Reading the two ancient authors taught Camões where to begin, namely, in the middle, *in medias res*, as Latin commentators had called it, at the point when Gama had already made it to the eastern coast of Africa, leaving the earlier rounding of the Cape to be told later. More important, the two authors taught Camões how to give his story cosmic significance. In Homer, Odysseus was protected by Athena and pursued by Poseidon, while in Virgil, Aeneas was persecuted by Juno and rescued by Jupiter. Camões decided to use the Olympian gods as well, but he carefully selected those that were most fitting for his story. To represent the interests of Asia against Portuguese intrusion, he chose Bacchus, the god of masks, theater, and wine, whom the Greeks, using the name Dionysus, had associated with the East.

Camões also borrowed *ekphrasis*, the extended descriptions of a picture through words. Homer had used this technique brilliantly by giving his listeners an account of the earth, the stars, the constellations, and peaceful life in Greece by describing Achilles's shield, on which images of these scenes had been carved. Another technique was the Homeric *simile*, an extended comparison that can go on for several stanzas.

While Homer supplied literary techniques, Virgil supplied vision. He had given his hero Aeneas the all-important purpose of founding Rome, using epic poetry to create the foundational myth of an entire nation. Camões wanted to replicate this success for Portugal, which is why he included its entire history, from humble beginnings to present glory.

We are so used to admiring classical antiquity that it is easy to forget just how strange, even far-fetched this recapture of the distant past can seem. Early modern Portugal was nothing like ancient

Greece or Rome. Fifteen hundred years had passed since Virgil wrote his epic, and over two thousand since Homer had written his. There were plenty of more recent, medieval stories Camões could have used, not to mention the Old and New Testaments (Camões lived, after all, in an intensely Christian country). But he and his contemporaries were transfixed by the gods, architecture, and literature of the remote culture of ancient Greece housed in the library of Coimbra. Classical literature, an epic, was the form he would use.

Though Camões used classical learning to make sense of Portugal's new empire, he also believed that the Portuguese had exceeded the accomplishments of ancient heroes. Odysseus and Aeneas had sailed the Mediterranean, a large and wild sea in which many sailors had drowned, but that sea was an inland lake in comparison to the Atlantic, the Indian Ocean, and the South China Sea, not to mention the vast expanse of the Pacific. (Camões downplayed the accomplishment of Magellan, who had traversed the Pacific on behalf of rival Spain.) He bragged that Odysseus and Aeneas had not sailed "By oceans where none had ventured," and that only the Portuguese had gone where no man had gone before.[17]

The scope of Portuguese exploration was beyond anything the ancients could have imagined; it even exceeded the domains of their lively cast of gods. The Cape of Good Hope with its dangerous cross-currents, adverse winds, and all the other hazards of the passage to India called for Camões to invent, in the most dramatic passage of his poem, an entirely new god: Adamastor, a grotesque giant, pale of skin, with a grizzled beard, decaying teeth, and sunken, coal-black eyes.

Camões also felt that he surpassed his ancient models in the power of his personal experience. Who knew what Homer, who was reported to have been blind, had ever experienced first-hand? The philosopher Plato had questioned his expertise. And while Virgil had traveled from his native Italy to Greece, he had never visited most of the locations in his poem. Homer and Virgil, in other words, were just making

things up. Camões knew first-hand what it was like to sail down the
western coast of Africa, round the Cape, and cross the Indian Ocean.
He knew what a typhoon felt like; he even knew what it was like to
be shipwrecked and almost die. He missed no opportunity to remind
his readers: "I saw"; "I went." Homer and Virgil were fabulists, but he
was not making things up. He had earned his epic through personal
experience, which made it superior to the classics:

> *If the philosophers of old, who visited*
> *So many lands to study their secrets,*
> *Had witnessed the marvels I witnessed,*
> *Spreading my sail to such different winds*
> *What great writings they would have left us!* [18]

The Lusiads is the first epic to mention everyday details of long
sea voyages, including scurvy, the illness from which so many sailors
suffered and died.[19] Unbeknownst to the sailors, the cause was vitamin C deficiency, which set in whenever ships went weeks or months
without fresh food. It would begin with fatigue, nausea, diarrhea, and
fever, and then proceed to swelling of the gums, all of which Camões
put in his epic. Unlike his ancient models, Camões cared about the
common sailors and soldiers—not surprising, since he had been one
of them. He even mocked the book-learning of the educated classes,
who doubted the unlikely sights reported by "rude sailors." Among
the marvels Camões described was St. Elmo's fire, a glowing ball of
light visible in the middle of a storm—a rare phenomenon caused by a
strong electric field in the atmosphere. He also captured a waterspout,
or water tornado, in fine-grained detail that speaks of his first-hand
experience:

> *I saw it distinctly (and do not presume*
> *My eyes deceived me) rise in the air,*

A little vapor and subtle smoke
Rotating a little from the wind's drag;
From there could be seen a tube extending
To the very heavens, but so slender
The eye could scarcely make it out; it seemed
Tenuous as a mist or something dreamed.
It went on growing little by little
To the thickness of a mast-head;
Though here narrow, and there wider as
It drew up great gulps of water;
Its foot undulated with the waves;
On the top, a black cloud condensed,
Growing heavier by the moment and sup-
purating with the huge volume taken up.[20]

Neither Homer nor Virgil, nor the classical scholars of Coimbra, could compete with what Camões had seen with his own eyes.

Camões the sailor also knew that Portuguese exploration was based on all kinds of practical arts, including shipbuilding and navigation. He was the first to mention, in an epic poem, an astrolabe, the ingenious device that enabled sailors to locate their precise latitude by reading the position of the sun or the stars, an analog to GPS.[21] It was this instrument that allowed the Portuguese to redraw the Ptolemaic maps.

It wasn't always easy to combine the classical, humanist learning housed at the university in Coimbra with the practical experience recorded in the documents of India House. In *The Lusiads*, Greek gods and modern technology, Adamastor and the astrolabe, exist uneasily next to each other, sometimes threatening to tear the work apart. As a compromise, Camões described the Greek gods as a poetic device, meaning that they should not be seen as real. This was part of the larger strategy pursued by Renaissance poets and scholars: they would revive pagan antiquity, including the Greek gods, only as long as this didn't interfere with Christianity. Classical learning could be practiced only with respect to human affairs (and poetry); but theologically speaking, the gods on Mount Olympus needed to remain dead.

Cultures survive and flourish in part by stealing from the past the way Camões did, but also by the surprises they find in other cultures they encounter. Camões took advantage of this source of inspiration, too. *The Lusiads* is a fascinating record of a great clash of cultures, full of misunderstanding, ignorance, arrogance, and violence, but also of mutual assistance and benefit, though unequally distributed.

Drawing both on his own experiences and those of other travelers, Camões considered with great interest the interactions that Portuguese explorers had had with inhabitants along the coast of Africa. These encounters were a matter of survival: each time the Portuguese attempted a landing, they were out of provisions, suffering from scurvy, and needing to repair their storm-damaged ships. Often they knew nothing about the people they encountered and found themselves thrown back on their own standards of judgment. The Portuguese view of whether a group was civilized or barbaric did not depend on the manner of their clothing, the food they ate, or the style of their dwellings. Camões described these things according to his own preconceptions. The main criterion was whether the strangers used money, gold or gems, and whether they knew anything about the spice trade with India. Only if they did were the Portuguese ready to regard them as civilized. It was a value judgment typical of explorers hoping to engage in long-distance trade.

As Gama (and later Camões, following in his path) sailed up the eastern coast of Africa, he encountered spice traders who were part of the network connecting Africa and India, and were therefore "civilized" in his eyes. People in this trading network participated in a money-based economy and enjoyed the wealth created by it. They had impressive houses and harbors, and their ships rivaled those of the

Portuguese. The Indian Ocean, it became clear, was not uncharted territory which no man had visited before; it was only the Portuguese who were new here. Everyone here had been sailing and trading for a long time. The sea voyage around the Cape, such a grand new undertaking for the Portuguese, was new only insofar as it joined two hitherto unconnected maritime networks.[22]

Being on good terms with these worldly traders up the East Africa coast was all the more important for the Portuguese because it meant they could anchor in fine harbors, find the wherewithal to repair their ships, and take on fresh provisions. Remaining on land for weeks or even months, they knew, was the only way to cure, or at least alleviate, scurvy. Above all, the African traders knew the wind systems of the Indian Ocean, and it was only with this local navigational knowledge that the Portuguese could ever hope to reach India.

From the perspective of the Portuguese, there was one problem with these impressively civilized and often very helpful people: they were Muslims. Not long before, large parts of the Iberian peninsula had been under Arab occupation and were known as al-Andalus. In many ways, being part of the Muslim sphere of influence was a blessing, in that it connected Portugal to such centers of learning as Baghdad's Storehouse of Wisdom, where some of the texts of classical learning had survived only thanks to Arab commentators and librarians. Arab rulers were usually tolerant, which meant that al-Andalus also became a center of Jewish learning, turning Portugal and Spain into a unique combination of Christian, Muslim, and Jewish scholarship and culture.

But these advantages weren't enough to keep the Arabs on the Iberian peninsula forever. Territory by territory, Christian rulers had pushed them back in what was called the Reconquest, which ended in 1492 when the last Arab stronghold fell. Triumphant, the new Christian rulers forced all remaining Muslim inhabitants to convert to the one true faith, Roman Catholicism (they did the same with Jewish

inhabitants) and then periodically accused them of hypocrisy, leading
to waves of expulsion (doing the same to Jewish converts). Coming on
the heels of this history, Camões regarded himself as the defender of a
distinctly Christian Europe that was caught in an eternal war against
Muslims and Jews.

If the Muslim presence in East Africa was unfortunate, at least it
meant that a few of the Portuguese could use Arabic to talk to these
people. The Portuguese also noticed that some of the African languages they encountered contained Arabic words. (Camões mentions
one such language in the epic without naming it, Swahili, the lingua franca of eastern Africa.)[23] Throughout their complicated dealings
with Muslims, the Portuguese kept looking for Christians, driven by
rumors of a Christian king, but to their great regret, they found only
Muslims all the way up the coast.

Finally, and with the help of Muslim navigators, Vasco da Gama's
four ships made it across the Indian Ocean to India. The Portuguese
were overjoyed and awed by what they found there. There were markets
rich with spices and gems, crowded ports, and lively trade. Yes, this
was what they had come to find: a sea route that would circumvent the
Arab-controlled Middle East. Even better, in India there were Christians everywhere. True, their saints often sprouted elephant trunks for
a nose and too many arms and they were all a little too colorful. But
Gama and his companions were willing to disregard these details; it
felt good to be among coreligionists so far from home.

If there was one lingering annoyance, it was that here, too, Muslims controlled maritime trade and seemed to exert all kinds of influence over these native Christians. But Gama was sure that he could
push aside these pesky Muslim rivals and make a deal with their sup-
posedly Christian overlords.

This is how Gama's crew and passengers described their first
impressions of India, and their opinions governed the Portuguese attitude at first. But by the time Camões traveled to India half a century

later, the Portuguese had come to realize just how mistaken these early accounts were. There was no fabulously powerful Christian king in eastern Africa (although the Portuguese would indeed make contact with embattled Ethiopians and aid them in their struggles against Muslims); the Indian statues the Portuguese travelers had taken for Christian saints were Hindu gods; and parts of the Indian subcontinent were under the control of Muslim rulers, the Mughals, who often left local Hindu rulers in place or made alliances with them. Camões incorporated this new knowledge into his epic, eliminating some of the more egregious misunderstandings that had characterized Gama's first voyage.

Once Gama had established contact with local Muslims and Hindus, he had another shock waiting for him: he had nothing anyone wanted to buy. The gifts and samples he had brought were laughably primitive—worth almost nothing. His soldiers and sailors had invested in fabrics and other commodities, hoping to sell them at high prices, but found that they fetched significantly less than what the goods had cost them back in Portugal. Almost everything was more expensive and more impressive here, not just the spices. The markets were overflowing with gems that were rare at home. Artisans were more skilled; merchants, richer; and the palaces grander than in Portugal. These riches weren't just recent. The Portuguese also marveled at ancient ruins much more elaborate than any they had seen in Europe. Slowly, they began to realize that in the rich trade network of the Indian Ocean, it was they who were poor and backward.[24]

After contact had been made and presents exchanged, the Hindu kings were greatly disappointed by these crude travelers who said that they had come from thousands of miles away to trade in spices but had nothing worth selling. In Camões's poem, Gama blamed the Muslims for this lukewarm reception and came up with an excuse: "I come simply as explorer," he pleaded. Trust me, when I return, "you will see then what merchandise you earn."[25] It didn't sound very convincing.

But Gama was true to his word. He did return, and with better merchandise as well as better ships and better maps. By the time Camões wrote his poem, Gerardus Mercator had come close to mapping the world as we know it today, along with the projection method associated with his name, although this new type of map was kept from circulating widely.

New maps were something of interest to Muslim and Hindus, something that could be traded and bragged about. Slowly, the Portuguese understood what they could sell and at what price (and they collected this knowledge at India House). Trade was supplemented by power politics when the Portuguese learned to play local Hindu rulers off against Muslims. Sometimes, the Hindu rulers were glad to get rid of their Muslim overlords, though often they came to regret their decision when they learned how ruthless the Portuguese could be, how trigger-happy with their powerful cannons, how quick to take and kill hostages, how ready to burn entire towns to the ground. For the most part, the Portuguese didn't seek large territorial possessions, but they sought to interrupt the Muslim trading network with warships outfitted for that purpose, taking the war of the seas deep into the Persian Gulf and the Red Sea.

≡

ALONE, IMPOVERISHED, WITH NOTHING TO HIS NAME BUT A MANU-script after the shipwreck in the South China Sea, Camões finally made it home, his legal troubles forgotten or dismissed. After returning to Macao, he caught a ship to the eastern coast of Africa and from there another one to Lisbon. To publish his work, he had to get permission from the new young king. Camões dedicated his book to him, urging him to continue the fight against the Muslims and to carry it to their heartland in North Africa. Additionally, before he could publish his work, Camões needed to get the blessing of the Inquisition.

Fortunately, the Church authorities understood that Camões's pagan gods were only poetic devices and gave its permission. With this last hurdle cleared, Camões was able to take *The Lusiads* to the printer.[26]

Print was a technology unknown in India and the Arab world at the time. Recently, Portuguese Jesuits had set up the first printing press in Goa to better convert the people they now understood were not Christians. Camões may have come across Chinese woodblock print—a technology already hundreds of years old by then—during his three years in Macao. But thanks to global trade, this Chinese invention, in the form recreated by Gutenberg, now came to a part of Asia where it had never been used before.

If Camões was able to print his poem on paper, it was thanks to the very Muslims against whom his poem polemicized—who had wrested the secret formula for paper-making from the Chinese, nurtured it in Baghdad, and brought it to Europe through al-Andalus. The world was becoming more interconnected.

Despite the new printing press at Goa, it didn't make sense for Camões to print *The Lusiads* there because his target audience was at home. Only in Portugal would he find a readership that would appreciate the classical references, people who had studied the new humanist canon at Coimbra. Specifically, the poem was directed at the young King Sebastião—Camões, like Dürer, needed royal patronage for a pension. Sebastião seems to have liked the poem, for he granted a pension, though it was rather meager. Fortunately, Camões had learned to make do with little and lived on it for the rest of his life.

We don't know exactly what motivated King Sebastião to assemble an army of nobles and attack North Africa, but it is possible that Camões's poem, which predicted a final victory over the Muslims, contributed to his decision. Of the entire Portuguese army, almost none returned, and the country's entire nobility was wiped out. The disaster was the end of Portugal as an independent entity. Soon, the Portuguese trading network in Asia was challenged by better-financed newcomers, above all the British East India Company, which would ultimately control large parts of the subcontinent.

No matter its role in the downfall of the Portuguese empire, *The Lusiads* is a good reminder that making meaning is a dangerous undertaking. It is dangerous to use the past to justify the present; it is dangerous to engage other cultures with ignorance and violence; it is dangerous to use the power of literature to motivate your readers— especially in the age of print.

But for all its faults, *The Lusiads* shows us how to use ancient lit-erary models to express the human thrill of modern exploration; the reason we see voyages into space as a *Space Odyssey*; why *Star Wars* used classical models; why *Star Trek* used Camões's slogan, "going where no man has gone before." Fortunately, we have learned some-thing from the violence undertaken in the name of *The Lusiads* and other modern explorers and epics. The code of conduct by which the Star Fleet operates is to avoid interfering with any life forms it may encounter on its voyage into the unknown. For this, too, we have to thank Camões—or rather, his critics, who turned his captivating work into a cautionary tale.

One of the architectural monuments of Portugal's brief world-wide empire is the Jerónimos Monastery in Lisbon, dedicated to the guardian saint of sailors. The monastery was commissioned by King Manuel, who had sent Vasco da Gama on his voyage, with funds that had flowed in from the Asian trade. The large structure contains late Gothic as well as Renaissance elements, borrowed from Greek and Roman models, but most surprising are its rich ornaments, which include shells and other maritime themes as well as plants from the East. In a daring decision, architects and sculptors decided to depart from traditional models and incorporate the world of the East, as *The Lusiads* would do in its own way.

Inside the monastery are the tombs of three men whose fates were closely interlinked: Camões, Gama, and King Sebastião. Of the three tombs, two are occupied. Gama did not return from his third voyage, though his remains were brought back and buried, and Sebastião did not return from his fatal war against the Muslims. Only Camões made it back alive.

The tomb of Camões in the Jerónimos Monastery, Lisbon.

(JERÓNIMOS MONASTERY, LISBON. PHOTO BY SAILKO)

CHAPTER 12

ENLIGHTENMENT IN SAINT-DOMINGUE AND IN A PARISIAN SALON

Anne-Louis Girodet de Roussy-Trioson, portrait of J. B. Belley, Deputy for Saint-Domingue, 1797. (VERSAILLES PALACE)

The portrait shows a Black man in elegant dress leaning casually against a pedestal. He has his head turned away and stares into the distance, while his elbow rests on the pedestal so that his shoulder partially hides the bust behind him. Light and shadows accentuate the rich color palette of the man, who wears beige trousers, a dark coat with yellow lapels, and a white scarf. The pedestal against which he leans is made of dark marble rich with veins in different colors, and the entire composition is set in a green landscape, under a blue sky. In contrast to this colorful composition, the bust is worked in pale marble and shows the bald head of an old man, his brow furrowed, looking with concentration or disapproval. Below him is an inscription, only partially visible, that says "T. Raynal." Who is T. Raynal? And who is the man paying homage to him but also giving him the cold shoulder?

The bust represents Abbé Raynal, a French Jesuit who became an Enlightenment philosopher. His bust is painted in the style of Roman antiquity—a reminder that revolutions often begin not with a hope for rupture but with a yearning for a return to the past, in this case, the political institutions of the Roman Republic.

The man casually leaning against the bust is Jean-Baptiste Belley, born in Senegal, forcibly abducted by slave-traders and brought to the French colony of Saint-Domingue (today's Haiti).[1] The portrait shows him wearing the typical dress of the French revolutionary convention, signaled especially by his full-length trousers instead of the "culottes," or knee-breeches, that were common at the time. (The French revolutionaries were called "sans-culottes," or "without knee-breeches," due to this choice of dress.) It was painted in 1797, in Paris, by Anne-Louis Girodet, who had studied with Jacques-Louis David, the most famous painter of the French Revolution (in 1793 David had painted the *Death of Marat*, a leader of the revolution murdered in his bath).

The portrait brings together people who contested slavery, economic exploitation, and imperial ambitions. To this end, they drew on the political institutions of ancient Rome, which were almost two thousand years old, as well as on actions, experiences, and thoughts ricocheting across the Atlantic, bringing revolt against slavery in the colonies, ideas about natural rights developed in salons, and insights into the economics of empires into constant and sometimes violent contact. Out of this combustible system, Belley and Raynal, together with countless others, reshaped the Atlantic world.

=

TO FULLY DECIPHER THIS PORTRAIT, ONE MUST TURN A FEW YEARS back, to 1793, when another formerly enslaved inhabitant of Saint-Domingue, Toussaint Bréda, decided to change his name. He would keep his given name, Toussaint, a contraction of Tous Saints, All Saints, but he no longer wanted to be called Bréda, which was the name of the plantation on which he had been born. A grandson of Africans abducted from Benin, he had been the property, along with all buildings, livestock, and other enslaved people of African descent, of a French aristocrat, Monsieur de Bréda.[2] Toussaint was almost fifty years old when he changed his name, and he had spent most of those years within the closed world of the Bréda plantation, located on the plains between the mountains and the sea on the northern coast of Saint-Domingue.

Henceforth, he would be known as L'Ouverture (or Louverture), which meant "the opening." The new name may have been a reference to a gap between his teeth or else to his knack for creating openings in battle, but in the end, the opening Toussaint L'Ouverture created was much larger than anything he could have possibly imagined in the spring of 1793: a revolution culminating in an independent state run by formerly enslaved people.[3]

Like most plantations, Bréda included various kinds of livestock and fields dedicated to coffee and vegetables, but most of its cash crop was sugar cane, a labor-intensive plant that required a large workforce. At first, that workforce had been supplied by the native population, whom the Spanish colonists forced into indentured labor.[4] But the inhuman working conditions, along with imported diseases, had decimated their number within two generations in a staggering act of annihilation.[5] To make up for the loss, the Spanish imported people from the western coast of Africa and sold them to plantation owners in need of laborers.[6]

Slavery had existed in other societies, but this form of it was new. Never had such large numbers of people been brought from so far away for the purpose of being brutally exploited as in the Caribbean and throughout the New World. Being a third-generation Saint-Dominguan, like L'Ouverture, was relatively rare because of high mortality rates. Of the enslaved people in Saint-Domingue, 41 percent were born on the island (despite harsh conditions) while the remaining 59 percent had been abducted in Africa.[7] More unusual was his age, since most enslaved people died well before their fifties (only 5 percent passed the age of sixty). The workforce was constantly replenished from Africa, where slave traders traveled further and further inland to capture people and transport them to the coast and then, under brutal conditions, across the Atlantic.[8]

L'Ouverture rose in the hierarchy of the plantation by doing work that required ever greater responsibility, often supervising the work of other enslaved people. In recognition of this, he was given his freedom while he was still in his early thirties. But even after having obtained his freedom he stayed on the plantation, in part because he had been given forty acres on which to grow coffee. He couldn't imagine this enterprise without using enslaved labor himself, so thoroughly did slavery structure the world of Saint-Domingue. The problem could not be solved on an individual basis; it required systemic change. Where would change come from?

Two events had unexpected consequences for this system of slavery. The first occurred just a few hundred miles from Saint-Domingue: the American War of Independence. To be sure, American revolutionaries did not propose to end slavery, since many of them were either owners of enslaved people or profited from their labor indirectly, and the government they formed would protect the interests of the slave-owning class. Instead, the American revolutionaries targeted a specific aspect of the colonial system: the role of taxes. All exports from the colonies were taxed by the home country. Commodities often had to be shipped there first before they could be traded with the rest of the world, yielding rich profits to the homeland. These taxes were imposed by parliaments in the far-away metropoles, without giving colonists political representation. The idea that a colony could rebel against the political system upholding such taxes, declare independence, and win a revolutionary war, as had happened in the thirteen North American colonies, sent shivers down the spines of European powers with colonial interests in the Americas, above all France and Spain. They did not want to lose their precious possessions the way Great Britain had.

The second event was the overthrow of the monarchy in France. Partly inspired by the American Revolution, the rebellion in France turned into a civil war pitting a rising bourgeoisie and urban poor against a system that kept them as second-class citizens, fueled by anti-monarchical and anti-clerical ideas proposed by some of the more radical Enlightenment thinkers and activists. The uprising had begun as a protest against aristocratic grandees who were seen as abusing their political and economic privileges, but it quickly developed its own dynamic, with the urban poor storming the Bastille, the prison that stood for the old order, and radical political clubs and associations attacking the monarchy and demanding new political rights. Initially, the revolt demanded checks on the absolute monarchy, with the hope of returning France to an earlier time when, allegedly, fewer aristocratic abuses of power occurred. To this end, the Roman Republic was held up as an inspiration—as expressed in the Roman-style bust of Raynal in the portrait. But despite this initial return to the past, the revolt ended with demands for an entirely new order. Even the word "revolution" changed its meaning. Originally it had meant a cyclical movement, such as the one performed by the stars (Copernicus had called his 1543 book on astronomy *De Revolutionibus*). Over time, it came to mean the opposite: a break with the old order, the beginning of something entirely new.[9]

How would these two events, the American Revolution and the French Revolution, affect Saint-Domingue? Among the colonists in this rich French possession, there was little talk of independence on the model of the United States, except among poor whites.[10] And most revolutionaries in Paris initially said little about France's overseas possessions except to reaffirm property rights, which included the right to own people. This served not only the interests of large plantation owners such as Count Noé, who had inherited the Bréda plantation from his uncle in 1786, but also those of southern port cities, such as Bordeaux, which had grown rich from the colonies.

And yet, both revolutions brought into question the system of authority and control that had allowed a small population of French people to control a large population of enslaved Africans and people of African descent. The result was a series of rebellions, beginning in 1791, in which L'Ouverture participated. At first, rival powers—especially Great Britain and Spain, which controlled the other part of the island, Santo Domingo (now the Dominican Republic)—armed the rebels and invaded, and L'Ouverture donned a Spanish uniform.[11] But foreign powers quickly lost control over the troops they had armed and trained. L'Ouverture in particular used the training and arms he received to create his own highly effective army-within-the-army.[12] Formerly enslaved people were making their own history.

They did so under the most complex circumstances. Besides enslaved people, the island contained free people of color, who sometimes owned their own plantations; the so-called "small whites," French colonists without major holdings; and finally major plantation owners. (*Créole* was a term used for people born on the island, mostly whites but also some people of mixed race.) As the revolution went on, there were increasing numbers of maroons, enslaved people who had escaped their plantations and formed settlements in the interior.[13]

Each group had its own interests and engaged in its own shifting alliances. In France proper, the situation was no less complicated. Even though the major landlords were French aristocrats whose dominance was now challenged, the bourgeois revolutionaries themselves often profited handsomely from the colonies and had no interest in dismantling the institution of slavery and of colonial exploitation. A small group of revolutionaries, called the "Friends of the Blacks," demanded an expansion of rights of citizenship, but only to include mixed-race free people.

To this complicated web were added international pressure groups pursuing different goals. In Britain, abolitionists demanded the end of slavery, but they looked with horror at the assault on the French monarch.[14] Vocal groups in the New England states and New York also advocated for the abolition of slavery, but were opposed by those who profited from it, both in northern cities and in the Southern states. Spain, staunchly monarchical, abhorred the assault on the monarchy in France but looked for every opportunity to weaken France's grip on its most lucrative colony. All these groups supported various troops on Saint-Domingue, sometimes with money, sometimes with shipments of arms and uniforms, sometimes by landing military advisors, leading to an ever-shifting patchwork of alliances.

L'Ouverture and other leaders quickly realized that they needed more durable allies; siding with the Spanish, who supported the slave economy and monarchy, was against the fundamental values of the rebellion. Meanwhile, the rebellion grew in size and confidence, and it was at this point, in 1793, that L'Ouverture chose to shed his old identity and name, a product of the plantation system, and to seek a new opening.

To mark this new identity, he issued an appeal:

Brothers and Friends. I am Toussaint L'Ouverture, my name is perhaps known to you. I have undertaken vengeance. I want liberty and equality to reign in Saint-Domingue. I work to bring them into existence. Unite yourselves to us, brothers, and fight with us for the same cause etc. Your very humble and obedient servant. TOUSSAINT L'OUVERTURE, General of the Armies of the King, for the Public Good.[15]

Vengeance was something L'Ouverture had spoken of from the beginning, but the language of liberty and equality was new. He needed to walk a fine line. By styling himself a "general" working in the "armies of the King," he signaled that he did not intend to throw over the monarchy or his relation to France, but by referring to "liberty," "equality," and the "public good" he used a term common among the French Jacobins to articulate his own ambitions. It aligned him with the Enlightenment.

The new language of the Enlightenment had been audible, above all, in the American Declaration of Independence (1776) and the French Universal Declaration of the Rights of Man and of the Citizen (1789), which had used the language of natural rights, applicable to everyone, universally. No more special privileges. These ideas had not been, in any simple sense, the cause of the two revolutions. Rather, they had been used to justify, explain, and understand events as they were happening.

Like actions, ideas often have unintended, or only dimly perceived, consequences, and the idea of natural rights was one of them. Few of the signatories of the Declaration of Independence were thinking that the new language of natural rights would apply to women and enslaved people. The framers didn't have to be explicit about these exceptions. They were not regarded as exceptions to a rule; they were understood as natural omissions that went without saying. Slavery, like patriarchy, was a fact of life, part of the social and economic system that had enriched France and the thirteen North American colonies. Everyone knew that.

But ideas such as "Men are born and remain free and equal in rights," the first sentence of the Universal Declaration, and "We hold these truths to be self-evident, that all men are created equal," as stated in the Declaration of Independence, can develop a dynamic of their own, overshoot their target, and be seized for new purposes. This happened because the declarations were heard not only by people who knew, without it having to be said, that women and enslaved people were clearly not included, but also by people such as L'Ouverture who applied them to themselves.

The consequences of these actions and ideas culminated half a year after L'Ouverture changed his name. On February 4, 1794, or rather, on the 16th of Pluviôse, Year II—revolutionary France had changed its calendar, several times in fact, declaring 1792 year one of the revolution, and renaming the months—three delegates from Saint-Domingue appeared before the Revolutionary Convention and were quickly admitted as members of the Convention.[16] One was Jean-Baptiste Mills, a free person of mixed race; the second was Louis-Pierre Dufaÿ, a white French colonist; and the third was the man in the portrait with which this chapter began, Jean-Baptiste Belley.

Belley's biography in some ways resembles that of L'Ouverture. According to his own account, he was born on Gorée, an island off the coast of Senegal, was brought to Saint-Domingue as an enslaved worker, and managed to buy his freedom, perhaps through skills which later supported him as a wigmaker.[17] He first entered a military unit composed of formerly enslaved people and participated in attacks on Savannah, Georgia, in 1779, where he was wounded and was distinguished for bravery, earning him the honorific "Mars." After leaving the military, he returned to his profession as wigmaker, becoming a respected member of the community of freedmen and freedwomen. Like L'Ouverture, Belley purchased and sold a number of enslaved workers.[18]

Though not an active, military revolutionary like L'Ouverture,

Belley was chosen as a delegate to the Revolutionary Convention. In many ways he was the perfect representative: he was someone who had experienced slavery; he had himself possessed a number of enslaved people; and he was eager to abolish the entire system of slavery as practiced in the New World.

On the 16th of Pluviôse, he stood before the Revolutionary Convention as the first Black delegate. His arrival was loudly applauded. Dufaÿ, his white colleague, delivered a speech appealing to the self-interest of revolutionary France, exhorting it to do what had hitherto been unthinkable to most: declare the enslaved people of Saint-Domingue free. The British, Dufaÿ pointed out, were planning an attack on Saint-Domingue. Then another delegate, Levasseur of Sarthe, proposed the abolition of slavery in the colonies. Another, Lacroix, declared: "President, don't allow the Convention to dishonor itself by a longer discussion."[19] Instead, a motion should be passed by acclamation. The motion read: "The National Convention declares slavery abolished in all the colonies. In consequence it decrees that all men, without distinction of color, domiciled in the colonies, are French citizens and enjoy all the rights assured under the constitution."[20] The assembly stood up in agreement, as the meeting protocol notes, and the "president proclaims the abolition of slavery, amid applause and thousands of repeated cries of Long live the Republic! Long live the convention!"[21] There was no direct connection between L'Ouverture and Belley, who had even been on opposite sides for a time, but their actions and ideas had forced the French colonizers to capitulate.

Where did the ideas claimed and elaborated by L'Ouverture and Belley, and now resounding in the Convention, originate? The answer to this question leads us back to the bust against which Belley is leaning in Girodet's portrait, the Roman-style bust bearing the inscription of T. Raynal.

PARIS, 1755

If you were in Paris and in search of new ideas and the people who held them in the 1750s, the best address was 372 rue Saint-Honoré. Of course, you couldn't just show up and ring the bell. You needed an invitation because the person who resided at that address was Madame Geoffrin, otherwise known as the Queen of Saint-Honoré. Her salon welcomed starving (and non-starving) artists, foreign nobility, diplomats, musicians, philosophers, and anyone who was chasing the latest gossip or the latest idea. Monday dinners were reserved for artists and were therefore less formal; the main gathering happened on Wednesdays, when writers, philosophers, and other purveyors of ideas enjoyed a lavish dinner and readings.[22] The painter Anicet Charles Gabriel Lemonnier captured a memorable evening of the year 1755, depicting some fifty men and women, elegantly attired, gathered in a room lined with paintings, and listening to a reading of a tragedy by the polemical writer and Enlightenment thinker who had chosen the pen name of Voltaire.

In eighteenth-century Paris, salons were a well-established institution. They were invariably centered on a woman with the financial resources and social connections to gather around her a group of regulars from different walks of life. Usually, it was important to decide which salon to belong to; hopping from salon to salon was frowned upon. Each was its own small universe, and the salons competed with one another.[23] If a prominent member moved from one salon to another, it caused a small scandal. Of all the salons, Madame Geoffrin's was the most interesting.

No one would have predicted that Madame Geoffrin would rise to preside over a salon, let alone a prominent one. She was born into a bourgeois family; her father enjoyed a court appointment as *valet de chambre* and her mother came from a banking family, but they did not make the education of their daughter a priority. Young Marie Thérèse

Anicet Charles Gabriel Lemmonier, *Reading of Voltaire's Tragedy of the Orphan of China in the Salon of Marie Thérèse Rodet Geoffrin in 1755*, c. 1812.

(CHÂTEAU DE MALMAISON, FRANCE)

was primarily brought up by her grandmother, with whom she went to live at the age of seven. The lack of formal schooling would haunt her for the rest of her life, leaving her, the future *salonnière*, with an uncertain grasp of French grammar and spelling. At the age of thirteen, her schooling ended abruptly when her parents arranged her marriage to a fifty-year-old businessman. The marriage was consummated on Maire Thérèse's fourteenth birthday.[24]

Without the benefit of higher education, the newly minted Madame Geoffrin made up for it with determination. Her husband kept a tight grip on finances, despite a flourishing business in Venetian glass whose clients included the court. But she knew what she wanted. She was inducted into the art of keeping a salon by an older *salonnière*, Madame de Tencin, the mother of the philosopher Jean d'Alembert.

Two deaths, in quick succession, paved the way for the realization of Madame Geoffrin's ambitions. One was the death of her husband, which allowed Madame Geoffrin to gain control over her finances. For the rest of her life, she would take an active part in the business of being a purveyor of glass to the royal court, which included connections to bankers in Geneva. Madame Geoffrin became, among many other things, a businesswoman, although she would not have used that term.[25]

The other death was that of Madame de Tencin, who had taught Madame Geoffrin how to build and maintain a salon. Geoffrin made sure she inherited Tencin's A-list clientele. Her goal was to create, in eighteenth-century Paris, gatherings similar to the scene in a Renaissance painting she happened to own a copy of: Raphael's *The School of Athens*, which depicted the self-understanding of the Italian Renaissance as the rebirth of ancient Greece.[26]

She threw herself into the work. In her hands, a salon became more than a mere gathering place or a biweekly dinner party; it became what we today would call an incubator of new ideas. Geoffrin built a network of connections and promoted those who had the privilege of being under her patronage. She bought paintings from artists who needed income, and attended, each year, the exhibition of new paintings at the Louvre, to keep up with the latest developments. In music, she followed the debate between French versus Italian music, and hosted Wolfgang Amadeus Mozart when he came to Paris.[27]

Members of Madame Geoffrin's salon insisted on being guided by reason rather than established authority. This meant that they challenged the opinions of formerly revered ancient philosophers, the Catholic Church, and any other institution that asserted its beliefs in forms other than reasoned argument. Among those at the forefront of this movement were freethinking philosophers such as Madame de Tencin's son, d'Alembert.[28] Voltaire, the most biting of these writers, had attended Geoffrin's dinners before the days of the salon and followed her doings with interest from Prussia, where he was attempting to turn King Frederick into an enlightened philosopher-king (with mixed results). Even though Madame Geoffrin herself did not seek the limelight and harbored a conservative outlook, she had somehow managed to cultivate the most radical thinkers of her time. Her salon became known as the "fortress of free thought."[29]

The work that summed up the world view of the Enlightenment was the *Encyclopédie*, which aimed to gather all knowledge accumulated by humanity as long as it was seen in light of reason. Denis Diderot and Jean d'Alembert were the minds behind this massive undertaking, which would eventually fill seventeen volumes. Despite its size and comprehensive nature, it was the most recent attempt at a *summa*, such as those composed by philosophers in the Storehouse of Wisdom or, later, the Christian Middle Ages. But in addition to serving as a gathering of knowledge, it was also a rallying cry for the Enlightenment and came to be called, half-jokingly, "a manifesto in seventeen volumes."

While short manifestos were cheap, a seventeen-volume collection of all true knowledge was not. The *Encyclopédie* was significantly supported by Madame Geoffrin, to the tune of 100,000 livres; without her funding, this massive undertaking, which captured the spirit of the age like no other, might never have been realized.[30] Among those in the know, her support led to yet another name for 372 rue Saint-Honoré, *le bureau d'esprit*—the office of the intelligentsia—with the implication that Madame Geoffrin was its president.

The attacks on established authority, inevitably, created a backlash. Enlightenment thinkers attracted the ire of the Jesuits, the influential order which saw itself as the intellectual defense force of the Church. Even Madame Geoffrin, though she operated behind the scenes, did not escape entirely unscathed and was spoofed in a play. (A good number of philosophers, beginning with Socrates, have been mocked in plays.)[31]

While d'Alembert and the *Encyclopédie* captured the limelight, another member of Geoffrin's salon directed Enlightenment ideas against a different enemy: European colonialism. He was the model for the pale bust in the portrait of Jean-Baptiste Belley, and his full name was Guillaume Thomas François Raynal.

To be sure, Raynal shared the Enlightenment hatred of religion, which to him meant unfounded authority, an outdated world view, superstition, and a life without reason, leading necessarily to fanaticism. Raynal had been educated by Jesuit priests and even ordained, which meant that he would never miss an opportunity to attack the Catholic Church in general and Jesuits in particular. He was almost as scathing about the priests of other religions, reserving his particular ire for Buddhism: "of all fanaticisms," Raynal writes, using fanaticism as a synonym for religion, "it is the most terrible."[32]

Raynal's main interest, however, was not in attacking the Catholic Church but in analyzing the enormous colonial possessions Europeans had acquired over the past centuries. In a sweeping four-volume book, he provided his readers with an economic analysis of the history of colonialism. He began with the Portuguese rounding of the Cape of Good Hope and the lucrative trade with India. From there, he surveyed India and China, where he praised the system of imperial examination and attacked Buddhism, with sidelong glances at the cultural relations between India and Greece in the ancient world (including those earlier discussed in this book). Having surveyed the East, Raynal moves west, to the moment when Spanish explorers make contact with the Americas. He relates Cortés's conquest of Tenochtitlan and the brutal suppression of the native population that resulted from it, including the shocking depopulation of the Americas. He did not know the extent to which this was due to smallpox, and attributed it, not incorrectly, to what he called "slow tyranny," the systematic and brutal subjection of the Indigenous population.[33]

Depopulation sets the stage for Raynal's main topic: slavery. Raynal describes in unflinching terms how European colonists made up for the depopulation they had caused by importing enslaved people from Africa. Africans were captured, or bought, and then forced onto the feared Middle Passage across the Atlantic Ocean in such inhuman conditions that more than 20 percent perished.[34] As a Frenchman, Raynal focuses his ire on his country's overseas possessions in both India and the West Indies, hence the title of his work: *Philosophical and Political History of the Two Indies* (1770).

Even though the work describes itself as a philosophical and political history, the engine of Raynal's analysis is something else: commerce. Like a true Enlightenment philosopher, he dismisses the ancient philosophers. They were happy to give long rhetorical speeches on the nature of the world, but for a modern philosopher, something else was needed. Raynal called it "experimental" philosophy, by which he meant what we would call science, a body of knowledge that rests on evidence.[35] It was philosophy in the sense that the *Encyclopédie* was devoted to, and Raynal fully approved of this undertaking. Experimental philosophy could mean what we would describe as the natural sciences, such as Benjamin Franklin's celebrated experiments with electricity (Franklin also stopped by Madame Geoffrin's address while in France and exchanged arguments with Raynal, since the Frenchman had misunderstood one of his texts). But in the case of Raynal, the historian of European colonialism, experimental philosophy meant an analysis of economic relations.

Raynal had realized that a new commercial era defined the world. The sea route from Portugal to India, and the contact between Europe and the Americas, had forced more and more parts of the world into an increasingly integrated trade network: commerce was what made this modern world go round, driven by the European companies at the forefront of colonial exploitation. This meant that the philosopher hoping to explain it would have to be an economist, or what Raynal decided to call a "commercial philosopher."[36] European colonialism, he realized, was deeply woven into the fabric of capitalism.

Raynal was no friend of slavery. Like a number of other Enlightenment thinkers, he saw it as an institution that went against nature.

But as a commercial philosopher, he did something more: he analyzed the commercial system of exploitation on which the entire colonial enterprise rested. He didn't just say that colonialism was brutal. He explained how it worked, who profited from it, and how those profits were realized. In analyzing slavery, he followed the money.

It was this latter feature that made his book such a powerful weapon: it explained the economic roots of the entire system and justified revolt against it. This feat turned him into a celebrated member of Madame Geoffrin's Enlightenment salon. It also set him apart from its other members. True, Diderot had included a scathing attack on slavery in his *Encyclopédie*. But that attack was couched in terms of natural rights, the language of the later Declaration of Independence and the Universal Declaration of the Rights of Man. That language was useful as far as it went, but it lacked the punch of Raynal's economic analysis, which brought the system of colonialism home, showing how France profited from the violence perpetrated in far-flung places such as western Africa and the West Indies.

The debates raging in Madame Geoffrin's salon highlighted the ambiguities of the Enlightenment. Abstract ideas such as questioning authority and invoking natural rights could be used by those, such as the framers of the American Constitution, who wanted to maintain slavery as part of a compromise with the southern states, just as they could be used by the many delegates to the French National Convention who wanted to maintain the country's colonial possessions. Sometimes, Enlightenment ideas could even be used to justify colonialism and other expansionist activities by such countries as Great Britain or France with the argument that less enlightened countries or populations needed to be forcibly rid of their hidebound ideas, or "fanaticisms." At the same time, Enlightenment ideas could also be used against those maintaining colonialism or oppression. As a tool of liberation, the Enlightenment could provide a powerful critique of slavery, one quite effective alongside other critiques based on emotional or, in the language of the time, "sentimental," evocations of suffering victims.

The recently freed Toussaint Bréda, still bearing the name of the plantation on which he had lived all his life, also read Raynal's book. (It was relatively unusual for an enslaved person to know how to read and write. L'Ouverture had learned it from his godfather, Pierre Baptiste, a free man who also worked on the Bréda plantation.) Needless to say, L'Ouverture knew about the brutality of the Middle Passage from fellow enslaved people and about the dehumanizing conditions prevailing on the plantations of Saint-Domingue from his own experience. But Raynal showed how deeply slavery was woven into the economic system that tied Saint-Domingue to France. Raynal could explain why even a freedman such as L'Ouverture would feel the need to employ enslaved people to work the fields given to him upon his emancipation.

From this perspective, slavery was brutal not simply because overseers and landlords were inhuman. It was brutal because an entire economic system was based on the exploitation of a group of people, which meant that everybody was somehow entangled in it and therefore dependent on it: not just plantation owners but also former freedmen, mixed-race free people, French colonists who didn't themselves own plantations, the bourgeoisie of Bordeaux and Paris, all the way up to the king. This system of profiteers also explained why the slave rebellion on Saint-Domingue was so complicated, with different groups on the island forming various pacts and temporary alliances.[37]

Above all, Raynal illustrated the way in which the salon of Madame Geoffrin and the rebel camp of Toussaint L'Ouverture were connected, something also captured in Girodet's painting of Belley leaning against a bust of Raynal.

=

THE ABOLITION OF SLAVERY IN SAINT-DOMINGUE WAS PROPOSED and adopted, without a debate, in the National Convention of France in

1794. It took more than just philosophy; it also took self-interest. Cunningly, radical Republicans and revolutionaries from Saint-Domingue had pointed out to the delegates that abolition would allow the arming of formerly enslaved people against possible incursions by the British or Spanish. It was an alliance of convenience as much as one based on lofty ideas.

Meanwhile, back in Saint-Domingue, L'Ouverture continued to consolidate power against the many other interests at work on the island, including plantation owners and an army of mixed-race forces, sometimes supported by weapons shipped from abroad, which had aligned against the people they considered slaves. He acquired arms, trained soldiers, and built a proper military force. He was gaining a better grip on the colony, though he was never quite its undisputed ruler.

While L'Ouverture maintained the initiative on the island, things were changing rapidly in revolutionary France, where a brash young general by the name of Napoleon Bonaparte planned to model himself on Alexander the Great. He managed to outmaneuver the warring revolutionary factions by declaring himself First Consul of the Republic.

In the colonies, as in France, Napoleon didn't seek to undo the revolution entirely, but among the revolutionary ideas he deemed too disruptive for his purposes was the abolition of slavery.[38] He sent a large force to Saint-Domingue to retake control, but yellow fever decimated his soldiers and denied him the quick victory he was hoping for. When a quick military solution proved elusive, Napoleon tried diplomacy and offered L'Ouverture safe passage to France. L'Ouverture accepted, but Napoleon didn't honor his end of the bargain and arrested L'Ouverture, who died in 1803 while imprisoned in Fort de Joux in eastern France.[39]

Belley suffered a similar fate. After his moment at the National Convention, he returned to Saint-Domingue to take up another military post, as an officer in the gendarmerie. For reasons that are unclear, he, too, found himself transported to France and imprisoned in 1802. He died in prison, abandoned and forgotten, two years after L'Ouverture, in 1805. By that time, Napoleon had revoked the abolition of slavery. Everything L'Ouverture and Belley had fought for seemed to have failed.

But Napoleon, victorious in countless battles and against many states, had miscalculated. What L'Ouverture and Belley had begun could not be undone. Jean-Jacques Dessalines, a former enslaved person whom L'Ouverture had cultivated and appointed a high-ranking general, defeated Napoleon's forces. In 1804, the year Napoleon crowned himself Emperor of France, Dessalines declared Saint-Domingue an independent republic and named it Haiti. An initial draft of the declaration was partially inspired by the American Declaration of Independence, but the final version focused on brutal actions of French colonizers and the history of racism.[40] In the unequal fight between L'Ouverture and Napoleon, L'Ouverture prevailed from beyond the grave, earning himself the soubriquet "the Black Napoleon."

L'Ouverture's success struck fear in the hearts of colonists everywhere, and they hit back with sanctions and threats, hoping to show that a state governed by formerly enslaved people from Africa could not prevail. Haiti had to fight for its survival, surrounded by imperial powers who wanted to keep it down.

The Haitian revolution was long ignored as a major event in world history, its example sidelined in the standard histories of the revolutionary era, which focused on America and France. There were notable exceptions to this rule. In the nineteenth century, the African American writer William Wells Brown included Toussaint L'Ouverture in a series of biographical sketches, and social reformer and abolitionist Frederick Douglass spoke admiringly of him.[41] Another admirer was Marcus Garvey, who would turn to the Ethiopian epic *Kebra Nagast* to lay claim to the legacy of Africa's ancient civilizations, and who protested the occupation of Haiti by the United States between 1915 and 1934.

In 1938 the Caribbean historian C. L. R. James wrote *Black Jaco-bins*, which gave Toussaint L'Ouverture the central place in the history of independence and revolution he deserved. James wrote his book during the rise of fascism in Europe, when many parts of Europe's colonial empires were still in place. He predicted, correctly, that Africa would soon cast off its colonial overlords: "Africa awakes now as Toussaint did then."[42]

For too long, Saint-Domingue has been regarded as peripheral to the Enlightenment. This is a great mistake, because there is no place that better reveals the force, but also the ambiguities, of Enlightenment ideas. Above all, Saint-Domingue demonstrates that ideas don't change the world by themselves; they must be seized by individuals who understand them according to their own needs and who use them for their own ends. The philosopher G. W. F. Hegel once described Napoleon as the embodiment of the spirit of the time: history on horseback. The phrase is apt, for Napoleon did redraw the map of Europe. But L'Ouverture would have been the better example: astride his horse, he showed that slavery could be abolished and thereby redrew the map of the entire world.

CHAPTER 13

GEORGE ELIOT PROMOTES THE SCIENCE OF THE PAST

I t was during her honeymoon, in Rome, that Dorothea Brooke began
to have doubts about her marriage to Edward Casaubon. While she
was touring the city, exploring its ruins and feeling the layers of its past,
Casaubon spent most of his time in the Vatican Library.[1] He, too, was
immersed in the past, but he was pursuing it with a particular idea in
mind: finding the key to all mythologies.[2] The project sounded gran-
diose, but what better time to undertake it than now, in the middle of
the nineteenth century, when empires and world-spanning commerce
had drawn the world closer together, and when all kinds of mythologies had been recorded, ready to be scrutinized? There was certainly
no better place to find such a key than in the Vatican Library, where
the Catholic Church had collected not only its own history but also
books from other cultures that had been stolen and brought back by
missionaries, adventurers, and colonists (including Aztec codices).

Casaubon's scholarship, his dedication to ideas, was why Dorothea
Brooke had married him. She had imagined herself as his student and
assistant, becoming part of this exciting grand project. How much
would she learn in the process and how much might she be able to
contribute? Casaubon was unworldly and clearly needed her. But now,

during the honeymoon, she was beginning to wonder whether her plan of putting his notes in order and of presenting the results to the learned world in triumph would ever come to pass, whether her husband would ever find the key to all mythologies.

These fictional events and worries are part of Mary Ann Evans's masterwork, *Middlemarch* (1871), which she published under the name of George Eliot. In the novel, Dorothea's doubts about her husband and his scholarship continue to grow. Before long, it becomes clear that Casaubon is morally limited, rigid and coldhearted, and ultimately seeks to control Dorothea beyond his own death by drawing up a will that curtails her freedom. In the last paragraph of the novel, the narrator suggests that Dorothea clearly should not have married him.[3]

Eliot's own relationship was a great deal more unconventional than Dorothea's marriage: her romantic partner was the critic George Henry Lewes, who was married with three children but was separated from his family. Despite his wife's refusal to grant him a divorce, Lewes and Eliot decided to live openly together, in violation of Victorian social norms. This way of life meant a loss of social status for both, but especially for Eliot, given that Victorian society was more censorious of women than men. The censure provoked by this relationship induced Eliot to assume her pen name, since the scandal of her private life would hurt the public reception of her books.[4] But while the relationship with Lewes brought great difficulty to Eliot, it also brought her great support.

Eliot depicted Casaubon negatively not only because of his retrograde attitude toward marriage but also because of his retrograde attitude toward the past. She named Casaubon after Isaac Casaubon (1559–1614), one of the most celebrated classical scholars of the English Renaissance. The historical Casaubon was a forceful proponent of the new science of philology, which he applied to a mysterious group of writings called *Corpus Hermeticum*, a wide-ranging assembly of wisdom texts seemingly drawing on Egyptian knowledge.[5] The *Corpus* had created a craze for ancient Egypt and was thought to be of great antiquity, but the historical Casaubon showed that it was of a much later date, having been composed in the first centuries of the Common Era. This was precisely the kind of humanist scholarship that the priest Lorenzo Valla had pioneered by showing through close critical examination of its language that the Donation of Constantine, carefully preserved in the Vatican Library, was a forgery.[6] Why would Eliot use Casaubon's name for her negative portrayal of a nineteenth-century philologist looking for the key to all mythologies?

For Eliot, the problem with the fictional nineteenth-century Casaubon was not his interest in the past; it was that his search for a single key to all mythologies was based on the wrong methods. Nineteenth-century Britain was experiencing an enormous boom in the past. Along with wealthy Europeans and Americans, British collectors brought large numbers of art objects, precious artifacts, texts, and even parts of entire buildings. To be sure, elite individuals in many parts of the world had been collecting objects forever, transporting one of Ashoka's pillars to Delhi, a South Asian statuette to Pompeii, and pre-Aztec objects to Tenochtitlan. But in the nineteenth century, the collection of remnants of the past accelerated, and was increasingly concentrated in European capitals. The past was becoming a prestige project, a popular pastime, a national obsession, and big business.

The recovery of the past was infused with colonialism, as was made clear when Napoleon invaded Egypt in the late eighteenth century and brought along scholars eager to explore its famous ruins and transport treasures home to Europe. One of these treasures was the Rosetta Stone, which enabled the humanist Jean-François Champollion to decipher the script that had been illegible for two thousand years. This feat allowed a completely different kind of access to ancient Egypt than the dubious *Corpus Hermeticum* studied by the historical Casaubon. Similarly out for loot was Lord Elgin, who removed half of the sculptures on the Parthenon and brought them to London, where they remain to this day, to the continuing consternation of Greece. (Recently, the Greek government built a museum for the remaining friezes right underneath the temple, with empty spaces for the ones abducted to London as a permanent plea to return them to where they belong.)

Eliot was writing *Middlemarch* at a time when new discoveries about Greek antiquity were making headlines, most spectacularly so when the German-American con man and amateur archeologist Heinrich Schliemann thought he had discovered the historical Troy described in the *Iliad*. Schliemann was not a trained archeologist because archeology as a discipline was just in the process of coming into its own, and he destroyed much of this ancient site by digging what archeologists now call, dismissively, the Schliemann trench. Despite his mistakes, he not only discovered different epochs of Troy but also established the principle of labeling layers of the past by identifying nine distinct strata.[7]

Meanwhile, agents of the British East India Company, the vast private company that held the monopoly for exploiting South Asian trade and ended up controlling most of the subcontinent, had become interested in the culture they controlled. They, too, brought back stolen treasures, including manuscripts.[8] In 1801, the East India Company opened an East India Museum in its offices on Leadenhall Street in London.[9] Agents working for or associated with the company translated many documents into English for the first time, while drawing on knowledge from South Asian scholars. It was here that the Brahmi script was deciphered, thus enabling people to read Ashoka's pillars once again. A few decades after the publication of *Middlemarch*, archeology had become a true science and was put into action by Mohammed es-Senussi, who was working for a Prussian expedition when he carefully unearthed the extraordinary bust of Nefertiti, only to see her transported to Berlin, where she remains to this day.

Europeans also changed how the past was represented by organizing their holdings to give visitors a sense of historical progression. Previously, collections—sometimes called cabinets of curiosities—had been arranged according to the whims of their owners. The new collections, by contrast, had a firm idea of how the past should be organized: not based on curiousness but on ideas about world civilizations and artistic excellence. To mark this change, collections also acquired a new name and were henceforth called museums, derived from the Greek word for "place of the Muses," the patron deities of the arts.[10]

The idea of organizing the past according to a conception of how art progresses may seem obvious to us now, even though we would question many of the particular ideas prevalent in the nineteenth century about what counted as high art or as a civilization, and how to categorize particular artifacts (often according to provincial European conceptions). Like all ideas, the sense that history proceeds along a single axis of evolutionary progress had to be invented, and it was fully established only in the eighteenth and nineteenth centuries.[11] To be sure, ancient chronicles had also organized information along a single timeline in genealogies of gods or kings—such as the Egyptian list of monarchs from which Nefertiti's name was erased. But these chronicles didn't suggest that history was progressing and evolving in important and fundamental ways. Other conceptions of time had humanity depart in successive stages from a golden age to a silver and then on to lesser metals such as bronze (the Greek poet Hesiod used those terms), but this decline was explained by moral failings. In yet another group of accounts, including Jewish, Christian, and Muslim scriptures, a golden age had been lost but could be regained on Judgment Day. In none of these accounts was change driven by the work of history itself or of historical forces.

The idea of progressive history was the result of a society that believed itself to be irrevocably moving forward, whether that meant politically through emancipation and democratization, technologically through ever more powerful machines, or materially because more goods were becoming available to more people. This bundle of progressions didn't occur everywhere. It coalesced most powerfully in nineteenth-century Britain, whose inhabitants, or at least those who shaped public opinion, saw themselves on a trajectory of political emancipation, technical innovation (exemplified by the steam engine), and the accumulation of wealth extracted from its colonial possessions.

The feeling that things were progressing in many different domains at once had an unexpected consequence: people were rapidly moving away from the past, not just in the trivial sense that one year was followed by the next, but qualitatively, by changing in ways that made the past more and more alien. There was a new recognition that things were subject to transformation, that new circumstances were changing people, their lives and experiences, and therefore their thoughts and feelings. These weren't random transformations. Change had been experienced by people living in all kinds of circumstances. What mattered was that the change was now seen as going only in one direction: forward. As a consequence, the past was receding and dwindling not only because buildings might get destroyed and manuscripts lost, but also because the movement forward meant that more and more distance was put between the present and the past. With each day, it became more difficult to recover and understand what was slipping away. In this situation, museums became a way back, a time capsule that allowed visitors to move against the flow of time, if only for a moment.

In order to preserve fragments of the past, it was not enough to recover objects and arrange them chronologically. Modern assumptions about what people thought and felt, how they lived, and what they believed in no longer applied to a past now understood to have been substantially different from the present. The past, in all its difference, needed to be carefully deciphered and reconstructed, like a text written in an ancient language. Philology, with its techniques of dating texts, provided one model, and science provided another—a model for subjecting ideas about the past to scrutiny, for testing hypotheses and meeting ideas with skepticism and rigorous, evidence-based study. The new science of the past was called historiography.

Nineteenth-century historians had many older models to consider and learn from. Much of the information in this book comes from the writings of past chroniclers, travel writers, bibliographers, and collectors, all of whom were interested in sources and other forms of evidence: from Egyptian priests, Greek writers such as Thucydides, scholars working at the Baghdad Storehouse of Wisdom, to all those who preserved and transmitted stories orally. But only now was writing about the past subject to a specific protocol of testing hypotheses, assembling evidence, and weighing counterevidence backed up by a conception of historical change, which is why it took until the nineteenth century for a historian to declare that the point of history was "to uncover the nature of past experience."

While some historians emphasized new methods, others focused on narrative, none more so than the British aristocrat Thomas Babington Macaulay. Macaulay exemplified the new focus on social and local history, painting a picture of events moving inexorably forward toward greater liberty and prosperity. This conception of progress was inflected by geography, especially his experience as a colonial administrator in India. For Macaulay, the forward thrust of history culminated in a particular place, Victorian England, while other places, such as the colonies, were backward and therefore in need of modernization. To aid in the so-called civilizing mission of European colonists, an idea used to prop up the brutalities of colonialism, he instituted an educational system in India focused on English literature and history as well as a new penal code.[12] (He also published a collection of narrative poems about ancient Rome to inspire his British readers in the creation of a new empire.)[13] His two careers, as historian and colonial administrator, are a reminder that the new science of the past was entangled with colonial exploitation and with deeply flawed ideas of who was progressing and who wasn't.[14]

Macaulay contributed to the lopsided exchange that was typical of the nineteenth century: while colonial officers dug up archeological sites, purchased manuscripts, and translated literary texts from the cultures they had colonized, thereby importing non-European culture and showcasing it in European museums, they also exported British history and literature to the colonies. This didn't mean they could always control what happened to their exports. (As if in answer to the India Museum constructed by the East India Company, Indian noblemen started to build up collections of Western art.[15]) The science of the past did not mean that historians became more objective—Macaulay knew what kind of history he wanted to write before he considered the evidence, hence the dominance, in his case, of narrative over method. But it meant that he felt nevertheless compelled to marshal evidence, data, and documents in support of his progressive history. Later, these same tools would be used to dismantle the kinds of narratives he spun from his assortment of facts.

The new science of history had other consequences. While objects were carefully preserved in museums, ruins were now left untouched and admired *as ruins*. This attitude, so familiar to us, was both novel and counterintuitive. Why, if you cared about an old building, would you not rebuild it so that it looked like it did when it was first erected? Why should a vase or painting that had suffered damage not be repaired to look as new as possible? The science of the past dictated that the past remain unreconstructed, imperfect, left alone. Ruins were no longer seen as eyesores but as almost magical lessons from the past that should be admired as such, learned from, and left untouched. Inevitably, a cult of the original emerged, which served to dismiss copies of famous paintings and sculptures. Earlier collectors had prided themselves on such possessions—Madame Geoffrin with her copy of Raphael's *The School of Athens* among them—but suddenly such copies were seen as shallow, devoid of precisely the patina of age and antiquity that made actual ruins and art objects worthy of reverence, and priceless (or, in any case, very expensive).

=

GEORGE ELIOT WAS AT THE FOREFRONT OF THE NEW SCIENCE OF the past, a surprising position to achieve for the daughter of an estate agent. But Mary Ann Evans was lucky in that she received more education than was typical for a woman of her class, at two boarding schools. Even so, instruction at those schools was constrained by evangelical Christianity. Not content with these limitations, the intellectually curious Mary Ann supplemented her education with more wide-ranging reading, some of which she found in the grand library of the estate administered by her father, and with the study of languages, including German.

When her mother died and her brother took over the family home, her father moved to the city of Coventry, taking Mary Ann with him. There, she befriended an intellectually curious group of people who favored intellectual independence from narrow forms of Christianity. Through them, she learned about modern, progressive thinkers such as Herbert Spencer, who distilled the sense of progress in political, technical, and economic matters, drawing heavily on the new ideas of evolution developed by Charles Darwin.[16]

Eliot not only absorbed these new ideas of progress, she also made them her own. Her first significant published work was a translation of an important contribution to the new freethinking, progressive science of history: David Strauss's *Das Leben Jesu, kritisch bearbeitet* (1835), which she rendered as *The Life of Jesus, critically examined.*[17] A significant portion of the new science of the past was being developed in Germany, and Strauss was at its radical edge.[18] Uncovering how people in ancient Rome or Baghdad lived and what they really thought was one thing; applying the same principle to the life of Jesus, quite another.

The life of Jesus had already been written by the Evangelists, it was holy scripture, but Strauss proposed to write the life of Jesus based on historical evidence and to "examine it critically"—not to find fault with Jesus or his teachings, but to signal that Jesus was a historical figure who had lived in a particular place and time. Being "critical" meant writing history according to the science of the past.

Unsurprisingly, the work met with fierce resistance, both in its original German and in its English translation, which was published in 1846. The Earl of Shaftesbury is said to have called it "the most pestilential book ever vomited out of the jaws of hell."

Eliot, who published this and other works under her original name, also translated a work by an even more radical thinker, if such a thing were possible: the German philosopher who would become a major influence on Karl Marx, Ludwig Feuerbach. Feuerbach distilled the new science of the past, with its emphasis on actual sources and evidence, into what he called materialism, the belief that historically specific circumstances shape people's ideas. This may seem an innocuous enough approach, but Feuerbach added that this was all there was to it, that there was nothing else, no other source of human imagination or thought. Humans, shaped by their historically bound lives, created social roles, philosophies, and art. His most pithy formulation, one that riled up all the Earls of Shaftesbury of the world, was: "Man created God after his own image."[19]

Feuerbach did not invent this kind of radical historical thinking alone. He drew heavily on the difficult but influential work of G. W. F. Hegel, whose philosophy roamed widely in world history and who imagined philosophy as the owl of Minerva flying across vast expanses of time and space. Hitherto philosophy had been primarily concerned with uncovering truths, abstract principles such as those sketched by Aristotle and elaborated by Ibn Sina. While it had always been clear that different philosophers had come up with different ideas at different times, the point of studying them was to see whether any of their ideas could be used as jumping-off points for gaining a comprehensive view of the world, for example through a *summa*, a commentary, or a new treatise. Similarly, Enlightenment philosophers such as the ones assembled under the auspices of Madame Geoffrin might reject older philosophers as useless because they were beholden to false pieties and authorities, but they nevertheless continued to read the ancients in case an idea might be found that could be useful in the present.

The new principle Hegel introduced into philosophy was the primacy of historical change. He insisted that philosophy as a discipline had to learn to think historically, by which he meant studying the progression by which thinking had evolved over time. The past should no longer be studied for morsels of truths; it needed to be studied *as the past*. Philosophers would become historians of ideas. (Despite this breakthrough idea, Hegel was not immune to the skewed mindset of many Europeans with respect to the non-European world. He privileged modern European societies as the most advanced, something for which he was later justly criticized.)

Hegel's approach crystallized the debate about what the driving force of progressive history really was. For Hegel, it was ideas. For Feuerbach, it was material circumstances. For Charles Darwin, it was environmental pressures on populations and species.

These new approaches to history were the reason why Eliot, in *Middlemarch*, felt it necessary to ridicule Casaubon for his search for the key to all mythologies. The problem was not Casaubon's study of old manuscripts. It was that he was not conversant with the latest methodological debates, especially those coming out of Germany, in part because he didn't even read German. Like everything else, mythologies had evolved in different ways in different places; they, too, were subject to the grand process of historical change and evolution. The only viable key to all mythologies was that of historical change. Casaubon was simply not up to Eliot's new historicist standards.

≡

THE TRANSLATIONS OF FEUERBACH AND STRAUSS LAUNCHED
Eliot's career, allowing her to move to London and become the editor of the *Westminster Review*, an important journal for new ideas and writing. Finding herself at a turning point in her life, she made two decisions that turned her into the writer we know today: to adopt a pen name, taking George Lewes's first name as her own while picking a simple last name to go with it: George Eliot. The other decision was to write fiction, beginning with her first novel, *Adam Bede*, and culminating in her masterpiece, *Middlemarch*.

As Eliot would have been the first to point out, the novel as a literary genre had itself a history. An important practitioner was Murasaki Shikibu, the eleventh-century author of *The Tale of Genji*. Eliot could not have known *The Tale of Genji* because it hadn't been translated into a Western language, but she would have known other narrative experiments from the distant past. Yet despite its deep and varied roots, the novel became a dominant form of storytelling only with the age of print, leading to such early best-sellers as Cervantes's *Don Quixote*, which was printed and pirated many times and quickly translated into English, in which language it reached Shakespeare, who based a (now lost) play on it.[20] The explosion of print led to rising literacy rates, which in turn increased the demand for books and newspapers, a virtuous cycle that continues to this day, accelerated by the development of the internet and e-books (this is how you may be reading this book).

These developments came to a head in the nineteenth century, when a mass market in literature made it possible for authors to live by their pen. Like other British novelists of the time, Eliot published her novels in installments in newspapers, then collated and republished them as complete books. Bound between hard covers, they could be purchased at a high price, intended for collectors who could afford private libraries, such as the estate on which her father had worked. For those who couldn't afford these expensively bound triple-decker books (three volumes bound together), there had emerged a network of private, for-profit lending libraries. It was through these lending services that most people would get their hands on published books to read at home, often aloud to family or groups of friends.

By turning to novel writing, Eliot was not giving up on her commitment to the new science of history; she merely turned it in a new direction. The novel had something important to contribute to the science of the past that was inaccessible to historians. If the past and its people were receding farther and farther away, this meant that new imaginative powers were needed to conjure it back into the present. Some of those powers were exercised by the new historians and scholars, who (unlike the fictional Casaubon), understood historical change. But the other group were novelists. As long as they used historical research and avoided the trap of thinking all humans were the same across time, novelists could convey to readers *how different* people in the past had actually been.

It was, therefore, no coincidence that the nineteenth century saw the invention of the historical novel as a distinct genre. In Britain, the most successful practitioner was Sir Walter Scott, who introduced his audience to the strangeness of the country's own past, remnants of which survived in remote parts of Scotland. This was another consequence of the new progressive timeline: it didn't move uniformly everywhere. There existed (allegedly) backward regions in the outer reaches of the empire, but also in the lands that English monarchs had colonized earlier, such as Wales, the Scottish Highlands, and parts of Ireland. By studying them, one could get a glimpse of the past, almost as in a museum. Those glimpses had to do with attitudes, life circumstances, and character, but also with language. Scott had studied the history of language and perfected a way of capturing older forms of English and non-standard dialect, allowing his readers to discover the past as a foreign country. Scott's career was a huge success. It turned out that there was a market for the past.

Where there is demand, there will be people to meet it, and the demand for all things Scottish was so high that Scott alone could not satisfy it. Others were eager to jump into the breach, and not only novelists. Particularly active were manufacturers of Scottish kilts, another example of an age-old tradition that was newly *en vogue*. Exactly how old? Actually, not old at all. While there were some traditions of kilts in Ireland, they had not existed in Scotland at all. Scottish kilts became an example of a phenomenon that historians call "invented tradition."[21] (This particular invented tradition also became popular in America through Brooks Brothers and other haberdashers.) Invented traditions satisfy people's desire for historical roots, creating ties to the past, even fictional ones. Humans have always invented their traditions to some extent, including Plato with his history of Atlantis. But during a period when people felt they were moving rapidly away from the past and relentlessly pushed forward by progress, the longing for the comfort of tradition was so intense that, when those traditions didn't exist, there was a large market for making them up from scratch or, more likely, from scraps of other traditions.

By the time Eliot turned to the historical novel, Scott's success had itself drifted into the past and been superseded by novelists whom Eliot considered third-rate, in part because they used only a veneer of history without either studying it or providing their readers with the experience of historical difference. Eliot wanted to return to the true historical novel as pioneered by Scott. But she also wanted her novels to be informed by the new science of the past, including more convincing depictions of people as shaped by their environments, and that meant that the novel should be historical in the Feuerbachian sense.

In a number of influential essays, some published in her own *Westminster Review*, Eliot outlined how she wanted to revolutionize fiction by committing it to respect the historical and material reality of its settings and people—what would come to be called realism. In one particularly harsh essay, entitled "Silly Novels by Lady Novelists," she accused a number of women novelists of using unrealistic dialogue and psychology, as well as being fixated on upper-class segments of society.[22] Their greatest sin was to use the past merely as a backdrop for characters who spoke and felt like contemporaries. Eliot's critique was not confined to these novelists. Everywhere she saw fellow novelists using cookie-cutter characters, clichéd dialogue, and contrived plots, violating both verisimilitude and history. All this had to change. The novel, that most flexible of all forms of storytelling, should be trained on the world. It ought to be suffused with information about people and their material circumstances, the forces that were now understood to be driving historical change.

In order to bring historical research and thinking to the novel, Eliot turned to a new breed of scholars, often working in Germany, who were focused on recovering folk traditions and the life circumstances not of kings and nobles but of servants, peasants, and artisans.[23] Lowly people had rarely received the attention of historians, who had been focused on the actions of kings and queens and the opinions and beliefs of the powerful, since only they were seen as being in a position to steer the course of human events. Now, historians became interested in the agency of all kinds of people from below. One such scholar was Wilhelm Heinrich Riehl, who had painstakingly studied German peasants, with close attention to their habits, their tools, their food, and other aspects of their daily lives.[24] This was the information novelists needed, so Eliot called for an English Riehl to set the course of the English novel right:

> . . . our social novels profess to represent the people as they are, and the unreality of their representations is a grave evil. . . . Art is the nearest thing to life; it is a mode of amplifying experience and extending our contact with our fellow-men beyond the bounds of our personal lot.[25]

This new program was, in many ways, an extension of what Feuerbach and Strauss had done, only now it was applied to fiction.

All of Eliot's novels were set in the past by at least several decades, but only one, *Romola*, was set in the distant past, namely in Renaissance Florence. Eliot wrote it with the intention of rehabilitating the historical novel.[26] *Romola* takes place right after the death of Lorenzo de' Medici, who had gathered some of the most important Renaissance artists and philosophers at his court.[27] When *Romola* begins, this heyday of Renaissance activity is on the decline, attacked by the popular preacher and friar Girolamo Savonarola, who detests the interest in the pagan past and seeks to lead a Christian revival. It is in this larger historical context that Eliot places her main character, the young woman Romola de' Bardi, who helps her humanist father with his work. De' Bardi is meticulous in his work and is in some ways a Casaubon-like figure, though more benign, his efforts on behalf of the past heroic but unrecognized.

Using invented characters to highlight the Renaissance recovery of the past was only part of Eliot's technique. The other was her own research. She hunted down books and sources in libraries and archives in Italian, Greek, French, and Latin, seeking out information on fifteenth-century economics, religion, and details of everyday life, including different dialects. She called her notebooks—full of references, lists, chronologies, and notes—"quarries," a term that dramatized just how far down into layers of history she felt she was digging.[28] The months of research turned into years, during which she also visited Florence to experience streets, buildings, and the hills surrounding the city at first hand. Lewes grew worried and urged a friend to plead with Eliot to stop the research and to start writing. Could the friend perhaps remind Eliot that she was not writing an encyclopedia but a novel?[29] Somehow, Eliot had gotten lost in the past, almost like Romola's father—or even like Casaubon. Was she looking for the key to the Italian Renaissance?

But unlike Casaubon and de' Bardi, Eliot pulled through. She ultimately acquired the detailed knowledge she felt necessary to write a historical novel that lived up to the new historical standards, full of distinct voices, smells, foods, tools, and habits. Lesser novelists, such as the ones Eliot criticized, used settings and objects economically to sketch a scene into which an action would unfold. But Eliot understood that a surplus of detail created the impression of historical reality. (The technique has been used ever since, including by our own historical novelists such as Hilary Mantel.)

Despite the relative success of the novel, the writing of *Romola* was not a process Eliot wanted to repeat. Even though she had hoped to produce a novel informed by Feuerbach, Riehl, and others emphasizing material circumstances, the end result was something closer to Hegel: a novel animated by ideas in which different characters represented different attitudes toward classical antiquity: active scholar (de' Bardi); research assistant (Romola); radical opponent (Savonarola). Eliot decided to approach her project of writing historical novels differently in the future. The result was her masterpiece: *Middlemarch*.

Middlemarch is a novel about progress on many levels, above all social and political progress. It is set during the debate over the First Reform Act, of 1832, which proposed changes to a voting system which, at the time, allowed only about 2.6 percent of the population to vote. The Reform Act expanded the franchise to include smaller landowners, shopkeepers, and tenant farmers, increasing the number of eligible voters from around 400,000 to 650,000. While previously women had been barred from voting by custom, which allowed for occasional exceptions, they were now explicitly excluded, since the Reform Act defined voters as male, a reminder that progress in one domain sometimes leads to regress in another. (In some boroughs, the Reform Act also disenfranchised some working-class voters.)

In *Middlemarch*, progress is debated not only in the form of the

First Reform Act, but also in other ways, as when a surveyor working for a railroad is attacked by those hoping to keep the company from extending rail lines. Progress is also featured in Dorothea's dedication to better housing conditions for her tenants, and in sanitary reforms and the building of hospitals based on the latest scientific research. Everywhere, these attempts at progress, at extending the vote, at improving the living conditions of the poor, at science, and at better transportation are blocked and ridiculed, sometimes by vested interests, sometimes by outdated attitudes. In *Middlemarch*, Eliot showed her readers—with the benefit of about forty years of hindsight—a society grappling with progress, and the reality of diminished expectations as lofty ideas hit harsh realities. Eliot wrote *Middlemarch* in the aftermath of the Second Reform Act, of 1867, which brought about much more fundamental change in the franchise by adding almost a million male voters, including many working-class men, something that would have been unthinkable for the characters in Eliot's novel.

The difference between the two reform bills created exactly what Eliot wanted: a historical perspective premised on progress. While her characters were struggling with the earlier, more modest reforms, her readers knew that the first bill had in fact succeeded and also that it would be superseded by another, much more far-reaching one. This perspective created the impression of historical momentum inevitably trending toward emancipation. Leaving her own struggles with *Romola* behind, Eliot created a novel that put all her earlier experiments with realism and historical novels to new use. The point was no longer to embed different ideas about the past in historically accurate settings, but to show the workings of history. In *Middlemarch*, Eliot wrote a novelistic counterpart to the work of the great historians.

Thanks to Eliot, the historical novel took its place alongside other institutions of historical preservation, such as museums, as well as works of narrative history, in spreading the new historicism and making it accessible to larger segments of the population. This, too, was part of the new understanding of progress: ideas were not just reserved for small elites, but for a broader readership.

We're still living in the era of historicism, an era that prizes meticulously researched historical novels (which usually now feature lists of historical sources), museums, original works, and fragments of the past, as well as libraries and archives. Since the nineteenth century, the world has been hurtling toward the future, which means that the past has become ever more precious precisely because it has been seen to be disappearing forever. While humans everywhere encountered remnants of the past that seemed strange and incomprehensible to them, forcing them to revive and reconstruct what had been lost, now that sense of loss is seen as inevitable. Thus we've created new institutions of preservation, from archeological sites to museums and libraries, and we rely on professionals, such as historians and trained curators, as well as novelists to bring the past back from the brink of permanent loss.

The new science of the past brought us much knowledge of the past and the diversity of human experience, even though many of its theorists and practitioners were in the thrall of skewed ideas about what counted as high culture, a masterwork, or a mark of civilization. This was in part because of the idea of progress driving this science, leading to biased ideas about who was ahead and who was behind. In the end, this science could tell people what it was they dug up, but it couldn't tell them what these dug-up objects meant, nor what should be done with them. We latecomers have to figure that out for ourselves.

CHAPTER 14

=

A JAPANESE WAVE TAKES
THE WORLD BY STORM

Katsushika Hokusai, color print, *The Great Wave off Kanagawa*, 1825–38.

The Great Wave rises like a mountain, towering over the narrow boats and their desperate rowers, ready to crash down on them with brutal force. It is massive, filling the sky with a wall of water, and dangerously alive, extending its tentacles of white foam and spray threateningly toward the rowers. These fragile humans are not the only ones in danger. So overwhelming is the wave that it even dwarfs Mount Fuji, which rises timidly in the distance, its snow-covered cap no match for the angry white convulsion ready to engulf it. The wave assaults everything: boats, rowers, mountain, even the sky.

It also took the world by storm. Created by the Japanese artist Katsushika Hokusai in the 1830s, it has become one of the most readily recognized icons in the world. What is the story behind the wave, and how did it rise above all other images?

People called its birthplace the *ukiyo*, or "floating world," which had nothing to do with water, waves, or sky but described the entertainment district of Edo (today's Tokyo), the place where art and desire intermingled to create exquisite but fleeting pleasures for those who could afford them. Male actors playing male and female roles used stylized gestures and poses that showcased their elegantly cut robes, the leading edge of fashion, to maximal effect. The plays themselves revolved around love, the most famous of them, *The Love Suicides of Amijima*, by Chikamatsu Monzaemon, celebrating the deep and impossible love of two star-crossed lovers. Like much in the floating world, Kabuki actors were associated with sexual pleasure, along with geishas, who combined the arts of music, sex, and dance. The floating world also provided martial entertainments, including sumo wrestling, a favorite spectator sport among the military class, or samurai.

The professionals of *ukiyo* also evolved a distinct art form: woodblock printing. Print was a technique of long standing which had originated in China, but Japanese artists working in the floating world perfected the technique of using woodblock print for multicolor images. For each color, a separate block had to be carved and keyed to the image, so that the different blocks could be printed on top of one another.[1]

The result was a strikingly new type of image, one that was quite different from the aesthetic ideals of traditional Japanese painting, which was done with watercolor or ink. Painters belonging to different schools had created images of people and landscapes of shimmering elegance, often exploiting the soft contours of watercolor to create an effect of misty vagueness, which might be contrasted with a few elegant lines drawn in black ink. Shades of watercolor could flow into each other, turning one color into another, while leaving much of the page white. Painters worked by subtle hints, a few leaves of grass suggesting a larger meadow, a faintly sketched mountain an entire range, and human figures indicated by a characteristic pose. *Wabi* was the term used to describe the flawed beauty of simplicity; *sabi*, the melancholy patina of age; and *yugen*, mystery and depth.[2] One such school, the Kano school, adopted as its dictum: "one brush unchanged for a thousand generations."[3] Even though neither Kano nor any other school remained static, it was clear that they all revered old works, learned their craft by imitating these paintings, and stayed close to the aesthetic ideals embodied by them.

The new multicolor prints couldn't have been more different. Instead of misty shades of watercolor, they were confined to a half-dozen colors per image, which had to be sharply delineated. Instead of mysterious depth, these prints presented flat, vividly colored surfaces. Instead of simple tranquility, they excelled at stark, often asymmetrical shapes; and instead of reverence for old masters, they suggested something entirely new.

A study of a painting by Mu Qi, a Chinese Chan (Zen) Buddhist painter of the Song dynasty (960–1279). The study was made centuries later, in 1670, by the painter Kano Tan'yu (1602–74). (METROPOLITAN MUSEUM OF ART, NEW YORK)

Even though these prints were not considered high art, they were perfect for the floating world, so much so that they came to be named after it: *ukiyo-e*, or "pictures of the floating world." At first they were used to advertise Kabuki theaters, and soon other establishments as well. Cheap monochrome booklets served as guidebooks to the entertainment district, allowing visitors to navigate its labyrinths of pleasure. But it was the multicolor prints that expressed its essence. Their unusual outlines could capture the striking poses assumed by Kabuki actors, depict the fall of a sleeve, the elegance of a pose, or the daring of a dance move. Vivid colors would catch the eye of potential clients or admirers of a particular actor or geisha. Even sumo wrestlers were made to look threatening less through their sheer weight than through their fierce attitude.[4] Best of all was that the prints were reproducible, which meant that they could reach large audiences cheaply.

Katsushika Hokusai, *ukiyo-e* (multicolor print) of the sumo wrestlers Takaneyama Yoichiemon and Sendagawa Kichigorō.

(METROPOLITAN MUSEUM OF ART, NEW YORK)

A depiction of a professional courtesan by *ukiyo-e* (multicolor print) artist Kitagawa Utamaro (1753?–1806).

(NATIONAL MUSEUM OF TOKYO. PHOTO: JEAN-PIERRE DALBÉRA)

Only the wealthy could afford to visit the pleasure quarter, which was reached through a single gate that served both to control who entered and who was allowed to leave. Needless to say, the pleasure quarter was a great deal less pleasurable to those who were forced to work in it: many, especially the women, had been sold by their parents as teens and were working off ten-year terms as indentured servants. Their often harsh working conditions were kept hidden from view, and the clients did not care to know about them. The reality was papered over by the atmosphere of glamor radiated by the vivid prints, which allowed the many who could not afford entry to glimpse the quarter's famous actors, geishas, and sumo wrestlers, whose images circulated like Instagram posts today.

Hokusai, born around 1760, was apprenticed to an *ukiyo-e* artist in his teens.[5] His early images were of Kabuki actors and geishas, and he also created examples of erotic art. Not content with reproducing these familiar subjects, he began to illustrate written books. Collaborating with writers took him away from the floating world and allowed him to experiment with a large variety of subjects, including scenes of everyday life—and landscapes, not a discipline traditionally associated with this art form.

Hokusai had the seeming misfortune to be born well after *ukiyo-e* had reached its zenith of quality and popularity in the late eighteenth century.[6] Despite being a latecomer, or perhaps because of it, Hokusai acquired versatility with an unusually broad range of images. At the age of fifty, he could celebrate a career as a print artist of some thirty years, and commissioned a printed catalogue of his work to be used by art students and collectors who could not afford originals. (Japanese paintings, likewise, had become more accessible since print technology enabled them to be reproduced and bound in books, whereas the originals were always painted on scrolls, which had to be hung on walls and periodically stored for reasons of preservation.)[7]

At the age of seventy, Hokusai decided to embark on an ambitious new project. He advertised it at the end of a popular novel, in 1830, announcing that he would present thirty-six views of Mount Fuji.[8] In this choice of subject, Hokusai knew that he had a shot at producing a best-seller, since that mountain was a frequently painted motif and had come to stand in for Japan itself.

The Great Wave became the most famous image of the series, but the whole series was a glorious achievement. Hokusai created his own color scheme (which included an imported pigment called Prussian Blue), and found ever more ingenious ways of featuring Mount Fuji: sometimes it is almost hidden, as if daring the viewer to find it, while at other times it brazenly dominates the image.[9] The focus on this one object allowed Hokusai to show off the versatility he had acquired over the past fifty years. He didn't manage to revive color print or turn it into a highly revered art form. But he managed to show that even now, in the first half of the nineteenth century, color printing could be used to stunning effect in the hands of an accomplished craftsman and artist.

Hokusai's *Thirty-Six Views of Mount Fuji* was a late flowering both in the history of color print and in his own career. Looking back on his life, he singled out his quest for perfection:

> From the age of six, I had a penchant for copying the form of things, and from about fifty my pictures were frequently published; but until the age of seventy, nothing I drew was worthy of notice. At seventy-three years, I was somewhat able to fathom the growth of plants and trees, and the structure of birds, animals, insects and fish. Thus when I reach eighty years, I hope to have made increasing progress, and at ninety to see further into the underlying principles of things, so that at one hundred years I will have achieved a divine state in my art, and at one hundred and ten, every dot and every stroke will be as though alive.[10]

Hokusai's long and productive life, it turned out, marked the end of an era. He died in 1849, at the age of eighty-eight, just before Japan's self-understanding was violently challenged from outside.

=

JAPAN IS AN ARCHIPELAGO OF ISLANDS, BUT THAT DOESN'T MEAN it was ever isolated. Separated from Korea and China by only a narrow strait, it was part of the Sinosphere through its imperial missions to the mainland, while a series of islands in the south created a connection to Taiwan and the Philippines. Japan's geography allowed both: relative isolation and exchange with neighbors.

To this long-established network of cultural contacts was added a new one when a Chinese junk, manned by the Chinese crew and three Portuguese traders, was blown off course and landed on the island of Tanegashima in 1543.[11] It was a fateful encounter. The Portuguese brought firearms, which were soon eagerly used by Japanese warlords, as well as Christianity. It also made the king of Portugal sense a new opportunity. Using Goa, on the South Asian subcontinent, as a base, the Portuguese sent more ships to Japan, even though they were not welcomed. But the Portuguese had become good at exploiting internal conflicts and were able to use rifts between Japan and China, as well as divisions within Japan, to secure their trading status. (When, just a few years later, Luís de Camões disembarked in Goa, Japan had become part of the Portuguese trading network.)

Japan's experience with the Portuguese and other Western powers was decidedly mixed, but a brewing civil war left it, for the time being, at the mercy of these intruders. The period of passive acquiescence didn't last long. The civil war was resolved into a new feudal military order, presided over by an emperor. The real power, however, was in the hands of the clans actually running the country, who were now able to turn their attention to the ships arriving in ever greater numbers on their shores and forcing their wares on the population. The new rulers decided to minimize Japan's exposure to foreign trade empires. Existing relations, including with the Portuguese, were tightly regulated, and foreign missionaries expelled. Christianity was forbidden and suspected Christians killed. In 1621, Japanese were forbidden to travel abroad or board foreign vessels without special permission. By 1635, only ships from China and Korea were allowed to anchor and send people ashore, with one further exception: the Dutch, who had created their own trading company, the VOC (short, in Dutch, for United East-Indian Company), and who were allowed to maintain a trading settlement on the island of Deshima in Nagasaki Bay.[12]

For the next two hundred years, Deshima was Japan's main contact with the West. Through Deshima, Japan kept track of events abroad even as Dutch sailors and officers of the VOC supplied information on Japan to their home audiences in Europe. Deshima was also a source of fascination for the Japanese, even though—or because—access to the small Dutch settlement was tightly controlled and extremely limited.[13] One way in which Deshima became known in the rest of Japan was through color prints, known as *Nagasaki-e*, which supplied stylized accounts of life in this Dutch enclave.[14] These prints of Europeans were one reason printmakers became interested in Western painting, including the technique of central perspective.

Hokusai was among them. One of his students had made a point of applying the Japanese technique of multicolor print to Western-style paintings. Not to be outdone by his students, Hokusai experimented with the technique himself. Of his thirty-six views of Mount Fuji, some are built around a central vanishing point, while others are modeled on traditional Chinese painting, allowing viewers to compare the two traditions side by side.

While Hokusai absorbed some Western influences through Deshima, the Dutch settlement was also how the West learned about Japanese multicolor prints. The Dutch acquired some of these images

Depiction of a Dutch man in Deshima, the Dutch trading post near Nagasaki, by a Japanese multicolor print artist. The Japanese caption identifies the man as a "captain." Japanese-style multicolor prints of foreign sailors, mostly Dutch and Chinese people, became known as *Nagasaki-e*.

(RIJSKMUSEUM AMSTERDAM)

and probably even commissioned others to be sold in the West. Hokusai's *Thirty-Six Views of Mount Fuji* may have been among the prints that first traveled to the West in this way.

As the only European trade settlement in Japan, Deshima maintained its status for two hundred years, occasionally challenged by the British navy. But in the end, it was not the British Empire, nor any of the other European nations with imperial ambitions that forced Japan to expand trading rights. It was the United States.

Matthew Perry had always been a modernizer. For most of his career, this impulse was directed at the US Navy, where, having overseen the construction of the nation's second steamship, the USS *Fulton*, he became legendary as the "Father of the Steam Navy." (He also modernized the curriculum of the United States Naval Academy.) In the US–Mexican war, he tested the effectiveness of this modernized navy, commanding the assault and capture of Tabasco, in southern Mexico.

That war over, Perry set his sights on other targets. In 1852, he received one from President Fillmore: to force Japan to open trade relations with the US through what has come to be known as gunboat diplomacy. He steered his steam frigate to Macao, the main Portuguese settlement, and from there to the southern island of Okinawa, where he arrived in 1853. Having established a base there, he sailed into Edo Bay, in full view of the capital, and showed off his firepower in a demonstration. Shortly thereafter, he was allowed to land. In 1854, he returned with nine ships and came ashore at Kanagawa, just south of Edo (where Hokusai's *Great Wave* is set). The treaty Perry forced upon Japan, called the Convention of Kanagawa, effectively ended Japan's control over its trade relations and established American trading rights in two ports.

If, before 1854, trade between Japan and the West had been only a trickle, now it became a flood. All kinds of goods flowed through the two ports, satisfying Western interest in Japanese products, multicolor prints prominent among them. Their elegant designs, striking colors, and distinctive motifs seemed typically Japanese to Western eyes. The prints were part of a craze known as *japonaiserie*, the fascination with all things Japanese, with Hokusai's *Thirty-Six Views of Mount Fuji* a typical example. It didn't matter that *ukiyo-e* were not at all representative of traditional Japanese painting, being instead a much more recent, commercial, and popular art form. Nor did it matter that in the hands of artists such as Hokusai, multicolor print artists had, in fact, incorporated some Western techniques. The only thing that mattered was that the series was easily reproducible, which was why these images, above all *The Great Wave off Kanagawa*, as the full title has it, became the image that, more than any other, represented Japan to a world that happened to have been remade by the Convention of Kanagawa.

=

IF THE EFFECT OF PERRY'S TREATY ON WESTERN ART WAS SIGNIFI-cant, its effect on Japan was infinitely greater: "It was like the fizzing of a champagne bottle which has just forced out its own cork."[15] The person who wrote these lines was Ernest Fenollosa, and he was in a very good position to know. Even though he had not been part of the signing of the Convention of Kanagawa, he became one of the Americans who transformed Japan in its wake. Fenollosa didn't make the champagne bottle pop, but he was there for the party.

It wasn't a party for everyone, and Fenollosa knew it. Perry's gunboat diplomacy had demonstrated the weakness of the old military government, with its strict hierarchies, inefficiencies, and inequities; the limiting of contact with outsiders was perhaps its least significant handicap. Once that regime had crumbled, Japan's new rulers realized that the country needed to modernize.[16] They invited foreigners to teach them everything there was to know about the West, Fenollosa among them. He stayed for much longer than expected and with consequences he would not have been able to fathom.

Born to an immigrant father in Salem, then a worldly port town just north of Boston, Fenollosa had gone to Harvard, where he received an education based on some of the new progressive thinkers who had appeared in George Eliot's orbit, including Charles Darwin, Herbert Spencer, and G. W. F. Hegel.[17] These were the figures that Japan now wanted to know about. To facilitate this transfer of knowledge, the Japanese emperor created a new university and invited young Fenol-

losa to teach there. Fenollosa had recently married Elizabeth Goodhue
Millett, and the couple decided to move to Japan.

Even though Fenollosa was in Japan to teach the very latest in
modern thought, his true passion was art. His daughter Brenda, who
was born in Tokyo, recalled their household:

> Our house, from time to time, became filled with objects of art:
> screens of gold leaf, over which were painted in brilliant colours
> scenes of Japanese life, of birds, and of landscapes; kakemonos in
> their rich brocade frames; wood-block prints of many famous art-
> ists; bronze hibachis-braziers in which the Japanese burn char-
> coal and over which they sit on padded mats, warming their
> hands; bronze vases and bronze candlesticks; bronze bells from
> the temples; brass and silver incense-burners; cloisonné trays and
> boxes, exquisite lacquer tanses and an infinite variety of porce-
> lain. How wonderful they were and how I gloried in looking at
> each new object after their arrival! And they mysteriously disap-
> peared, only to be followed by others, until these latter also went
> the way of the first.[18]

Fenollosa was immersing himself in the history of Japan, turning his house into a private museum that included woodblock prints.
Prior to moving to Japan, he had studied at the school associated with
the prestigious Museum of Fine Arts in Boston. In Japan, he found
himself confronted with a deep and complex tradition of art that he
knew little about; he decided to learn as much about it as he possibly
could. First, he studied, with different teachers, the history of Japanese
art, only to realize that in order to understand it, he also needed to
understand its Chinese source. Not content with the academic study of
both traditions, he took lessons in ink drawing, acquiring significant
skills as a painter. Later, he would take the same approach of combining historical study with practical instruction to the highly stylized

Noh theater (the more elegant, courtly cousin of Kabuki), reaching an almost professional level. He was praised as the foreigner who had learned this difficult art better than any before him.[19]

Fenollosa's interest in the history of Japan made him notorious as an eccentric personage: an antiquarian.[20] Perry's gunboat diplomacy had led Japan to devalue its own traditional arts, which came to be seen every bit as outdated as the military government and the self-imposed isolation of the previous era. Himself a product of this drive toward Western-style modernization, Fenollosa nevertheless began looking for neglected or locked-away objects from the distant past with the hope of bringing them back to light.

In the summer of 1884, Fenollosa traveled to the great temple of Horyu-ji with authorization from the central government to demand that the monks open their shrines to let him inspect their statues.[21] This was not something the monks were happy to do, considering it something close to sacrilege, but Fenollosa, armed with his letters, insisted.

> Finally we prevailed, and I shall never forget our feelings as the long disused key rattled in the rusty lock. Within the shrine appeared a tall mass closely wrapped about in swathing bands of cotton cloth, upon which the dust of ages had gathered. It was no light task to unwrap the contents, some 500 yards of cloth having been used, and our eyes and nostrils were in danger of being choked with the pungent dust. But at last the final folds of the coverings fell away, and this marvellous statue, unique in the world, came forth to human sight for the first time in centuries. It was a little taller than life, but hollow at the back, carved most carefully from some hard wood which had been covered with gilding, now stained to the yellow-brown of bronze. The head was ornamented with a wonderful crown of Corean [Korean] openwork gilt bronze, from which hung long streamers of the

same material set with jewels. But it was the aesthetic wonders of this work that attracted us most.[22]

Fenollosa's sense of discovery, as he continues to praise the statue, its lines and proportions, its pose and the smile of the head, is captivating. In the same pages, he compares it to the best of Greek art and also to Leonardo da Vinci's *Mona Lisa*, the Gothic statues of Amiens, and archaic Egyptian art. Fenollosa had become a discoverer, delighting in locating objects such as this statue, and it is no surprise that his mind ran to Schliemann, the bold excavator of Troy.[23]

In embarking on this mission of unearthing (or unwrapping) objects from the past, Fenollosa was motivated by a different Western idea—not the works of Darwin and Spencer he was supposed to teach, but the new science of the past. To this end, he helped create the Tokyo School of Fine Arts and the Tokyo Imperial Museum, thus bringing those nineteenth-century institutions, with their distinct approach to the past, to Japan. Driven by a similar impulse, he created an inventory of national treasures, ferreting out works in monasteries and attics, the Korean Buddha having inspired him to seek out more such objects. He helped draft a law for the preservation of temples and artworks. The emperor of Japan, perhaps in recognition of this new science of the past, praised Fenollosa (according to Fenollosa's own account): "you have taught my people to know their own art. In going back to your own country, I charge you, teach them also."[24]

But what happened to all the paintings and objects Fenollosa brought home, or rather, why were they constantly arriving and then leaving again, as his daughter remembered it? Was Fenollosa using his house as a storage depot for the future art museum in Tokyo? Unfortunately, no. Fenollosa was taking advantage of the temporary devaluation of Japanese art to create a collection of his own, which he then sold to a wealthy collector in Boston. The Fenollosa–Weld collection, all 948 artifacts of it, now forms the basis of the Boston Museum of Fine Arts' East Asian holdings. (Other objects were sold to New York.) Fenollosa's position was therefore highly ambiguous: by day, he was part of the influx of foreign ideas that led to the devaluing of traditional Japanese art; by night he profited from that devaluation by buying cheap and selling dear, even as he genuinely cared about preservation, built museums and sought to elevate the status of Japanese art by applying to it the new science of the past, and was respected in Japan for his efforts.

Upon his return from Japan, Fenollosa became the curator of the department of Oriental art at the Boston Museum of Fine Arts. He was dismissed after a divorce (still scandalous at that time). For the rest of his life, he curated exhibitions, gave lectures, moved between Japan and the West, and wrote a comprehensive history of Chinese and Japanese art that introduced the subject to Western audiences with unparalleled insight and sophistication. Fenollosa did not dismiss popular works such as Hokusai's *Great Wave*—on the contrary, he included the painter in an exhibition on multicolor print—but he made sure that this one image did not dominate or define Japanese art. If anything, he set the record straight, showing just how unusual and different from traditions of visual art in Japan that woodblock of Mount Fuji really was.

All mediators are ambiguous figures. Fenollosa went to Asia as part of a modernizing invasion yet became deeply engaged in its history. He bought and exported treasures of Japanese art, and yet helped Japan create institutions to preserve its own heritage, according to nineteenth-century Western ideas of how the past should be treated. He uncovered treasures, but sometimes against the resistance of their owners, who would have preferred to let these treasures reside within their shrines. He taught Japan about Western figures such as Spencer, then spent most of his life teaching Western audiences about the history of Asian art. Fenollosa engaged in almost all activities related to the past in all their ambivalence: he unearthed works from the past, and acquired them under dubious historical circumstances; he sold and displayed his acquisitions; and he studied them with dedication and care. His life's work demonstrates everything that is admirable and reprehensible about these activities.

Fenollosa, the translator, had one more role to play—or rather, his second wife did. When Fenollosa died in 1908, he left behind many unpublished notes, translations, observations, lectures, and book manuscripts. What should Mary McNeil Fenollosa do with them? She had been pursuing her own career as a writer, publishing several novels, some set in Japan, under the pseudonym Sydney McCall. As a writer knowledgeable about Asian art, she thought she might try to complete some of her late husband's works-in-progress. The first project she tackled was the largest, his unfinished multivolume attempt to offer a grand history of Asian art. Devoting enormous time and effort to the task, Mary McNeil Fenollosa managed to complete this work and even went back to Japan to check factual details before publishing it, with a preface of her own, in 1912. Combining world history, partially inspired by Hegel, and detailed discussions of aesthetics, the work quickly became the standard introduction to Asian art and remains a touchstone to this day.

This mammoth task completed, and while continuing to publish novels under her pseudonym, Mary McNeil began looking for someone to take over her late husband's translations of Chinese poetry and Noh drama. Her choice fell on an American poet living in London by the name of Ezra Pound. It was an unusual choice. Pound was not a specialist in Japan or China and knew neither language. But he was starting to make a career as a poet, presenting a new approach known as imagism, based on stark, simple images. As a writer and poet herself, Mary McNeil felt that, despite the obvious drawbacks, he was the right person for the job. Decades later, Pound proudly recalled: "After meeting Mrs Fenollosa at Sarojini Naidu's in or about 19[13] she read some of my verse and decided that I was 'the only person who could deal with

her late husband's notebooks as he would [have] wished.'"[25] Despite
Pound's rather annoying self-praise, his remark was not wrong: Mary
McNeil had made a brilliant choice.

Pound used Fenollosa's own literal translations and transcriptions
and turned them into the kind of poetry he had been perfecting on his
own. It was an unusual undertaking, neither an authoritative translation nor an original work of poetry. Amy Lowell, herself an imagist
poet, wrote to her friend Florence Ayscough: "[Pound] got his things
entirely from Professor Fenelosa [sic], they were not Chinese in the first
place, and Heaven knows how many hands they went through between
the original Chinese and Professor Fenelosa's Japanese original. In
the second place, Ezra has elaborated on these until, although they
are excellent poems, they are not translations of the Chinese poets."[26]
Lowell, whose rivalry with Pound speaks through these lines, was
right. Pound's creations were not translations; he did get a lot from
Fenollosa; and the result, as Lowell admitted, *was* excellent. The main
problem was what to call it. T. S. Eliot, a close collaborator of Pound,
declared, with deliberate provocation, that Pound was "the inventor of
Chinese poetry for our times."[27] In retrospect, there is a better term for
what happened in the unusual mash-up of Chinese poetry, Japanese
Noh drama, Fenollosa, his teachers, Mary McNeil, and Ezra Pound:
modernism.

Pound had a different slogan for the same idea: *make it new!* When
seen from one angle, modernism was a deliberate attempt to throw
over the past. In itself, this was, of course, nothing new. Humans
had done so ever since Nefertiti and Akhenaten decided to move out
from under the shadow of the pyramids and start a new city, with new
buildings, a new god, and new forms of art. But around the turn of the
twentieth century, the past had acquired a new, overwhelming force.
In many of the countries that felt themselves on a forward trajectory
of progress, whether through political emancipation, industrializa-
tion, or foreign force, the past was being recovered and displayed in

institutions such as museums and libraries, and brought into a system by the science of the past. Modernism defined itself against these institutions of cultural storage and instead made common cause with the progressive movement of industry. Art was no longer on the side of tradition; it was now on the side of progress, along with emancipation and machines.

Pound was in the vanguard of this movement. In fact, this is what some of these modernist radicals called themselves: the avant-garde. Originally used to describe the advance corps of an army, the avant-garde felt itself to be ahead, leaving behind tradition and the tastes of the vast middle, the masses.[28]

But there was more to modernism than rejection of the past, as the unusual collaboration emerging from Fenollosa's papers shows. Modernists such as Pound were confronted not only with the past in the form of museums; they were also confronted, often for the first time, with the artistic creation of distant cultures that came flooding into the West through colonial adventures and global trade. Some Western observers had felt the trickles of this flood earlier: German writer Johann Wolfgang von Goethe had coined the term "world literature" in 1827, after being exposed to Sanskrit drama, Persian and Arabic poetry, and Chinese novels. Western art, which had become self-satisfied and insular, was forced to take in an increasing number of masterworks and popular art from distant lands—some recently excavated, such as the *Epic of Gilgamesh*; some recently translated, such as Sei Shōnagon's *Pillow Book* and Murasaki Shikibu's *Tale of Genji* (both were translated only in the wake of Perry's gunboat diplomacy and thanks to mediators such as Fenollosa); and some only recently achieving worldwide circulation, such as Hokusai's *Great Wave*.

The effect was a profound shattering of tradition. This shattering could be perceived as disorienting, an inability to assimilate so many newly available artworks and ideas. But it could also be perceived as liberating, allowing artists to experiment with new forms, new combinations of old and new, familiar and unfamiliar. Modernists were in the second group: they regarded the disorientation not as a calamity but as a necessary, even welcome, condition, one that could allow for something new to emerge. This, too, was what Ezra Pound meant when he exhorted his fellow artists to "make it new": not to throw over the past, but to use the disorientation of the age in creative ways.

Pound also edited some of the Noh plays Fenollosa had translated and published an essay on this unusual form of theater. Noh theater couldn't have been more different from Western theater: on a bare stage, lined with musicians on two sides, elaborately dressed actors sang, murmured, and shouted highly arcane lines, based on a canon of plays that was hundreds of years old. They did not impersonate characters in any obvious way but performed a set of precisely prescribed gestures and poses, which carried specific meanings (moving one outstretched hand slowly toward the eye signified weeping, for example). The plays often centered on places haunted by a ghost.

Western dramatists, who had grown weary of the increasingly realistic sets and dialogue that characterized theater in the second half of the nineteenth century, were mesmerized by this genre. Having sought alternatives to Western realism, they were suddenly presented with a ready-made solution.

One of these dramatists and directors was also a poet, William Butler Yeats. Having experimented with poetic stylization, he used Noh theater, as translated by Fenollosa and published by Pound, to forge a new style of drama. He often chose as his subject traditional Irish figures, but the plays he created around them, especially one called *At the Hawk's Well*, were strange, stylized, and heavily reliant on Noh. So enamored was he with this distant art that he hired a Japanese dancer, Michio Ito, to perform in his troupe.[29] It didn't matter that Ito had not received any Noh training and had, in fact, learned his craft in Germany. Yeats felt that Ito would be able to give these Irish–Japanese plays something of that revered Japanese tradition. Subsequently, Ito moved to Hollywood and then, after the Second World War, accompanied the American troops to Japan, where he performed for the occupying army: ever a go-between, seen sometimes as a translator, sometimes as a traitor, much like Fenollosa.

Brought to Europe and America by mediators such as Fenollosa and Ito, Asian art continued to have disruptive effects on Western art. After watching a performance by the Chinese opera performer Mei Lanfang in Russia, the German playwright Bertolt Brecht built an entire art of estrangement around what he believed to be the essence of Chinese opera, whose stylization spoke to him much as the stylizations of Noh theater had spoken to Yeats. In fact, Brecht was also interested in Noh theater and wrote an adaptation of one particular Noh play, *Taniko*.[30] When the French provocateur Antonin Artaud, a key figure in the French avant-garde, saw a performance of Balinese shadow-puppet theater, he felt that it would guide him out of the dead end of Western culture.[31]

Unlike Fenollosa, none of these figures immersed themselves in Asian art. Some of them, especially Pound, learned more than others, but their reception of foreign works was marked by misunderstanding and projection, driven by their own artistic need for innovation. Such has ever been the case with cross-cultural encounters.

Much, if not all, of what we call modernism was born from these and similar experiences. Modernism is often described as a Western phenomenon that spread to other parts of the globe. But what Mary McNeil recognized by persuading Pound to work with Fenollosa's notes, which Fenollosa had created thanks to his various Japanese teachers, was something different: a mash-up of traditions from Asia and the West, created by different intermediary figures, sometimes working together, sometimes at cross purposes. The modernism all these figures created was much more interesting than a supposed Western export product; it was an extremely modern and thoroughly mesmerizing mess.

CHAPTER 15

THE DRAMA OF NIGERIAN INDEPENDENCE

Ladigbolu I, king of Oyo, died on Tuesday, December 19, 1944. He was buried that night, having reigned over the city and a substantial territory for thirty-three years. The death of a king, especially one who had ruled for so long, was a major event; elaborate ceremonies and rituals had evolved to help this society adapt. One of the highest positions in the realm was held by the King's Horseman, Jinadu, who had enjoyed the many privileges and favors bestowed on the person occupying this role. Because the king's reign had been unusually long, Jinadu had savored these privileges for much longer than he could have reasonably expected. But from the beginning, he had known that they came with a price: upon the death of the king, the King's Horseman would have to die as well, to lead the king's horse and dog to the land of the ancestors.[1] And so, upon hearing of the king's death, Jinadu traveled to Oyo, where he arrived on January 4, 1945, dressed all in white, and began dancing through the streets, making his way toward the house of Bashorun Ladokun as a preparation for committing suicide.

Like much of Africa, the Yoruba state of Oyo had been carved up at the Berlin Conference of 1884–85, where the major European nations divided Africa among themselves, giving Oyo to the British. The conference formalized the European control over western Africa that had its origins centuries earlier, when Portuguese ships crept down the coast looking for passage to the Indian Ocean. European encroachment had intensified when Portuguese, Spanish, and British colonists began establishing trading posts, enslaving Africans and transporting them to work on sugar and cotton plantations in the New World. (Because Yoruba-speaking Africans were overrepresented among those enslaved and transported to the New World, their culture left a particular imprint on such places as Haiti and the Sea Islands off the coast of South Carolina.)

The Berlin Conference had taken the de facto European control over territory in Africa and formalized it. The result was arbitrarily drawn borders that cut across linguistic, tribal, and religious groups. Oyo found itself part of a large administrative entity that would become Nigeria, a vast state containing a multitude of groups—some estimate over five hundred tribes and languages and dialects. To retain control over such a large territory and diverse peoples, the British had instituted a system of indirect rule, whereby they retained local customs and laws as much as possible, elevating local rulers willing to cooperate with the colonial overlords.

King Ladigbolu was a prime example of this policy. After his death, the system of indirect rule and non-interference in local affairs hit a limit when the British colonial district officer Captain J. A. MacKenzie learned about the impending suicide of the King's Horseman. He stepped in and ordered the King's Horseman arrested, thus interrupting the ritual.[2] In doing so, the district officer didn't realize that he was destabilizing an entire system of political authority. How to solve this crisis? Murana, the youngest son of the King's Horseman, found a way. With his father imprisoned and incapable of action, he decided to assume his father's title, and as the new King's Horseman committed suicide in his father's stead. It was a desperate act, but the only possible way to solve the breach caused by British interference.

The events surrounding Ladigbolu, his horseman, and the horseman's son were only a small episode in the history of European colonization, but they resonated with a widespread sense that the system of colonial rule was crumbling. The demise of European colonialism was hastened when, at the end of World War I, Woodrow Wilson enshrined the principle of self-determination in the new League of Nations, raising the hopes of national independence that had been harbored ever since the example of Haiti's revolution over a hundred years earlier. World War II pushed European nations to the brink. Germany, which had acquired colonies late, had lost both wars and with them all claim to overseas possession. The two world wars had also depleted the other European empires, above all England and France, which had barely survived, and only thanks to Russia and the United States; smaller colonial powers such as the Netherlands, Belgium, Italy, and Portugal were in a similar position. In addition, the colonies had contributed to the war effort on the side of their overlords, including the kingdom of Oyo under Ladigbolu, and now they demanded freedom in return. The result of these events was an extraordinary reordering of political geography over the next twenty years, with the number of nation-states quadrupling, from fifty to two hundred.

Political independence, it quickly became clear, was not enough. The new nations also needed to tell themselves new stories and find new meaning in the world after colonialism. In other words, they needed to forge new cultural identities, hence the flowering of different forms of art, above all novels, the dominant form of storytelling in the middle of the twentieth century. Through these novels, writers from former colonies became the voices of their nations, seeking to claim cultural independence by creating new national stories out of older ones as well as by borrowing from elsewhere. The burden put upon these writers was a significant, almost impossible one: how could they hope to excavate local traditions, which had often been neglected or even actively repressed during the period of colonial rule? How to stitch together an identity from disparate groups forced together by arbitrary colonial borders? How to address the history of violence brought on by colonialism? And to what extent should they rely on the cultural heritage of the former colonists, including their languages (and alphabets), whether English, French, Portuguese, Dutch, German, Italian, or Spanish, which had been instituted in schools and the bureaucratic apparatus left behind by the departing colonists?

The Caribbean poet Derek Walcott wrote *Omeros*, an epic poem about Saint Lucia that took Homer as a model, giving ordinary people Homeric names and conferring on their lives an epic dignity. Other artists drew on their cultures' own traditions, including oral storytelling. In Mali, not far from Nigeria, traditional singers had told stories of the medieval king Sunjata and now turned those stories into written literature, creating what we call *The Epic of Sunjata*.

=

ONE WRITER WHOSE CAREER HAS BEEN SHAPED BY THESE EXPECTAtions and dilemmas is Wole Soyinka. Born in 1934, Soyinka's formative years were spent in colonial Nigeria. His parents belonged to a class of Nigerians thoroughly marked by colonial rule: they were both Christian, his father a schoolteacher and his mother coming from a distinguished Anglican family.[3] His schooling was based on an English curriculum, which also included some Greek literature, whose purpose it was to educate an elite of colonial subjects into the cultural world of their rulers. Soyinka attended high school and then Government College Ibadan, both examples of this educational policy. (This type of colonial curriculum was first created by Macaulay in India, to make the colonial elite "English," before it was broadly implemented in England and across the empire.)[4]

Typically, the top students emerging from this educational system would be invited to spend some time in England, Soyinka among them. In 1954, he traveled to England by ship to attend the University of Leeds, a city in England's former industrial heartland, now booming in the postwar period since it had suffered no damage during the war. There he studied the canon of Western theater, above all Shakespeare, under the tutelage of distinguished Shakespearean scholar G. Wilson Knight. After graduating from Leeds in 1957, Soyinka began to write plays and found work as a reader for the Royal Court Theatre in London, deepening his knowledge of Western theater.

Originally, Soyinka had expected to return to the colony to work in the British-led administration, but the anticolonial movement, which had been gaining speed since the end of the war, suddenly changed the purpose of Soyinka's career. When he returned in 1960, Nigeria had just obtained nationhood. Instead of helping the British rule this vast territory, he would help Nigeria understand its new independence.

The way Soyinka chose to tackle this task was through theater. It was a canny move. His fellow Nigerian Chinua Achebe had taken the novel as his literary form, winning acclaim with *Things Fall Apart*, published just two years before independence, in 1958. But even though the novel as a genre enjoyed many advantages, including that of reaching a potential mass audience, it had an immense disadvantage. On the most basic level, it required people to be able to read, which many Nigerians could not. Also, the novel as a genre was seen as a Western import (the non-Western novelistic traditions of Asia were not widely known). Achebe had had to exercise considerable ingenuity to make this literary form, with all its colonial baggage, his own.

Recognizing these disadvantages, Soyinka saw that theater could tap into Yoruba traditions more easily and speak more directly to a broader range of people.[5] Theater, too, had been part of the British export to its colonies, but it was not considered to be as exclusively Western as the novel in part because theater relied on music, dance, and ritual—all of which were deeply rooted in the Yoruba world, which Soyinka, despite his Western schooling, had absorbed through his extended family. One of his first efforts was *Dance of the Forest*, which he wrote explicitly for Nigeria's independence, a festival drama that revolves around the gathering of different tribes and includes many references to Yoruba poems, incantations, figures of speech, and idioms.

Translating these Yoruba patterns into English posed a problem, however, for English was the language of the colonizers. Upon independence, a number of small but politically active theater groups had sprung up seeking to decolonize Nigeria's culture by performing in Nigerian languages. One such playwright and theater-maker was Duro Ladipo. One of his well-known plays was called *Oba Waja*, which translates as *The King Is Dead*. It is a hard-hitting dramatization of the events following the death of Ladigbolu I, the interference of the British colonizers, and the death of the horseman's son. For Ladipo, this episode captured perfectly the cultural colonization Nigeria had suffered under the British and was therefore a good place to start the difficult process of cultural decolonization. Written in 1964, four years after independence, the play was meant to help the newly independent nation reckon with the violence of British rule. For Ladipo, there was no question that he should write in Yoruba. Unlike Soyinka, he did not have significant formal schooling in English to make that language a viable option; he was deeply formed by Yoruba oral and written literatures and performance; and he wanted to address the Yoruba-speaking population. And English, of course, came with colonial baggage.

Cultural decolonization didn't stop at reckoning with British violence. It also involved recovering cultural traditions that had been sidelined by colonization. Oyo was one of the oldest urban civilizations in this part of Africa, going back to 800–1000 CE.[6] Originally a city-state protected by walls, Oyo had expanded and ultimately became a major empire between 1608 and 1800. Remnants of this once glorious period remained, or were waiting to be excavated, including sculptures made from durable materials such as stone, terracotta, and wood. The variety of styles and traditions was staggering, with realistic heads of women going back to the eleventh century.[7] Equally striking were more abstract depictions of human and animal heads, both in sculptures and in masks worn during particular rituals. Among those rituals, the Egungun ritual, centered in Oyo, was especially important. It was performed during a festival dedicated to ancestors, who were believed to be residing in an invisible world. In order to establish a connection with that world, the ritual performers made themselves invisible through masks and elaborate dresses made from layers upon layers of cloth covering the entire body.

In his own approach to recovering Yoruba traditions and creating a culture of independence, Soyinka did not follow Ladipo in his choice of language and instead opted for English, founding a troupe

Fragment of a terracotta head from Osun State, Nigeria, dated 1100–1500. The head shows that Yoruba sculpture was highly developed at the time.

(COLLECTION OF ROBIN B. MARTIN, BROOKLYN MUSEUM. PHOTO: BROOKLYN MUSEUM)

An Egungun mask worn by Yoruba dancers for ceremonial purposes.

(AMERICAN MUSEUM OF NATURAL HISTORY, AFRICAN COLLECTION. PHOTO: DADEROT)

that was meant to establish English-speaking theater for a newly independent Nigeria. The choice of language was part of his more general attitude toward cultural mixture. Unlike some of his contemporaries, he did not find it necessary to jettison what he had absorbed of English, French, and Greek literature, including his intensive study of Shakespeare. British colonial rule had shaped him, and shaped Nigeria; it was now inextricably part of the country's history and culture.[8] Gaining cultural independence didn't mean somehow subtracting colonialism from this history as if it were a poison that could be drawn from a wound. The heritage of colonialism needed to be confronted, it needed to be overcome, but this could be accomplished by using some of its cultural resources and turning them against the colonists themselves.[9]

By creating the country of Nigeria in utter disregard of its various traditions, the British had forced together, into a single entity, several hundred languages and dialects. The three major ones were Hausa in the north, Igbo in the east, and Yoruba, Soyinka's primary cultural context, in the west. These linguistic identities were further complicated by tribal and religious affiliations, including Islam in the north, Christianity (as in Soyinka's family), and various polytheistic belief systems.

During colonial rule, this artificial creation was maintained by military force and by propping up local rulers, such as Ladigbolu I of Oyo. But once independence arrived, these artificial boundaries made the creation of a functioning political system extremely difficult. In the case of Nigeria, the result was a terrible civil war known as the Biafran War (1967–70), in which Igbo speakers sought unsuccessfully to gain independence by establishing the republic of Biafra.[10] The war resulted in widespread violence and horrific atrocities, with the greatest number of casualties in the Igbo region.[11]

As an increasingly visible playwright, writer, and intellectual, Soyinka sought to prevent the war and mediated between the parties, with the result that he was deemed insufficiently loyal to his own Yoruba group and imprisoned. He spent twenty-seven months in prison, the major part in solitary confinement in a four-by-eight-foot cell, a grueling experience he later described in his autobiographical work *The Man Died* (1972).[12] With this work, he joined the long list of African writers, which includes Nelson Mandela, who have contributed to the heroic genre of prison writing. Since Soyinka's release, his life in Nigeria has been interrupted by periods of exile, many of them forced upon him by hostile rulers who could not tolerate this fearless writer, one of the first playwrights to critique the rise of African dictators.[13]

The terrible years of civil war and his own imprisonment sharpened Soyinka's attitude toward cultural independence. They demonstrated just how insidious the legacy of colonialism really was, how difficult, almost impossible, it was for artificial entities such as Nigeria to emerge as functioning states. Paradoxically, this political and linguistic reality was also the reason why Soyinka continued to write in English, despite its colonial heritage—because it would allow him to communicate across the different language groups. (At times, Soyinka has advocated for the use of Swahili as a pan-African lingua franca.) To this day, he has deplored the arbitrary boundaries drawn by the former colonizers and has held out hope that Africans might be able to reimagine the political organization of their continent beyond the boundaries inherited from colonialism. At the same time, he became a participant in high-profile debates, for example with Nigerian intellectual Biodun Jeyifo about Marxism.

It was after having become one of Nigeria's most important writers and political dissidents that Soyinka remembered the story of the King of Oyo, his horseman, and the horseman's son, so memorably dramatized by Ladipo, and decided to write his own adaptation of the material. The result was *Death and the King's Horseman* (1974), the play that explored in new ways his relation to colonialism, Yoruba culture, and theater. It would ultimately define his career and lead to

the Nobel Prize in Literature, making him the first African writer to
win this distinction.

The bare bones of the story remained the same: the king is dead,
and the district officer intervenes by arresting the King's Horseman
to prevent him from committing suicide, thus prompting the son of
the King's Horseman to commit suicide in his stead. Into this basic
constellation, Soyinka weaves layers of entanglement that prevent
audiences from reducing the play to a simple confrontation between
arrogant colonizers and their colonial victims.

Soyinka's first change was to the district officer's wife: no longer
Ladipo's manipulative and ignorant villain, she is the most sympathetic British character, one who at least seeks to understand what is
going on. In a crucial scene, she and the son of the King's Horseman
debate the ethics of the ritual suicide, with the son drawing her attention to heroic, self-sacrificing actions being celebrated by the British
during the war: "[after a moment's pause] Perhaps I can understand
you now," she concedes, though her understanding of Yoruba tradition
remains limited.[14]

This change makes the district officer the main agent of interference, though even he is portrayed with a grain of sympathy through
another twist: the son of the King's Horseman turns out to be his pro-
tégé; the district officer had made it possible for the son to study medicine in England. While in Ladipo's version the son hears of the king's
death in a bar in Ghana, in Soyinka's version he rushes home from
England—a figure, like Soyinka himself, who knows both worlds and
finds himself in a position of having to mediate between the two. The
son is thus a modernizing figure, one who finds himself between cultures, and perhaps dreams of a future in which his two experiences
can be reconciled. This future, however, is taken away by the district
officer's interruption of the suicide ritual, which forces the son to rescue
a tradition from which he had distanced himself.

If British interference remains the precipitating action of the play,

Soyinka also refined the figure of the King's Horseman. In his version, it's not just interference from outside that undermines the burial ritual with its mandated suicide. Here, the King's Horseman himself has doubts, hesitates, and postpones the ritual by claiming a young bride for himself. Even without interference, something is going wrong—the old ways are no longer accepted without question. It is almost as if the King's Horseman is asking to be arrested by the district officer so that he doesn't have to go through with the suicide. When the son finally takes over for the father, he is repairing something broken not only by the district officer and his wife, but also by his own father.

Soyinka was not particularly interested in the historical circumstances of these events (he got the year wrong, for example), but he captured their wider significance: in the first half of the twentieth century, the necessity of ritual suicide was being questioned, and there is reason to believe that it might have changed anyway. British interference did not just force the son to complete the act; it prevented the ritual from going through its own process of gradual transformation and modernization.

These changes made the play more complex, more entangled, more tragic. But they alone would not have turned *Death and the King's Horseman* into the masterpiece that it is, one of the great plays of the twentieth century. In rewriting the story of the King's Horseman, Soyinka mobilized everything he knew about theater and tradition and turned this piece into a deep investigation into ritual, arguably humanity's oldest form of meaning-making.

Soyinka's key insight is that the Horseman's suicide is not the only ritual being performed. Thinking so would mean accepting that the Yoruba, or Africans more generally, are the only people who perform rituals, while colonists are the ones interrupting them. This was precisely what the colonialist mindset would suggest, the mindset Soyinka was trying to unsettle. His way to unsettle it was not merely to show that interrupting rituals is bad. It was to show the ignorance of people who don't understand how profoundly rituals organize all societies, including the British.

=

IN ANALYZING THE RITUALISTIC DIMENSION OF THE CONFLICT, Soyinka drew on anthropology and its view that all cultures are based on symbolic actions. It took a while for the discipline to arrive at this insight when it was conceived in the nineteenth century. While (mostly Western) archeologists, collectors, librarians, and interpreters were busy recovering ruins, sculptures, and manuscripts from the (mostly) non-Western world, a second group of scholars took aim at immaterial practices and belief systems. The attempt to understand what non-Western people believed and how they lived became the new discipline of anthropology.

The original idea was that some non-Western groups were living as if in an earlier stage of human development, giving anthropologists a chance to recover an understanding of how all humans had lived in pre-modern times. The only way to study this was to live with remote tribes and learn how they saw the world. How did they organize their society? What were their belief systems? What was their "primitive" mindset? Anthropologists developed protocols so that they would not project their own systems and values onto these societies. They viewed them as precious remnants from the Stone Age that would allow machine-age anthropologists a glimpse into their own past.[15]

Studying the past by studying living relics was based on a notion of "advanced civilization" or "high culture," understood as exceptional achievements by extraordinary artists, the pinnacles of advanced civilization. These might include the greatest temples and churches, masterpieces of sculpture and painting, the grandest symphonies, and the most important pieces of literature. Greatest according to whose standard? Often it was Western cultures that established these rankings, in which they included select cultures of the past, such as Greece or Egypt, that were believed to be the cultural wellsprings of modern Europe. It didn't matter that Bronze Age Greece, as depicted in Homer, was arguably more remote from modern Europe than, say, from the Arab Middle Ages. Greece was simply adopted, retroactively, as the origin of Europe—nor did it matter that the concept of Europe hadn't even existed at the time.

But even though the notion of cultural masterpieces was keyed to this constructed notion of Europe and its cultural origins, the idea of masterpieces could, in principle, be extended to other cultures. Hence the search, among archeologists and librarians, for buried or forgotten masterpieces such as the bust of Nefertiti, Aztec codices, Buddhist temples, or Yoruba sculptures.

The problem with this "pinnacles of culture" approach, even of the expanded sort, was that it ran into trouble with societies that didn't have the forms of culture that had evolved in Europe. Nomadic or semi-nomadic peoples, for example, who didn't have writing, were regarded as living in a previous stage of culture, one that had not yet achieved the pinnacles of, say, Ancient Egypt, Tang-era China, or fifteenth-century Mexico let alone modern London or Paris.

Over the course of the twentieth century and in the face of the movement to decolonize culture, anthropology changed. The idea that studying isolated groups of humans gave you access to the remote past became increasingly suspect. It was based on a colonial mindset that pitted an "advanced" Western world against "primitive" remnants of the distant past. In response, a new generation of anthropologists jettisoned the idea of "high cultures" and focused on structures of belief, especially kinship systems. All societies had them, so studying them didn't mean buying into the old colonialist mindset of advanced nations and those that had not yet caught up.[16]

Thus, culture was no longer a matter of pinnacles of creation achieved only by select individuals in select cultures: now all humans had culture. It manifested in the foods they ate and the ones they refused to eat; in their mode of dwelling; in storytelling, whether oral or written; in belief systems of all kinds; and in dance, music, and ritual.[17]

The new anthropological approach was so powerful that other disciplines borrowed from it, including sociology. Through this work, something unexpected happened: anthropologists began to turn their attention to their own societies. If it no longer made sense to be preoccupied solely with discovering forgotten masterpieces abroad, perhaps it also didn't make sense to focus only on masterpieces at home? If all groupings of humans produced culture, then this meant that culture didn't just happen in museums, concert halls, and libraries; it happened everywhere.

Sometimes drawing on nineteenth-century scholars interested in European folk art, anthropologists and sociologists now started to study England and other European countries with the same tools they had developed in studying colonized cultures, analyzing eating habits, tastes, value systems, beliefs, and rituals, including those of working-class people who had hitherto been excluded from the realm of culture.[18] This inward turn was sometimes derided as cultural relativism: the idea that all cultures were equal. But this description was only partially true; the approach looked relativistic only when seen through the lens of the old "pinnacles" model.

In truth, the two notions of culture could be combined. Extraordinary works of all kinds could still be admired as extraordinary without the old hierarchy of cultures attached. One could value an oral epic such as *Sunjata* as a supreme distillation of Mali culture, or elaborate Egungun masks for their ritual function with deep roots in Yoruba tradition, without worrying whether they were "as good as" Chinese porcelain or Egyptian death masks. The question "are they as good as" simply didn't make sense anymore. Works were worthy of attention for different reasons, sometimes because they were particularly valued within the culture that produced them, sometimes because they mesmerized foreign visitors (like Xuanzang in India), sometimes because, like Hokusai's *Great Wave*, they had circulated widely both within a culture and outside of it without necessarily being regarded as "the best" or even typical. As Soyinka put it in a recent work, cultural relativism can only be the beginning of an exploration into culture, not the end.[19] This book is based on the same assumption.

=

TURNING AN ANTHROPOLOGICAL EYE TOWARD ENGLAND WAS PRE-cisely what Soyinka did in *Death and the King's Horseman*. The English colonists perform an elaborate masque in the Residency to celebrate a visit from a royal prince. They have assembled, in various gowns and costumes, to perform particular dance moves to mark this important, symbolic occasion. A band plays "Rule Britannia," badly. The participants go through what Soyinka calls a "ritual of introductions" as they are each presented ceremonially to the prince. The district officer and his wife wear Yoruba headdresses associated with the annual festival celebrated in honor of departed ancestors. Clearly, they don't know anything about this ritual, but they imitate some of the movements superficially, seeking to amuse the prince and the other colonists. This quaint rite is then interrupted by the trouble over the king's burial. At this moment, two societies, each bound by their own rituals, confront each other, to devastating effect.

The clash of cultures is not inevitable: it is brought about by ignorance (the kind of ignorance anthropologists and artists such as Soyinka sought to work against). Oblivious to their own rituals, the British blithely interfere in Yoruba practices in the mistaken belief that any ritual is outdated and barbaric. Soon, the returning son of the King's Horseman will lecture them, and the audience, on the sacrilege they commit by wearing Yoruba costumes out of context. Soyinka is showing us a world held together by rituals; what we need is a map of how to navigate them. The son of the King's Horseman, the go-between, does his best to provide one, but no one takes him seriously. Soyinka, another go-between, clearly hoped that he would fare better.

In the middle of these clashes, the district officer snaps at his wife, Jane: "Just when did you become a social anthropologist?"[20] It is an apt question, and keyword, for this is exactly what Soyinka, if not the district officer's wife, had become. Or rather, social anthropology was what Soyinka drew upon in viewing all societies, including England, in terms of ceremony and ritual.

Soyinka's expanded notion of culture brought into focus intriguing correspondences across his own far-flung sphere of interest, above all between the ritual world of ancient Greece and the equally ancient Yoruba world. His main interest was the Yoruba god Ogun, the god associated with creativity—the most important Yoruba god, in Soyinka's view, because he was associated with what Soyinka called "transition," including the passage to the world of the ancestors.[21] Ogun also reminded Soyinka of Dionysus, the Greek god of theater.[22] In some ways, Soyinka was doing with Greek gods what Romans had done, namely adapting them for his own purposes from a position of distance.

Soyinka's interest in Ogun and Dionysus allowed him to address a crucial question connected to his anthropological understanding of culture: what is the relation between ritual and theater? The work in which he addressed this question most explicitly was his adaptation of Euripides's *The Bacchae*.

The youngest of the three tragedians, Euripides had written this play to explore the origin of theater and its relation to ritual—Greek tragedies were performed as part of a Dionysus festival—which is why *The Bacchae* lent itself particularly well to Soyinka's question. In the Greek pantheon, Dionysus was a latecomer, a foreign god introduced from the east. Euripides's play explores the violence that comes from the resistance to this god and his ritual, as the King of Thebes attempts to keep the god away. The plot is not so different from *Death and the King's Horseman*; it involves the interference, on the part of an ignorant politician, in the conduct of a ritual that the population demands and deems right. (The Dionysus cult was primarily for the lower classes, a fact Soyinka used in his adaptation by introducing a chorus of enslaved people.)

The theme of ritual and how it relates to theater runs through the entire play, beginning with its opening scene, in which members of the chorus are being whipped. We think we are watching a ritual being enacted, one that demands the drawing of real blood. But then there is confusion about how much this whipping is supposed to hurt, suggesting that this is not a ritual at all, but something governed by different rules, namely those of theater, which would explain why the actors are outraged at being asked to suffer actual pain.

In this and other scenes, Soyinka shows that while theater may have originally emerged from ritual, it now carries different expectations for both actors and audiences. Another way of saying this is that unlike ritual, theater is no longer primarily a religious event. Theater is important, it fulfills all kinds of civic and cultural functions, bringing an audience and a community together; it is a meaning-making or at least meaning-exploring activity, but one that has been removed from its ritualistic origin. This dynamic was at work in Euripides's play, which looked back at the origin of the Dionysus cult and hence of Greek tragedy, just as it is part of Soyinka's adaptation, which asks how and what Yoruba rituals can mean today.

In Soyinka's hands, theater turned out to be the perfect vehicle for asking this crucial question about ritual and culture. It allowed him to absorb rituals, both Yoruba and Greek, but also to examine them. It allowed him to criticize aspects of Yoruba tradition without denouncing it as primitive; it allowed him to integrate different theatrical traditions, from Euripides to Shakespeare. By leaving behind the old hierarchy of cultures, he produced something exceedingly rare: a masterpiece.

Soyinka still shapes modern Nigerian culture, which has survived the horrors of colonialism and of the slave trade, by drawing on his country's immense artistic resources. He has imagined the future of Nigerian and, more broadly, of African culture as a revival, a renaissance, a term no longer restricted to the Italian Renaissance but one that can be understood as the primary mechanism of how human culture is produced everywhere. Above all, Soyinka has been exemplary in preserving Yoruba cultural traditions by reusing them in new ways and by freely combining them with other traditions. Rather than shutting himself off from Greek and other European theaters, he made them his own, despite the history of violence associated with their presence in Nigeria, by remixing them with Yoruba traditions, both old and new. His work does not deny or erase the extreme forms of violence inflicted by European colonialism or its attempts to belittle and erase Yoruba culture. Instead, Soyinka bears witness to that history by drawing on all the cultural resources at his disposal.[23]

=

IN ENCOURAGING AN AFRICAN RENAISSANCE, SOYINKA AS WELL AS Duro Ladipo had another, unexpected role to play: they laid the foundation for the extraordinary flowering of Nigerian film that has come to be known as Nollywood. One of the films often associated with the beginnings of Nollywood is *Kongi's Harvest* (1970), adapted by Soyinka from his 1965 play. Soyinka himself starred in the leading role of Kongi, the dictator of an imaginary African nation. For the putative goal of modernizing the country, Kongi has deposed the traditional king and rules as an increasingly erratic dictator, intent on eliminating all opposition and changing traditional rites, including the all-important Yam festival, to increase his power.

While Soyinka worked in English-language cinema, Ladipo focused on Yoruba cinema, including *Ajani Ogun* (1976), the story of a young hunter who fights a corrupt politician. (Ladipo played a role in the film and received music credits.) Along with *Kongi's Harvest, Ajani Ogun* began a golden age of Nigerian film.

That golden age, in its original form, did not last long. By the 1980s, the role of cinemas began to be replaced by videocassettes available in the marketplace. But the new format also created a demand for more content, a demand that was met with extremely limited budgets and in high numbers. The straight-to-video films were aimed not at the cultural elite but at people who had come from villages to work in service jobs in the city; it was a huge market, and the films became popular successes, giving rise to a large industry that soon moved from VHS tapes to DVDs and to television. Today, Nollywood produces more films than Hollywood and Bollywood. As Femi Odugbemi, a Nollywood veteran, described it recently: "Now you have a multi-fiduciary channel for Nollywood. Today Nollywood is sold in the market, Nollywood has got cinemas, Nollywood is on cable TV, Nollywood is on Netflix. Nollywood is at your beck and call, your arm's reach, via all media regardless of where you are."[24]

The sheer size of Nollywood has given rise to a large number of stars, and those new stars are in turn creating new forms of theatrical performance. My favorite is *Hear Word!: Naija Women Talk True* (2014), a play written and directed by Ifeoma Fafunwa. Fafunwa assembled some of Nollywood's stars, including Taiwo Ajai-Lycett, Joke Silva, Bimbo Akintola, Omonor, Elvina Ibru, Ufuoma McDermott, Zara Udofia-Ejoh, Lala Akindoju, Rita Edward, Deborah Ohiri, and Odenike. These women tell stories revolving around life in today's Nigeria, especially as it affects women. The piece was inspired by *Four Colored Girls Who Have Considered Suicide/When the rainbow is Enuf* (1976), a play of twenty monologues written by the African American writer Ntozake Shange, and by Eve Ensler's *Vagina Monologues* (1996), a play about sexuality, relationships, and violence against women that has been performed by many actors on what has been rebranded as "V-Day," February 14.[25]

Hear Word!—a Nigerian expression that means "listen and comply!"—is based on monologues spoken in English, accompanied by Yoruba songs. Combining different theatrical and performance traditions, the piece's original cast channeled the fame of Nollywood and redirected it to domestic violence and other challenges faced by women in Nigeria. Fafunwa conceived of the piece as an alternative to what she described as "angst-filled and angry" work coming out of Europe, which led her to emphasize music, dance, and humor. Her piece resonated beyond its original conception. After the first performance, she found that "women started to gather in the lobby after the show and exchange stories. It was permission, all of a sudden, to speak."[26] *Hear Word!* was offering a space for actors and audiences to examine their condition, something particularly precious, as she observed, in a culture that has tended to stigmatize therapy.

After premiering in Nigeria, *Hear Word!* found a second audience abroad, one that includes the Nigerian exile communities attuned to Nollywood but also audiences less knowledgeable about this industry and its stars. The show went to the Edinburgh Theater Festival and to the United States, where it was presented at such venues as the Public Theater in New York and at Harvard University.[27] Taiwo Ajai-Lycett, one of the stars in the original cast, reflected on the success of *Hear Word!* by urging her audiences to pay more attention to theater as a vehicle for social change. "This is where the intellectual narrative is being made. . . . We have started changing Nigeria intellectually and this is where they should join us."[28] Ajai-Lycett's career captures the history of Nollywood and its relation to theater. She is mostly known to audiences for movie roles ranging from soap operas to action thrillers, while also working as a television presenter, but like Nollywood itself, her roots go back to the theater—her first stage appearance was playing a village girl in *The Lion and the Jewel*, by Wole Soyinka. Along with her follow Nollywood veterans, she was rediscovering the power of theater.

Both Soyinka and *Hear Word!* remind us that culture thrives on syncretism, not on purity, on borrowing cultural forms rather than locking them away. Great playwrights and performers will find material wherever they can to forge from it artworks that speak to their own time and place. Theater is an intensely local art, taking place in a particular location in front of a particular audience, while answering a basic human need for congregating in special places of meaning-making; it is in such places, as Ajai-Lycett put it, that the true narratives are made.

WILL THERE BE A LIBRARY IN 2114 CE?

In 2015, Margaret Atwood boarded one of the noiseless electric streetcars that zip around Oslo and let herself be pulled into the hills above the city. From the station, she took a well-preserved forestry road straight up into the woods, the path marked by white arrows. She was accompanied by a couple of dozen people, all decked out in hats and raincoats, or carrying umbrellas, due to a persistent drizzle. As this colorful flock made its way through the woods, the road gave way to a hiking path, reinforced with occasional planks to guide the hikers safely to their destination, a circular clearing in the woods. Trees had been recently cut down, but new ones had been planted, the small saplings, six to eight inches tall, carefully protected from pests by a white coating. Between the saplings, Margaret Atwood and her companions were received with hot coffee, brewed in cast-iron pots over open fires, and chocolates. People stood around in groups or sat on the ground, taking pictures and talking, waiting for the ceremony to begin.

The first to speak was Katie Paterson, the creative mind behind the event. Hailing from Scotland, she had made a name for herself as an artist seeking to bring small- and large-scale processes, those too small or too large to be readily perceived by humans, into the perceptible realm. In her speech, she briefly rehearsed why they had assembled here, in the woods above Oslo. Then Atwood said a few words, before the main part of the ceremony could begin.

Atwood, whose dystopian novels depict the horrors of patriarchal control over women, the dangers of corporate oligarchs, and the potential consequences of genetic engineering, had brought a box tied with purple ribbons. The box contained a text called *Scribbler Moon*, Atwood explained; but that's all she was allowed to say about it, according to the rules set up by Paterson, except perhaps to express the thinking behind the title, which she said was meant to bring together the idea of writing with that of time. Then Paterson approached and gave Atwood a quick peck on the cheek before taking the box and handing it over to a representative of the Oslo Public Library. "Be careful with the box," she joked, or half-joked, or perhaps she was actually worried. These gestures and acts didn't have the rehearsed seriousness of a religious ceremony, nor were they mere theater; they were something in between (as readers of Soyinka might appreciate). The representative then also delivered a brief speech, promising to take care of the box containing *Scribbler Moon* and to hand it over to its next guardian when the time came. After the ceremony, Atwood gave a brief interview, urging her audience not to kill the ocean. Then everyone slowly made their way home.[1]

Atwood was the first author Paterson had invited to contribute to an art project that combines an idea of long-term cultural storage with environmental sustainability. The clearing in the woods above Oslo is part of this project and is marked as such by a wooden sign screwed to a tree. In red letters it informs anyone who passes by that the clearing is part of Framtidsbiblioteket, a word translated into English as Future Library. Next to the three words are concentric circles that look like the rings of a tree.

Paterson's idea was that for each of the following ninety-nine years, one writer would write a text, commit to keep everything about it, except its title, secret, and participate in the handing-over ceremony. The boxes containing the manuscripts are to be transported to a special room in the Oslo Public Library, where visitors can enter and look at the titles, but not read them or check them out. The texts will be kept under lock and key until the year 2114. At that point, they will be printed on paper made from the trees planted as saplings back in 2014. As the title of the project, Future Library, indicates, it is, like so much of Atwood's fiction, about the future.

In a short text written for the occasion, Atwood mused:

> Will any human beings be waiting there to receive it? Will there be a "Norway"? Will there be a "forest"? Will there be a "library"? How strange it is to think of my own voice—silent by then for a long time—suddenly being awakened, after 100 years. What is the first thing that voice will say as a not-yet-embodied hand draws it out of its container and opens it to the first page?[2]

As Atwood added in an interview following the ceremony, writing for the future is what everyone has been doing, in the sense that writing is a technology that makes speech endure over time. What was different here was that Future Library created a deliberate interruption, a hiatus of ninety-nine years in the case of Atwood and diminishing each year, so that the final participant will see almost immediate publication, just as in a normal production cycle.

This artificial interruption reproduces a feature of cultural history that has been crucial to this book: what happens when a cultural object is recovered after a hiatus? Usually, interruption is not something brought about deliberately but something that happens through chance, such as the landfall covering the entrance to the Chauvet cave, wars, environmental change, or cultural changes in what is seen as worthy of preservation. In the case of Future Library, the interruption is engineered to occur at the moment of inception.

What does this experiment reveal? Through the handing-over ceremony, the solemn pledge of silence, and the guardianship of the library, Future Library calls attention to the institutions that allow cultural objects to be stored and conveyed into the future. "Will there be a 'library'?" Atwood asked in her interview, putting cautious quotation marks around the word, perhaps worried that the very idea of the library might be undergoing change, or that it may cease to exist at all. Norway, or the city of Oslo, could decide that libraries are a useless expenditure and sell off its holdings. The fate of the library, for Atwood, is bound up with a larger one: what will happen to Norway? If that state no longer exists, the library will be in the hands of some other governing entity or of no one at all.

Atwood's question, "Will there be a 'forest'?" shifts the discussion from states and institutions to the environment. Of the three parts of the project, the forest is the most unusual, the one that speaks to our gathering sense of environmental crisis and the need for sustainable practices. It is also the most vulnerable. Climate change might mean that the saplings planted in 2014 will be unable to survive, threatened by new pests, extreme storms, forest fires, or the adverse effects of some desperate geo-engineering project gone wrong. But the forests of Norway are vast, and Norway is not high on the list of countries most threatened by climate change. In this sense, Paterson's choice is an apt one. Perhaps she was also inspired by the fact that Norway has become particularly engaged in environmentalism, boasting the highest percentage of electric vehicles, among other achievements.

Things get slightly more complicated when one remembers that these achievements were paid for, at least indirectly, by Norway's large oil reserves, which are also fueling, if that is the word, its enormous sovereign wealth fund. It's this fund, together with Norway's fortunate geographic position with respect to climate change, that is perhaps the best guarantee that there will indeed be a Norway and, therefore, a library. So, in a sense, it's precisely Norway's oil money, which is contributing to climate change, that is most likely to ensure that Norway will survive until the year 2114, even if its forests don't.

Of course, future librarians might decide to jettison the part of the project stipulating that these works be printed on paper made from those trees and instead put them up on the internet, which might be environmentally preferable (provided that the electricity powering it is produced in a sustainable manner). Cloud storage might also offer the best chances for survival, though some have worried about the longevity of electronic storage, given how quickly formats change and become illegible. The long history of culture presented in this book adds a cautionary note for all projects of long-term preservation. An overwhelming amount of written literature has been lost, and the rare fragments that have been dug up had become illegible by the time they were recovered, either because the language or the writing system had been forgotten or because the physical writing surface had decayed.

Like King Ashoka, Future Library places its trust in the written word. Since the rise of writing five thousand years ago, the written word has been endowed with prestige based in part on its supposed longevity, in contrast to the fleeting nature of the spoken word, which tends to be devalued as fleeting and ephemeral (there are exceptions to this rule: traditions of secret knowledge deemed too precious to be entrusted to writing). In truth, oral traditions can be surprisingly resilient, offering distributed storage based on dedicated humans rather than on external storage devices and symbolic recording systems that can easily be destroyed. Oral traditions can also be more flexible than written ones, adapting to new environments, whereas writing is dependent on a particular recording system and code. And yet, we keep sending text messages across time—even though we have so often forgotten how to read them.

Thus far, most of the authors who have contributed to the project are from the global north—the Canadian Margaret Atwood and the English David Mitchell were followed by the Icelandic poet Sigurjón Birgir Sigurðsson and the Norwegian Karl Ove Knausgård. They were joined by authors who are predominantly based in the global north, such as Elif Shafak, a novelist from Turkey who has been partly living in London, and Ocean Vuong, a Vietnamese-born poet and novelist who mostly grew up in the United States and lives in western Massachusetts. Han Kang, a poet and novelist from South Korea, lives outside the anglosphere, but she has found great acclaim in the English-speaking world since winning the London-based International Booker Prize for her novel *The Vegetarian* in 2016. Only the eighth and, so far, most recent contributor, the Zimbabwean novelist, playwright, and filmmaker Tsitsi Dangarembga is from and continues to be based in the global south. She came to international prominence through another international prize, the Commonwealth Writer's Prize, which she received for her 1988 novel *Nervous Conditions*, written in English.

Collectively, these eight writers represent a version of world literature that slants not only northward but also anglophone (on the Future Library website, their titles are listed only in English, regardless of the language of the works themselves). In this, Future Library mirrors world literature and its system of publishing conglomerates and prizes, which tend to be based in northern Europe and North America. The Nobel Prize in Literature, after all, was created in Sweden and is presided over by the Swedish Academy and its members. To be sure, the Nobel Prize committee has made efforts to honor writers from the global south, beginning with the 1913 award to Rabindranath Tagore, through the 1986 award to Wole Soyinka to the 2021 award to Abdulrazak Gurnah, the latter bestowed, in the words of the Academy, "for his uncompromising and compassionate penetration of the effects of colonialism and the fate of the refugee in the gulf between cultures and continents." It will be interesting to see how Future Library—and publishing markets more generally—will evolve over the course of the next ninety-some years until 2114. Will more writers from the global south gain entrance? Will English diminish or increase in importance? Will new institutions and prizes emerge that are based in the global south, the region also most likely to suffer disproportionally from the effects of climate change?

The hope of preserving culture for the future is something that Future Library shares with time capsules, attempts to seal off cultural objects and send them into the future undisturbed. The creation of time capsules seems to coincide with periods of desperation and doom. In the twentieth century, an early exemplar was a sealed container that was lowered into the ground of Queens, New York, as part of the 1939 World's Fair, just before the outbreak of World War II. It contained everyday objects but also microfilmed literature and images, a microfilm reader, a dictionary, and texts translated into many languages, as well as greetings by Thomas Mann (in English), Albert Einstein (in German), and Robert Millikan, a physicist (in English). Only two printed books were included: the Bible and a booklet containing a list of the contents of the capsule. Copies of this *Book of Record* were also distributed to libraries so that the contents of the time capsule as well as knowledge of its existence and location might be preserved. (In this, the *Book of Record* exemplifies a second mode of preservation, one that trusts not in sealed containers but in wide distribution of multiple copies. I read it on the internet.[3])

The 1939 World's Fair time capsule was intended to sit untouched for five thousand years. Unfortunately, Corona Park in Flushing Meadows is only seven feet above sea level, which means that long before the year 6939, the time capsule will likely be at the bottom of the Atlantic Ocean. Anticipating such catastrophes on earth, other time capsules have been sent into space, beginning with the first interstellar crafts, *Pioneer 10* and *11*, and culminating with the golden records fixed to the *Voyager 1* and *2* interstellar probes.[4] These discs are safe from floods and wars, but they will be difficult to retrieve; they are safe from human interference, but for whom are they intended? Either an alien intelligence or future humans who have mastered the art of intergalactic travel, both considerable long shots.

An alternative solution was carried out in 1969, when the *Apollo 11* mission took a disc containing recordings of goodwill messages from around the world into space and deposited it on the moon, along with an American flag.[5] (Buzz Aldrin almost forgot to leave it behind; Neil Armstrong reminded him at the last minute to toss it to the surface of the moon as Aldrin was boarding the lunar module to head back to earth.[6]) In all of these cases, the selection of cultural expressions— recorded oral greetings, written symbols—was haphazard, an afterthought to the construction of the time capsules and their recording devices, yet another example of the divergence, in our time, between engineering and the humanities.

The fate of these time capsules shows how difficult it is to anticipate future threats and destruction, and not only on a scale of thousands of years. The Future Library was interrupted in 2020, only six years after its launch, by the coronavirus. The smooth workings of the project, which by then boasted a brand-new room in a brand-new library building, the saplings growing nicely in the forest, the annual ritual of the handing-over ceremony attracting visitors, many sleek videos produced, edited, and posted on the project's simple but elegant website, aided by a well-functioning publicity apparatus—all this came to a screeching halt.

The trouble began with Knausgård. Because he lived in the UK, he was not able to travel to Norway for the handing-over ceremony due to virus-related travel restrictions. Meanwhile, Vuong had accepted the invitation to contribute but was having trouble writing due to the disruptions brought on by the pandemic.[7] And so, the project was, at least temporarily, on hold, much sooner than anyone had expected.

This sudden interruption of a project premised on longevity highlights the fragility of the infrastructure necessary for the preservation of culture. If one hundred years seem a rather short time frame when compared to the 37,000 years of the Chauvet paintings or the 5,000 years of writing (and of the Queens time capsule), the virus showed just how prone to failure cultural institutions are all the time. We can build a wonderful new library supported by one of the most stable democracies and underwritten by a sovereign wealth fund, but a tiny virus, itself the product of environmental change, can bring travel and much else—though not the internet—to a standstill.

The future is unpredictable, reminding us that culture is, at best, a broken chain that we keep repairing in every generation. In the end, what will allow Future Library to continue after an interruption that came so much earlier than anyone would have predicted is something other than the longevity of trees, libraries, or Norway. It is whether people—Katie Paterson, writers, the press, the public—will still care about a project such as Future Library.

Will they? Future humans, for whom nature as we now know it might have become unavailable, might well consider the felling of trees for paper-making a grave ethical failing, and judge us every bit as severely as we now judge the authors of the past for their deviations from our legal, social, and moral norms (among the participants, only Han Kang expressed sadness at the thought of felling trees).[8] The future might denounce Future Library as the typical product of a generation that wrecked the planet, on the grounds that planting some trees does not make up for the heavy environmental footprint of the entire project, with its significant carbon costs in travel and construction.

What Future Library must hope, then, is that future readers will accept this difference in values, that they will be willing to engage with humans from the past whose behavior they will almost certainly see as falling woefully short. This is the greatest trust that Future Library requires: a trust that the future will judge us less harshly than it may have reason to do, or at least appreciate and preserve our cultural creations despite their inadequacy by future standards.

This trust rests on shaky grounds. Cultural history is a history of destruction caused by environmental disasters like landslides and volcanoes as well as by foreign invaders and colonists acting out of ignorance and malice. But culture was also destroyed by latecomers beholden to new values and beliefs. The chroniclers who erased Nefertiti's name were probably genuinely disturbed by the new Aten cult, just as Confucians in China genuinely felt that Buddhist monks were shirking their duty to the state. Likewise, medieval Christians could not imagine putting pagan Greeks and Romans on an equal footing with Christian ones. There are significant differences in the nature and extent of violence wrought during these and other cultural encounters, but they have in common that they resulted in the deliberate ruination of cultural objects, in addition to the loss of countless human lives.

To be sure, we've learned some lessons from the history of destruction that runs through culture. New laws have clamped down on outright theft, and more museums are returning artifacts that were extracted under colonialism, acquired under dubious circumstances or outright stolen.[9] We are more sophisticated in preserving culture through UNESCO heritage sites and grass-roots initiatives, while also being more attentive to immaterial cultural practices such as dance and performance traditions as well as other forms of knowledge that are transmitted orally from teacher to student, from body to body. These are significant accomplishments in the handling of culture and need to be tirelessly promoted and implemented more broadly.

But the larger lessons of cultural survival are harder to learn, because the past keeps challenging our most cherished opinions and values. Every single text or object mentioned in this book survived by beating the overwhelming odds of destruction not only from natural disaster but also from deliberate sabotage. They survived despite the fact that they were at odds with the societies by which they were found and by which they were preserved. The Buddhist texts and statues that survived in China did so even though they disagreed with dominant

Confucian and Taoist mores, just as Greek philosophers survived in Baghdad even though they were not followers of the Prophet Muhammad. Likewise, some Christian Europeans, during one of their several revivals, were ready to reacquaint themselves with classical antiquity even though those authors were pagan, just as Aztecs incorporated objects of previous cultures into their own rituals despite their difference. Similarly, the rebels of Saint-Domingue used Enlightenment ideas even though these had emerged from the country that had enslaved them, just as the inhabitants of former European colonies repurposed elements of European culture, such as Greek tragedy in the case of Soyinka, for the goal of independence.

In all of these cases, cultural objects and practices survived even though they could be understood as threats to those who nevertheless assured their survival. These objects certainly challenged any sense of cultural purity. Again and again, cultural history shows that it is purists and puritans, those invested in ideas of spotless virtue of whatever stripe, that are most likely to engage in acts of cultural destruction.

Purists also deprive their own cultures of valuable resources by limiting access to meaning-making strategies from the past and from other societies. Cultures thrive on the ready availability of different forms of expression and meaning-making, on possibilities and experiments, and to the extent that cultural contact increases those options, it stimulates cultural production and development. Those invested in purity, by contrast, tend to shut down alternatives, limit possibilities, and police experiments in cultural fusion. By doing so, they impoverish themselves while condoning or encouraging the neglect and destruction of those aspects of the past that do not conform to their own, narrow standards.

Against such purists stand the heroes of this book, the people who dedicated their lives to the transmission and continuation of cultural traditions, including those who committed to memory long stories such as those of the Trojan War, and those who perfected cultural

techniques such as building pillars and creating mosaics, fresco paintings, and writing systems such as Egyptian hieroglyphics and Aztec
picture-writing. Equally heroic are those who built institutions dedicated to preservation and transmission, including storehouses of wisdom such as the one in Baghdad, monasteries such as the one created
by Hildegard of Bingen, museums inspired by the new science of the
past promoted by George Eliot, and artists dedicated to continuing
performance traditions such as Wole Soyinka. Also included are those
who facilitated (peaceful) cultural encounters, such as Xuanzang with
his travels to India, Ennin with his travels to China, and Sei Shōnagon
grappling with the legacy of Chinese culture in Japan. Despite the
incomplete and often mistaken views about the countries these travelers visited (or heard about), they sought out encounters with other
cultures in order to challenge their own assumptions and beliefs.

I like to imagine that readers of this book have done the same.
None of the ancient works or their creators discussed here are without
blemish. The cultures that shaped them had values and practices different from our own; they were products of societies few of us would like
to live in. Like the societies that produced them, these works carry the
values and injustices of their eras. Considering them worth preserving, and accepting them as part of our common cultural heritage, does
not require that we agree with the values of their era or single them
out as moral examples to be emulated in the here and now. None of
the works mentioned in this book would hold up to this standard, not
Nefertiti's exploitative Egypt, its monuments a famous example of the
enslavement of the workers who erected them, nor Ashoka the Fierce,
who regretted the bloodbaths he was responsible for but did not give
up the territories he had won through them, not the arrogant Greeks
and certainly not the Romans with their legions, let alone al-Ma'mun,
who killed his brother to gain power before conversing with Aristotle
in his dream. The raiders of the Ark do not deserve to be admired for
this act (if it actually occurred), not to speak of European colonists

who decimated the population of an entire hemisphere, and much of its culture as well. The nineteenth-century historicists and archeologists, such as Fenollosa, intent on preserving the past, often destroyed it inadvertently and were guilty of theft on a grand scale. All creators of culture must grapple with the violence and exploitation that is also part of cultural history, accept differences in values, and trust that the future will show them similar forbearance.

Today's qualms about cultural borrowing and ownership are driven not only by the history of violence that runs through human culture but also by anxieties about how social media makes the circulation of culture seem frictionless. A good example is a recent wave—not Hokusai's *The Great Wave off Kanagawa* but the "Korean Wave," or Hallyu, which emerged alongside the internet in the late nineteen nineties. It crested in 2012 with the release of the music video for "Gangnam Style" by the South Korean singer, rapper, and producer PSY. Named after the most expensive district in Seoul, "Gangnam Style" includes racing stables and motorboats but cross-cuts these scenes of luxury with run-down highways, an ordinary bus offhandedly spruced up with disco balls, and PSY sitting on a toilet. The video was the first to attract over a billion views on YouTube, thanks to its winking knowingness, cheerful embrace of camp, and fun set pieces: drinking coffee in a fancy setting, PSY on the floor of an elevator between the legs of another man making grinding dance moves.

The Korean Wave was able to reach such a large audience because, from the beginning, it was based on a mixture of styles including rock, jazz, reggae, and Afrobeat. Its musical signature relies on R & B dance tracks with heavy beats, melodic bridge sections, and "soft" rap interludes, mostly sung in Korean with occasional English phrases (like "Gangnam style"). The videos often feature synchronized dance moves, which are less common in US-produced popular culture though well known in other traditions, including Bollywood. Also notable is what's not there: the violence and obscenity that often feature in US- and UK-based pop and rap culture. (The image of K-pop as "clean fun" also explains the fierce reactions K-pop singers must endure when they violate the high expectations of moral integrity harbored by their fans.)[10]

K-pop's rise has been accompanied by an anti-Korean backlash as well as by claims that it isn't Korean at all.[11] While it is true that K-pop doesn't represent traditional or typical Korean art (just as *The Great Wave off Kanagawa* didn't represent traditional or typical Japanese art), it is equally true that K-pop has deep roots among Korea's girl groups, including those that performed in the 1950s at American military bases. These peppy groups evolved through the 1960s and 1970s in part because they managed to evade censorship during Korea's military dictatorships, though by the late 1970s and early 1980s, this cultural form seemed to be on the wane.[12]

The great wave of Korean pop actually started as a revival, when the country returned to civilian rule in 1987 and the government began supporting its nascent cultural industry. The first group to enjoy great success, Seo Taiji and Boys, was followed by other boy bands and girl groups. After the financial crisis of 1997, K-pop reinvented itself yet again, with more English names and titles—it was then that "K-pop" replaced Hallyu (Chinese for "Korean Wave") as a label for the new phenomenon—attracting significant teen audiences in Japan and soon in Australia, Latin America, parts of Africa, North America, and Europe. (I remember sitting down at the breakfast table with Norwegian friends in Oslo to find their youngest poring over a textbook; this twelve-year-old was studying Korean, by himself, before breakfast, to gain a deeper understanding of his idols.)

It's worth pointing out that the K-pop wave, which has long spilled over into TV series and video games, occurred before the rise of Tik-Tok, thanks to which we now find ourselves living, truly, in a Gangnam world. This is nowhere as clear as in the countless imitations the video has inspired. The most-watched version involves a group of animated fruits and vegetables fronted by Annoying Orange (which is, in fact, annoying), and the inevitable "Gunman Style," featuring gun-slinging cowboys. There is also "Johnson Style," which celebrates NASA's Johnson Space Station in Houston, Texas, though this video doesn't come close, in terms of popularity, to a shot-by-shot remake on Minecraft. These imitations speak to the inventive energies of K-pop's international fan base, including over forty imitations from Malaysia alone.[13] More recently, K-pop singers have crossed into visual art, while V (Kim Tae-hyung), from the boy band BTS, has made use of masks, with their deep history in East Asian theater and performance traditions.

Has cultural "sharing" gone too far? I don't think so, in part because it's impossible to draw the line between "good" and "bad" sharing; ultimately, we must choose between isolation or circulation, purity or mixture, possessing culture or sharing it. Popular art serves many functions; one of them is as an index of the ways in which culture circulates at a given time. "Gangnam Style" captured something important about consumer culture and globalization for an audience that had grown up with it, and was therefore clued in about its images. While we don't need to hail every form of cultural mobility, every act of revival, and every internet phenomenon as an act of great significance, K-pop is a good reminder that the arc of cultural history bends toward circulation and mixture.

If we want to support and sustain cultural invention, we need every means at our disposal. Unlike biological evolution, which is built into human life, culture can never be taken for granted. It depends on the people who take it upon themselves to preserve and revive culture in every generation, including archeologists, museum curators, librarians, artists, and teachers, and specifically it depends on their ability to inspire future generations (very much including the Minecraft-playing, Korean-studying K-pop fans around the world).

The work of these teachers and intermediaries is more important than ever today, a time when universities, one of the institutions charged with preserving culture, tend to focus on technology and other STEM subjects. But it is not enough to blame others for the decline in the humanities as it is occurring in the United States and some other countries. The problem is in part home-made. We humanists have not always lived up to our role in the promotion of a diverse cultural history, just as we have lost the public at large—the readers, parents, and students who should be our primary audience (at my university, 8 percent of the incoming class of 2021 declared a primary interest in the arts and humanities). I believe that only if we win back the broader public, only if we manage to communicate the significance and excitement of cultural diversity to the next generation, only if we keep alive the cultural treasures that our forebears wrought, will the arts and humanities thrive.

There is much the arts and humanities have to contribute. Our era is enamored with technological innovation and the promise that breakthrough solutions to our most pressing problems are just around the corner. But we can't engineer our way out of today's most intractable conflicts, which are based on age-old troubles involving clashing identities, colliding interests, and opposing beliefs. These conflicts can only be addressed if they are understood as reaching deep into the cultural past, which can only be achieved with the use of tools provided by the humanities.

The culture of the past is the ground in which new cultures grow—not for nothing is the word "culture" borrowed from agriculture. Culture needs to be tended by connecting humans living today with our distant ancestors, and with one another, so that the work of meaning-making can continue. We need all the cultural resources we can find to face our uncertain future, which will include massive disruptions from wars, migration, and climate change, as registered by Future Library.

Among the participants in Future Library, several were prompted by the project to contemplate the long history of culture. Atwood went all the way back to its distant origins, thereby providing this book with a fitting conclusion:

> I picture this encounter—between my text and the so-far non-existent reader—as being a little like the red-painted handprint I once saw on the wall of a Mexican cave that had been sealed for over three centuries. Who now can decipher its exact meaning? But its general meaning was universal: any human being could read it. It said: "Greetings. I was here."[14]

ACKNOWLEDGMENTS

=

This book began as a conversation with my partner, Amanda Claybaugh, and our friends Alison Simmons and Luke Menand over dinner. We were lamenting, as one does these days, the decline of the humanities. Suddenly I realized that I had no idea what the humanities were, and that I therefore lacked the basis on which to judge whether they were declining, improving, or just chugging along as usual. Following this unsettling realization, I developed the habit of asking everyone who would listen what they understood "the humanities" to be. The answers left me even more confused. Clearly, the collection of disciplines now grouped in humanities divisions in North American universities is highly contingent, more the product of accidents and local arrangements than of a grand vision of how knowledge should be organized. Also, the term "humanities" does not translate easily into other languages and cultures, though one can find rough equivalents at different moments in history, from Tang-era China and the golden age of Arabic letters to the *sciences humaines* and *Geisteswissenschaften* in continental Europe. At some point, it began to dawn on me that I had been asking the wrong question. What I was really after was not a justification, after the fact, of one particular strand of the humanities, but something underlying all of these traditions: an engagement with the human-made cultural objects and practices of the past for the purpose of redefining the present. If there is a definition of the humanities underlying this book, it is a concern with the history and the continuing vitality of human culture, why we, as a species, have created it, how it continues to shape us, and what we should do with it.

Many people were crucial in helping me turn the book into what it has become, including my dear agent, Jill Kneerim. Sadly, Jill did not live to see the book published, but she guided me though the process of completing it with her usual finesse, and her spirit is on every page. This book, and every book I will write in the future, is deeply indebted to her. I also want to thank my editor at W. W. Norton, Alane Mason, with her surefire instinct for what works—and what doesn't. Alane was a partner in this undertaking from the beginning and accompanied the book tirelessly through many drafts, sprinkling her insights generously across each of them. Special mention is also due to Norton editor Sarah Touborg, with whom I am working on an "Introduction to the Arts and Humanities" that will draw on material from this book. Our conversations made me realize the importance of teaching, of making culture relevant to each generation. And continuing with Norton, a great thanks is due to the friends and colleagues with whom I have been editing the *Norton Anthology of World Literature*, including Emily Wilson, Wiebke Denecke, Suzanne Akbari, Barbara Fuchs, Caroline Levine, Pericles Lewis, and Pete Simon (in the chronological order of their expertise, which is how I think of them). Working with this team first introduced me to the pleasures of big-picture work in the humanities, without which this book would not exist. Finally, I am greatly indebted to Allegra Huston for her superb copyediting, which improved every single page of this book in ways that often went beyond the fixing of errors (of which, I am sorry to say, there were many), and Mo Crist for their assistance in seeing the book through the production process.

A book such as this one is based on the work of countless special-ists, and whenever I go through the endnotes, a feeling of deep grati-tude rises in my breast for the generations of scholars whose tireless and often underappreciated work made this book possible. Many are mentioned, but some also provided invaluable feedback on individ-ual chapters in acts of great generosity. They include Wendy Belcher, Josiah Blackmore, David Damrosch, Wiebke Denecke, Maya Jasanoff, Biodun Jeyifo, Michele Kenfack, Nayanjot Lahiri, Jon McGinnis, Luke Menand, Erez Naaman, Parimal Patil, Alison Simmons, Elena Theodorakopoulos, Camilla Townsend, and Nicholas Watson. Felipe Fernández-Armesto read the entire manuscript and gave extremely valuable and wide-ranging feedback on every chapter.

Among the friends and colleagues whom I regaled with ques-tions about the humanities are Christopher Balme, Rens Bod, David Damrosch, Michael Eskin, Blake Gopnik, Roby Harrington, Noah Heringman, Paulo Horta, Maya Jasanoff, Yoon Sun Lee, Yu Jin Ko, Sarabinh Levy-Brightman, Luke Menand, Bernadette Meyler, Mon-ica Miller, Klaus Mladek, Claudia Olk, Parimal Patil, Heike Paul, John Plotz, Tore Rem, Bruce Robbins, Alison Simmons, Matthew Smith, Doris Sommer, Charlie Stang, Kathrin Stengel, Carl Wenner-lind, Yan Haiping, and Rebecca Walkowitz. I was able to present a very early version of this project as the Hölderlin Lecture at the Goethe University of Frankfurt, at the invitation of Nikolaus Müller-Schöll and Ramona Mosse, and at the MIT Comparative Global Humanities Conference organized by Wiebke Denecke, whose work on cultural translation was an inspiration for several chapters of this book.

An additional shoutout is due to the informal group of people at Harvard forging connections between the humanities and professional schools, including Bharat Anand, Rohit Deshpande, Tarun Khanna, Rebekah Mannix, Doris Sommer, and Suzanne Smith.

I wrote this book during the COVID-19 pandemic and the work kept me halfway sane, so I want to thank everyone mentioned above for having helped me through this difficult period, as well as my brothers, Stephan and Elias, and my mother, Anne-Lore.

Above all, I want to thank Amanda Claybaugh, who is ever my first interlocutor and most astute reader. Her support and love during the past two years, and the twenty-five years before them, have sustained everything I do. This book is dedicated to her.

NOTES

=

INTRODUCTION: INSIDE THE CHAUVET CAVE, 35,000 BCE

1. Jean Clottes, *Chauvet Cave: The Art of Earliest Times*, translated by Paul G. Bahn (Salt Lake City: University of Utah Press, 2003), 41.
2. Jean-Marie Chauvet, Eliette Brunel Deschamps, and Christian Hillaire, *Dawn of Art: The Chauvet Cave. The Oldest Known Paintings in the World*, translated by Paul G. Bahn (New York: Harry N. Abrams, 1996), 99. This is the publication produced by the team that discovered the cave.
3. Chauvet et al., *Dawn of Art*, 96.
4. Jean Clottes even sees a systematic connection between animal scratches and later paintings made by humans "as if the former attracted the latter"; *Chauvet Cave*, 62.
5. Sometimes, humans scratched engravings on top of animal marks. Chauvet et al., *Dawn of Art*, 99.
6. Clottes, *Chauvet Cave*, 72.
7. Anita Quiles et al., "A high-precision chronological model for the decorated Upper Paleolithic cave of Chauvet-Pont d'Arc, Ardèche, France," *Proceedings of the National Academy of Sciences of the United States of America* 113, no. 17 (April 26, 2016): 4674; www.pnas.org/cgi/doi/10.1073/pnas.1523158113.
8. For an account of ritual in the caves, see Jean Clottes and David Lewis-Williams, *The Shamans of Prehistory: Trance and Magic in the Painted Caves*, translated by Sophie Hawkes (New York: Harry N. Abrams, 1998). Also see Gregory Curtis, *The Cave Painters: Probing the Mysteries of the World's First Artists* (New York: Knopf, 2006), 217ff.
9. I recommend a documentary film about music in prehistoric caves: *Swinging Steinzeit*, directed by Pascal Goblot (France: ARTE F, 2020).
10. For a sense of the parallels between the humanisms developed in China and Europe, see *The Norton Anthology of World Literature*, 5th edition, volume C,

cluster on Humanism, edited by Wiebke Denecke and Barbara Fuchs (New York: Norton, forthcoming).

11.   Also see Rens Bod, *A New History of the Humanities: The Search for Principles and Patterns from Antiquity to the Present* (Oxford: Oxford University Press, 2013), 5ff.

CHAPTER 1: QUEEN NEFERTITI AND HER FACELESS GOD

1.   Not many commentators honor es-Senussi's pivotal role in this excavation. One exception is Evelyn Wells, *Nefertiti: A Biography of the World's Most Mysterious Queen* (New York: Doubleday, 1964), 8.

2.   The account of es-Senussi's discovery is based on the diary of the excavation: Ludwig Borchardt, *Tagebuch*, quoted in Friedericke Seyfried, "Die Büste der Nofretete: Dokumentation des Fundes und der Fundteilung 1912–1913," in *Jahrbuch Preußischer Kulturbesitz* 46 (2010): 133–202.

3.   For an account of these excavations, see Cyril Aldred, *Akhenaten: King of Egypt* (London: Thames and Hudson, 1988), 15ff. Also see Erik Hornung, "The Rediscovery of Akhenaten and His Place in Religion," *Journal of the American Research Center in Egypt* 29 (1992): 43–49.

4.   The best book on Nefertiti, from the perspective of art history, is Joyce Tyldesley, *Nefertiti's Face: The Creation of an Icon* (Cambridge, MA: Harvard University Press, 2018), 31.

5.   Klaus Dieter Hartel and Philipp Vandenberg, *Nefertiti: An Archaeological Biography* (Philadelphia: Lippincott, 1978), 68.

6.   Tyldesley, *Nefertiti's Face*, 15. Also see Aldred, *Akhenaten*, 148ff.

7.   Hartel and Vandenberg, *Nefertiti*, 114ff.

8.   See Aldred, *Akhenaten*, 220–22.

9.   For a description of the role of Amun, see Aldred, *Akhenaten*, 134ff.

10.   Tyldesley, *Nefertiti's Face*, 12ff.

11.   To date, no evidence has been found to contradict the claim made by Akhenaten that he founded the city on a site entirely devoid of human habitation. Aldred, *Akhenaten*, 60.

12.   Tyldesley, *Nefertiti's Face*, 12–13.

13.   Hartel and Vandenberg, *Nefertiti*, 99–113.

14.   Wells, *Nefertiti*, 68.

15.   Aldred, *Akhenaten*, 21.

16.   Hornung, "The Rediscovery of Akhenaten," 43.

17.   For the most convincing argument against a naturalistic interpretation of these depictions, see Dorothea Arnold, *Royal Women of Amarna* (New York: Abrams, 1997), 19ff.

18.   Tyldesley, *Nefertiti's Face*, 109.

19.   Tyldesley, *Nefertiti's Face*, 41.

20.   Tyldesley, *Nefertiti's Face*, 100.

21.   Arnold, *Royal Women of Amarna*, 47.

22.   Arnold, *Royal Women of Amarna*, 67.

23.   Aldred, *Akhenaten*, 32.

24.   "The Great Hymn to the Aten," in Miriam Lichtheim, *Ancient Egyptian Literature*, vol. 2, *The New Kingdom* (Berkeley: University of California Press, 2001).

25. Arnold, *Royal Women of Amarna*, 10ff.

26. Carl Niebuhr, *The Tell El Amarna Period: The Relations of Egypt and Western Asia in the Fifteenth Century B.C. According to the Tell El Amarna Tablets*, translated by J. Hutchinson (London: David Nutt, 1903).

27. G. R. Dabbs and J. C. Rose, "The Presence of Malaria Among the Non-Royal of the North Tombs Cemetery," *Horizon* 16, no. 7 (2015); G. R. Dabbs and M. Zabecki, "Abandoned Memories: A Cemetery of Forgotten Souls?," in B. Porter and A. Boutin, eds., *Remembering the Dead in the Ancient Near East* (Boulder: University Press of Colorado, 2014), 236–38.

28. Tyldesley, *Nefertiti's Face*, 43.

29. Also see James C. Scott, *Against the Grain: A Deep History of the Earliest States* (New Haven: Yale University Press, 2017).

30. This is the story narrated in the Torah, also known as the five books of Moses.

31. The most prominent contemporary person to have pursued these questions is Jan Assmann, in his various highly regarded but also occasionally contested books, including *The Price of Monotheism* (translated by Robert Savage; Stanford: Stanford University Press, 2009) and *Of God and Gods: Egypt, Israel, and the Rise of Monotheism* (Madison: University of Wisconsin Press, 2008).

32. Thomas Mann, *Joseph and His Brothers*, translated by John E. Woods (New York: Everyman's Library, 2005).

33. Sigmund Freud, *Moses and Monotheism* (New York: Alfred A. Knopf, 1939).

34. Akhenaten seems to have proscribed some rituals connected to other gods, such as Osiris. See Aldred, *Akhenaten*, 244ff.

35. See Martin Puchner, *The Written World: The Power of Stories to Shape People, History, and Civilization* (New York: Random House, 2017), 46ff.

36. Assmann, *The Price of Monotheism*, 46.

37. Tyldesley, *Nefertiti's Face*, 15–20.

CHAPTER 2: PLATO BURNS HIS TRAGEDY AND INVENTS A HISTORY

1. Plato, *Timaeus*, 22b.

2. For an incisive meditation on the status of latecomers in culture, to which I am greatly indebted throughout this book, see Wiebke Denecke, *Classical World Literature: Sino-Japanese and Greco-Roman Comparisons* (Oxford: Oxford University Press, 2014). Denecke compares the relation of Japanese culture to China with the relation between Rome and Greece. Her book begins with Plato's story of Solon and the Egyptian priests.

3. Diogenes Laertius, "Plato," in *Lives of Eminent Philosophers*, translated by R. D. Hicks (Cambridge, MA: Harvard University Press, 1972), vol. 1, 3:6.

4. There has been a debate since at least 1776 about whether women actually attended Greek theatrical performances. Some sources omit them, while others suggest that women attended, including Plato in his dialogue *Laws*, 817c. See Marilyn A. Katz, "Did the Women of Ancient Athens Attend the Theater in the Eighteenth Century," *Classical Philology* 93, no. 2 (April 1998): 105–24. Also see Jeffrey Henderson, "Women at the Athenian Dramatic Festivals," *Transactions of the American Philological Association* 121 (1991): 133–47.

5. Laertius, "Plato."

6. See Thomas G. Rosenmeyer, *The Art of Aeschylus* (Berkeley: University of Cali-

fornia Press, 1982); David Wiles, *Tragedy in Athens: Performance Space and Theatrical Meaning* (Cambridge: Cambridge University Press, 1997).

7.   For the role of women in tragedy, see Froma Zeitlin, *Playing the Other: Gender and Society in Classical Greek Literature* (Chicago: University of Chicago Press, 1996).

8.   For a vivid portrait of Socrates, see Emily Wilson, *The Death of Socrates* (Cambridge, MA: Harvard University Press, 2007).

9.   Laertius, "Plato."

10. See Martin Puchner, *Drama of Ideas: Platonic Provocations in Theater and Philosophy* (Princeton: Princeton University Press, 2006).

11. S. Sara Monoson, *Plato's Democratic Entanglements: Athenian Politics and the Practice of Philosophy* (Princeton: Princeton University Press, 2000).

12. Andrea Wilson Nightingale, *Genres in Dialogue: Plato and the Construction of Philosophy* (Cambridge: Cambridge University Press, 1995). Socrates's death, as depicted by Plato, spawned an entire tradition of plays about Socrates. See Puchner, *The Drama of Ideas*, 37–71. Also see Wilson, *The Death of Socrates*.

13. For the best history of the Socratic dialogue, see Charles H. Kahn, *Plato and the Socratic Dialogue* (Cambridge, MA: Harvard University Press, 1972).

14. Also see Jonas Barish, *The Anti-Theatrical Prejudice* (Berkeley: University of California Press, 1981).

15. Eric A. Havelock, *Preface to Plato* (Cambridge, MA: Harvard University Press, 1963); Walter J. Ong, *The Technologizing of the World* (London: Methuen, 1982).

CHAPTER 3: KING ASHOKA SENDS A MESSAGE TO THE FUTURE

1.   This is based on *Tarikh-I-Firoz Shahi*, an account of Firoz Shah's sultanate by the contemporary historian Shams-i Siraj 'Afif. An English translation was published as *Medieval India in Transition: Tarikh-i-Firoz Shahi*, edited by R. C. Jauhri (New Delhi: Sundeep Prakashan, 2001), 180ff.

2.   Siraj 'Afif, *Tarikh-I-Firoz Shahi*, 113.

3.   Siraj 'Afif, *Tarikh-I-Firoz Shahi*, 177ff.

4.   William Jeffrey McKibben, "The Monumental Pillars of Firuz Shah Tughluq," *Ars Orientalis* 24 (1994): 105–18, esp. 111.

5.   Firoz Shah was not the first ruler who attempted to remove this pillar; several of his predecessors had tried and failed. McKibben, "The Monumental Pillars," 111.

6.   Jauhri, *Medieval India in Transition*, 176; also see John S. Strong, *The Legend of King Asoka: A Study and Translation of the Asokavadana* (Delhi: Motilal Banarsidass Publications, 1989), 10.

7.   Xuanzang, *Record of the Western Regions*, translated by Samuel Beal as *Si-Yu-Ki: Buddhist Records of the Western World*, 2 vols. (London: Trübner, 1884), 2:85 and 91. Hwui Li, *The Life of Huien-Tsiang*, translated by Samuel Beal (London: Kegan Paul Trench, Trübner, 1914), 82, 93, 102. Overall, Xuanzang identified a number of pillars, some with inscriptions, but the pillar of Topra is not among them. Also see Erik Zürcher, *The Buddhist Conquest of China: The Spread and Adaptation of Buddhism in Early Medieval China* (Leiden: Brill, 2007).

8.   Strong, *The Legend of King Asoka*, 7.

9. Marlene Njammasch, "Krieg und Frieden unter den Mauryas," in *Altorientalische Forschungen* 14, no. 2 (January 1, 1987): 322–33, esp. 324.

10. Xuanzang, *Record of the Western Regions*, 9.

11. Strong, *The Legend of King Asoka*, 210ff.

12. *The Legend of King Asoka*, 199ff. Also see Strong, "The Legend and Its Background," in *The Legend of King Asoka*, 17.

13. The *Asokavadana* was so widely read that it suggested to its readers a connection between stupas and Ashoka. Strong, "Aśoka and the Buddha," in *The Legend of King Asoka*, 109.

14. In his grand history of the earth, of which the author is an ardent fan, H. G. Wells proclaimed Ashoka to be one of the great high points in the history of mankind. H. G. Wells, *A Short History of the World* (New York: Macmillan, 1922), 163ff. The best scholarly book on Ashoka is by Nayanjot Lahiri, *Ashoka in Ancient India* (Cambridge, MA: Harvard University Press, 2015).

15. For a detailed critique of dharma and other political categories in ancient India in relation to political violence, see Upinder Singh, *Political Violence in Ancient India* (Cambridge, MA: Harvard University Press, 2017).

16. Peter Harvey, *An Introduction to Buddhism: Teachings, History, and Practices*, 2nd ed. (Cambridge, MA: Cambridge University Press, 2013). Richard F. Gombrich, *How Buddhism Began: The Conditioned Genesis of the Early Teachings*, 2nd ed. (London: Routledge, 1996). Similar ideas can also be found among the Jains, and according to legend Ashoka's grandfather had died as a Jaina, which means that this idea was part of a larger tradition and not merely Buddhist.

17. Strong, *The Legend of King Asoka*, 211.

18. *The Edicts of Asoka*, edited and translated by N. A. Nikam and Richard McKeon (Chicago: University of Chicago Press, 1959), 56.

19. Romila Thapar, *Asoka and the Decline of the Mauryas* (Oxford: Clarendon Press, 1961), 74.

20. Christopher I. Beckwith, among a minority of scholars, questions whether all edicts should be attributed to Ashoka. Christopher I. Beckwith, *Greek Buddha: Pyrrho's Encounter with Early Buddhism in Central Asia* (Princeton: Princeton University Press, 2015), 234.

21. Thapar, *Asoka*, 137.

22. John Irwin, "Aśokan Pillars: A Reassessment of the Evidence," *Burlington Magazine* 115, no. 848 (November 1972): 706–20, esp. 717ff.

23. Also compare Lahiri, *Ashoka in Ancient India*, 275ff.

24. Nikam and McKeon, *Edicts of Asoka*, 27 (Rock Edict XIII).

25. Strong, *The Legend of King Asoka*, 14. It is possible that the text postdates Ashoka, however.

26. Irwin, "Aśokan Pillars," 717.

27. Lahiri, *Ashoka in Ancient India*, 120ff. The role of early writing in India is a hotly debated subject. Richard Gombrich, in "How the Mahayana Began," *Buddhist Forum* 1 (1990): 27, claims that no writing existed before the life of the Buddha was written down. I also consulted Harry Falk, *Schrift im alten Indien* (Tübingen: Gunter Narr, 1993), 337. Peter Skilling, in "Redaction, Recitation, and Writing: Transmission of the Buddha's teaching in India in the early period," in Stephen C. Berkwitz, Juliane Schober, and Claudia Brown, eds., *Buddhist Man-*

uscript Cultures (Basingstoke, UK: Routledge, 2009): 63, assumes that some writing existed, but that it was only used for administrative purposes. There is also the puzzle of the so-called Indus Valley Script, considerably older, which may or may not be a linguistic script and which has not yet been deciphered. See Peter T. Daniels and William Bright, eds., *The World's Writing Systems* (Oxford: Oxford University Press, 1996), 165ff.

28. Uses of the Brahmi script before Ashoka's time have been found in Kodumanal and Porunthal in south India.

29. One of the few historians of the humanities to mention this extraordinary figure is Rens Bod, in *A New History of the Humanities: The Search for Principles and Patterns from Antiquity to the Present* (Oxford: Oxford University Press, 2014), 14ff.

30. Thapar, *Asoka*, 9, 162ff. Also see Falk, *Schrift im alten Indien*, 104–05.

31. For an account of Alexander's effect on the East, see Amélie Kuhrt and Susan Sherwin-White, eds., *Hellenism in the East: The Interaction of Greek and Non-Greek Civilizations from Syria to Central Asia after Alexander* (Berkeley: University of California Press, 1988). I also consulted Daniels and Bright, *The World's Writing Systems*, and Falk, *Schrift im alten Indien*.

32. Plutarch, *Lives*, translated by Bernadotte Perrin, Loeb Classical Library 99 (Cambridge, MA: Harvard University Press, 1919), VIII, 2–3.

33. Lahiri, *Ashoka in Ancient India*, 166ff. Even though there is no archeological evidence, it is likely that the Brahmi script was used in the north before Ashoka's time, as it had been in southern India and Sri Lanka.

34. Thapar, *Asoka*, 367. It is even possible, though unlikely, that Ashoka himself had some Greek parentage. See Thapar, *Asoka*, 25.

35. Lahiri, *Ashoka in Ancient India*, 120ff.

36. J. R. McNeill and William H. McNeill, *The Human Web: A Bird's-Eye View of World History* (New York: Norton, 2003), 41ff.

37. Jared Diamond, *Guns, Germs, and Steel: The Fates of Human Societies* (New York: Norton, 1997).

38. Thapar, *Asoka*, 147ff.

39. McNeill and McNeill, *The Human Web*, 36ff.

40. See among many other sources, Diamond, *Guns, Germs, and Steel*.

41. Thapar, *Asoka*, 159.

42. Compare to Karl Jaspers, *The Origin and Goal of History* (Basingstoke, UK: Routledge, 2011).

43. Ven. S. Dhammika, *The Edicts of King Ashoka* (Kandy, Sri Lanka: Buddhist Publication Society, 1993), 27. Also see Nikam and McKeon, *The Edicts of Asoka*, where the line reads: "He has achieved this moral conquest repeatedly both here and among the peoples living beyond the borders of his kingdom, even as far away as six hundred Yojanas, where the Yona king Antiyoka rules, and even beyond Antiyoka in the realms of the four kings named Turamaya, Antikini, Maka, and Alikasudara, and to the south among the Cholas and Pandyas as far as Ceylon" (29).

44. Compare Peter Frankopan, *The Silk Roads: A New History of the World* (London: Bloomsbury, 2015).

45. Nikam and McKeon, *The Edicts of Asoka*, 38.

46. Dhammika, *The Edicts of Ashoka*, 34; Nikam and McKeon, *The Edicts of Ashoka*, 36.

47.   Thapar, *Asoka*, preface. Also see William Dalrymple, *The Anarchy: The East India Company, Corporate Violence, and the Pillage of an Empire* (London: Bloomsbury, 2019).

48.   For an account of James Princep, see Charles Allen, *Ashoka: The Search for India's Lost Emperor* (New York: Little, Brown, 2012), 120ff.

CHAPTER 4: A SOUTH ASIAN GODDESS IN POMPEII

1.   Mirella Levi D'Ancona, "An Indian Statuette from Pompeii," *Artibus Asiae* 13, no. 3 (1950): 166–80, esp. 168ff.

2.   See Elizabeth Ann Pollard, "Indian Spices and Roman 'Magic' in Imperial and Late Antique Indomediterranea," *Journal of World History* 24, no. 1 (March 2013): 1–23, esp. 7.

3.   Grant Parker, "Ex Oriente Luxuria: Indian Commodities and Roman Experience," *Journal of the Economic and Social History of the Orient* 45, no. 1 (2002): 40–95, esp. 73. For a fuller account of long-distance trade, see Kasper Grønlund Evers, *Worlds Apart Trading Together: The Organization of Long-Distance Trade between Rome and India in Antiquity* (Oxford: Archaeopress, 2017), 22ff. Evers doubts that the statue represents Lakshmi due to significant differences between the statue and common representations of the goddess.

4.   Parker, "Ex Oriente Luxuria," 44, 48.

5.   Parker, "Ex Oriente Luxuria," 68ff. Also see Pollard, "Indian Spices and Roman 'Magic'," 8.

6.   Pollard, "Indian Spices and Roman 'Magic'," 2. On Pompeian villas and luxury, see Martha Zarmakoupi, *Designing for Luxury and the Bay of Naples: Villas and Landscapes (c. 100 BCE–79 CE)* (Oxford: Oxford University Press, 2014).

7.   New evidence about Pompeii's bar and food establishments continues to emerge. In 2020, evidence of a "snack bar" was unearthed. Elisabetta Povoledo, "Snail, Fish and Sheep Soup, Anyone? Savory New Finds at Pompeii," *New York Times*, December 26, 2020, https://www.nytimes.com/2020/12/26/world/europe/pompeii-snack-bar-thermopolium.html?searchResultPosition=2.

8.   The most recent and excellent study of the eruption, with particular attention to Pliny, is Daisy Dunn, *The Shadow of Vesuvius: A Life of Pliny* (New York: Liveright, 2019).

9.   The discovery of a temple dedicated to an Egyptian god in a Roman city was so startling to the eighteenth century, when the discovery was made, that it contributed to a revival of interest in Egypt; one of those inspired by it was Wolfgang Amadeus Mozart, whose opera *The Magic Flute* uses Isis and her husband Osiris, as well as other Egypt-inspired motifs. Mary Beard, *The Fires of Vesuvius: Pompeii Lost and Found* (Cambridge, MA: Belknap Press, 2008), 303. Another, probably more prominent influence on Mozart was Napoleon's expedition. See Jan Assmann, *Moses the Egyptian: The Memory of Egypt in Western Monotheism* (Cambridge, MA: Harvard University Press, 1997), 16.

10.   Dexter Hoyos, *Rome Victorious: The Irresistible Rise of the Roman Empire* (London: I. B. Tauris, 2019), 29.

11.   Beard, *Fires*, 254.

12.   Importing large exotic animals, including elephants, became a big business

after Romans developed a taste for gladiatorial games. Pollard, "Indian Spices and Roman 'Magic'," 7.

13.   Beard, *Fires of Vesuvius*, 143.

14.   D'Ancona, "Indian Statuette," 180.

15.   For a description of Etruscan influence on Rome, see Mary Beard, *SPQR: A History of Ancient Rome* (New York: Liveright: 2015), 108ff. For specific case studies of Etruscan culture in Italy before and during Roman times, see Sinclair Bell and Helen Nagy, *New Perspectives on Etruria and Early Rome, in honor of Richard Daniel De Puma* (Madison: University of Wisconsin Press, 2009).

16.   Horace, Epistle 2.156–7: *Graecia capta ferum victorem cepit et artis intulit agresti Latio.*" Translated by Elena Theodorakopoulos, unpublished. For the larger context of the Romans' use of Greece, see Wiebke Denecke, *Classical World Literatures*, 36ff.

17.   Denis Feeney, *Beyond Greek: The Beginnings of Latin Literature* (Cambridge, MA: Harvard University Press, 2016), 58.

18.   For a general introduction to Roman drama, see Gesine Manuwald, *Roman Drama: A Reader* (London: Duckworth, 2010).

19.   George Fredric Franko and Dorota Dutsch, *A Companion to Plautus* (Hoboken, NJ: John Wiley & Sons, 2020), 11.

20.   Sebastiana Nervegna, "Plautus and Greek Drama," in Franko and Dutsch, *Companion to Plautus*, 33. Also see Elaine Fantham, "Roman Experience of Menander in the Late Republic and Early Empire," *Transactions of the American Philological Association* 114 (1984): 299–309.

21.   Franko and Dutsch, *Companion to Plautus*, 19. Timothy J. Moore, "The State of Roman Theater c. 200 BCE," in Franko and Dutsch, *Companion to Plautus*, 24.

22.   David Damrosch, *What Is World Literature?* (Princeton: Princeton University Press, 2003).

23.   Feeney, *Beyond Greek*, 43.

24.   The other exception is Japan, as outlined so incisively by Denecke, *Classical World Literatures*.

25.   An alternative description of this phenomenon is provided by Michael von Albrecht in *A History of Roman Literature* (Leiden: Brill, 1997); he calls Roman literature "the first 'derived' literature" (12).

26.   Denecke, *Classical World Literatures*, 21.

27.   Denecke, *Classical World Literatures*, 157.

28.   Virgil used some local legends, such as one that Trojans landed in Sicily; there also existed legends relating to Aeneas in Etruria. For a discussion of these sources, see Karl Galinsky, *Aeneas, Sicily, and Rome* (Princeton: Princeton University Press, 2015).

29.   Helene Foley, *Reimagining Greek Tragedy on the American Stage* (Berkeley: University of California Press, 2012).

CHAPTER 5: A BUDDHIST PILGRIM IN SEARCH OF ANCIENT TRACES

1.   The following account is based on Xuanzang's own account of his travels, *Si-Yu-Ki: Buddhist Records of the Western World*, translated from the Chinese of Huien Tsiang by Samuel Beal, 2 vols. (London: Trübner, 1884), and on the biography most likely written by one of Xuanzang's students, *The Life of Huien-*

Tsiang, by the Shaman Hwui Li, translated by Samuel Beal (London: Kegan Paul Trench, Trübner, 1914), 191. The best general introduction to East Asia is Charles Holcombe, *A History of East Asia: From the Origins of Civilization to the Twenty-First Century*, 2nd ed. (Cambridge: Cambridge University Press, 2017). I am also greatly indebted to Wiebke Denecke, whose headnotes in the *Norton Anthology of World Literature*, for which we both serve as editors, have taught me much about East Asia.

2. Li, *The Life of Huien-Tsiang*, 10–13.
3. Li, *The Life of Huien-Tsiang*, 13–17.
4. Michael Nylan, *The Five "Confucian" Classics* (New Haven: Yale University Press, 2001).
5. Wiebke Denecke, *Dynamics of Masters Literature: Early Chinese Thought from Confucius to Han Feizi* (Cambridge, MA: Harvard University Press, 2011).
6. Li, *The Life of Huien-Tsiang*, 2.
7. Li, *The Life of Huien-Tsiang*, 3.
8. Compare Peter Frankopan, *The Silk Roads: A New History of the World* (London: Bloomsbury, 2015).
9. Li, *The Life of Huien-Tsiang*, 4–7.
10. Peter Harvey, *An Introduction to Buddhism: Teachings, History, and Practices*, 2nd ed. (Cambridge, MA: Cambridge University Press, 2013). Richard F. Gombrich, *How Buddhism Began: The Conditioned Genesis of the Early Teachings*, 2nd ed. (London: Routledge, 1996).
11. Li, *The Life of Huien-Tsiang*, 44.
12. Xuanzang, *Record of the Western Regions*, translated by Samuel Beal in *Si-Yu-Ki: Buddhist Records of the Western World*, 2 vols. (London: Trübner, 1884), vol. 1, 32.
13. Xuanzang, *Record of the Western Regions*, 51.
14. For more on how the legend and idea of Ashoka shaped the perception of Xuanzang and other Chinese travelers, see John Kieschnick and Meir Shahar, *India in the Chinese Imagination* (Philadelphia: University of Pennsylvania Press, 2013), 5ff.
15. Xuanzang, *Record of the Western Regions*, 2:91.
16. Shashibala, ed., *Kumarajiva: Philosopher and Seer* (New Delhi: Indira Gandhi National Centre for the Arts, 2015).
17. Li, *The Life of Huien-Tsiang*, 10.
18. Xuanzang, *Record of the Western Regions*, 2:135.
19. Li, *The Life of Huien-Tsiang*, 167ff.
20. Li, *The Life of Huien-Tsiang*, 168.
21. Xuanzang, *Record of the Western Regions*, 2:15.
22. Li, *The Life of Huien-Tsiang*, 191.
23. Li, *The Life of Huien-Tsiang*, 209ff.
24. The Dunhuang caves also harbored an important cache of old texts that include the oldest surviving printed scroll in the world, a copy of the Diamond Sutra. See Martin Puchner, *The Written World: The Power of Stories to Shape People, History, and Civilization* (New York: Random House, 2017), 90ff.
25. Li, *The Life of Huien-Tsiang*, 215.
26. Wiebke Denecke, *Classical World Literatures: Sino-Japanese and Greco-Roman Comparisons* (Oxford: Oxford University Press, 2014). Denis Feeney, *Beyond Greek: The Beginnings of Latin Literature* (Cambridge, MA: Harvard University Press, 2016).

CHAPTER 6: *THE PILLOW BOOK* AND SOME PERILS OF CULTURAL DIPLOMACY

1. This story is based on Sei Shōnagon, *The Pillow Book*, translated by Meredith McKinney (London: Penguin, 2006), 198–99. For this chapter, I am greatly indebted to Wiebke Denecke and our work on the *Norton Anthology of World Literature*.

2. Sei Shōnagon, *The Pillow Book* (trans. McKinney), 3, 46.

3. Sei Shōnagon, *The Pillow Book* (trans. McKinney), 55, 87.

4. Helen Craig McCullough, *Okagami, The Great Mirror: Fujiwara Michinaga (966–1027) and His Times* (Princeton: Princeton University Press, 1980).

5. Sei Shōnagon, *The Pillow Book* (trans. McKinney), 101.

6. Sei Shōnagon, *The Pillow Book of Sei Shōnagon*, translated and edited by Ivan Morris (New York: Columbia University Press, 1991), 175; Sei Shōnagon, *The Pillow Book* (trans. McKinney), 246.

7. Sei Shōnagon, *The Pillow Book* (trans. McKinney), 39.

8. See Edwin Reischauer, *Ennin's Travel in T'an China* (New York: Ronald Press, 1955).

9. *Ennin's Diary: The Record of a Pilgrimage to China in Search of the Law*, translated from the Chinese by Edwin O. Reischauer (New York: Ronald Press, 1955), 50.

10. Compare Charles Holcombe, *The Genesis of East Asia, 221 B.C.–A.D. 907* (Honolulu: University of Hawai'i Press, 2001).

11. See Wiebke Denecke, *Classical World Literatures: Sino-Japanese and Greco-Roman Comparisons* (Oxford: Oxford University Press, 2014). There was another difference from Rome's relation to Greece: Romans needed translations of Greek works, while Japanese readers did not need translations of Chinese works.

12. For a good description of "brush talk," see headnote by Wiebke Denecke, "Japan's Classical Age," in *Norton Anthology of World Literature*, 4th ed., vol. B (New York: Norton: 2012), 1161–69.

13. *Ennin's Diary*, 45.

14. *Ennin's Diary*, 86ff.

15. *Ennin's Diary*, 102ff.

16. *Ennin's Diary*, 230, and Reischauer's comments, 198.

17. Dietrich Seckel, *Buddhist Art of East Asia*, translated by Ulrich Mammitzsch (Bellingham, WA: Western Washington University, 1989), 10.

18. Seckel, *Buddhist Art*, 24.

19. Seckel, *Buddhist Art*, 25ff.

20. Seckel, *Buddhist Art*, 27.

21. *Ennin's Diary*, 332.

22. *Ennin's Diary*, 341

23. *Ennin's Diary*, 382.

24. *Ennin's Diary*, 370–71.

25. Ivan Morris, *The World of the Shining Prince: Court Life in Ancient Japan* (New York: Knopf, 1964).

26. Haruo Shirane, *The Bridge of Dreams: A Poetics of "The Tale of Genji"* (Stanford: Stanford University Press, 1978).

27. Noriko T. Reider, *Seven Demon Stories from Medieval Japan* (Boulder: University of Colorado Press, 2016), 89ff.

28.   Kibi no Makibi scroll, in Noriko T. Reider, *Seven Demon Stories from Medieval Japan* (Boulder: University Press of Colorado, 2016).

29.   Sei Shōnagon, *The Pillow Book* (trans. McKinney), 255–56.

CHAPTER 7: WHEN BAGHDAD BECAME A STOREHOUSE OF WISDOM

1.   The dream is reported in two sources, in slightly different versions, by Abdallah ibn Tahir and by Yahya ibn 'Adi. Both versions are quoted and discussed in Dimitri Gutas, *Greek Thought, Arabic Culture: The Graeco-Arabic Translation Movement in Baghdad and Early 'Abbasid Society (2nd–4th/8th–10th centuries)* (London: Routledge, 1998), 97–98.

2.   Gutas, *Greek Thought*, 52.

3.   This was part of a larger pattern of nomadic conquerors adopting writing. See, for example, Robert Tignor et al., *Worlds Together, Worlds Apart: A History of the World*, 2nd ed. (New York: Norton, 2008), 99, 105, 252.

4.   J. R. McNeill and William H. McNeill, *The Human Web: A Bird's-Eye View of World History* (New York: Norton, 2003). Also see James C. Scott, *Against the Grain: A Deep History of Earliest States* (New Haven: Yale University Press, 2017).

5.   For a discussion of Scott's *Against the Grain*, see my review essay "Down With the Scribes?," *Public Books*, April 16, 2018, https://www.publicbooks.org/down -with-the-scribes/. I should add that I have since come around to Scott's point much more than I did when I first read and reviewed his book.

6.   David M. Carr, *Writing on the Tablet of the Heart: Origins of Scripture and Literature* (Oxford: Oxford University Press, 2005), 47–56. Also see David Damrosch, *The Buried Book: The Loss and Rediscovery of the Great Epic of Gilgamesh* (New York: Henry Holt, 2006).

7.   Gutas, *Greek Thought*, 54ff. For the best general introduction to the *Arabian Nights*, see Robert Irwin, *The Arabian Nights: A Companion* (London: Palgrave Macmillan, 2004).

8.   Jonathan M. Bloom, *Paper Before Print: The History and Impact of Paper in the Islamic World* (New Haven: Yale University Press, 2001), 48–51. Also see Nicholas Basbane, *On Paper: The Everything of its Two-Thousand-Year History* (New York: Vintage, 2013), 48–49.

9.   De Lacy Evans O'Leary, *How Greek Science Passed to the Arabs* (London: Routledge, 1948).

10.   Gutas, *Greek Thought*, 52.

11.   Gutas, *Greek Thought*, 61ff. For an excellent article describing the translation of Greek texts into Arabic, see A. I. Sabra, "The Appropriation and Subsequent Naturalization of Greek Science in Medieval Islam: A Preliminary Statement," *History of Science* 25 (September 1987): 223–43.

12.   Amélie Kuhrt and Susan Sherwin-White, eds., *Hellenism in the East: The Interaction of Greek and Non-Greek Civilizations from Syria to Central Asia after Alexander* (Berkeley: University of California Press, 1988). Peter Green, *Alexander the Great and the Hellenistic Age: A Short History* (London: Weidenfeld & Nicolson, 2007), 63. I also consulted M. Rostovtzeff, *The Social and Economic History of the Hellenistic World*, vol. 1 (Oxford: Clarendon Press, 1941), 446ff.

13.   Roy MacLeod, ed., *The Library of Alexandria: Centre of Learning in the Ancient*

World (London: Tauris, 2000). F. E. Peters, *The Harvest of Hellenism: A History of the Near East from Alexander the Great to the Triumph of Christianity* (New York: Simon and Schuster, 1970).

14.   Another source of Greek learning in the Arab Empire was the Eastern Church. In the first phase of the Arab conquest, there was little forced suppression of other religions, which meant that the Arab Empire contained various religious communities, from Zoroastrians (mostly in Persia) and Manichaeans to Christians living throughout the Middle East and Mesopotamia, including in a monastery conveniently located just south of Baghdad. These Christians, Greek-speaking or at least conversant in Greek, since the New Testament was written in that language, were able to translate Greek texts for their new Arab rulers; one text was even translated by the Patriarch of Alexandria himself.

15.   Dimitri Gutas, "Origins in Baghdad," in Robert Pasnau, ed., *The Cambridge History of Medieval Philosophy* (Cambridge: Cambridge University Press, 2011), 9–25, esp. 12ff.

16.   Paul Speck, "Byzantium: Cultural Suicide?" in Leslie Brubaker, ed., *Byzantium in the Ninth Century: Dead or Alive?*, Thirteenth Spring Symposium of Byzantine Studies, Birmingham, March 1996 (London: Routledge, 2016), 73–84, esp. 76.

17.   Translation by Franz Rosenthal in *Knowledge Triumphant, The Concept of Knowledge in Medieval Islam* (Leiden: Brill, 2006), 182.

18.   Warren Treadgold, "The Macedonian Renaissance," in Warren Treadgold, ed., *Renaissances Before the Renaissance: Cultural Revivals of Late Antiquity and the Middle Age*s (Stanford: Stanford University Press, 1984), 81. Gutas speculates that demand across the Arab Empire would have created financial incentives for Byzantine scribes to copy classical texts; *Greek Thought*, 185.

19.   For an excellent account of the role of Greek philosophy in the Islamic world, see Joel L. Kraemer, *Humanism in the Renaissance of Islam: The Cultural Revival during the Buyid Age* (Leiden: Brill, 1986), and its companion volume, *Philosophy in the Renaissance of Islam: Abū Sulaymān Al-Sijistānī and his Circle* (Leiden: Brill, 1986).

20.   L. E. Goodman, *Avicenna* (London: Routledge, 1992). For the best introduction to Avicenna, see Jon McGinnis, *Avicenna* (Oxford: Oxford University Press, 2010).

21.   Gutas, *Greek Thought*, 162; also see Rosenthal, *Knowledge Triumphant*, 50ff.

22.   Biographical information is partly based on Ibn Sina's own autobiographical text, in Dimitri Gutas, ed., *Avicenna and the Aristotelian Tradition*, vol. 89 of *Islamic Philosophy, Theology and Science: Texts and Studies*, edited by Hans Daiber, Anna Akasoy, and Emilie Savage-Smith (Leiden: Brill, 2014), 11–19.

23.   Goodman, *Avicenna*, 48ff.

24.   Ibn Sina, "Autobiography," in Gutas, *Avicenna and the Aristotelian Tradition*, 19.

25.   Ibn Sina, "Autobiography," in Gutas, *Avicenna and the Aristotelian Tradition*, 150ff.

26.   In an excellent article, the scholar Erez Naaman uses the twin terms "appropriation and naturalization" to describe the process by which Ibn Sina and others used Greek philosophy and made it their own, including the Aristotelian

concept of *habitus*. "Nurture over Nature: Habitus from al-Fārābī through Ibn Khaldūn to 'Abduh," *Journal of the American Oriental Society* 137, no. 1 (2017): 10ff.

27.   Rosenthal, *Knowledge Triumphant*, 195.

28.   Goodman, *Avicenna*, 80.

29.   Ibn Sina, "Autobiography," in Gutas, *Avicenna and the Aristotelian Tradition*, 111.

30.   There were also rival Aristotelians to contend with. In one treatise, Ibn Sina contrasted his approach, which he called "Eastern Philosophy" since it was developed in the eastern part of the Islamic World, to "Western Philosophy," the one developed in Baghdad. (The difference amounted to different understandings of Aristotle and his legacy.) Since Aristotle's life, there had accrued many layers of commentary, ways of turning these old texts into useful tools for later times, from classical Athens to Alexander the Great (Gutas, *Greek Thought*, 153). The same happened in the course of the Arabic translation project, which had begun in Baghdad but since spawned other approaches and schools, culminating in Ibn Sina's own work.

31.   Ahmed H. al-Rahim, "Avicenna's Immediate Disciples: Their Lives and Works," in Y. Tzvi Langermann, ed., *Avicenna and His Legacy: A Golden Age of Science and Philosophy* (Turnhout, Belgium: Brepols, 2010): 1–25.

32.   Al-Rahim, "Avicenna's Immediate Disciples."

33.   For an excellent partial edition of this text, see Jon McGinnis, *Avicenna: The Physics of The Healing: A Parallel English-Arabic Text* (Provo, UT: Brigham Young University Press, 2009).

CHAPTER 8: THE QUEEN OF ETHIOPIA WELCOMES THE RAIDERS OF THE ARK

1.   "Aksum," *Encyclopedia Britannica*, March 28, 2019, https://www.britannica .com/place/Aksum-Ethiopia.

2.   Also see Stuart Munro-Hay, *The Quest for the Ark of the Covenant: The True History of the Tablets of Moses* (London: I. B. Tauris, 2005), 27ff.

3.   David Allan Hubbard, *The Literary Sources of the Kebra Nagast*, PhD thesis, University of St. Andrews, 1956, 330.

4.   Munro-Hay, *Quest*, 28.

5.   Exodus 19:1–34:28.

6.   Book of Ezra; Book of Nehemiah. Also see Lisbeth S. Fried, *Ezra and the Law in History and Tradition* (Columbia: University of South Carolina Press, 2014), and Juha Pakkala, *Ezra the Scribe: The Development of Ezra 7-10 and Nehemiah 8* (Berlin: Walter de Gruyter, 2004).

7.   1 Kings 10:1–13; 22 Chronicles 9:1–12 (KJV). It is unclear, from the text, where that country is. Many scholars presume that it is in Yemen. If so, the *Kebra Nagast* reinterprets the story as referring to ancient Ethiopia, just across the Bab-el-Mandeb strait.

8.   Carl Bezold, *Kebra Nagast, Die Herrlichkeit der Könige, nach den Handschriften in Berlin, London, Oxford und Paris, zum ersten Mal im äthiopischen Urtext hrsg. und mit deutscher Übersetzung versehen* (Munich: G. Franz, 1905). For work in progress on the *Kebra Nagast*, see Wendy Laura Belcher, "The Black Queen

of Sheba: A Global History of an African Idea," https://wendybelcher.com/african-literature/black-queen-of-sheba/, accessed November 22, 2021. For an excellent article on the subject of the Queen of Sheba, see Wendy Laura Belcher, "African Rewritings of the Jewish and Islamic Solomonic Tradition: The Triumph of the Queen of Sheba in the Ethiopian Fourteenth-Century Text *Kəbrä Nägäst*," in Roberta Sabbath, ed., *Sacred Tropes: Tanakh, New Testament, and Qur'an as Literary Works* (Boston/Leiden: Brill, 2009), 441–59.

9.   Harold G. Marcus, *History of Ethiopia* (Berkeley: University of California Press, 1994), 19ff.

10.   Luke 4:16ff; 21:22; 22:37; Matthew 5:17. On the education of the historical Jesus, especially his knowledge of Hebrew, see John P. Meier, *A Marginal Jew: Rethinking the Historical Jesus*, vol. 1, *The Roots of the Problem and the Person* (New York: Doubleday, 1991), 264ff. Meier believes that the famous formulation of Jesus "fulfilling" the Law is a later creation; *A Marginal Jew*, vol. 4, *Law and Love* (New Haven: Yale University Press, 2009), 41. Also see Geza Vermes, *Christian Beginnings: From Nazareth to Nicaea (AD 30–325)* (London: Allen Lane, 2012).

11.   Acts 9:4–18.

12.   There is one possible exception: the scene in which Jesus writes with his finger in the sand, but we do not learn what he wrote and the writing disappears immediately, presumably blown away by the wind; John 8:6.

13.   William M. Schniedewind, *How the Bible Became a Book: The Textualization of Ancient Israel* (Cambridge: Cambridge University Press, 2004). Also see David M. Carr, *Writing on the Tablet of the Heart: Origins of Scripture and Literature* (Oxford: Oxford University Press, 2005).

14.   Taddesse Tamrat, *Church and State in Ethiopia 1270–1527* (Oxford: Clarendon Press, 1972), 23ff.

15.   Also see Hubbard, *Literary Sources of the Kebra Nagast*, 123ff.

16.   Edward Ullendorf, *Ethiopia and the Bible*, Schweich Lectures on Biblical Archaeology, 1967 (Oxford: Oxford University Press, 1968), 12.

17.   Compare Ullendorf, *Ethiopia and the Bible*, 20ff.

18.   Stuart Munro-Hay, "A Sixth-Century Kebra Nagaśt?," in Alessandro Bausi, ed., *Languages and Cultures of Eastern Christianity* (London: Routledge, 2012), 313–28.

19.   Donald Levine, *Greater Ethiopia: The Evolution of a Multiethnic Society* (Chicago: University of Chicago Press, 1974), 96ff.

20.   Serge A. Frantsouzoff, "On the Dating of the Ethiopian Dynastic Treatise Kabrä nägäśt: New Evidence," *Scrinium* 12 (2016): 20–24. Also see Gizachew Tiruneh, "The Kebra Nagast: Can Its Secrets Be Revealed?," *International Journal of Ethiopian Studies* 8, no. 1 & 2 (2014): 51–72, esp. 53.

21.   Levine, *Greater Ethiopia*, 70ff.

22.   Ullendorf, *Ethiopia and the Bible*, 21.

23.   Hubbard, *Literary Sources of the Kebra Nagast*, 133.

24.   Marcus, *History of Ethiopia*, 13.

25.   Qur'an, Sura 27:15–45.

26.   Levine, *Greater Ethiopia*, 70ff.

27.   Tamrat, *Church and State*, 231.

28. Marcus, *History of Ethiopia*, 31.
29. Munro, *Quest*, 104. Intrigued by reports of a Christian in eastern Africa, King John II of Portugal had sent the adventurer Pêdro da Covilhã to make contact with Prester John around 1490 by land and again, a few years later, by sea.
30. Marcus, *History of Ethiopia*, 34.
31. Munro, *Quest*, 190.
32. Gizachew Tiruneh, "The Kebra Nagast: Can Its Secrets Be Revealed?," in *International Journal of Ethiopian Studies* 8, no. 1 & 2 (2014): 52.
33. E. A. Wallis Budge, "Introduction," in *The Kebra Nagast* (New York: Cosimo Classics, 2004): xxvii. Quoted in Tiruneh, "The Kebra Nagast," 52.
34. Homer, *Odyssey*, 1.23. Also see Frank M. Snowden, Jr., *Blacks in Antiquity: Ethiopians in the Greco-Roman Experience* (Cambridge, MA: Belknap Press, 1970).
35. Rupert Lewis, *Marcus Garvey* (Kingston, Jamaica: University of the West Indies Press, 2018), 19, 35.
36. For the role of Garvey, see Barry Chevannes, *Rastafari: Roots and Ideology (Utopianism and Communitarianism)* (Syracuse: Syracuse University Press, 1994), 87ff.
37. Ennis B. Edmonds, *Rastafari: A Very Short Introduction* (Oxford: Oxford University Press, 2012), 7.
38. See, for example, G. G. Maragh a.k.a. The Rt. Hon. Leonard Percival Howell, *The Promised Key* (London: Hogarth Blake, 2008). This text was originally published in Jamaica around 1935. Howell was one of the original founders of the movement.
39. Lewis, *Marcus Garvey*, 83; Chevannes, *Rastafari*, 42.
40. Edmonds, *Rastafari*, 43. Others relate the hairstyle to that of certain African tribes such as Gallas, Somalis, Maasai, or Mau Mau fighters. Chevannes reports that some Rastafarians thought of dreadlocks as an homage to King Selassie's crown (*Rastafari*, 145).
41. Chevannes, *Rastafari*, 21.
42. Marizia Anna Coltri, *Beyond Rastafari: A Historical and Theological Introduction*, Religions and Discourse 56 (Bern: Peter Lang, 1015), 202. See for example Gerald Hausman, *The Kebra Nagast: The Lost Bible of Rastafarian Wisdom and Faith* (New York: St. Martin's Press, 2020), with a foreword by Ziggy Marley, "which explores the importance of the Kebra Nagast as a powerful and sacred text both in Rastafarian tradition and in a broader sense."

CHAPTER 9: ONE CHRISTIAN MYSTIC AND THE THREE REVIVALS OF EUROPE

1. There had been no Roman emperor since 476 in Rome, though there continued to be emperors in Byzantium, the eastern Rome. See Wilfried Hartmann, *Karl der Große* (Stuttgart: W. Kohlhammer, 2010), 206ff.
2. Luc-Normand Tellier, *Urban World History: An Economic and Geographical Perspective* (Québec: Presses de l'Université du Québec, 2009), 158.
3. Johannes Fried, *Charlemagne* (Cambridge, MA: Harvard University Press, 2016), 339.
4. Charlemagne, "Epistola Generalis," quoted in Fried, *Charlemagne*, 23.

5. Hartmann, *Karl der Große*, 179.

6. Douglas Bullough, *The Age of Charlemagne* (New York: Exeter, 1980), 41.

7. Hartmann, *Karl der Große*, 177. Also see Fried, who imagines Charlemagne reading even in his youth (*Charlemagne*, 25).

8. Fried, *Charlemagne*, 238.

9. Fried, *Charlemagne*, 268, 275.

10. Bullough, *The Age of Charlemagne*, 100ff.

11. Sarah L. Higley, *Hildegard of Bingen's Unknown Language: An Edition, Translation and Discussion* (New York: Palgrave Macmillan, 2007), 151.

12. One of the figures to bring knowledge from al-Andalus was the Spanish Goth Theodulf. See Bullough, *The Age of Charlemagne*, 102.

13. Fried, *Charlemagne*, 246.

14. For a detailed discussion of the sources pertaining to Hildegard's biography, see Michael Embach, "The Life of Hildegard of Bingen (1098–1179)," in Jennifer Bain, ed., *The Cambridge Companion to Hildegard of Bingen* (Cambridge: Cambridge University Press, 2021), 11–36, esp. 14.

15. Some have speculated that the parents may have run out of money. Honey Meconi, *Hildegard of Bingen* (Champaign: University of Illinois Press, 2018), 4.

16. See Saint Benedict, *The Holy Rule of St. Benedict*, translated by Rev. Boniface Verheyen (Grand Rapids, MI: Christian Classics Ethereal Library, 1949), 67.

17. Gottfried und Theodorich, "Hildegards Leben," in *Schriften der Heiligen Hildegard von Bingen*, edited and translated by Johannes Bühler (Leipzig: Insel Verlag, 1922), 18. Also see Embach, "The Life of Hildegard of Bingen," 17.

18. For a description of everyday life in a convent, see Alison I. Beach, "Living and Working in a Twelfth-Century Women's Monastic Community," in Bain, *The Cambridge Companion to Hildegard of Bingen*, 37–51.

19. Richard R. Gombrich, *How Buddhism Began: The Conditioned Genesis of the Early Teachings*, 2nd ed. (London: Routledge, 1996).

20. Peter Harvey, *An Introduction to Buddhism: Teachings, History and Practices*, 2nd ed. (Cambridge: Cambridge University Press, 2013).

21. Embach, "The Life of Hildegard of Bingen," 20.

22. Alfred Haverkamp, ed., *Hildegard von Bingen in ihrem historischen Umfeld: Internationaler wissenschaftlicher Kongreß zum 900 jährigen Jubiläum, 13–19 September 1998, Bingen am Rhein* (Mainz: Philipp von Zabern, 2000), 164.

23. Embach, "The Life of Hildegard of Bingen," 24.

24. Victoria Sweet, "Hildegard of Bingen and the Greening of Medieval Medicine," *Bulletin of the History of Medicine* 73, no. 3 (Fall 1999): 381–403.

25. Peter Dronke, *Women Writers of the Middle Ages: A Critical Study of Texts from Perpetua to Marguerite Porete* (Cambridge: Cambridge University Press, 1984), 171. Also see Faith Wallis, "Hildegard of Bingen: Illness and Healing," in Bain, *The Cambridge Companion to Hildegard of Bingen*, 144–69.

26. Fiona Bowie, ed., *Hildegard of Bingen: Mystical Writings* (Pearl River, NY: Crossroad Classics, 1990), 68.

27. Bowie, *Hildegard*, 73.

28. Haverkamp, *Hildegard von Bingen*, 334ff.

29. Embach, "The Life of Hildegard of Bingen," 21–22.

30. Haverkamp, *Hildegard von Bingen*, 289, 69. Also see Lori Kruckenberg, "Lit-

eracy and Learning in the Lives of Women Religious in Medieval Germany," in Bain, *The Cambridge Companion to Hildegard of Bingen*, 52–84, esp. 54ff.

31. *Illuminations of Hildegard of Bingen*, with commentary by Matthew Fox (Rochester, VT: Bear, 1985). Also see Nathaniel M. Campbell, "Picturing Hildegard of Bingen's Sight: Illuminating her Visions," in Bain, *The Cambridge Companion to Hildegard of Bingen*, 257–79, esp. 263ff. For an account of Hildegard's use of the scriptorium, see Margot Fassler, "Hildegard of Bingen and Her Scribes," in Bain, *The Cambridge Companion to Hildegard of Bingen*, 280–305.

32. Kent Kraft, "Hildegard of Bingen: The German Visionary," in Katharine M. Wilson, *Medieval Woman Writers* (Athens, GA: University of Georgia Press, 1984), 109–30. Also see Jennifer Bain, "Music, Liturgy, and Intertextuality in Hildegard of Bingen's Chant Repertory," in Bain, *The Cambridge Companion to Hildegard of Bingen*, 209–33, and Alison Altstatt, "The Ordo virtutum and Benedictine Monasticism," in Bain, *The Cambridge Companion to Hildegard of Bingen*, 235–56.

33. Marianne Pfau and Stefan Johannes Morent, *Hildegard von Bingen: Der Klang des Himmels* (Köln: Böhlau, 2005), 45.

34. Higley, *Hildegard of Bingen's Unknown Language*.

35. Gerald MacLean and William Dalrymple, *Re-Orienting the Renaissance: Cultural Exchanges with the East* (New York: Palgrave Macmillan, 2005), 6. For an excellent survey article presenting a global view of the Renaissance, with an emphasis on non-European parallels and influences as well as the export of the Renaissance by European missionaries, see Peter Burke, Luke Clossey, and Felipe Fernández-Armesto, "The Global Renaissance," *Journal of World History* 28, no. 1 (March 2017): 1–30.

36. George Makdisi, *The Rise of Colleges: Institutions of Learning in Islam and the West* (Edinburgh: Edinburgh University Press, 1981).

37. Marcello Simonetta, *The Montefeltro Conspiracy: A Renaissance Mystery Decoded* (New York: Doubleday, 2008).

38. Leah R. Clark, "Collecting, Exchange, and Sociability in the Renaissance Studiolo," *Journal of the History of Collections* 25, no. 2 (2013): 171–84.

39. Marcello Simonetta and J. J. G. Alexander, eds., *Federico da Montefeltro and his Library* (Milan: Vatican City, 2007), 33.

40. Jan Lauts and Irmlind Luise Herzner, *Federico da Montefeltro, Herzog von Urbino* (Munich: Deutscher Kunstverlag, 2001).

41. James Turner, *Philology: The Forgotten Origins of the Modern Humanities* (Princeton: Princeton University Press, 2014).

42. Rens Bod, *A New History of the Humanities: The Search for Principles and Patterns from Antiquity to the Present* (Oxford: Oxford University Press, 2013), 146ff.

43. R. W. Southern and others have used the term "scholastic humanism" to describe the use of classical texts in the twelfth-century revival at work in cathedral schools and universities. R. W. Southern, *Scholastic Humanism and the Unification of Europe*, vol. 1, *Foundations* (Oxford: Blackwell, 1995).

44. Robert Kirkbridge, *Architecture and Memory: The Renaissance Studioli of Federico de Montefeltro* (New York: Columbia University Press, 2008).

45. Frances Yates, *The Art of Memory* (London: Routledge, 1966).

CHAPTER 10: THE AZTEC CAPITAL FACES ITS EUROPEAN ENEMIES AND ADMIRERS

1. Inga Clendinnen, *Aztecs: An Interpretation* (Cambridge: Cambridge University Press, 1991), 32. The best book on Aztec culture I consulted for this chapter is Camilla Townsend's *Fifth Sun: A New History of the Aztecs* (Oxford: Oxford University Press, 2019). Also see the very good book by David Carrasco, *The Aztecs: A Very Short Introduction* (Oxford: Oxford University Press, 2011).

2. Earlier estimates of up to 200,000 have been revised down. Susan Toby Evans, *Ancient Mexico and Central America: Archaeology and Cultural History* (London: Thames & Hudson, 2008), 549.

3. José Luis de Rojas, *Tenochtitlan: Capital of the Aztec Empire* (Gainesville: University of Florida Press, 2012), 49.

4. Anna McCarthy, *An Empire of Water and Stone: The Acuecuexco Aqueduct Relief*, masters thesis, University of Texas at Austin, 2019.

5. Barbara E. Mundy, *The Death of Aztec Tenochtitlan, the Life of Mexico City* (Austin: University of Texas Press, 2015), 46ff.

6. Rojas, *Tenochtitlan*, 5ff.

7. Clendinnen, *Aztecs*, 257. Also see David Carrasco, *City of Sacrifice: The Aztec Empire and the Role of Violence in Civilization* (Boston: Beacon Press, 2000).

8. Linda Manzanilla, "Teotihuacan," in *The Aztec Empire*, curated by Felipe Solis (New York: Guggenheim Publications, 2004), 114–17.

9. Elizabeth Boone, *Cycles of Time and Meaning in the Mexican Books of Fate* (Austin: University of Texas Press, 2007), 178.

10. Jane S. Day, *Aztec: The World of Moctezuma* (New York: Robert Rinehart, 1992), 100.

11. Rojas, *Tenochtitlan*, 13. Clendinnen, *Aztecs*, 38.

12. Boone, *Cycles*.

13. Rojas, *Tenochtitlan*, 3ff, 73ff.

14. Bernardino de Sahagún, *General History of the Things of New Spain: Florentine Codex*, paleography, translation, introduction and notes by Arthur J. O. Anderson and Charles E. Dibble (Santa Fe: School of American Research, 1905–82), vol. 12, ch. 3.

15. Peter Hess, "Marvelous Encounters: Albrecht Dürer and Early Sixteenth-Century German Perceptions of Aztec Culture," *Daphnis* 33, no. 1–2 (2004): 161ff.

16. Martin Puchner, *The Written World: The Power of Stories to Shape People, History, and Civilization* (New York: Random House, 2017), 159.

17. Martin Brecht, *Martin Luther: Sein Weg zur Reformation, 1483–1521* (Stuttgart: Calwer, 1981), 199.

18. Elizabeth L. Eisenstein, *The Printing Press as an Agent of Change: Communications and Cultural Transformations in Early-Modern Europe*, 2 vols. (Cambridge: Cambridge University Press, 1979).

19. *Albrecht Dürer's Tagebuch der Reise in die Niederlande*, edited by Dr. Friedrich Leitschuh (Leipzig: Brockhaus, 1884).

20. Ernst Rebel, *Albrecht Dürer: Maler und Humanist* (Gütersloh: Orbis Verlag, 1999), 86–87.

21. Caroline Campbell, Dagmar Korbacher, Neville Rowley, and Sarah Vowles, eds., *Mantegna and Bellini* (London: National Gallery, 2018).

22. For the best assessment of self-portraiture during this formative period, see

Joseph Leo Koerner, *The Moment of Self-Portraiture in German Renaissance Art* (Chicago: University of Chicago Press, 1993).

23. Rudolf Hirsch, *Printing, Selling and Reading, 1450–1550* (Wiesbaden: Harrassowitz, 1974), 67–78.

24. Recent research suggests that the pro-Lutheran portion of the diary may have been a later addition, inserted by Luther sympathizers. But Dürer's support for Luther, or at least his sympathy for Luther, is confirmed by other sources.

25. *Albrecht Dürer's Tagebuch*, 58.

26. Hernán Cortés, *Letters from Mexico*, translated, edited, and with a new introduction by Anthony Pagden (New Haven: Yale University Press, 2001), 45.

27. Barbara Stollberg-Rilinger, *The Holy Roman Empire: A Short History*, translated by Yair Mintzker (Princeton: Princeton University Press, 2018), 12.

28. See also Hess, "Marvelous Encounters," 170.

29. Matthew Restall, *When Moctezuma Met Cortés: The True Story of the Meeting that Changed History* (New York: Ecco, 2018), 118ff.

30. Rebel, *Albrecht Dürer.*

31. Rebel, *Albrecht Dürer*, 318.

32. Rojas, *Tenochtitlan*, 36ff.

33. Louise M. Burkhart, "Meeting the Enemy: Moteuczoma and Cortés, Herod and the Magi," in Rebecca P. Brienen and Margaret A. Jackson, eds., *Invasion and Transformation: Interdisciplinary Perspectives on the Conquest of Mexico* (Boulder: University Press of Colorado, 2008), 14. Important for questioning Cortés's own account of the encounter, which portrays Moctezuma as subservient, is Restall, *When Montezuma Met Cortés*. However, Restall does believe the detail that Cortés tried to embrace Moctezuma.

34. Cortés, *Letters*, 113.

35. Rojas, *Tenochtitlan*, 38ff.

36. Accounts of the plague date from about a hundred years later. It is difficult to verify when exactly it began but it is likely to have played a role in this civil war.

37. Rojas, *Tenochtitlan*, 38ff.

38. Viviana Diaz Balsera, "The Hero as Rhetor: Hernán Cortés's Second and Third Letter to Charles V," in Brienen and Jackson, *Invasion and Transformation*, 57–74.

39. *The Memoirs of the Conquistador Bernal Diaz del Castillo, Written By Himself, Containing A True and Full Account of the Discovery and Conquest of Mexico and New Spain*, translated by John Ingram Lockhart (London: J. Hatchard and Son, 1844). See David Carrasco's edition of this work, David Carrasco, ed., *The History of the Conquest of New Spain by Bernal Díaz del Castillo* (Albuquerque: University of New Mexico Press, 2008).

40. Fray Bernardino de Sahagún, *Historia general de las cosas de Nueva España*, edited by Francisco del Paso y Troncoso, 4 vols. (Madrid: Fototipia de Hauser y Menet, 1905). For the best account of the daily life of the Aztecs, see David Carrasco and Scott Sessions, *Daily Life of the Aztecs: People of the Sun and Earth* (New York: Hackett, 2008).

41. Thomas Patrick Hajovsky, *On the Lips of Others: Moteuczoma's Fame in Aztec Monuments and Rituals* (Austin: University of Texas Press, 2015), 6ff.

42. Susan D. Gillespie, "Blaming Moteuczoma: Anthropomorphizing the Aztec Conquest," in Brienen and Jackson, *Invasion and Transformation*, 25–55.

43. Fábrega had access to the codices known as Vaticanus B, Vaticanus A, and the Codex Cospi, as well as the Codex Borgia, to which he devoted the first important commentary. José Lino Fábrega, "Interpretación de Códice Borgiano," in *Anales del Museo Nacional de México*, vol. 5 (Mexico City: Museo Nacional de México, 1900). Also see Boone, *Cycles*, 6.

44. The most ingenious contemporary interpreter of these codices is Elizabeth Boone, in *Cycles*.

45. For a fascinating account of how the Nahuas kept their history alive, see Camilla Townsend, *Annals of Native America: How the Nahuas of Colonial Mexico Kept their History Alive* (Oxford: Oxford University Press, 2016).

CHAPTER 11: A PORTUGUESE SAILOR WRITES A GLOBAL EPIC

1. Henry H. Hart, *Luís de Camoëns and the Epic of the Lusiads* (Norman: University of Oklahoma Press, 1962), 143ff. On the subject of shipwreck in Camões's work, see the excellent Josiah Blackmore, "The Shipwrecked Swimmer: Camões's Maritime Subject," *Modern Philology* 109, no. 3 (2012): 312–25.

2. Hart, *Luís de Camoëns*, 124. Some details are based on his work.

3. Hart, *Luís de Camoëns*, 138. Clive Willis, *Camões, Prince of Poets* (Bristol, HiPLAM, 2010).

4. For a history of the Mediterranean world, see Fernand Braudel, *The Mediterranean and the Mediterranean World in the Age of Philip II*, vol. 1, translated from the French by Siân Reynolds (Berkeley: University of California Press, 1996).

5. Hart, *Luís de Camoëns*, 55ff.

6. Álvaro Velho, *Journal of Vasco da Gama's Trip of 1497* (Porto: Diogo Kopke, 1838).

7. Also see Landeg White, introduction to Luís de Camões, *The Lusiads*, translated by Landeg White (Oxford: Oxford University Press, 2001).

8. Roger Crowley, *Conquerors: How Portugal Forged the First Global Empire* (New York: Random House, 2015), 97.

9. Crowley, *Conquerors*, 10. Also see Katharina N. Piechocki, *Cartographic Humanism: The Making of Modern Europe* (Chicago: University of Chicago Press, 2019), 30.

10. Joyce Chaplin, *Round About the Earth: Circumnavigation from Magellan to Orbit* (New York: Simon and Schuster, 2012), 43; Crowley, *Conquerors*, 132.

11. White, introduction to Camões, *Lusiads*, 2.

12. Hart, *Luís de Camoëns*, 144.

13. Hart, *Luís de Camoëns*, 54. Also see Willis, 182.

14. Amadeu Ferraz de Carvalho, "Camões em Coimbra," *Instituto Revista Scientifica e Literária* 71, no. 6 (June 1924): 241–61.

15. Piechocki, *Cartographic Humanism*, 15.

16. Camões, *Lusiads*, canto 3, verse 97.

17. Camões, *Lusiads*, canto 1, verse 1. Second passage translated by author.

18. Camões, *Lusiads*, canto 5, verse 23.

19. Camões, *Lusiads*, canto 5, verses 81–82.

20. Camões, *Lusiads*, canto 5, verse 17.

21. Camões, *Lusiads*, canto 5, verse 25.

22. Bernhard Klein, "Camões and the Sea: Maritime Modernity in *The Lusiads*," *Modern Philology* 111, no. 2 (November 2013): 158–80, esp. 163ff. For an excel-

lent account of Portuguese writings about Africa, see Josiah Blackmore, *Moorings: Portuguese Expansion and the Writing of Africa* (Minneapolis: University of Minnesota Press, 2008).

23.   Klein, "Camões and the Sea," 176.

24.   For a fuller critique of this poem from an Asian perspective, see the excellent article by Balachandra Rajan, "The Lusiads and the Asian Reader," *English Studies in Canada* 23, no. 1 (March 1997): 1–19.

25.   Camões, *Lusiads*, canto 8, verse 68.

26.   Hart, *Luís de Camoëns*, 193.

CHAPTER 12: ENLIGHTENMENT IN SAINT-DOMINGUE AND IN A PARISIAN SALON

1.   Christine Levecq, *Black Cosmopolitans: Race, Religion, and Republicanism in the Age of Revolution* (Charlottesville: University of Virginia Press, 2019), 76.

2.   Madison Smartt Bell, *Toussaint Louverture: A Biography* (New York: Pantheon, 2007), 76.

3.   Robin Blackburn, *The Overthrow of Colonial Slavery 1776–1848* (London: Verso, 1988), 218.

4.   When Christopher Columbus landed on the island in 1492, there were an estimated half million Tainos living there. Philippe Girard, *Haiti: The Tumultuous History—from Pearl of the Caribbean to Broken Nation* (New York: Palgrave Macmillan, 2005), 19.

5.   Girard, *Haiti*, 20.

6.   Laurent Dubois and John D. Garrigus, *Slave Revolution in the Caribbean, 1789–1804: A Brief History with Documents* (Boston: Bedford/St. Martin's, 2006), 6.

7.   David P. Geggus, "Toussaint Louverture and the Slaves of the Bréda Plantation," *Journal of Caribbean History* 20, no. 1 (1985), 35.

8.   On the omnipresence of death in Caribbean slave societies, see the excellent book by Vincent Brown, *The Reaper's Garden: Death and Power in the World of Atlantic Slavery* (Cambridge, MA: Cambridge University Press, 2008). More enslaved Africans were brought to Saint-Domingue than to the United States; Girard, *Haiti*, 26.

9.   Martin Puchner, *Poetry of the Revolution: Marx, Manifestos and the Avant-Gardes* (Princeton: Princeton University Press, 2006). The process took over a hundred years, from the Glorious Revolution (1688) to the French Revolution (1789).

10.   Dubois and Garrigus, *Slave Revolution*, 25ff.

11.   See Dubois and Garrigus, *Slave Revolution*, 19ff.

12.   C. L. R. James, *The Black Jacobins: Toussaint L'Ouverture and the San Domingo Revolution* (New York: Vintage, 1989), 145ff.

13.   For a description of the importance of maroons in the Haitian revolution, especially its aftermath, see Johnhenry Gonzalez, *Maroon Nation: A History of Revolutionary Haiti* (Cambridge: Cambridge University Press, 2019).

14.   Blackburn, *The Overthrow of Colonial Slavery*, 170ff.

15.   Blackburn, *The Overthrow of Colonial Slavery*, 218.

16.   Dubois and Garrigus, *Slave Revolution*, 122–25, esp. 122.

17.   Jean-Louis Donnadieu, "Derrière le portrait, l'homme: Jean-Baptiste Belley,

dit 'Timbaze', dit 'Mars' (1746–1805)," *Bulletin de la Société d'Histoire de la Guadeloupe* 170 (January–April 2015): 29–54.

18.   Donnadieu, "Derrière le portrait," 40ff.

19.   Dubois and Garrigus, *Slave Revolution*, 24.

20.   Blackburn, *The Overthrow of Colonial Slavery*, 224–25.

21.   Dubois and Garrigus, *Slave Revolution*, 124.

22.   Janet Aldis, *Madame Geoffrin: Her Salon and Her Times, 1750–1777* (London: Methuen, 1905), 59.

23.   G. P. Gooch, "Four French Salons," *Contemporary Review*, January 1, 1951: 345–53.

24.   A. Tornezy, *Un Bureau d'Esprit au XVIIIe Siècle: Le Salon de Madame Geoffrin* (Paris: Lecène, 1895).

25.   Maurice Hamon, "Madame Geoffrin: Femme d'affaires au temps des Lumières," *Revue Française d'Histoire Économique* 2, no. 6 (2016): 12–25.

26.   Tornezy, *Un Bureau d'Esprit*, 46.

27.   Aldis, *Madame Geoffrin*, 137.

28.   Maurice Hamon, "Marie-Thérèse Geoffrin, une inconnue célébre?," in Jacques Charles-Gaffiot, Michel David-Weill, and Małgorzata Biłozór-Salwa, eds., *Madame Geoffrin, une femme d'affaires de d'esprit* (Paris: Silvana Editoriale, 2011), 17–29.

29.   Aldis, *Madame Geoffrin*, 87.

30.   Aldis, *Madame Geoffrin*, 90.

31.   A play by Charles Palissot de Montenoy called *Les philosophes* cast her in the role of Cydalise. Aldis, *Madame Geoffrin*, 307.

32.   Raynal, *A Philosophical and Political History of the Settlements and Trade of the Europeans in the East and West Indies*, translated by J. O. Justamond, 10 vols. (London: A. Strahan, T. Cadell, jun. and Wl Davies, 1798), 1:201.

33.   Raynal, *A Philosophical and Political History*, 2:403.

34.   Raynal also subscribed to views that sound strange, outdated, and racist today, including an idea of biological degeneration of humans in the Americas (in which he included white French settlers). He believed that the last part of his book aided the struggle for American independence. See A. Owen Aldridge, "Raynal, Guillaume-Thomas-François," American National Biography (1999), https://doi.org/10.1093/anb/9780198606697.article.1602192.

35.   Raynal, *A Philosophical and Political History*, 8:225.

36.   Raynal, *A Philosophical and Political History*, 2:341.

37.   Some scholars cast doubt on whether Toussaint really read Raynal, as he claimed to have done. There is an alternative explanation, which is equally instructive. According to this explanation, Toussaint planted an article written by one of his supporters, in which his reading of Raynal was highlighted, shortly before his return to France, during his standoff with Napoleon. If this was true, this meant that Toussaint used Raynal to explain his rebellion in terms the French could understand, that is, in terms of Enlightenment and "commercial" philosophy. Philippe R. Girard and Jean-Louis Donnadieu, "Toussaint before Louverture: New Archival Findings on the Early Life of Toussaint Louverture," *William and Mary Quarterly* 70, no. 1 (January 2013): 41–78, esp. 76.

38.   On Napoleon's restoration of slavery, see Lawrence C. Jennings, *French Anti-*

Slavery: The Movement for the Abolition of Slavery in France, 1802–1848 (Cambridge: Cambridge University Press, 2000), 5ff.

39.   Dubois and Garrigus, *Slave Revolution*, 27ff.

40.   Dubois and Garrigus, *Slave Revolution*, 30; also see David Armitage, *The Declaration of Independence: A Global History* (Cambridge, MA: Harvard University Press, 2008).

41.   William Wells Brown, *The Black Man: His Antecedents, His Genius, and His Achievements* (Boston: Robert F. Wallcut, 1865).

42.   James, *Black Jacobins*, 377.

CHAPTER 13: GEORGE ELIOT PROMOTES THE SCIENCE OF THE PAST

1.   George Eliot, *Middlemarch*, with an introduction and notes by Rosemary Ashton (London: Penguin Classics, 1994), 192–94.

2.   Eliot, *Middlemarch*, 63.

3.   Eliot, *Middlemarch*, 837.

4.   Rosemary Ashton, *George Eliot: A Life* (London: Penguin, 1997), 164ff.

5.   James Turner, *Philology: The Forgotten Origins of the Modern Humanities* (Princeton: Princeton University Press, 2014).

6.   Rens Bod, *A New History of the Humanities: The Search for Principles and Patterns from Antiquity to the Present* (Oxford: Oxford University Press, 2013), 146ff.

7.   David A. Traill, *Schliemann of Troy: Treasure and Deceit* (New York: St. Martin's Press, 1996).

8.   William Dalrymple, *The Anarchy: The East India Company, Corporate Violence, and the Pillage of an Empire* (London: Bloomsbury, 2019).

9.   John E. Simmons, *Museums: A History* (London: Rowman & Littlefield), 150.

10.   The term "museum" had existed earlier, but only now did it acquire its modern meaning. In 1755 Samuel Johnson still defined it as "repository of learned curiosities," while in 1889 George Brown Goode, the assistant secretary of the Smithsonian Institution, described a museum, somewhat jokingly, as a "collection of instructive labels, each illustrated by a well-selected specimen," emphasizing the pedagogical nature of the enterprise. See Simmons, *Museums*, 4.

11.   For an account of the narratives used by nineteenth-century historians, see Hayden White, *Metahistory: The Historical Imagination in Nineteenth-Century Europe* (Baltimore: Johns Hopkins University Press, 1973).

12.   Robert E. Sullivan, *Macaulay: The Tragedy of Power* (Cambridge, MA: Harvard University Press, 2009), 149ff.

13.   Sullivan, *Macaulay*, 251ff.

14.   Gauri Viswanathan, *Masks of Conquest: Literary Study and British Rule in India* (New York: Columbia University Press, 1989). Macaulay was an advocate for abolishing slavery in the British Empire; Sullivan, *Macaulay*, 51ff.

15.   Maya Jasanoff, *Edge of Empire: Lives, Culture, and Conquest in the East, 1750–1850* (New York: Knopf, 2005).

16.   Biographical information is based on Ashton, *George Eliot*, 33ff.

17.   David Friedrich Strauss, *The Life of Jesus, Critically Examined*, translated by Marian Evans (London: Edward Chapman and William Hall, 1846).

18.   Leopold von Ranke, *Die Geschichten der Romanischen und Germanischen Völker* (Berlin: Reimer, 1824), vi.

19. Ludwig Feuerbach, *Vorlesungen über das Wesen der Religion*, twentieth lecture, in *Ludwig Feuerbach's Sämmtliche Werke*, vol. 8 (Leipzig: Otto Wigand, 1851), 241.

20. For a history and modern adaptations of this lost play, see Stephen Greenblatt, *Cultural Mobility: A Manifesto* (Cambridge: Cambridge University Press, 2010).

21. Eric Hobsbawm and Terence Ranger, *The Invention of Tradition* (Cambridge: Cambridge University Press, 2012).

22. George Eliot, "Silly Novels by Lady Novelists," in *The Essays of George Eliot* (New York: Funk and Wagnalls, 1883), 178–204.

23. Bruce Robbins, *The Servant's Hand: English Fiction from Below* (New York: Columbia University Press, 1986).

24. One of them was Wilhelm Heinrich Riehl. George Eliot, "The Natural History of German Life," in *The Essays of George Eliot*, 141–77.

25. Eliot, "Natural History," 144.

26. Kelly E. Battles, "George Eliot's Romola: A Historical Novel 'Rather Different in Character'," *Philological Quarterly* 88, no. 3 (Summer 2008): 215–37.

27. George Eliot, *Romola* (London: Smith, Elder, 1863).

28. Andrew Thompson, "George Eliot as 'Worthy Scholar': Note Taking and the composition of Romola," in Jean Arnold and Lila Marz Harper, eds., *George Eliot: Interdisciplinary Essays* (London: Palgrave, 2019), 63–95.

29. Thompson, "George Eliot," 65.

CHAPTER 14: A JAPANESE WAVE TAKES THE WORLD BY STORM

1. Julie Nelson Davis, *Partners in Print* (Honolulu: University of Hawai'i Press, 2015).

2. David Bell, *Ukiyo-e Explained* (Folkestone, UK: Global Oriental, 2004).

3. Attributed to Kano Yasunobu (1613–85). See Davis, *Partners in Print*, 27.

4. Davis, *Partners in Print*, 88ff.

5. Sarah E. Thompson: *Hokusai*, with an essay by Joan Wright and Philip Meredith (Boston: MFA Publications, 2015), 16.

6. Matthi Forrer, *Hokusai* (New York: Prestel, 2010).

7. Davis, *Partners in Print*, 30.

8. Thompson, *Hokusai*, 73.

9. Thompson, *Hokusai*, 21, 73.

10. Timothy Clark, "Late Hokusai, Backwards," in Timothy Clark, ed., *Hokusai: Beyond the Great Wave* (London: Thames & Hudson, 2017), 12–27, esp. 21.

11. Kenneth G. Henshall, *A History of Japan: From Stone Age to Superpower* (New York: Palgrave Macmillan, 2004), 43.

12. Henshall, *History of Japan*, 58ff. Also see David J. Lu, *Japan: A Documentary History*, vol. 1 (New York: Routledge, 2015), 220ff.

13. For an account of the kinds of cultural products that were exchanged during this period, see Marius B. Jansen, *The Cambridge History of Japan*, vol. 5, *The Nineteenth Century* (Cambridge: Cambridge University Press, 2008), 436ff.

14. Davis, *Partners in Print*, 63.

15. Ernest F. Fenollosa, *Chinese Written Character as a Medium for Poetry* (New York: Fordham, 2008), 149.

16. Henshall, *History of Japan*, 79ff.

17. Van Wyck Brooks, *Fenollosa and his Circle: With Other Essays in Biography* (New York: Dutton, 1962), 7. Also see Henshall, *History of Japan*, 81ff.

18.   Brooks, *Fenollosa and his Circle*, 58.
19.   Brooks, *Fenollosa and his Circle*, 34.
20.   Ernest F. Fenollosa, *Epochs of Chinese and Japanese Art: An Outline History of East Asiatic Design* (London: Heinemann, 1912), xiiiv ff.
21.   Fenollosa, *Epochs*, 50.
22.   Fenollosa, *Epochs*, 50.
23.   Fenollosa, *Epochs*, 53.
24.   Fenollosa, *Epochs*, xviii.
25.   Fenollosa, *Chinese Written Character*, 2.
26.   Quoted in Achilles Fang, "Fenollosa and Pound," *Harvard Journal of Asiatic Studies* 20, no. 1–2 (June 1957): 123–238, esp. 216.
27.   Quoted in Hugh Kenner, *The Pound Era* (Berkeley: University of California Press, 1971), 192.
28.   Martin Puchner, *Poetry of the Revolution: Marx, Manifestos, and the Avant-Gardes* (Princeton: Princeton University Press, 2006).
29.   Martin Puchner, *Stage Fright: Modernism, Anti-Theatricality and Drama* (Baltimore: Johns Hopkins University Press, 2002), 119ff; Carrie J. Preston, *Learning to Kneel: Noh, Modernism, and Journeys in Teaching* (New York: Columbia University Press, 2017).
30.   Puchner, *Stage Fright*, 145.
31.   Puchner, *Poetry of the Revolution*, 205.

CHAPTER 15: THE DRAMA OF NIGERIAN INDEPENDENCE

1.   James Gibbs, *Wole Soyinka* (New York: Macmillan, 1969), 117–18.
2.   See Henry Louis Gates, Jr., "Being, the Will and the Semantics of Death," in Wole Soyinka, *Death and the King's Horseman*, edited by Simon Gikandi (New York: Norton, 2003), 155–63, esp. 155.
3.   Simon Gikandi, introduction to Soyinka, *Death and the King's Horseman*, xi.
4.   Gauri Viswanathan, *Masks of Conquest: Literary Study and British Rule in India* (New York: Columbia University Press, 1989).
5.   For an account of the full range of Soyinka's theatrical engagement, see James Gibbs, "From Broke-Time Bar via the Radio-Station Hold-Up to Oyedipo at Kholoni and Thus Spake Orunmila—An Attempt to Establish a More Comprehensive Awareness of Soyinka's Dramatic Work," in Duro Oni and Bisi Adigun, ed., *The Soyinka Impulse: Essays on Wole Soyinka* (Ibadan, Nigeria: Bookcraft, 2019): 23–79.
6.   Henry John Drewal, John Pemberton III, and Rowland Abiodun, "The Yoruba World," in Allen Wardwell, ed., *Yoruba: Nine Centuries of African Art and Thought* (New York: Abrams, 1989), 13.
7.   Drewal et al., "The Yoruba World," 21.
8.   As the Nigerian intellectual Biodun Jeyifo has argued decisively, English should be considered an African language. Biodun Jeyifo, "English is an African Language—Ka Dupe!: For and against Ngũgĩ," *Journal of African Cultural Studies* 30, no. 2 (2018): 133–47, ihttps://doi.org/10.1080/13696815.2016.1264295.
9.   This attitude put Soyinka at odds not only with Ladipo but also with the African and Caribbean intellectuals who had formed a movement called *négritude* in Paris in the 1930s. (See Louis Menand, *The Free World: Art and Thought in the*

Cold War [New York: Farrar, Straus, and Giroux, 2021], 398.) Soyinka shared many of the intentions of this group, but ultimately felt that it trapped African artists in a purely "defensive role" based on a simple opposition between two entities called Europe and Africa. Wole Soyinka, "Myth, Literature, and the African World," reprinted in Soyinka, *I Am Because We Are*, edited by Fred Lee Hord and Jonathan Scott Lee (Amherst: University of Massachusetts Press, 2016), 104–13, esp. 106. While honoring the importance of the *négritude* movement, Soyinka wanted to chart a different course. (He also observed that the most dogmatic statements about the vision of *négritude* were made by white European intellectuals.) Soyinka, "Myth, Literature, and the African World," 109.

10. Toyin Falola and Matthew M. Heaton, *The History of Nigeria* (Cambridge: Cambridge University Press, 2008), 158ff.

11. Falola and Heaton, *History of Nigeria*, 180. The horrors of this war were captured in Chimamanda Ngozi Adichie's novel *Half of a Yellow Sun* (London: Fourth Estate, 2006).

12. Wole Soyinka, *The Man Died: His Classic Prison Writings* (London: Rex Collings, 1997). For a further description of this period, see Lucy K. Hayden, "'The Man Died': Prison Notes of Wole Soyinka: A Recorder and Visionary," *CLA Journal*, 18, no. 4 (June 1975): 542–52.

13. The best book on Soyinka's political work is Biodun Jeyifo, *Wole Soyinka: Politics, Poetics and Postcolonialism* (New York: Cambridge University Press, 2004).

14. Soyinka, *Death and the King's Horseman*, 44.

15. In the nineteenth century, this approach was called cultural evolutionism.

16. The new approach was pioneered by Franz Boas, a German-born American anthropologist, and further developed by A. L. Kroeber.

17. Among the pioneers of this movement was the American anthropologist Margaret Mead. Another variant was called social anthropology, developed by the French structuralist Claude Lévi-Strauss.

18. Raymond Williams, *Culture and Society: 1780–1950* (London: Chatto and Windus, 1958).

19. Wole Soyinka, *Of Africa* (New Haven: Yale University Press, 2012), 177.

20. Soyinka, *Death and the King's Horseman*, 23.

21. Also see Kathleen Morrison, "'To Date Transition': Ogun as Touchstone in Wole Soyinka's 'The Interpreters,'" *Research in African Literature* 20, no. 1 (Spring 1989): 60–71.

22. Or rather, since Ogun was also the god of metalwork, he was like a combination of Dionysus and Prometheus. Soyinka, "Myth, Literature, and the African World," 141.

23. For the most recent study of Soyinka, see Bola Dauda and Toyin Falola, *Wole Soyinka: Literature, Activism, and African Transformations* (New York: Bloomsbury, 2022).

24. Femi Odugbemi, "Prologue," in Emily Witt, *Nollywood: The Making of a Film Empire* (Columbia Global Reports, 2007), 19, https://www.jstor.org/stable/j.ctv1fx4h6t.3.

25. Holly Williams, "Playwright Ifeoma Fafunwa: 'It was permission, all of a sudden, to speak,'" *Guardian*, August 10, 2019; https://www.theguardian.com/

stage/2019/aug/10/ifeoma-fafunwa-interview-hear-word-edinburgh-festival
-nigerian-architect-playwright.

26.   Williams, "Playwright Ifeoma Fafunwa."

27.   As a director of Harvard's program in theater, dance, and media, I felt privileged to experience *Hear Word!* thanks to the engagement of Diane Borger,
executive producer at the American Repertory Theater, and Deborah Foster,
director of undergraduate studies at Harvard's program in theater, dance, and
media.

28.   Chux Ohai, "Cast of Hear Word! Call for Social Change," *Punch*, March 16,
2018. https://punchng.com/cast-of-hear-word-call-for-social-change/.

EPILOGUE: WILL THERE BE A LIBRARY IN 2114 CE?

1.   Account based on Future Library website, https://www.futurelibrary.no,
accessed January 30, 2022, and on video of the 2015 handover day with Margaret Atwood, https://vimeo.com/135817557, accessed January 30, 2022.

2.   Margaret Atwood, "Future Library," https://assets.ctfassets.net/9sa97ciu3
rb2/2hdAyLQYmESc0eYemIEcm2/09772ac1c62defc7ccf50fe6ea207a83/
Margaret_Atwood.pdf, accessed January 30, 2022.

3.   *The Book of Record of the Time Capsule of Cupaloy deemed capable of resisting the
effects of time for five thousand years. Preserving an Account of Universal Achievements. Embedded in the Grounds of the New York World's Fair 1939* (New York:
Westinghouse Electric and Manufacturing Company, 1938). Available at:
https://en.wikisource.org/wiki/Book_of_Record_of_the_Time_Capsule_
of_Cupaloy.

4.   Carl Sagan, F. D. Drake, Ann Druyan, Timothy Ferris, Jon Lomberg, and
Linda Salzman Sagan, *Murmurs of Earth: The Voyager Interstellar Record* (New
York: Ballantine, 1978).

5.   "Apollo 11 Goodwill Messages," NASA News Release No 69-83F, July 13, 1969.

6.   Eric M. Jones, "Corrected Transcript and Commentary" (Washington, DC:
NASA, 1995): 111:36:55, https://history.nasa.gov/alsj/a11/a11.clsout.html.

7.   Sian Cain, " 'You'll Have to Die to Get These Texts': Ocean Vuong's Next
Manuscript to Be Unveiled in 2114," *Guardian*, August 19, 2020, https://www
.theguardian.com/books/2020/aug/19/ocean-vuong-2114-book-future-library
-norway.

8.   Katie Paterson, "An Interview with Han Kang: The fifth author for Future
Library," https://vimeo.com/336320261, 9:00ff.

9.   Barnaby Phillips, "Western Museums are Starting to Return Colonial-Era
Treasures," *Economist*, November 8, 2021.

10.   Haerin Shin, "The dynamics of K-pop spectatorship: The Tablo witch-hunt and
its double-edged sword of enjoyment," in JungBong Choi and Roald Maliangkay, eds., *K-pop—the International Rise of the Korean Music Industry* (Abingdon,
UK: Routledge, 2015), 133ff.

11.   Eun-Young Jung, "Hallyu and the K-pop Boom in Japan: Patterns of con-
sumption and reactionary responses," in Choi and Maliangkay, *K-pop*, 116ff.
International fans also frequently reported being ostracized for their fandom;
"Introduction," 6.

12.   Roald Maliangkay, "Same Look Though Different Eyes: Korea's history of uni-

form pop music acts," in Choi and Maliangkay, *K-pop*, 24. Also see Gooyong Kim, *From Factory Girls to K-pop Idol Girls: Cultural Politics of Developmentalism, Patriarchy and Neoliberalism in South Korea's Popular Music Industry* (Lanham, MD: Lexington, 2019).

13. Gaik Cheng Khoo, "We Keep It Local—Malaysianizing 'Gangnam Style': A question of place and identity," in Choi and Maliangkay, *K-pop*, 146.

14. Atwood, "Future Library."

INDEX

===

abolition, 212, 223–25
Academy (of Plato), 34
actors, 31
adaptation, xxi–xxii, xxiii
Aeneas, 66–69, 127
Aeneid (Virgil), 65–68
Aeschylus, 27–28, 28
Africa
  arbitrary boundaries and, 274
  colonialism, 266–69, 271, 273
  cultural identity and, 268–69
  independence, 226, 268–69
  Oyo, 266–67, 271 (see also *Death and the King's Horseman*; Nigeria)
  Portugal and, 134, 189–90, 198–200, 267
  See also slavery: European slave trade; *specific countries*
Agathocles, 51
Ahuitzotl, 165
Ajai-Lycett, Taiwo, 285
Ajani Og (film), 283–84
Akhenaten/Amenhotep IV (king of Egypt), 3–4, 5, 6–12, *11*, 13–15, 18–21, 310n11
Alcuin, 143
Alexander the Great, 46–47, 48, 61, *61*, 110–11, 127
Amarna, 7–8, 310n11
Amda Seyon (king of Ethiopia), 126
Amenhotep III (king of Egypt), 6
American Declaration of Independence, 213–14
American War of Independence, 209–11, 213

anamorphosis, 162
Ancient Greece. *See* Greece
al-Andalus, 144, 199, 324n12
Andronicus, Livius, 63–64
animal markings and art, xiv, xv, 309nn4–5
animals and Ashoka, 42
Annoying Orange, 301
anthropology, 277–79, 334nn15–17
Apollo 11, 294
appropriation, xi, xii
aqueducts, 165
Arab empire
  Africa and, 199
  demand for classical texts, 320n18
  Ethiopia and, 131–33
  Europe and, 155, 156
  Greece and, 109–11, 320n14 (*see also* Aristotle)
  Kebra Nagast translations and, 131
  religions in, 199, 320n14
  rise in power, 106, 122
  See also specific countries
architecture
  House of Menander, 59
  pillars, 37–40, 39, 41, 42–44, 47, 50–51, 79
  Romanesque style, 143–44
  Rome taking from Greece, 68
Aristotle
  Arab empire and, 105, 110, 112, 113–19
  commentary, 321n30
  discovery in Europe, 155–56
  knowledge categories, 116–17
  preservation of, 34–35

Ark of the Covenant, 124–25, 126–27, 129

art
  animal markings and, xiv, xv, 309nn4–5
  avant-garde, 263–64
  cave art, xiv–xix, *xix*, 309nn4–5
  Dürer, 171–72
  engravings, 172, 175, 176, *177*, 203, 247, 248–49
  intarsia, 161–63, *162*
  Nagasaki-e, 253, *254*
  paintings (*see specific painters*)
  picture scrolls, 99–102, *102*
  progress and, 263
  Romanesque style, 143–44
  sculpting, 4, 8–12, 167, 258–59, 271, *271* (*see also specific sculptures*)
  watercolors, 247–48
Artaud, Antonin, 265
Ashoka, 40–47, 49–50, 85, 313n14, 314n34, 314n43
Ashoka pillars, 37–40, 41, 42–44, 47, 50–51, 79
Askum, Ethiopia, 123–39, 126, 132, 133, 134–35
astrolabe, 163, 197
Aten, 7, 10–11, 12–13, 18–19
Athens, 25–32. *See also* Greece
Atlantis, 25–26
Atwood, Margaret, 287–90, 302–3
avant-garde, 263–64
Avicenna. *See* Ibn Sina
Aztecs
  artworks of, 173, 175–76
  books of, 167, 181, 182–83
  rise in power, 164
  sacrifices to gods, 166, 175
  Tenochtitlan, 164–66, 175, *175*, 178–81, 184, 220
  Teotihuacan mythology, 166–67
  See also Moctezuma

The Bacchae (Euripides), 281–82
Baghdad
  geometry, 106–7
  al-Ma'mun and, 106
  paper making, 109

summa, 107, 118–19, 121 (*see also* Storehouse of Wisdom)
  urban revolution, 107–8
Bali, 265
barbarians, 23
Battle of Issus, *61*
Behaim, Martin, *188*, 190–91
Belgium, 171
Belley, Jean-Baptiste (J.B.), 206–7, *206*, 214, 224–25
Bellini, 170
Benedict of Nursia, 145, 146
Benedictine monasteries, 144–50, 163
Berlin Conference, 266–67
Bernard of Clairvaux, 151
Bernardino de Sahagun, 181–82
Biafran War, 273–74
Bible, 172, 293. *See also* Ark of the Covenant; Hebrew Bible/Old Testament
bibliographies, 121
Black Death, 170, 327n36
Black Jacobins (James), 226
Black Panthers, 139
Boas, Franz, 334n16
Bonaparte, Napoleon, 224–25, 226
books
  of Aztecs, 167, 181, 182–83
  burning, 167
  Dürer art, 171
  historical novels, 239–45
  in intarsia, 161
  mass production, 183, 238
  See also specific titles
borrowing as fraught, 100–101
Boston Museum of Fine Arts, 260
Brahmi script, 47, 50, 51, 230, 314n28, 314n33
Brecht, Bertolt, 265
Bréda, Toussaint, 208. *See also* L'Ouverture, Toussaint
Britain
  collecting India's artifacts, 51
  colonialism (*see* Africa; India; Nigeria)
  Ethiopia and, 134–35
  Greece and, 230
  Roman Empire and, 233

Soyinka in, 269–70, 275
studying history of, 279
British East India Company, 51, 204, 230
Brooke, Dorothea (character), 227–28, 244
Brown, William Wells, 225
brush talk, 92
Brussels, 171
BTS, 301
Buddha, 94–95
Buddhism
anti-Buddhist edicts, 96–97
Ashoka and, 40–42, 44, 45, 49–50
vs. Confucianism, 75
cultural flow and, 49–50, 74, 80–81, 85–86, 92, 98, 101
declining in India, 86
memorization and, 46
monastic community, 74, 75, 145 (see also Ennin)
Raynal and, 220
Silk Road and, 50
Taoism and, 95–96
translation of texts, 64, 80, 83–84
Xuanzang and, 75–77, 79–80, 81, 82–83
Zen, 101
Buddhist statues, 77–79, 78, 85, 94–95, 97
Byzantium, 111, 113

Camões, Luís de, 185–87, 191–92, 193–98, 200, 202–5, 205
Carolingian minuscule script, 143, 159
Carolingian Renaissance, 144
Carthage, 58
Casaubon, Edward (character), 227–28, 229, 237
Casaubon, Isaac, 228–29
Catholicism, 219–20. See also Vatican
Cato the Elder, 65
Cervantes, Miguel de, 237
Champollion, Jean-François, 229
Charlemagne, 140–44, 140, 145, 163
Charles V (king of Spain), 172–74
Chauvet cave, xiii–xix, xix

China
anti-Buddhist edicts, 96–97
Buddhism and, 74–75, 80
India and (see Buddhism; Xuanzang)
Japan and, 90, 98–100 (see also Ennin; Pillow Book)
opera, 265
Tang dynasty, 73–74, 84 (see also Ennin)
Taoism, 95–97
unauthorized departure of citizens, 70
Zhou dynasty, 72–73
See also various Confucius entries
choruses, 26, 27, 28, 29
Christianity
Aten/Joseph/Moses, 18
Crusades, 155
Enlightenment and, 219–20
in Ethiopia, 123–24, 127, 128–31, 133–34
Ethiopia and, 138–39
Inquisition, 202–3
Islam and, 156, 199–201
Judaism and, 127
monastic community, 144–45 (see also Benedictine monasteries)
new accounts of Jesus and, 128
persecuted, 97
redefining, 159–60, 172, 235
refusing recovery, 35
transcribing pagan texts, 111
Vatican, 140, 159–60
Vatican Library, 227
See also Jesus
Church of Maryam Syon, 123–24, 123, 133
Cicero, 161
climate zones, 48
Clottes, Jean, 309n4
cloud storage, 291
coins, 51, 54
collections, 229, 230–33, 234, 259–61
colonialism
overview, xxii–xxiii
in Africa, 266–69, 271, 273 (see also Death and the King's Horseman)
anthropology and, 278

colonialism (*continued*)
  collection and, 51
  end of, 268–69
  lopsided exchanges, 234
  modernization and, 233
  Raynal against, 219–21
  recovery and, 229, 234
Columbus, Christopher, 174–75
Confucian classics, 72–74
Confucianism, 74–75, 81, 82, 96
Confucius, 73
Constantine, 159–60
Convention of Kanagawa, 256
copying texts, 35, 103, 120, 144–45,
  147, 159, 320n18
Corinth, 58–59, 62
The Coronation of Charlemagne, 140, *140*
Corpus Hermeticum, 228–29
Cortés, Hernán, 173–74, 179–81, 220
Councils, 128
COVID-19 pandemic, 294–95
Crusades, 155
cultural evolutionism, 334n15
cultural grafts, 64–65, 68–69
cultural relativism, 279
culture
  as achieved by all humans, 278–80
  defined, xi–xii
  as owned, xi, xii, 299
  as shared, xi–xii, xxii, xxiii, 301

d'Alembert, Jean, 219
Dance of the Forest (Soyinka), 270–71
Dangarembga, Tsitsi, 292
Dante, 147–48
Darius of Persia, *61*
Das Leben Jesu, kritisch bearbeitet
  (Strauss), 235–36
David, Jacques-Louis, 207
Death and the King's Horseman (Soy-
  inka), 274–76, 280–82
Declaration of Independence, 213–14
decolonization. *See* independence
Delhi, 36–40. *See also* Ashoka
democracy, 32
Dengel, Lebna, 133–34
Dessalines, Jean-Jacques, 225
dharma, 41, 42, 44, 45, 49, 50

Diamond Sutra (printed scroll), 317n24
Díaz, Bernal, 181
Diderot, Denis, 219
digital content, xxiii
Dinamene, 186, 187, 192
Dionysia festival, 27, 29
Dionysus, 281–82, 334n22
disease, 14, 49
Disibodenberg, 145, 148–49
Don Quixote (Cervantes), 238
Donation of Constantine, 159–60
Douglass, Frederick, 225
Dufaÿ, Pierre, 214, 215
Dunhuang caves, 83, 317n24
Dürer, Albrecht, 169–73, 174–78, 183
Dutch empire, 253–54

earthquakes, 55
East India Company, 51, 204, 230
The Edicts of Asoka (Nikam and
  McKeon), 314n43
education (general), 35, 60–61
Egypt
  as defying time, 5–6
  Greece and, 23, 25–26, 34
  longstanding cultural tradition, 24
  performance in, 29–30
  Roman Empire and, 54, 58, 315n9
  storage revolution, 16–17
  See also Nefertiti; Thutmose
ekphrasis, 194
Elements (Euclid), 109–10
Elgin (Lord), 229–30
Eliot, George, 227–30, 235–36, 237–39,
  241–44
Eliot, T. S., 262
Encyclopédie, 219, 221
end of times, 151
engineering of Tenochtitlan, 164–66
engravings, 172, 175, 176, *177*, 203,
  247, 248–49
Enlightenment, 213, 219–20, 221–23,
  226, 236–37
Ennin, 90–94, 96–98, 101
environmentalism. *See* Future Library
  project
The Epic of Sunjata, 269
es-Senussi, Mohammed, 1–4, *3*, 11

Ethiopia
  Arab empire and, 130–33
  Ark of the Covenant, 126–27 (see
    also *Kebra Nagast*)
  Britain, 134–35
  Christianity and, 123–24, 127,
    128–31, 133–34, 138–39
  Jamaica and, 137–39
  Our Lady Mary of Zion church,
    123–24, *123*, 133
  Portugal and, 134
  as remote, 135
  See also *Kebra Nagast*
Etruria, 62, 63
Euclid, 109–10
Eugene II (pope), 151
Eurasian exchange network, 48
Euripides, 27–28, 59, 281–82
Europe, 155–56. *See also specific coun-
  tries*
Evans, Mary Ann (George Eliot). *See*
  Eliot, George
evolution, xv
Eyck, Jan van, 171

Fábrega, José Lino, 182
Fafunwa, Ifeoma, 284–85
falsafa, 114–15, 116
false attribution, 120
farming, 48, 107–8
Faxian, 80
Federico da Montefeltro, 157–59, *158*,
  160–63
Fenollosa, Brenda, 257
Fenollosa, Ernest, 256–62
Fenollosa, Mary McNeil, 261–62,
  265
Fenollosa–Weld collection, 259–61
Feuerbach, Ludwig, 236
Firoz Shah Tughlaq, 36–40, 51, 86
First Reform Act, 243
floating world, 247, 249–50
Florentine Codex, 182
France, xiii–xix, *xix*, 211–12, 224. *See
  also* Paris
Franklin, Benjamin, 221
French Revolution, 207, 210–11,
  213

French Universal Declaration of the
  Rights of Man and of the Citizen,
  213, 214
Freud, Sigmund, 18
Future Library project, 287–93, 294,
  295, 302–3

Gama, Cristovoa de, 134
Gama, Vasco da, 133–34, 189, 193–94,
  198, 200–202, 205
"Gangnam Style" (PSY), 299–301
Garvey, Marcus, 137, 225
Geoffrin, Marie Thérèse (Madam),
  216–19, *217*, 221, 223
geometry, 106–7
Germany, 21–22, 268
Girodet, Anne-Louis, 207
Global North, 291–92
Global South, 292–93
Go game, 100
gods, 6–8, 17–19. *See also specific gods*
Goethe, Johann Wolfgang von, 263
Goode, George Brown, 331n10
grain storage, 16–17, 108
graphic novels, 102
"The Great Hymn to the Aten" (hymn),
  12–13
Great Obelisk, *132*
The Great Wave off Kanagawa (Hoku-
  sai), *246*, 247, 251, 256, 260
Greece
  Arab empire and, 109–11 (*see also*
    Aristotle)
  Ashoka and, 314n34
  Britain and, 230
  Christianity and, 148
  Egypt, 23, 25–26, 34
  new accounts of Jesus and, 128
  as origin of Europe, 278
  Plato and, 31–34
  Plato's stories of Athens, 25–26
  Portugal and, 192–93
  rediscovery of ancient culture, 192–94
  revival in Europe, 155–56
  Roman Empire and, 54, 58–63, 63–69
  theatre, 26–32, 34, 59, 63, 116,
    281–82, 311n4
  See also Athens

gunboat diplomacy, 255, 256, 258
Gutas, Dimitri, 320n18
Gutenberg, Johannes, 159

Haile Selassie, 123–24, 137–38
Haiti, 225. *See also* Saint-Domingue
Hallyu, 299–301
Han Kang, 295
Han Yu, xx
Harun al-Rashid, 109, 112, 113
Hear Word!: Naija Women Talk True
    (Fafunwa), 284–85
Hebrew Bible/Old Testament, 17–19,
    64, 127–28, 129, 130, 132–33. *See
    also* Ark of the Covenant; Bible
Hegel, G. W. F., 226, 236, 237
heritage and culture, xi
Hildegard of Bingen, 144–46, 148–54,
    163
Hinduism, 201
historical novels, 239–45
historiography, 232–33, 233–36, 245,
    259. *See also* historical novels
Hokusai. *See* Katsushika Hokusai
Homer, 30–31, 65–68, 135, 147–48,
    194, 195–96, 269. See also *Iliad;
    Odyssey*
House of Menander, 59
Huitzilopochtli, 166
humanism, 160, 302
humanities (general), 302
hunting, 36

Ibn Sina, xx, 113–14, 117–22, 321n30
Igbo people, 273–74
ignorance, 280
Iliad (Homer), 31, 61, 66, 230. *See also*
    Homer
indentured servants, 250
independence, 209–11, 213–14, 226,
    268–69, 270–71, 273, 274
India
    Arab empire and, 109, 110
    British colonialism and, 51
    China and (*see* Buddhism; Xuan-
        zang)
    colonial elite, 269
    Eurasian exchange network and, 48

Lakshmi statue (*see* S. Indian statue
    in Pompeii)
    Portugal and, 186, 189, 200–202
    Roman Empire and, 54
    writing, 313–14n27
    See also Delhi; Xuanzang
India House, 190, 191, 197
Indigenous Peoples, 174–75, 176,
    208–9. *See also* Aztecs
Inquisition, 202–3
instruments, 153–54
intarsia, 161–63, *162*
interactions, xxii
interactions of cultures overview, xxii
invented tradition, 240
Ireland, 264
Isis, 58
Islam
    Christianity and, 156, 199–201
    Crusades, 155
    Ethiopia and, 131–32
    Greek thought and, 117–18
    knowledge seeking and, 112
    monotheism and, 19
    Muslim traders and Portuguese,
        199–200
    religious competition, 112–13
    rise of, 132–33
Israelites, 124, 125
Italian Renaissance, 157–58, 197–98,
    242
Italy, xx. *See also* Roman Empire
Ito, Michio, 264–65

Jains, 313n16
Jamaica, 136–39
James, C. L. R., 226
Japan
    Buddhism and, 92, 101 (*see also*
        Ennin)
    China and, 90, 98–100 (*see also*
        Ennin; *Pillow Book*)
    culture as government policy, 90
    Dutch empire and, 253–54, *254*
    Fenollosa, 256–59
    floating world, 247, 249–50
    The Great Wave off Kanagawa, 246,
        251

Hokusai, *246*, 247, *249*, 250–52, 253–54, 255–56, 260
Ireland and, 264
literacy, 98–99
Nagasaki-e, 253, *254*
Noh theatre, 30, 247, 249, 257–58, 264–65
Portugal and, 252–53
scroll art, 99–102, *102*
theatre, 30, 247, 249, 264–65
ukiyo-e, 248–49, *249*, 255
United States and, 255–61, 264, 265
watercolors, 247–48
japonaiserie, 255
Jesuits, 219
Jesus, 127–28, 150, 235–36, 322n12
Jeyifo, Biodun, 333n8
Jinadu (Oyo King's Horseman), 266, 267
Johnson, Samuel, 331n10
"Johnson Style," 301
Joseph, 17–19
Journey to the West (Wu), 86
Judaism
    in Arab empire, 199–200
    Aten cult and, 18–19
    Christianity and, 127
    Ethiopia and, 129–30
    Europe and, 156
    monastic life, 146
    translation of Bible, 64
    See also Hebrew Bible/Old Testament
al-Juzjani, 120–21

Kabuki, 247, 249
Kano school, 248
Kano Tan'yu, *248*
Karnak temple, 6–7
Katsushika Hokusai, *246*, 247, *249*, 250–52, 253–54, 255–56, 260
Kebra Nagast (Ethiopian text), 125–27, 129–32, 133, 135
Kibi no Makibi, 99–100, 101, 102
kilts, 240
The King Is Dead (Ladipo), 271
Kitagawa Utamaro, *249*
Knausgård, Karl Ove, 294

knowledge (general)
    Aristotle's four branches, 116–17
    Islam and, 118
    know-how, xvii
    know-why, xvii
    loss of (*see* loss)
    recovering, xix–xx (*see also* recovery)
    storing and transmitting, xv–xvi, xviii–xix, xxi, xxiii (*see also* oral traditions; writing)
    See also Storehouse of Wisdom
Kongi's Harvest (film), 283
Korea, 50, 91
Korean Wave, 299–301
K-pop, 299–301
Kumarajiva, 80

Ladigbolu I (king of Oyo), 266, 271, 274–76
Ladipo, Duro, 271–72, 283–84, 333n9
Lakshmi statue. *See* S. Indian statue in Pompeii
Legend of Ashoka (Buddhist text), 40–42, 44, 79
Lemonnier, Anicet Charles Gabriel, 216, *217*
Leo III (pope), 141
Lévi-Strauss, Claude, 334n16
Lewes, George Henry, 228
liberal arts, 152
libraries
    access to history and, 182
    India House, 190, 191, 197
    lending libraries, 239
    in Nineveh, 108
    private, 238
    University of Coimbra library, 193, 195
    Vatican, 227
    See also Benedictine monasteries; Future Library project; Storehouse of Wisdom; *studiolo* of Federico
Library of Alexandria, 34, 35, 111
The Life of Jesus, critically examined (Strauss), 235–36
lingua ignota, 154
linguistics, 46

literacy
    Homer texts and, 31
    Kana in Japan, 98
    in Nigeria, 270
    oral traditions and, 64
    printing press and, 238
    in Roman Empire, 141–42
    slavery and, 223
    women and, 98–99
    See also writing
literary production, 142–43. See also
    Benedictine monasteries; printing
    press
literati (wenren), 72
logic, 116
looting, 20–21
loss
    overview, xxi, xxiii
    Aztec books, 181
    Byzantium culture, 111
    Greek writing system, 25
    illegibility, 291
    India's early civilizations, 43
    new values/beliefs, 296
    writing on palm leaves, 46
    writing over, 148
    See also preservation
L'Ouverture, Toussaint, 208–9, 211,
    212–13, 214, 215, 223–26, 330n37
Lowell, Amy, 262
The Lusiads (Camões), 185, 193–98,
    203–4
Luther, Martin, 160, 172

Macaulay, Thomas Babington, 233–34,
    269
MacKenzie, J. A., 267
Magellan, Ferdinand, 190, 195
Malaysia, 301
Mali, 269
al-Ma'mun, 105–6, 110, 112, 113
The Man Died (Soyinka), 274
manga, 102
Mann, Thomas, 18
al-Mansur, 106–7
Mantegna, 170
Manuel (king of Portugal), 191
maps, 188, 190–91, 193, 202

maroons, 211
masks, 27, 194, 272, 272, 279, 301
materialism, 236
mathematics, 116, 152
The Matrix (film), 35
McCall, Sydney. See Fenollosa, Mary
    McNeil
McKeon, Richard, 314n43
Mead, Margaret, 334n16
medicine, 149–50
memorization, 46, 114
memory theaters, 162–63
Menander, 59, 60, 63
Menelik, 125–26
Mercator, Gerardus, 202
Mesopotamia, 108–9. See also Baghdad
metaphysics, 116
Mexico. See Aztecs; Moctezuma
Mexico City, 184
Miaphysite, 128–29
Middle Ages, xx
Middlemarch (Eliot), 227–30, 237,
    243–44
Mills, Jean-Baptiste, 214–15
misunderstandings, xxii
Moctezuma (emperor of the Aztec
    Empire), 164, 166, 167–68, 178–
    80. See also Aztecs: artworks of
modernism, 263–64, 265
monastic community, 74, 75, 144–45,
    146. See also Ennin
monks, 74, 75, 145. See also Benedictine
    monasteries
monotheism, 18–20
Moses, 17–18
Mount Fuji, 251, 253
Mount Wutai, 93–94, 96, 97
Mu Qi, 248
Muhammad, 112, 132–33
Muhammad ibn Tughlaq, 122
Murana (Oyo King's Horseman), 267,
    275, 276
Murasaki Shikibu, 99, 100, 238
museums, 232, 259, 331n10
music
    in Greece, 24
    Hildegard of Bingen and, 152,
        153–54

instruments in *studiolo* of Federico, 161, 162
K-pop, 299–301
in prehistoric caves, xvi

Nagasaki-e, 253, *254*
Napier, Robert, 134
Napoleon I (emperor of France), 224–25, 226
Native Americans. *See* Indigenous Peoples
natural philosophy, 117
Nefertiti (queen of Egypt), 2–3, *3*, 5, 6–12, *11*, 13–15, 18–22
négritude, 333–34n9
Nervous Conditions (Dangarembga), 292
New Testament, 128, 129, 132
Nigeria
    Berlin Conference, 267
    English language and, 333n8
    film industry, 283, 285
    independence, 270–71, 273, 274
    theatre (*see* Fafunwa, Ifeoma; Ladipo; Soyinka, Wole)
Nikam, N. A., 314n43
Nobel Prize, 292
Noh theatre, 30, 247, 249, 257–58, 264–65
Nollywood, 283–84, 285
nomadic people, 278
Norway, 287–91
novels, 239–42, 270
nuns, 144. *See also* Benedictine monasteries; Hildegard of Bingen
Nuremberg, 169–70, 172, 183

Oba Waja (Ladipo), 271
Odugbemi, Femi, 284
Odyssey (Homer), 31, 63–64, 66. *See also* Homer
Ogun, 281, 334n22
Old Testament, 128. *See also* Hebrew Bible/Old Testament
Olmecs, 167
Omeros (Walcott), 269
One Thousand and One Nights (Harun al-Rashid), 109
opera, 265

oral traditions
    in Egypt, 24
    in Greece, 24
    in India, 46, 47
    linguistics and, 46
    literacy and, 64
    in modern day, xxi
    as outlasting writing, 50–51
    as resilient, 291
organization, 230–32
origin, 103–4
Osiris, 58
Oslo. *See* Norway
Our Lady Mary of Zion church, 123–24, *123*, 133
ownership, 103–4
Oyo, 266–67, 271. See also *Death and the King's Horseman*

pagans, 111, 112, 147
painters. *See* watercolors; *specific artists*
palimpsest, 148
paper, 103, 109, 169, 203
papyrus, 109
Paris, 216–19, *217*, 221, 223
Paterson, Katie, 287–89, 290, 295. *See also* Future Library project
Paul the Deacon, 142
Perry, Matthew, 255
Persia, 43, 48, 108–9
The Persians (Aeschylus), 28
Petrarch, 160–61
philology, 159–60
Philosophical and Political History of the Two Indies (Raynal), 221
philosophy
    Enlightenment era, 236–37
    experimental, 221
    Ibn Sina shaping, 119
    natural, 117
    Plato turning to, 32, 33–34
    Plato's Academy, 34
    thinking historically, 237
    See also specific philosophers
physics, 116
picture scrolls, 99–102, *102*
Piero della Francesca, 135, *136*, 157, *158*

pillars, 37–39, *38*, 41, 42–44, 47, 50–51, 79
Pillow Book (Shōnagon), 87–88, 89–90, 92, 102–3
pinnacles of culture, 277–78, 279
plagues, 170, 327n36
Plato, 25–27, 30, 31–35, 148
Plautus, 63, 68
plays. *See* theatre
Pliny the Younger, 67
Plutarch, 68
poetry, 89–90, 100, 192, 233, 261–62, 264, 269. See also *The Lusiads*
Pompeii, 54–58, 59–61, 62, 68–69, 315n7
Portugal
    Africa and, 189–90, 198–200, 267
    Ethiopia and, 134
    forbidding maps, 191
    India and, 186, 189, 200–202
    Japan and, 252–53
    rediscovery of ancient cultures, 192–93
    ship explorations, 187–90, 195, 196–201
    war and nobility, 203
    writings of explorations, 191, 192, 193–98
    See also Camões, Luís de
Pound, Ezra, 261–63, 265
prehistoric humans, xii–xix, *xix*
preservation
    cities rebuilt and, 121
    copying, 35, 103, 120, 144–45, 147, 159, 320n18
    environmental destruction, 57 (*see also* Pompeii)
    of Ibn Sina's work, 120–21
    illegibility and, 291
    in modern day, xxiii
    new values/beliefs and, 296–97
    outsiders and, 182
    through mass production, 183
    as tireless, 296
    writing vs. oral tradition, 291
    See also loss

Prester John, 134, 232n29
Prinsep, James, 51
printing, xxi
printing press
    Federico's rejection of, 159
    in Goa, 203
    Gutenberg and, 159
    invention of, 159
    literacy and, 238
    Luther and, 160, 172
    as mass production, 183
    in Nuremberg, 169–70
prints, 171
prison writing, 273–74
progressive history, 230–34, 236–37
Prometheus, 334n22
Prophet Muhammad, 112, 132–33
PSY, 299–301
Ptolemy, 193
purists, 297–98

Queen of Sheba, 125–26, 129–30, 133, 135, *136*
Qur'an, 118, 133

Raphael, 140, *140*, 218
Ras Tafari. *See* Haile Selassie
Rastafari, 138–39
Raynal, Guillaume Thomas François, 206–7, *206*, 210, 220–23, 330n34, 330n37
realism, 240–43, 244
Reconquest, 199
Record of the Western Regions (Xuanzang), 72, 84–85
recovery
    overview, xix–xx, xxiii
    Ashoka pillars, 37–40, 47–48
    Cicero letters, 161
    collections and, 229–31
    colonialism and, 229
    decolonization and, 271
    Japanese arts, 258–59
    refusing, 35
    reused writing material, 148

regula Sancti Benedicti, 145, 146, 147, 149
religion
  in Arab empire, 199, 320n14
  Ashoka and, 44
  Chauvet cave and, xvi
  competition, 112–13
  See also specific religions
removing/moving culture, 37–39, 51.
  See also Ashoka pillars; collections
Renaissance, xx, 157–58, 197–98, 242
revolution, as term, 210–11
rewriting, 120
rhinoceros, 176–78
Riehl, Wilhelm Heinrich, 241
rituals, xvi, 276–77, 280–82
rituals of introductions, 280
Roman Empire
  overview, 54
  Arab empire and, 111
  Britain and, 233
  Christianity and, 148
  decline of, 141
  Egypt and, 58, 315n9
  emperors, 323n1
  exotic animals and, 315–16n12
  Greece and, 58–69
  inspiring revolt, 210
  literary production, 141–43
  Pompeii and, 54–55, 57
  Portugal and, 192–93
  rediscovery of, 192–93
  renewal of, 141–42
  revolt against slavery and, 207–8
  theatre, 59, 63
  See also Charlemagne
Romanesque style, 143–44
Romola (Eliot), 242–43
Romulus and Reumus, 65
Rosetta Stone, 229
Rotrude, 142
ruins, 234

S. Indian statue in Pompeii, 53–54, 55, 56, 57, 61, 69
sacrifices, 166, 175
St. Elmo's fire, 196

Saint Lucia, 269
Saint-Domingue, 207, 211–12, 214–15, 223–25, 226. *See also* Belley, Jean-Baptiste; L'Ouverture, Toussaint
salons, 216, *217*, 218–19, 221, 223
samurai, 247
Schliemann, Heinrich, 230
The School of Athens (Raphael), 218
science of past, 233–36, 245, 259. *See also* historical novels
Scotland, 239–40
Scott, Walter, 239–40
Scribbler Moon, 288
scriptorium, 144, 147, 151, 153
sculpting, 4, 8–12, 167, 258–59, 271, *271*
scurvy, 196
Sebastião (king of Portugal), 203, 205
Second Reform Act, 244
secret languages, 154
Sei Shōnagon, 88, 99. See also *Pillow Book*
Shakespeare, William, 238
A Short History of the World (Wells), 313n14
Silk Road, 50, 109
"Silly Novels by Lady Novelists" (Eliot), 241
simile, 194
simulated reality, 35. *See also* theatre
singers, 24
slavery
  abolition of, 212, 223–25
  economic system and, 223
  in Egypt, 17, 132
  Enlightenment critiquing, 222–23
  European slave trade, 136–37, 138–39, 207, 209, 220–23, 267
  literacy and, 223
  playwrights and, 63
  in Saint-Domingue, 211–12, 214–15, 223–25 (*see also* L'Ouverture, Toussaint)
  in United States, 209–10, 212, 213, 222
social anthropology, 334n16
Socrates, 30, 31–33

Solomon (king of Israel), 124, 125–26, 129–30, 133, *136*
Solon, 23, 25
Sophocles, 27–28
South Asia, 30
South Korea, 299–301
Southeast Asia, 50
Soyinka, Wole, 30, 269–70, 272–76, 280–83, 292, 333–34n9
space crafts, 293–94
Spain, 173, 212. *See also* Aztecs; Moctezuma; Saint-Domingue
spies, 85
Star Trek (TV series), 204
statues. *See* Buddhist statues; S. Indian statue in Pompeii
STEM, 302
storage
    overview, xxi, xxiii
    destruction and, 35
    environmental sustainability and, 288–89, 295
    of grain, 16–17, 108
    memory theaters, 162–63
Storehouse of Wisdom, 108–10, 111–13, 114–16, 117–19, 121–22, 156
stories, xvi
Strauss, David, 235–36
studiolo of Federico, 157–59, 160–62, *162*, 163
suffering, 41–42, 44–45, 49
suicide rituals, 276–77. *See also* Murana
summas, 107, 118–19, 121, 122, 155–56
sumo wrestling, 247, 249, *249*
Syracuse, 62

Tainos, 329n4
The Tale of Genji (Murasaki), 99, 238
Taliban, 79
Taoism, 95–97
taxes, 210
technology, 302
Ten Commandments, 124–25, 126–27, 129
Tenochtitlan, 164–66, 175, *175*, 178–81, 184, 220

Teotihuacan, 166–67
Terence, 63, 68
Tewodros II (emperor of Ethiopia), 134
theatre
    in Arab empire, 116
    Balinese shadow puppets, 265
    Chinese opera, 265
    democracy and, 32
    in Egypt, 29–30
    in Greece, 26–32, 34, 59, 63, 116, 281–82, 311n4
    in Japan, 30, 247, 249, 257–58, 264–65
    as local, 286
    in Nigeria (*see* Fafunwa, Ifeoma; Ladipo,Duro; Soyinka, Wole)
    Plato attacking, 33
    ritual and, 281–82
    in Roman Empire, 59–60, 63
    Socrates distrusting, 31
    in South Asia, 30
    Western realism, 264
    See also choruses
Things Fall Apart (Soyinka), 270
Thirty-Six Views of Mount Fuji (Hokusai), 251, 253–54
Thutmose (sculptor), 4–5, 7, 8–10, 108
Timaeus (Plato), 148
time capsules, 293–94. *See also* Future Library project
Times New Roman font, 143
Tlaloc, 166
Tlaxcalans, 178
Tokiwa Mitsunaga, 102
transformations, 232
translations
    Buddhist texts in China, 80 (*see also* Xuanzang)
    Das Leben Jesu, kritisch bearbeitet, 235
    of Fenollosa, 261–62
    as forgotten/omitted, 83–84
    Greek texts into Arabic, 110
    Greek texts into Latin, 63–64
    Kebra Nagast, 130–31
    Luther's Bible, 172
    of *Odyssey*, 63–64
    Persian texts in Arabic, 108–9

Yoruba into English, 271
See also Storehouse of Wisdom
transmission, xviii–xix, xxiii. *See also*
    oral traditions; writing
Trojans, 67, 68
Troy, 230
The Truman Show (film), 35
Tutankhamun/Tutankhaten, 14–15
typhoons, 185–86, 187

ukiyo, 247, 249–50
ukiyo-e, 248–49, *249*, 255
UNESCO heritage sites, 296
United States, 209–10, 255–61, 264, 265
Universal Negro Improvement Associa-
    tion (UNIA), 137
University of Coimbra, 193, 195
urban revolution, 107–8

Valla, Lorenzo, 160, 229
value judgements, 198–99
Vatican, 140, 159–60
Vatican Library, 227
vellum, 159
Virgil, 65–69, 127, 147–48, 194–96
visions, 150–52
vitamin deficiency, 196
VOC, 253
volcanoes. *See* Pompeii
Volmar, 153
Voltaire, 216, 218–19
voting, 243–44
Vuong, Ocean, 294

Walcott, Derek, 269
water, 165–66
watercolors, 247–48
waterspouts, 196–97
welfare state, 41–43
Wells, H.G., 313n14
Wilson, Woodrow, 268
women, 243, 284–85, 311n4
woodcuts, 171, 203, 247,
    248–49
world literature, 263

writing
    overview, xxi
    on Ashoka pillars, 39–40, 41, 44, 47,
        50–51
    Charlemagne and, 142
    Chinese characters in Japan, 90,
        91–92
    deciphering, 50–51, 143
    in Greece, 24–25, 29, 31, 33
    in India, 313–14n27
    kana in Japan, 98–99
    longevity and, 291
    in Mesopotamia, 108
    nomadic people and, 278
    on palm leaves, 46
    Plato critiquing, 33
    of Portuguese exploration, 191,
        192
    spreading of Greek alphabet,
        47
    as widely adopted, 46
    See also books; literacy
Wu Cheng'en, 86
Wuzong of Tang, 95–96

Xuanzang
    overview, 70–71
    Ashoka pillars and, 39–40
    Buddhism and, 75–77, 79–80, 81,
        82–83
    China and, 81
    crossing Hindu Kush, 83
    crossing Indus River, 71–72, 82
    fame of, 86
    journey as dangerous, 76–77
    Mahayana school and, 81
    Record of the Western Regions, 72,
        84–85
    recovering texts, 80, 81, 82–83
    studying texts, 72, 73–74, 75–76

Yeats, William Butler, 264
Yohannis (emperor of Ethiopia), 135
Yoruba people, 267, 270–71, *271*,
    273–74, 280–83. *See also* Oyo

CULTURE

Martin Puchner

CULTURE
Martin Puchner

DISCUSSION QUESTIONS

1. Discuss the two views of culture Martin Puchner presents in the preface to *Culture*. Why do people often cling to the first view? What are the advantages, hazards, and costs of the assumption that culture can be owned? Why does Puchner argue that the second view is messier but "more in keeping with how culture actually works" (p. xii)?

2. What do drawings in places such as the Chauvet cave teach us about intergenerational collaboration among humans? Why do you think early humans increasingly recorded "know-why" as opposed to "know-how" on cave walls? How do we organize and study "know-how" and "know-why" today? Do you think modern society values one domain (know-how or know-why) more than the other?

3. What does Puchner believe we can learn about culture by focusing on its storage, loss, and recovery throughout human history? Do you think technology has made us any better at sharing and preserving culture? Why do you suppose we fight over culture and it what means, perhaps now more than ever?

4. What do archeological discoveries from Akhetaten express about the relationship between religion and art? Why do you suppose humans in modern societies have tried to disentangle religion from art? Why do we continue to maintain neatly distinguished areas of art and belief? To what extent are the categories useful?

5. Puchner writes, "What is important is not *what* we borrow but *how* we borrow, what we make of what we find" (p. 19). How does *Timaeus* (Plato's dialogue inventing a glorious history for Greece) demonstrate this proposition? Why were the Greeks so receptive to Plato's "philosophical critique of everything" (p. 34) and "false histories" (p. 35)? How might Plato's writing and handling of history help us make sense of our computer- and social media–powered lives today?

6. What made Buddhism such an excellent cultural export? How did Ashoka use Buddhism to solidify and expand his power? What did he fail to understand about culture? What can the story of his reign teach us about cross-cultural contact and cultural artifacts?

7. According to Puchner, "Rome's most remarkable legacy is the art of the graft" (p. 69). What did the art of the graft look like in the Roman Empire? Why is Pompeii still the best place to observe cultural graft? Why is cultural grafting so often a contentious process in the United States? Do you think other countries import and adopt culture more successfully?

8. Why did Xuanzang ultimately decide to leave the heartland of Buddhism in India and return home to China? How did he handle his role as a cultural go-between? Why is his *Record of the Western Regions* regarded as "a classic in cultural mobility" (p. 85)? What valuable lessons might we take from it in the twenty-first century?

9. How did the caliph al-Ma'mun respond when Aristotle visited him in a dream? Why did he insist on having Greek knowledge translated into Arabic and preserved in Baghdad's Storehouse of Wisdom? How did the Persian scholar Ibn Sina make use of Aristotle's "unified system of knowledge" (p. 117)? How did he relate Aristotle to Islam and facilitate cultural borrowing as far away as western Europe?

10. How did Ethiopia's Church of Maryam Syon allegedly take possession of the Jewish people's original Ark of the Covenant? How did the alleged theft shape Ethiopian Christianity? How did the *Kebra*

Negast subsequently shape Ethiopia's fortunes? Why does Puchner believe the *Kebra Negast* should be recognized as a crucial text in the canon of world literature?

11. How did the court library of Charlemagne, the Benedictine scriptorium, twelfth-century universities, and the Italian *studiolo* differ in purpose and complement one another? Why does Puchner refer to the Italian Renaissance of the fifteen and sixteenth centuries as "a borrowed Renaissance" (p. 157)? How did this borrowed Renaissance ultimately assist in "transforming the world yet again" (p. 163)?

12. "If destruction sometimes preserves," Puchner writes, "continual use often destroys" (p. 184). How does the history of Tenochtitlan exemplify this principle? How did you react to the inscription on the Plaza de las Tres Culturas in Mexico City? To what extent does the inscription promote peace and a dynamic view of culture? Do you think the inscription is a suitable response to what happened to Tenochtitlan?

13. What literary techniques and models did Luís de Camões use to "recapture" the distant past in his epic work *The Lusiads*? What made *The Lusiads* the first epic of its kind? How did it impact the Portuguese empire as well as future literature about exploration? Why is it being rediscovered now?

14. Why did Toussaint L'Ouverture remain on the plantation where he'd been enslaved? Why couldn't he imagine a way forward without using enslaved labor? How did Guillaume-Thomas François Raynal articulate L'Ouverture's predicament for French intellectuals?

15. Why is there a painting in Versailles Palace showing L'Ouverture's contemporary Jean-Baptiste Belley dressed in French revolutionary clothes and posed beside a bust of Reynal? What does the painting capture? What does it communicate to us today?

16. How did George Eliot wish to revolutionize fiction? How did her masterpiece *Middlemarch* show the workings of history and society grappling with progress? Why does *Middlemarch* remain such a celebrated, influential novel?

17. How did the Western literary world react when Ezra Pound used Ernest Fenollosa's translations and transcriptions of Chinese poetry and Noh drama to create a new kind of poetry in English? Do you suppose a lesser poet could have gotten away with "mashing up" Asian art like this? How much do you think the language and spirit of modernism (with Pound's imperative to "make it new!" [p. 262]) forever changed cross-cultural encounters and resulting art?

18. What did Wole Soyinka mean when he wrote that "cultural relativism can only be the beginning of an exploration into culture, not the end" (p. 280)? How have Soyinka and other Nigerian artists demonstrated that "culture thrives on syncretism, not on purity, on borrowing cultural forms rather than locking them away" (p. 286)?

19. How do you predict the Future Library project will turn out? Do you think we'll still have brick-and-mortar libraries in 2114? Can you imagine the English language becoming less important over the next hundred years? Why or why not?

20. Do you agree with Puchner that those in thrall to "cultural purity" (p. 297) are the enemies of cultural survival? How, in Puchner's view, do the "purists" stand against the people dedicated to the transmission and continuation of cultural traditions? Should there be any rules for cultural "sharing"? If so, what should the rules be?

Meghan Kenny	*The Driest Season*
Nicole Krauss	*The History of Love*
Don Lee	*The Collective*
Amy Liptrot	*The Outrun: A Memoir*
Donna M. Lucey	*Sargent's Women*
Bernard MacLaverty	*Midwinter Break*
Maaza Mengiste	*Beneath the Lion's Gaze*
Claire Messud	*The Burning Girl*
	When the World Was Steady
Liz Moore	*Heft*
	The Unseen World
Neel Mukherjee	*The Lives of Others*
	A State of Freedom
Janice P. Nimura	*Daughters of the Samurai*
Rachel Pearson	*No Apparent Distress*
Richard Powers	*Orfeo*
Kirstin Valdez Quade	*Night at the Fiestas*
Jean Rhys	*Wide Sargasso Sea*
Mary Roach	*Packing for Mars*
Somini Sengupta	*The End of Karma*
Akhil Sharma	*Family Life*
	A Life of Adventure and Delight
Joan Silber	*Fools*
Johanna Skibsrud	*Quartet for the End of Time*
Mark Slouka	*Brewster*
Kate Southwood	*Evensong*
Manil Suri	*The City of Devi*
	The Age of Shiva
Madeleine Thien	*Do Not Say We Have Nothing*
	Dogs at the Perimeter
Vu Tran	*Dragonfish*
Rose Tremain	*The American Lover*
	The Gustav Sonata
Brady Udall	*The Lonely Polygamist*
Brad Watson	*Miss Jane*
Constance Fenimore Woolson	*Miss Grief and Other Stories*

Available only on the Norton website

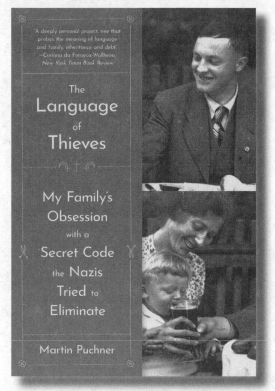